A YEAR OF MARVELS

Ryan North, Amy Chu, Yves Bigerel, Dennis Culver,
Paul Allor, Chuck Wendig, Chad Bowers, Chris Sims,
Nilah Magruder, Jeremy Whitley, Todd Casey, Elliott Casey,
Method Man & Charlamagne Tha God
WRITERS

Danilo Beyruth, Ryan Browne, Yves Bigerel, Leonardo Romero,
Diego Olortegui, Juanan Ramírez, Brian Level, Siya Oum,
Laura Braga, Paul Davidson, Anthony Piper,
Nelson Blake II & J.L. Giles
ARTISTS

Cris Peter, Ryan Browne, Andres Mossa, Ruth Redmond,
Rachelle Rosenberg, Jesus Aburtov, Jordan Boyd, Siya Oum,
Lee Loughridge & Anthony Piper
COLOR ARTISTS

Mast, Reilly Brown, Geoffo & Daniel Govar
LAYOUT ARTISTS

Jake Thomas, Heather Antos, Devin Lewis, Christina Harrington, Charles Beacham,
Alanna Smith, Darren Shan, Kathleen Wisneski, Mark Basso & Chris Robinson
EDITORS

VC's Travis Lanham
with Joe Sabino
LETTERERS

Annie Cheng
DIGITAL PRODUCTION & LAYOUT

Tim Smith 3
DIGITAL PRODUCTION MANAGER

Jordan D. White & Nick Lowe
SUPERVISING EDITORS

COLLECTION EDITOR JENNIFER GRÜNWALD ▪ ASSISTANT EDITOR CAITLIN O'CONNELL
ASSOCIATE MANAGING EDITOR KATERI WOODY ▪ EDITOR, SPECIAL PROJECTS MARK D. BEAZLEY
VP PRODUCTION & SPECIAL PROJECTS JEFF YOUNGQUIST ▪ SVP PRINT, SALES & MARKETING DAVID GABRIEL
BOOK DESIGNER JAY BOWEN

EDITOR IN CHIEF AXEL ALONSO ▪ CHIEF CREATIVE OFFICER JOE QUESADA
PRESIDENT DAN BUCKLEY ▪ EXECUTIVE PRODUCER ALAN FINE

A YEAR OF MARVELS. Contains material originally published in magazine form as A YEAR OF MARVELS: THE AMAZING #1, THE INCREDIBLE #1, THE UNSTOPPABLE #1, THE UNBEATABLE #1 and THE UNCANNY #1; GHOST RIDER X-MAS SPECIAL INFINITE COMIC #1; and MARVEL NEW YEAR'S EVE SPECIAL #1. First printing 2017. ISBN# 978-1-302-90295-7. Published by MARVEL WORLDWIDE, INC., a subsidiary of MARVEL ENTERTAINMENT, LLC. OFFICE OF PUBLICATION: 135 West 50th Street, New York, NY 10020. Copyright © 2017 MARVEL No similarity between any of the names, characters, persons, and/or institutions in this magazine with those of any living or dead person or institution is intended, and any similarity which may exist is purely coincidental. **Printed in the U.S.A.** DAN BUCKLEY, President, Marvel Entertainment; JOE QUESADA, Chief Creative Officer; TOM BREVOORT, SVP of Publishing; DAVID BOGART, SVP of Business Affairs & Operations, Publishing & Partnership; C.B. CEBULSKI, VP of Brand Management & Development, Asia; DAVID GABRIEL, SVP of Sales & Marketing, Publishing; JEFF YOUNGQUIST, VP of Production & Special Projects; DAN CARR, Executive Director of Publishing Technology; ALEX MORALES, Director of Publishing Operations; SUSAN CRESPI, Production Manager; STAN LEE, Chairman Emeritus. For information regarding advertising in Marvel Comics or on Marvel.com, please contact Vit DeBellis, Integrated Sales Manager, at vdebellis@marvel.com. For Marvel subscription inquiries, please call 888-511-5480. **Manufactured between 2/24/2017 and 3/28/2017 by LSC COMMUNICATIONS INC., SALEM, VA, USA.**

10 9 8 7 6 5 4 3 2 1

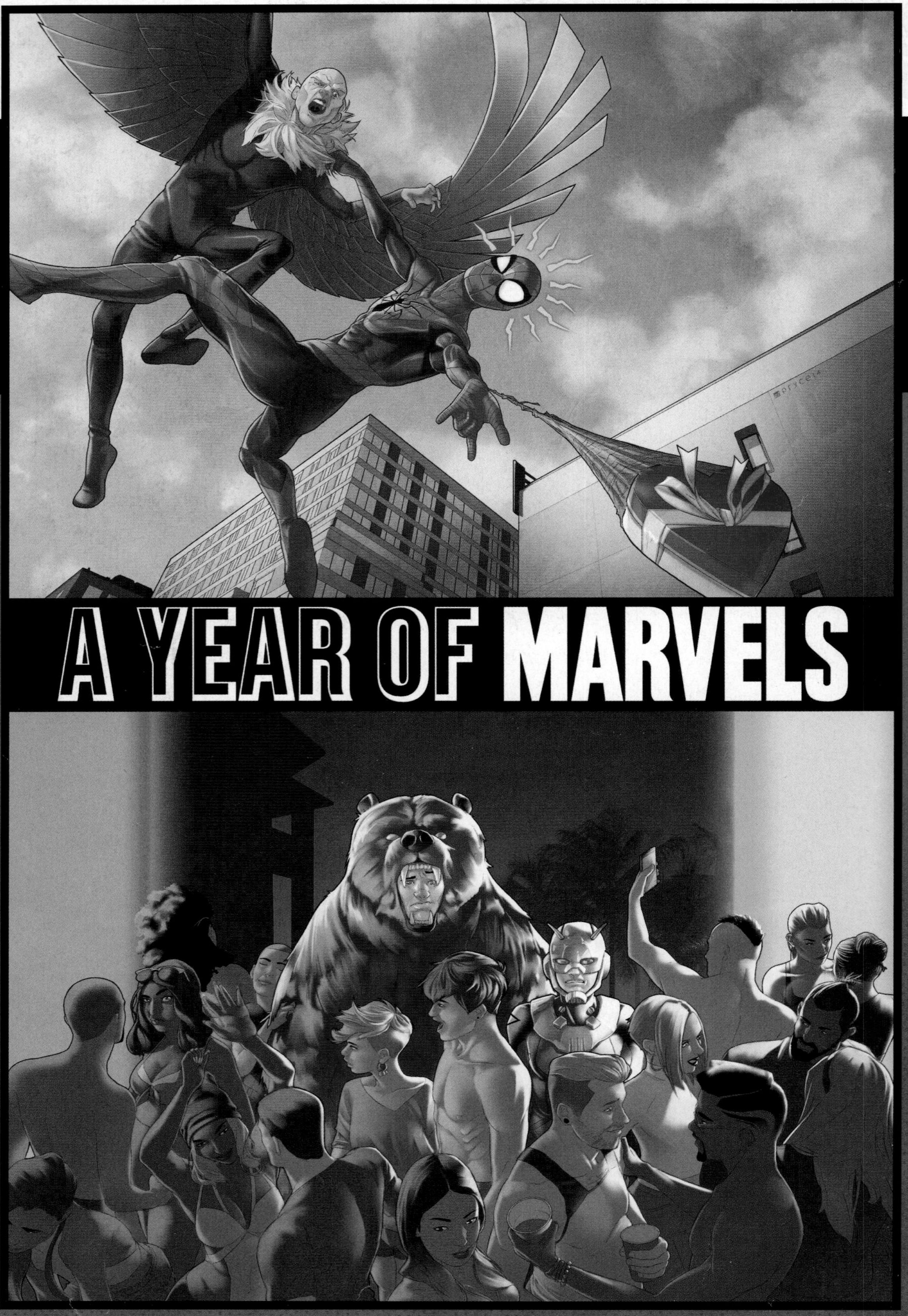
A YEAR OF MARVELS

THE AMAZING #1

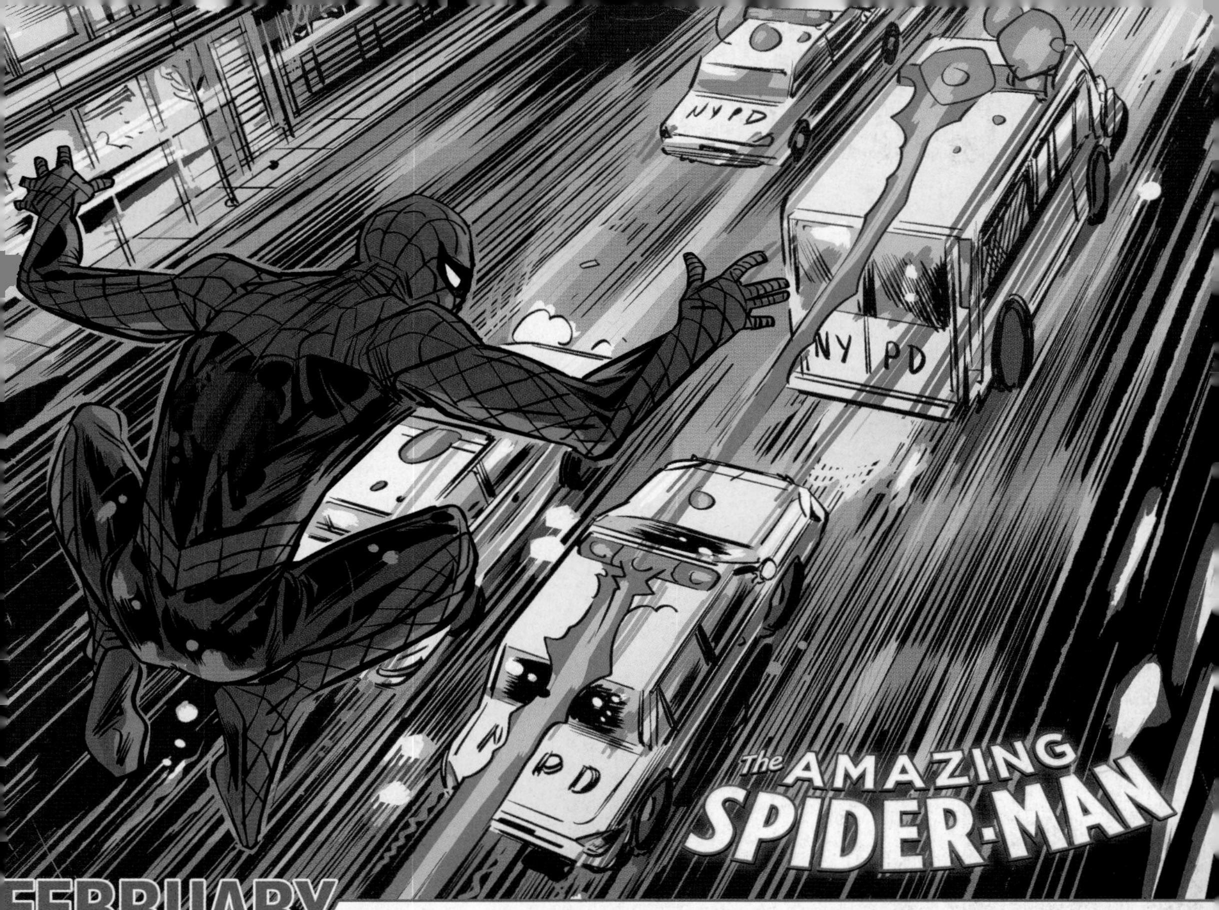
NYPD
NY PD
PD
The AMAZING SPIDER-MAN

FEBRUARY

SUNDAY	MONDAY	TUESDAY	WEDNESDAY	THURSDAY	FRIDAY	SATURDAY
	1	2 Groundhogs Day	3	4	5	6
7	8	10	11	12	13	14 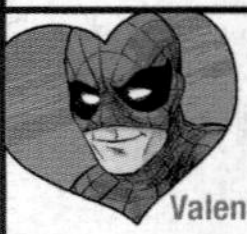 Valentine's Day
15	16 Presidents Day	17	18	19	20	21
22	23	24	25	26	27	28
29						

RYAN NORTH — WRITER
DANILO BEYRUTH — ARTIST
CRIS PETER — COLOR ARTIST
MAST — LAYOUT ARTIST
VC'S TRAVIS LANHAM — LETTERING

ANNIE CHENG & TIM SMITH 3 — PRODUCTION TEAM
CARLOS LAO — PRODUCTION DESIGN
JAKE THOMAS — EDITOR
JORDAN D. WHITE & NICK LOWE — SUPERVISING EDITORS

EDITOR IN CHIEF **AXEL ALONSO** CHIEF CREATIVE OFFICER **JOE QUESADA** PUBLISHER **DAN BUCKLEY** EXECUTIVE PRODUCER **ALAN FINE**

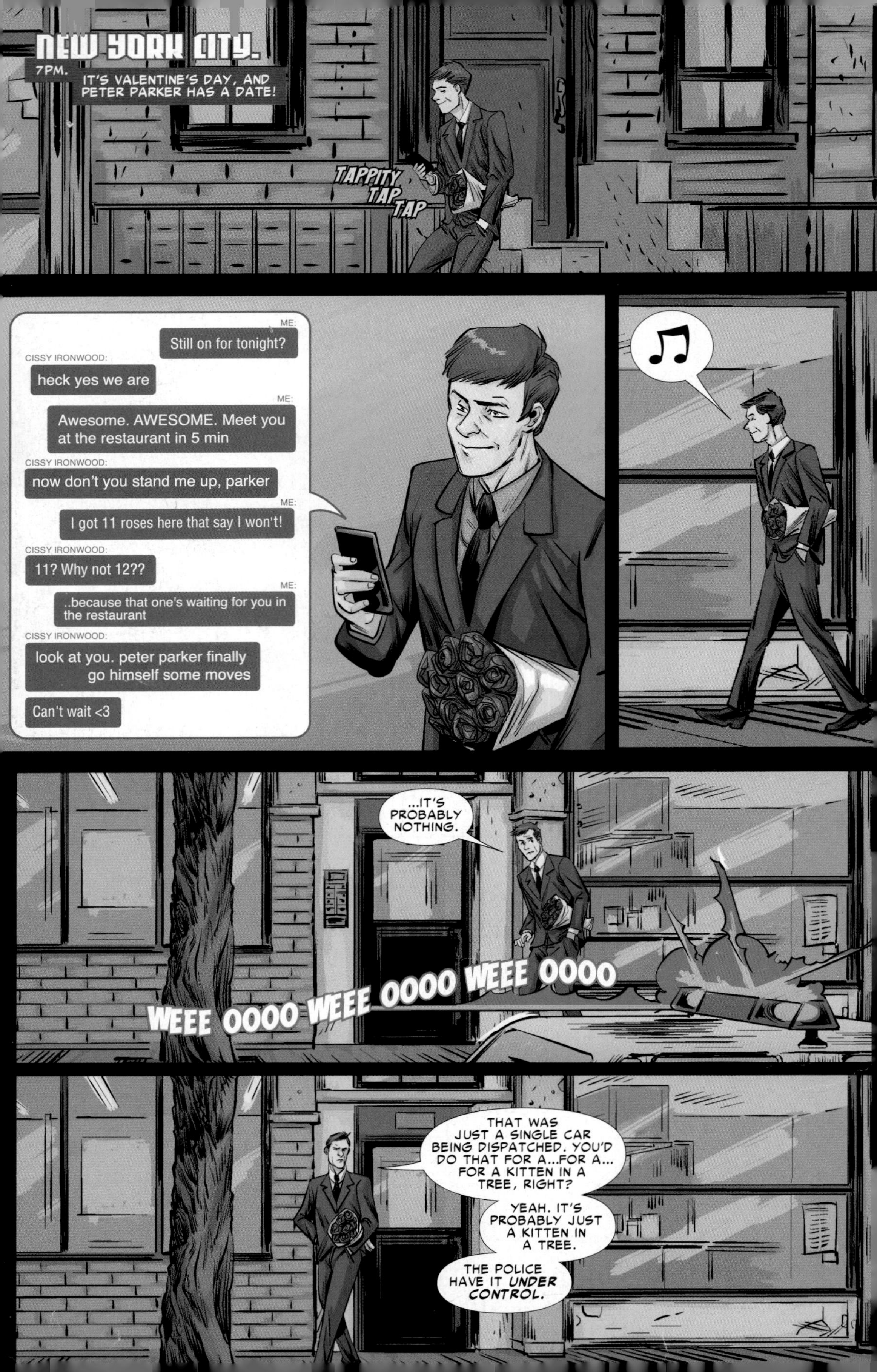
NEW YORK CITY.
7PM.
IT'S VALENTINE'S DAY, AND PETER PARKER HAS A DATE!
TAPPITY TAP TAP
ME:
Still on for tonight?
CISSY IRONWOOD:
heck yes we are
ME:
Awesome. AWESOME. Meet you at the restaurant in 5 min
CISSY IRONWOOD:
now don't you stand me up, parker
ME:
I got 11 roses here that say I won't!
CISSY IRONWOOD:
11? Why not 12??
ME:
..because that one's waiting for you in the restaurant
CISSY IRONWOOD:
look at you. peter parker finally go himself some moves
Can't wait <3
♫
...IT'S PROBABLY NOTHING.
WEEE OOOO WEEE OOOO WEEE OOOO
THAT WAS JUST A SINGLE CAR BEING DISPATCHED. YOU'D DO THAT FOR A...FOR A... FOR A KITTEN IN A TREE, RIGHT?
YEAH. IT'S PROBABLY JUST A KITTEN IN A TREE.
THE POLICE HAVE IT *UNDER CONTROL.*

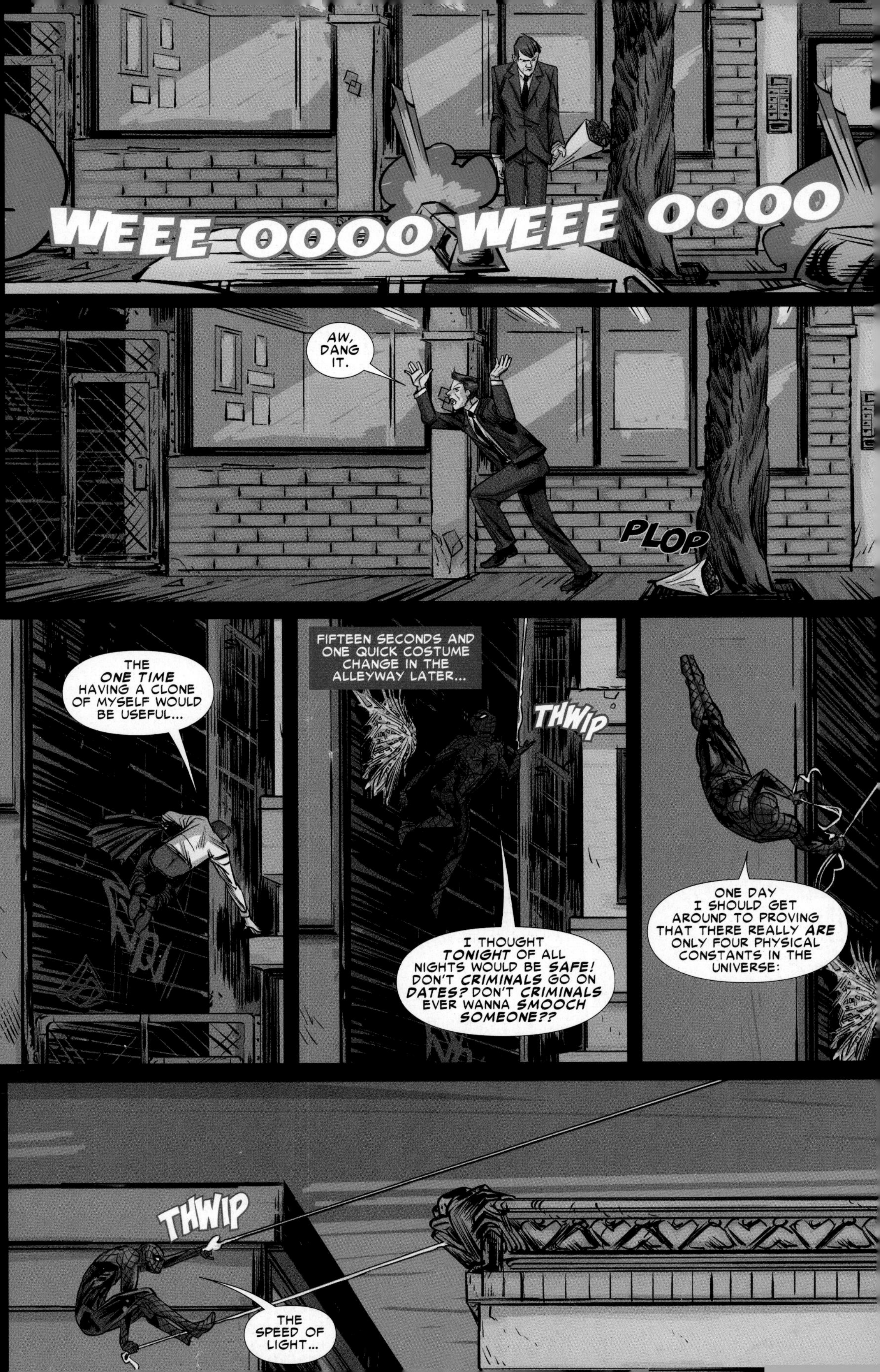
WEEE OOOO WEEE OOOO
AW, DANG IT.
PLOP
THE ONE TIME HAVING A CLONE OF MYSELF WOULD BE USEFUL...
FIFTEEN SECONDS AND ONE QUICK COSTUME CHANGE IN THE ALLEYWAY LATER...
THWIP
I THOUGHT TONIGHT OF ALL NIGHTS WOULD BE SAFE! DON'T CRIMINALS GO ON DATES? DON'T CRIMINALS EVER WANNA SMOOCH SOMEONE??
ONE DAY I SHOULD GET AROUND TO PROVING THAT THERE REALLY ARE ONLY FOUR PHYSICAL CONSTANTS IN THE UNIVERSE:
THWIP
THE SPEED OF LIGHT...

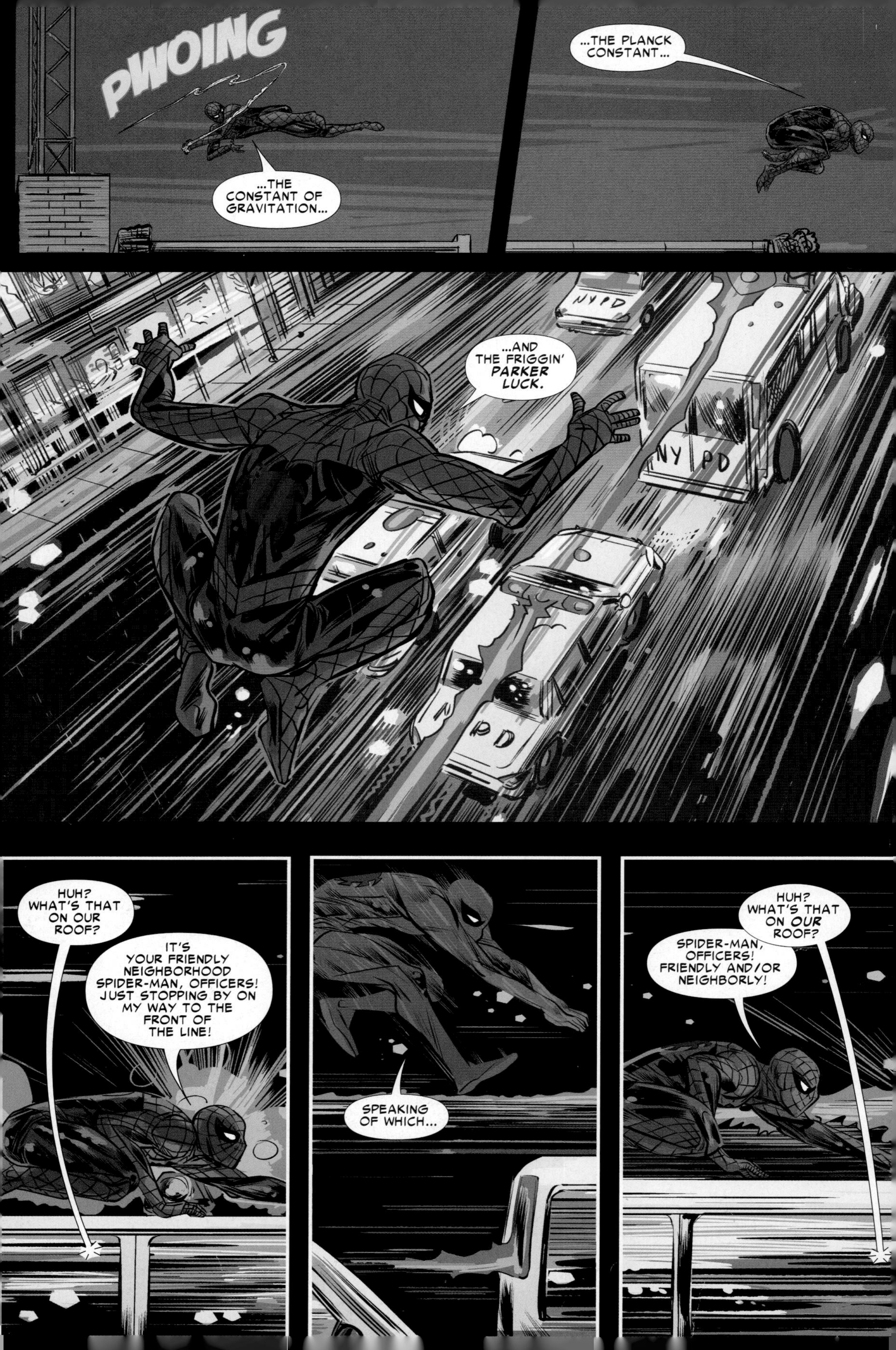
PWOING
...THE CONSTANT OF GRAVITATION...
...THE PLANCK CONSTANT...
...AND THE FRIGGIN' *PARKER LUCK.*
NYPD
NY PD
PD
HUH? WHAT'S THAT ON OUR ROOF?
IT'S YOUR FRIENDLY NEIGHBORHOOD SPIDER-MAN, OFFICERS! JUST STOPPING BY ON MY WAY TO THE FRONT OF THE LINE!
SPEAKING OF WHICH...
HUH? WHAT'S THAT ON *OUR* ROOF?
SPIDER-MAN, OFFICERS! FRIENDLY AND/OR NEIGHBORLY!

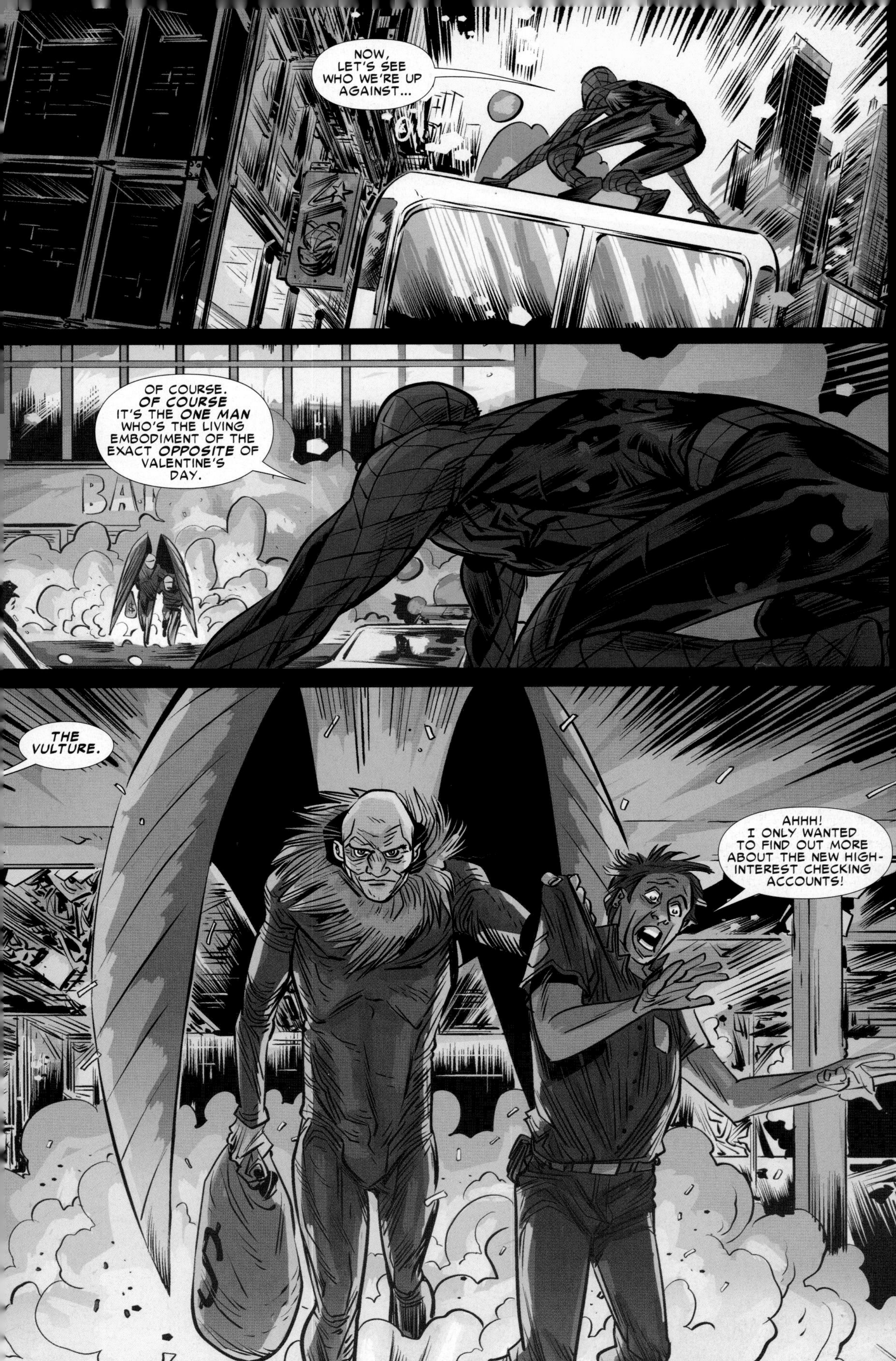
NOW, LET'S SEE WHO WE'RE UP AGAINST...
OF COURSE. *OF COURSE* IT'S THE *ONE MAN* WHO'S THE LIVING EMBODIMENT OF THE EXACT *OPPOSITE* OF VALENTINE'S DAY.
BA
THE VULTURE.
AHHH! I ONLY WANTED TO FIND OUT MORE ABOUT THE NEW HIGH-INTEREST CHECKING ACCOUNTS!

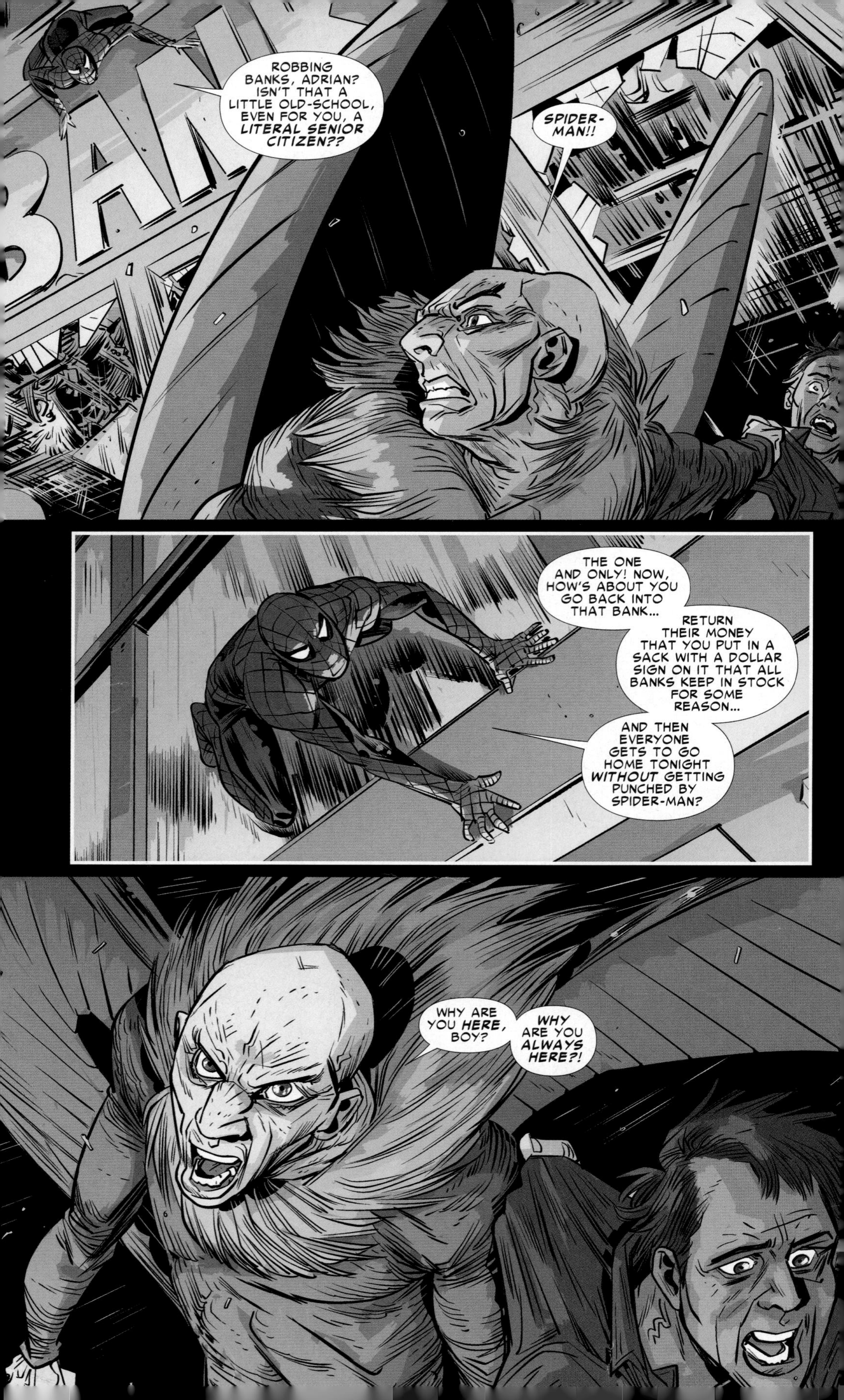

ROBBING BANKS, ADRIAN? ISN'T THAT A LITTLE OLD-SCHOOL, EVEN FOR YOU, A *LITERAL SENIOR CITIZEN??*
SPIDER-MAN!!
THE ONE AND ONLY! NOW, HOW'S ABOUT YOU GO BACK INTO THAT BANK...
RETURN THEIR MONEY THAT YOU PUT IN A SACK WITH A DOLLAR SIGN ON IT THAT ALL BANKS KEEP IN STOCK FOR SOME REASON...
AND THEN EVERYONE GETS TO GO HOME TONIGHT *WITHOUT* GETTING PUNCHED BY SPIDER-MAN?
WHY ARE YOU *HERE*, BOY?
WHY ARE YOU *ALWAYS HERE?!*

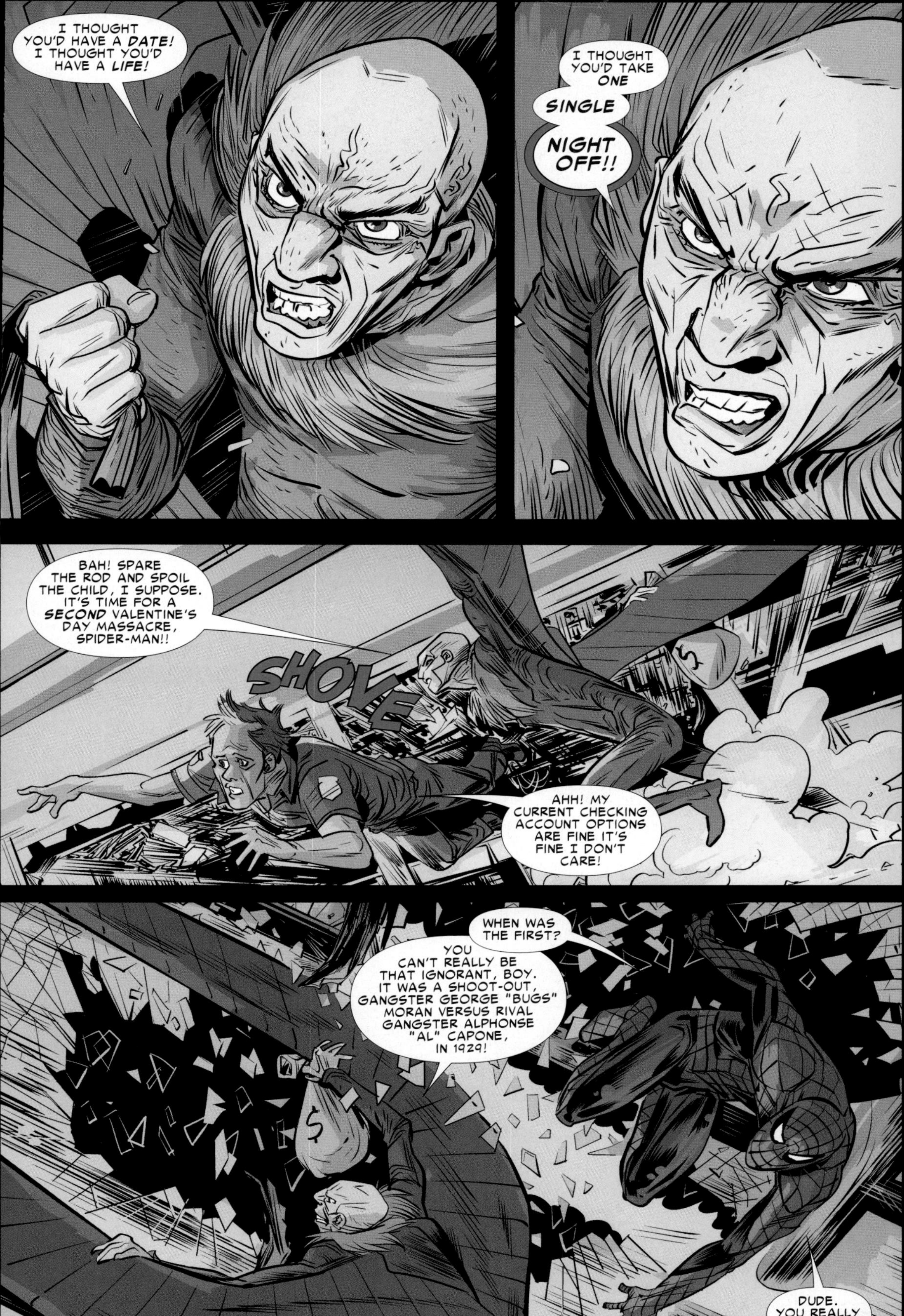

I THOUGHT YOU'D HAVE A *DATE!* I THOUGHT YOU'D HAVE A *LIFE!*
I THOUGHT YOU'D TAKE *ONE*
SINGLE
NIGHT OFF!!
BAH! SPARE THE ROD AND SPOIL THE CHILD, I SUPPOSE. IT'S TIME FOR A *SECOND* VALENTINE'S DAY MASSACRE, SPIDER-MAN!!
SHOVE
AHH! MY CURRENT CHECKING ACCOUNT OPTIONS ARE FINE IT'S FINE I DON'T CARE!
WHEN WAS THE FIRST?
YOU CAN'T REALLY BE THAT IGNORANT, BOY. IT WAS A SHOOT-OUT, GANGSTER GEORGE "BUGS" MORAN VERSUS RIVAL GANGSTER ALPHONSE "AL" CAPONE, IN 1929!
DUDE. YOU REALLY *ARE* OLD.

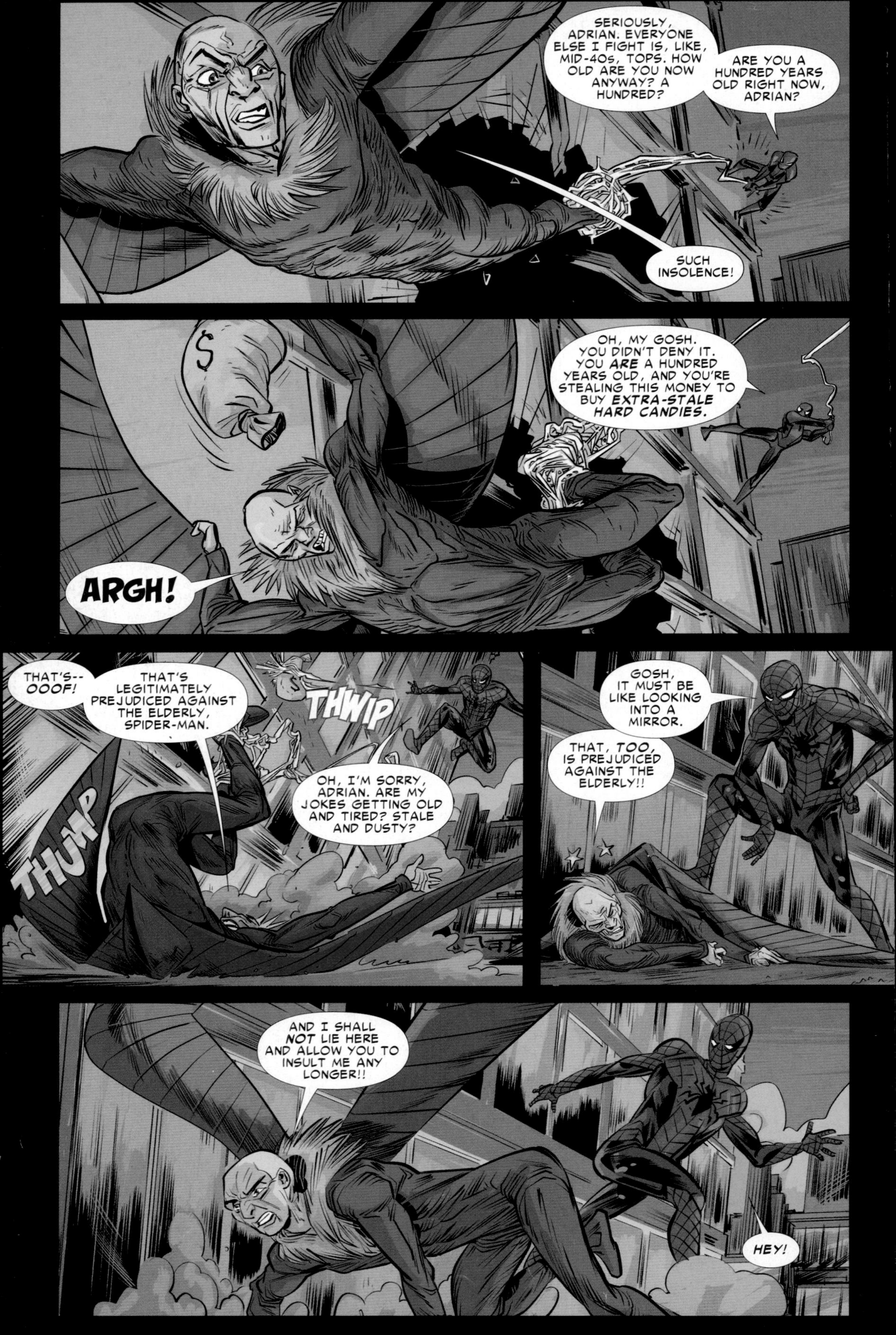
SERIOUSLY, ADRIAN. EVERYONE ELSE I FIGHT IS, LIKE, MID-40s, TOPS. HOW OLD ARE YOU NOW ANYWAY? A HUNDRED?
ARE YOU A HUNDRED YEARS OLD RIGHT NOW, ADRIAN?
SUCH INSOLENCE!
OH, MY GOSH. YOU DIDN'T DENY IT. YOU ARE A HUNDRED YEARS OLD, AND YOU'RE STEALING THIS MONEY TO BUY EXTRA-STALE HARD CANDIES.
ARGH!
THAT'S-- OOOF!
THAT'S LEGITIMATELY PREJUDICED AGAINST THE ELDERLY, SPIDER-MAN.
THWIP
THUMP
OH, I'M SORRY, ADRIAN. ARE MY JOKES GETTING OLD AND TIRED? STALE AND DUSTY?
GOSH, IT MUST BE LIKE LOOKING INTO A MIRROR.
THAT, TOO, IS PREJUDICED AGAINST THE ELDERLY!!
AND I SHALL NOT LIE HERE AND ALLOW YOU TO INSULT ME ANY LONGER!!
HEY!

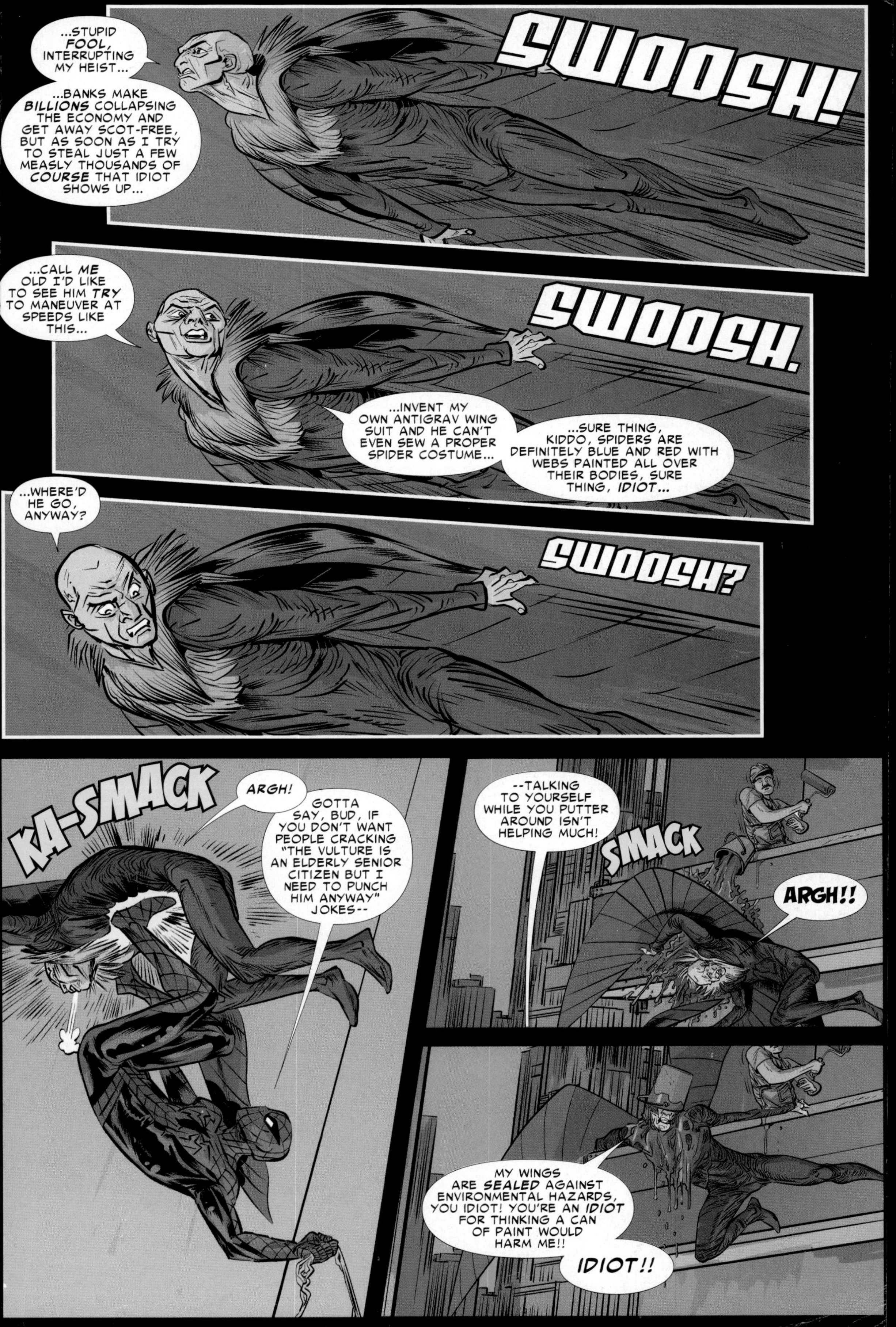

...STUPID FOOL, INTERRUPTING MY HEIST...
...BANKS MAKE BILLIONS COLLAPSING THE ECONOMY AND GET AWAY SCOT-FREE, BUT AS SOON AS I TRY TO STEAL JUST A FEW MEASLY THOUSANDS OF COURSE THAT IDIOT SHOWS UP...
SWOOSH!
...CALL ME OLD I'D LIKE TO SEE HIM TRY TO MANEUVER AT SPEEDS LIKE THIS...
SWOOSH.
...INVENT MY OWN ANTIGRAV WING SUIT AND HE CAN'T EVEN SEW A PROPER SPIDER COSTUME...
...SURE THING, KIDDO, SPIDERS ARE DEFINITELY BLUE AND RED WITH WEBS PAINTED ALL OVER THEIR BODIES, SURE THING, IDIOT...
...WHERE'D HE GO, ANYWAY?
SWOOSH?
KA-SMACK
ARGH!
GOTTA SAY, BUD, IF YOU DON'T WANT PEOPLE CRACKING "THE VULTURE IS AN ELDERLY SENIOR CITIZEN BUT I NEED TO PUNCH HIM ANYWAY" JOKES--
--TALKING TO YOURSELF WHILE YOU PUTTER AROUND ISN'T HELPING MUCH!
SMACK
ARGH!!
MY WINGS ARE SEALED AGAINST ENVIRONMENTAL HAZARDS, YOU IDIOT! YOU'RE AN IDIOT FOR THINKING A CAN OF PAINT WOULD HARM ME!!
IDIOT!!

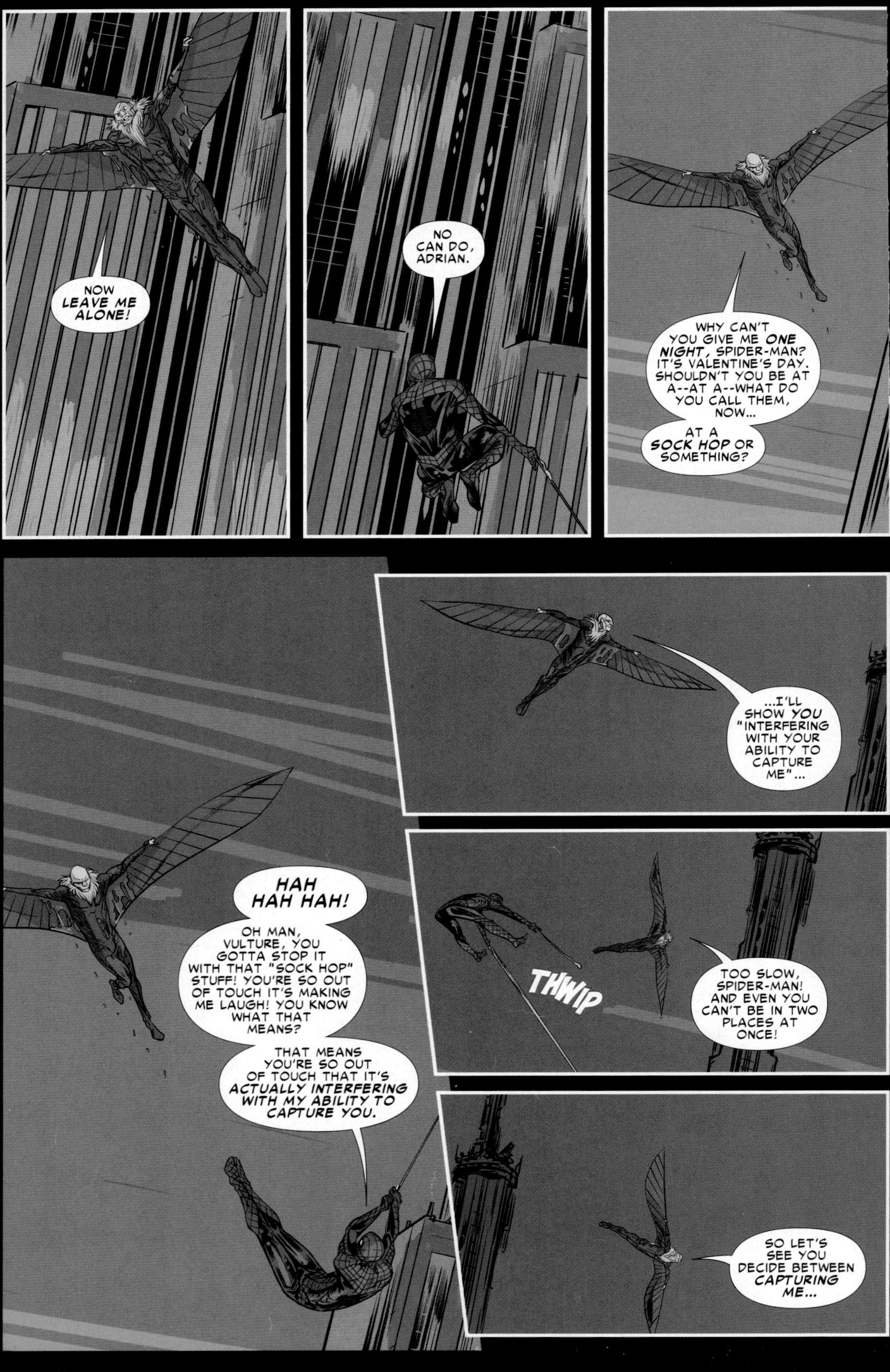

NOW LEAVE ME ALONE!
NO CAN DO, ADRIAN.
WHY CAN'T YOU GIVE ME ONE NIGHT, SPIDER-MAN? IT'S VALENTINE'S DAY. SHOULDN'T YOU BE AT A--AT A--WHAT DO YOU CALL THEM, NOW...
AT A SOCK HOP OR SOMETHING?
HAH HAH HAH!
OH MAN, VULTURE, YOU GOTTA STOP IT WITH THAT "SOCK HOP" STUFF! YOU'RE SO OUT OF TOUCH IT'S MAKING ME LAUGH! YOU KNOW WHAT THAT MEANS?
THAT MEANS YOU'RE SO OUT OF TOUCH THAT IT'S ACTUALLY INTERFERING WITH MY ABILITY TO CAPTURE YOU.
...I'LL SHOW YOU "INTERFERING WITH YOUR ABILITY TO CAPTURE ME"...
THWIP
TOO SLOW, SPIDER-MAN! AND EVEN YOU CAN'T BE IN TWO PLACES AT ONCE!
SO LET'S SEE YOU DECIDE BETWEEN CAPTURING ME...

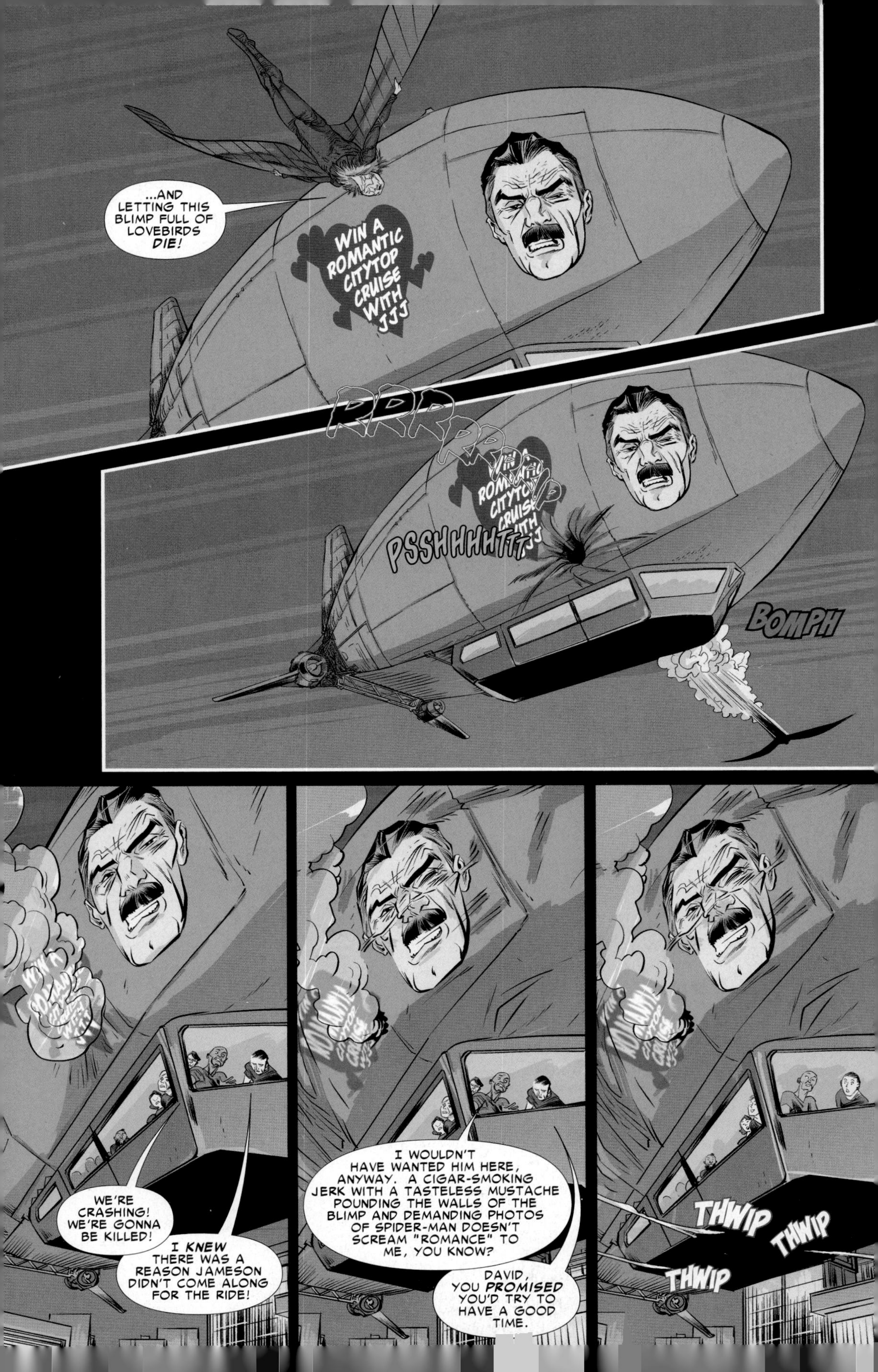
...AND LETTING THIS BLIMP FULL OF LOVEBIRDS *DIE!*
WIN A ROMANTIC CITYTOP CRUISE WITH JJJ
RRRRRRRIP
PSSHHHHTTT
BOMPH
WE'RE CRASHING! WE'RE GONNA BE KILLED!
I *KNEW* THERE WAS A REASON JAMESON DIDN'T COME ALONG FOR THE RIDE!
I WOULDN'T HAVE WANTED HIM HERE, ANYWAY. A CIGAR-SMOKING JERK WITH A TASTELESS MUSTACHE POUNDING THE WALLS OF THE BLIMP AND DEMANDING PHOTOS OF SPIDER-MAN DOESN'T SCREAM "ROMANCE" TO ME, YOU KNOW?
DAVID, YOU *PROMISED* YOU'D TRY TO HAVE A GOOD TIME.
THWIP
THWIP
THWIP

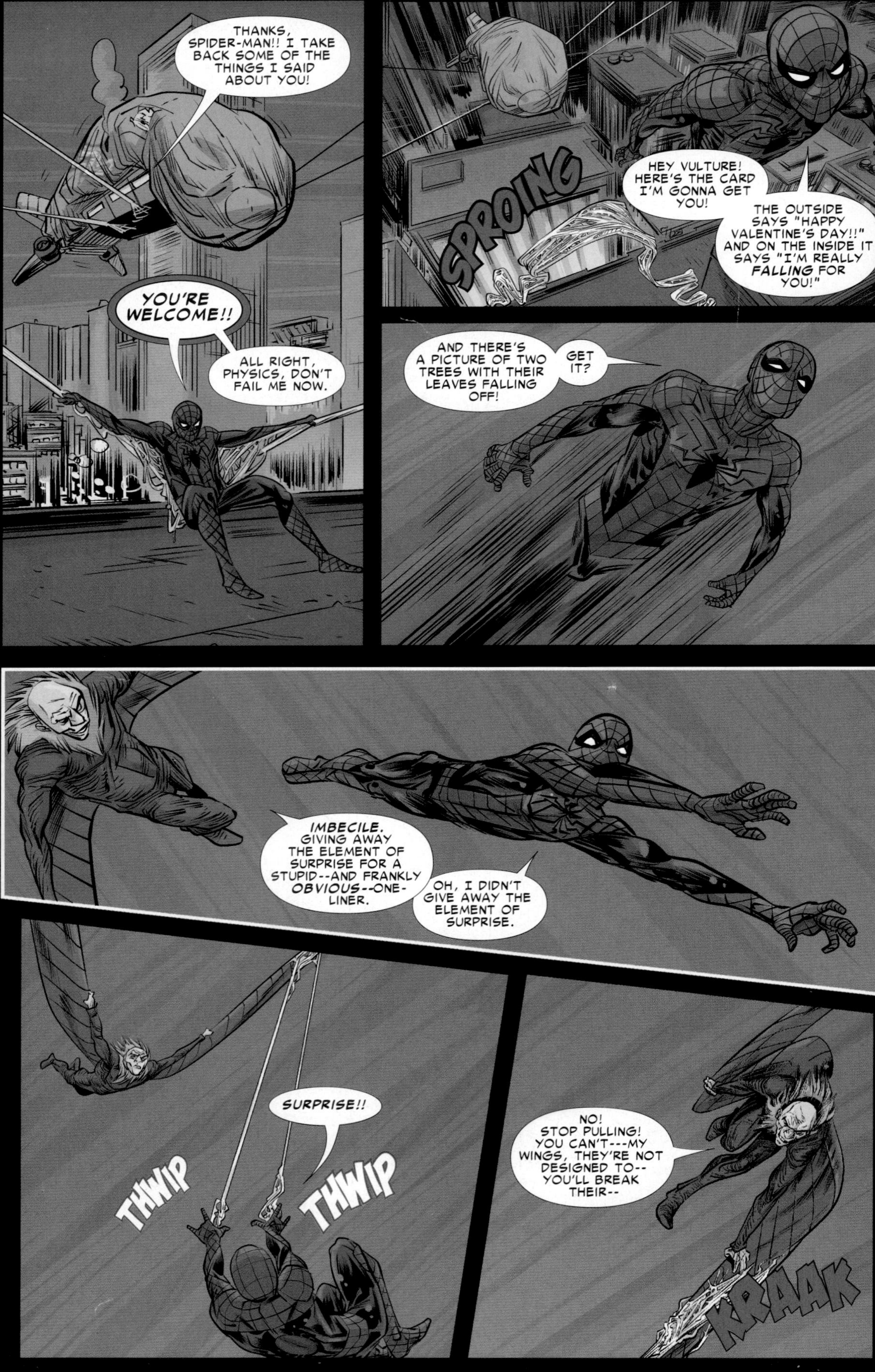
THANKS, SPIDER-MAN!! I TAKE BACK SOME OF THE THINGS I SAID ABOUT YOU!
YOU'RE WELCOME!!
ALL RIGHT, PHYSICS, DON'T FAIL ME NOW.
SPROING
HEY VULTURE! HERE'S THE CARD I'M GONNA GET YOU!
THE OUTSIDE SAYS "HAPPY VALENTINE'S DAY!!" AND ON THE INSIDE IT SAYS "I'M REALLY FALLING FOR YOU!"
AND THERE'S A PICTURE OF TWO TREES WITH THEIR LEAVES FALLING OFF!
GET IT?
IMBECILE. GIVING AWAY THE ELEMENT OF SURPRISE FOR A STUPID--AND FRANKLY OBVIOUS--ONE-LINER.
OH, I DIDN'T GIVE AWAY THE ELEMENT OF SURPRISE.
SURPRISE!!
THWIP
THWIP
NO! STOP PULLING! YOU CAN'T---MY WINGS, THEY'RE NOT DESIGNED TO--YOU'LL BREAK THEIR--
KRAAK

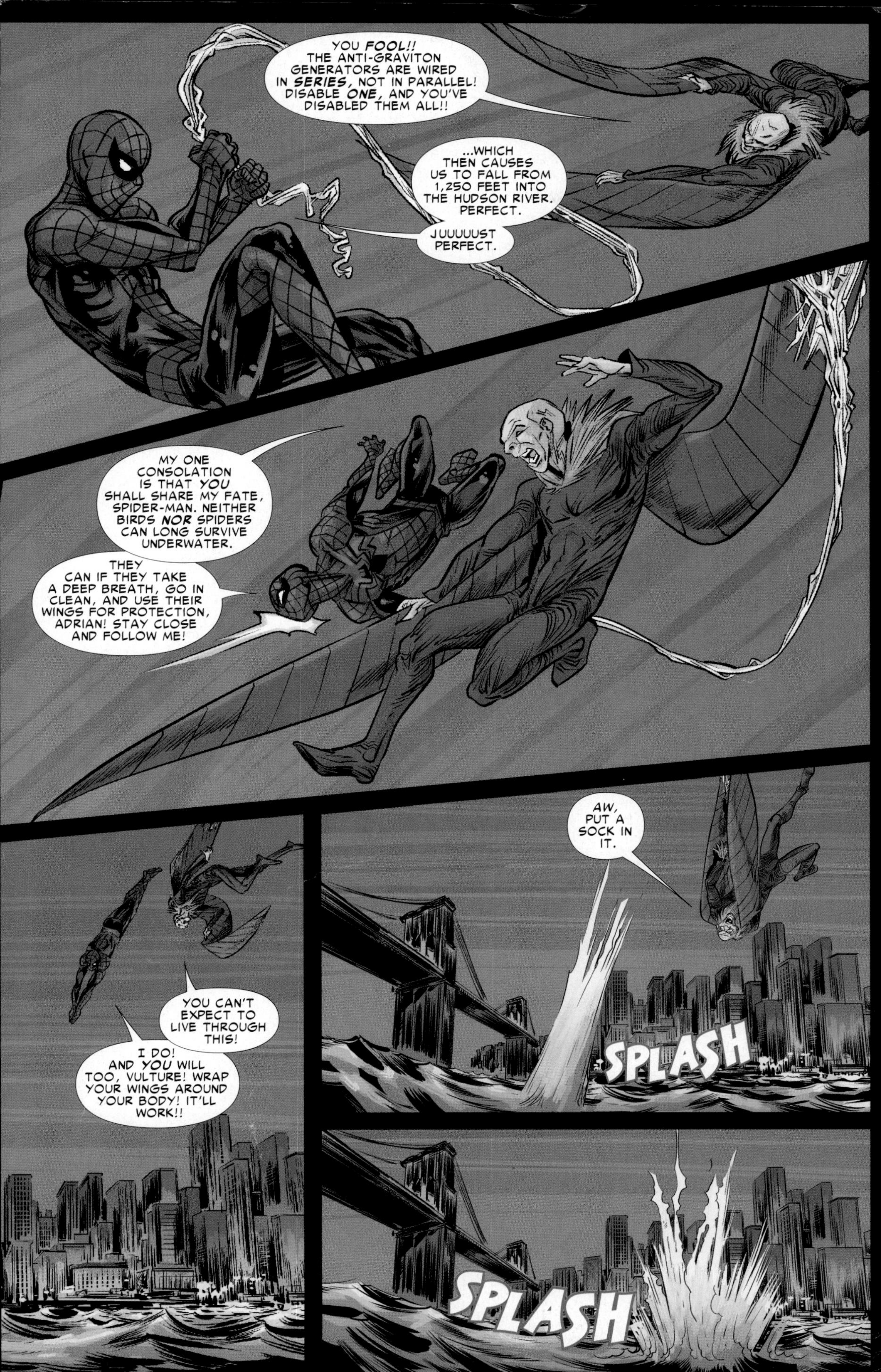
YOU FOOL!! THE ANTI-GRAVITON GENERATORS ARE WIRED IN SERIES, NOT IN PARALLEL! DISABLE ONE, AND YOU'VE DISABLED THEM ALL!!
...WHICH THEN CAUSES US TO FALL FROM 1,250 FEET INTO THE HUDSON RIVER. PERFECT.
JUUUUUST PERFECT.
MY ONE CONSOLATION IS THAT YOU SHALL SHARE MY FATE, SPIDER-MAN. NEITHER BIRDS NOR SPIDERS CAN LONG SURVIVE UNDERWATER.
THEY CAN IF THEY TAKE A DEEP BREATH, GO IN CLEAN, AND USE THEIR WINGS FOR PROTECTION, ADRIAN! STAY CLOSE AND FOLLOW ME!
YOU CAN'T EXPECT TO LIVE THROUGH THIS!
I DO! AND YOU WILL TOO, VULTURE! WRAP YOUR WINGS AROUND YOUR BODY! IT'LL WORK!!
AW, PUT A SOCK IN IT.
SPLASH
SPLASH

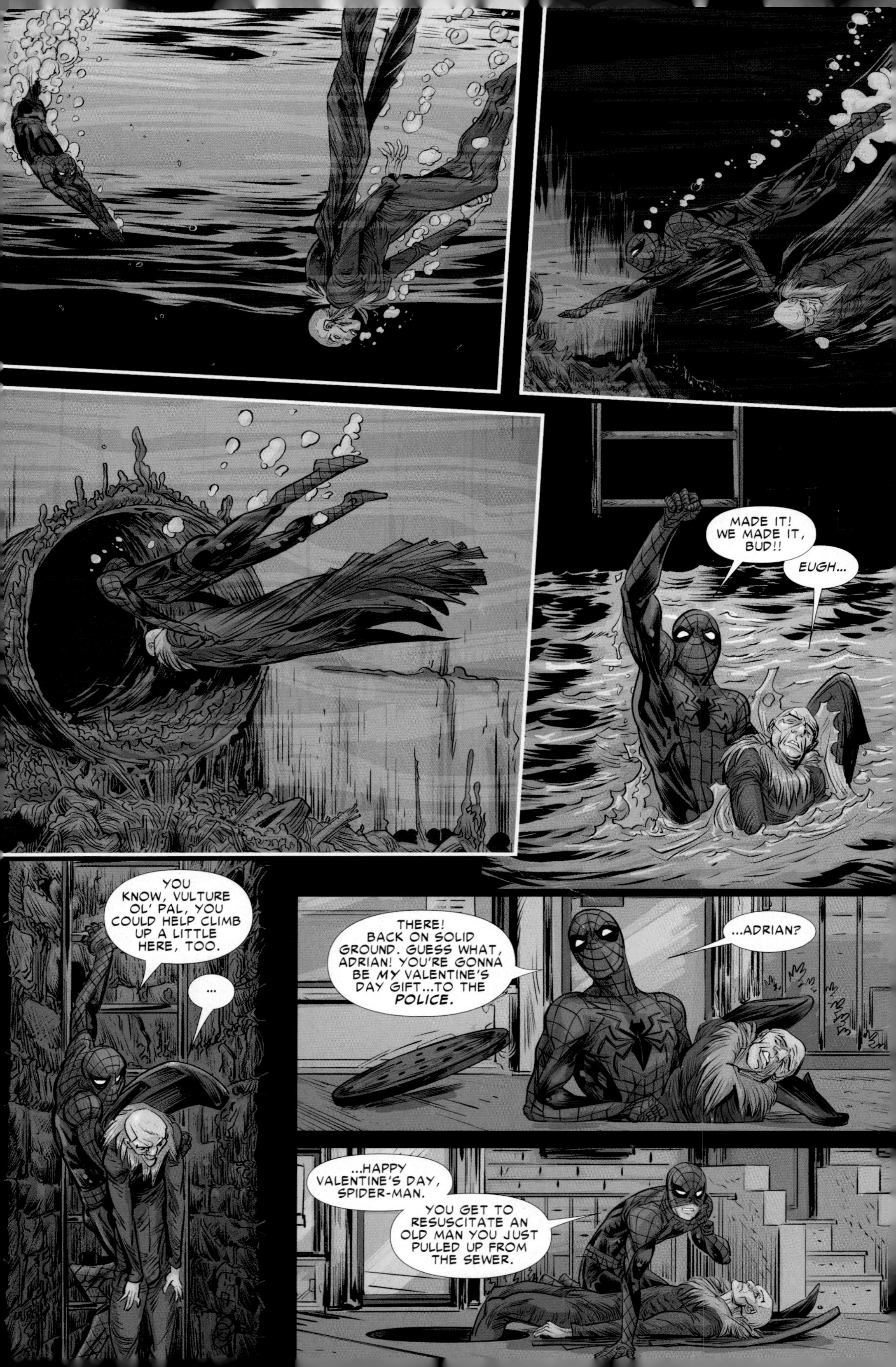
MADE IT! WE MADE IT, BUD!!
EUGH...
YOU KNOW, VULTURE OL' PAL, YOU COULD HELP CLIMB UP A LITTLE HERE, TOO.
...
THERE! BACK ON SOLID GROUND. GUESS WHAT, ADRIAN! YOU'RE GONNA BE MY VALENTINE'S DAY GIFT...TO THE POLICE.
...ADRIAN?
...HAPPY VALENTINE'S DAY, SPIDER-MAN.
YOU GET TO RESUSCITATE AN OLD MAN YOU JUST PULLED UP FROM THE SEWER.

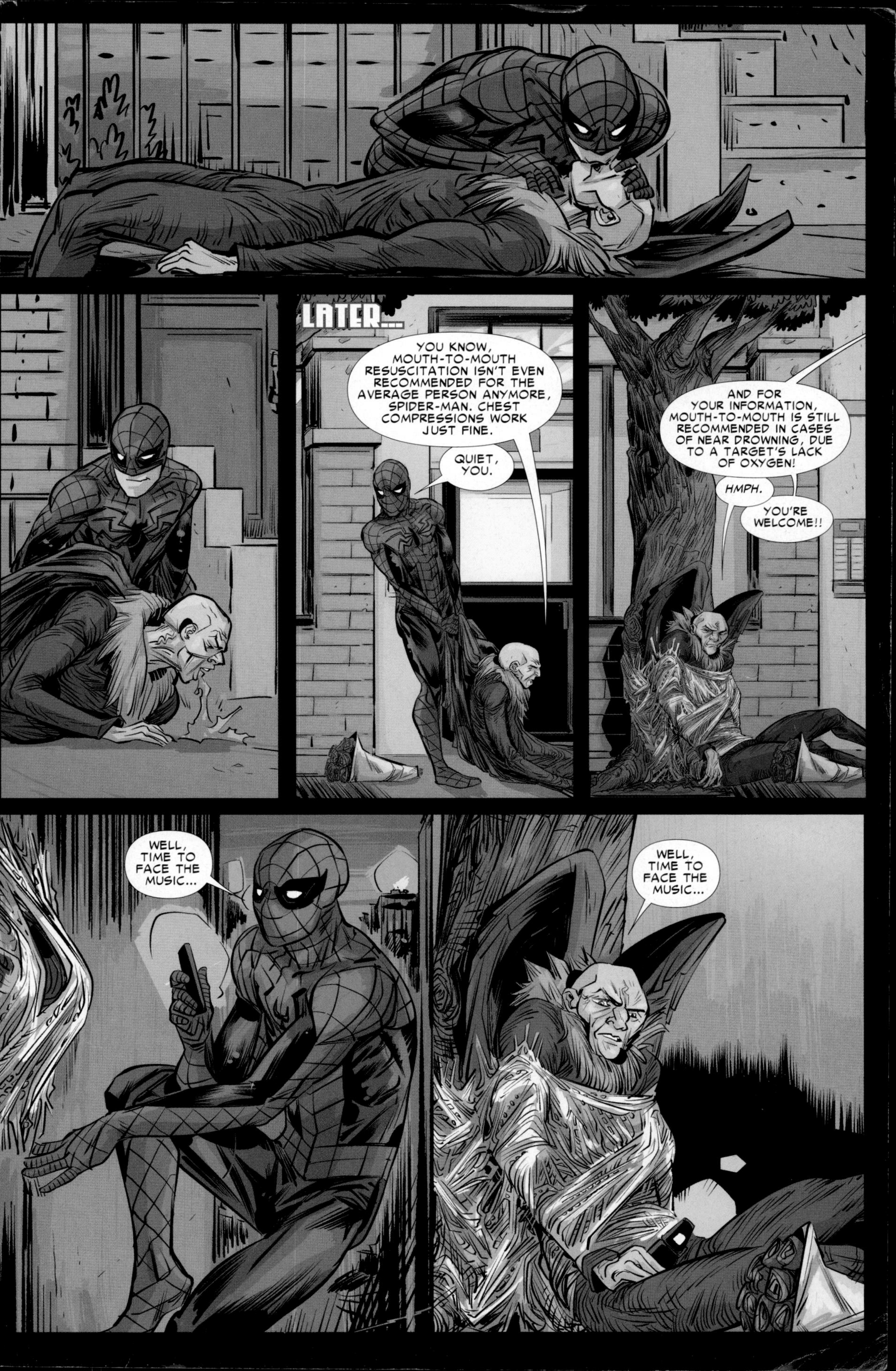
LATER...
YOU KNOW, MOUTH-TO-MOUTH RESUSCITATION ISN'T EVEN RECOMMENDED FOR THE AVERAGE PERSON ANYMORE, SPIDER-MAN. CHEST COMPRESSIONS WORK JUST FINE.
QUIET, YOU.
AND FOR YOUR INFORMATION, MOUTH-TO-MOUTH IS STILL RECOMMENDED IN CASES OF NEAR DROWNING, DUE TO A TARGET'S LACK OF OXYGEN!
HMPH.
YOU'RE WELCOME!!
WELL, TIME TO FACE THE MUSIC...
WELL, TIME TO FACE THE MUSIC...

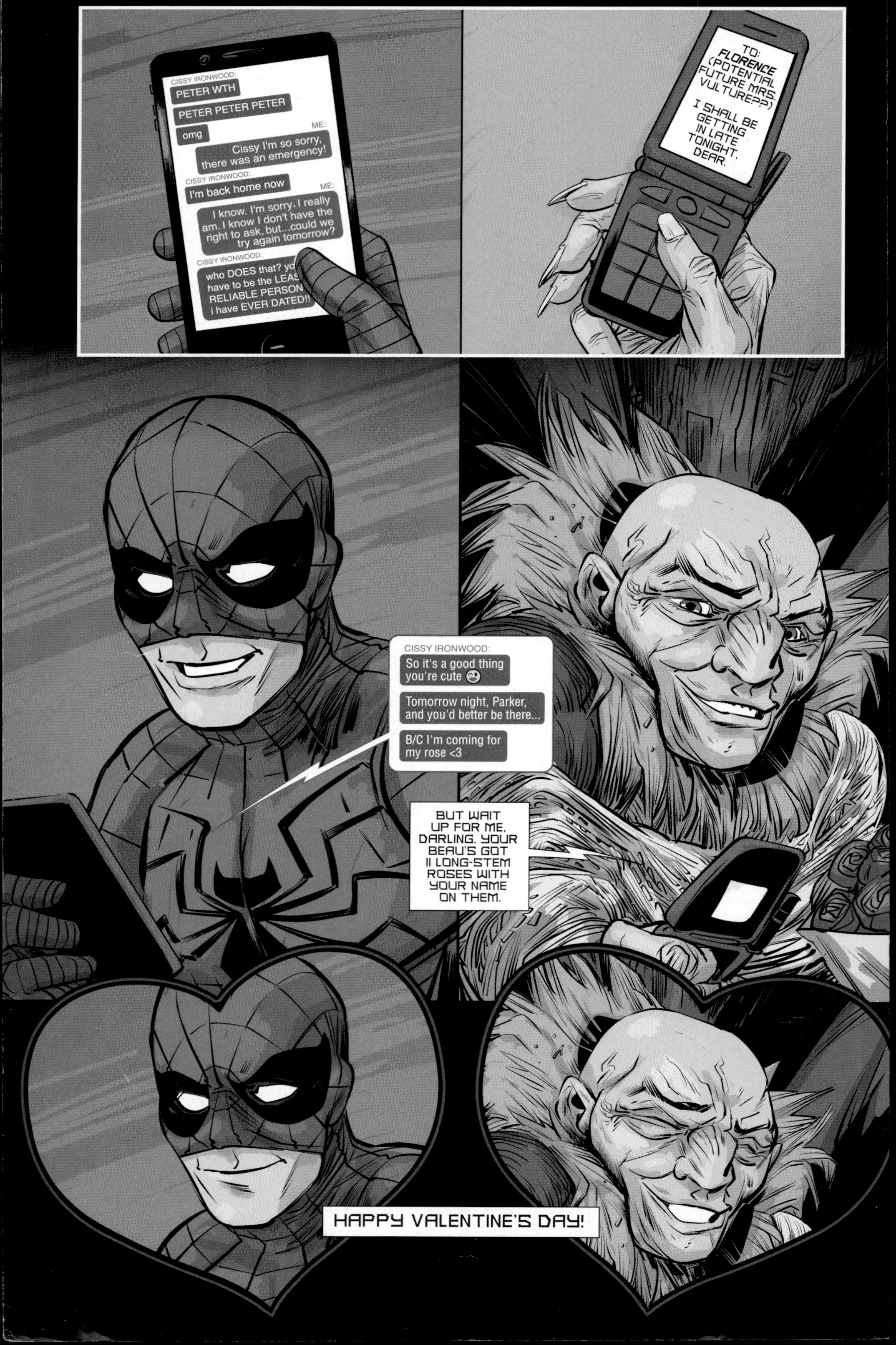
CISSY IRONWOOD:
PETER WTH
PETER PETER PETER
omg
ME:
Cissy I'm so sorry, there was an emergency!
CISSY IRONWOOD:
I'm back home now
ME:
I know. I'm sorry, I really am. I know I don't have the right to ask, but...could we try again tomorrow?
CISSY IRONWOOD:
who DOES that? yo
have to be the LEAS
RELIABLE PERSON
i have EVER DATED!!
TO: FLORENCE (POTENTIAL FUTURE MRS. VULTURE??)
I SHALL BE GETTING IN LATE TONIGHT, DEAR.
CISSY IRONWOOD:
So it's a good thing you're cute
Tomorrow night, Parker, and you'd better be there...
B/C I'm coming for my rose <3
BUT WAIT UP FOR ME, DARLING. YOUR BEAU'S GOT 11 LONG-STEM ROSES WITH YOUR NAME ON THEM.
HAPPY VALENTINE'S DAY!

THE ASTONISHING ANT-MAN

MARCH

SUNDAY	MONDAY	TUESDAY	WEDNESDAY	THURSDAY	FRIDAY	SATURDAY
	1	2	3	4	5	6
7	8	10	11	12	13	14 First Day of Spring
15 Daylight Savings Time Begins	16	17 St. Patrick's Day	18	19	20	21
22 Spring Break	23	24	25	26	27	28
29	30	31				

AMY CHU
WRITER

RYAN BROWNE
ARTIST

REILLY BROWN
LAYOUT ARTIST

VC'S TRAVIS LANHAM
LETTERING

ANNIE CHENG & TIM SMITH 3
PRODUCTION TEAM

CARLOS LAO
PRODUCTION DESIGN

HEATHER ANTOS
EDITOR

JORDAN D. WHITE & NICK LOWE
SUPERVISING EDITORS

EDITOR IN CHIEF **AXEL ALONSO** CHIEF CREATIVE OFFICER **JOE QUESADA** PUBLISHER **DAN BUCKLEY** EXECUTIVE PRODUCER **ALAN FINE**

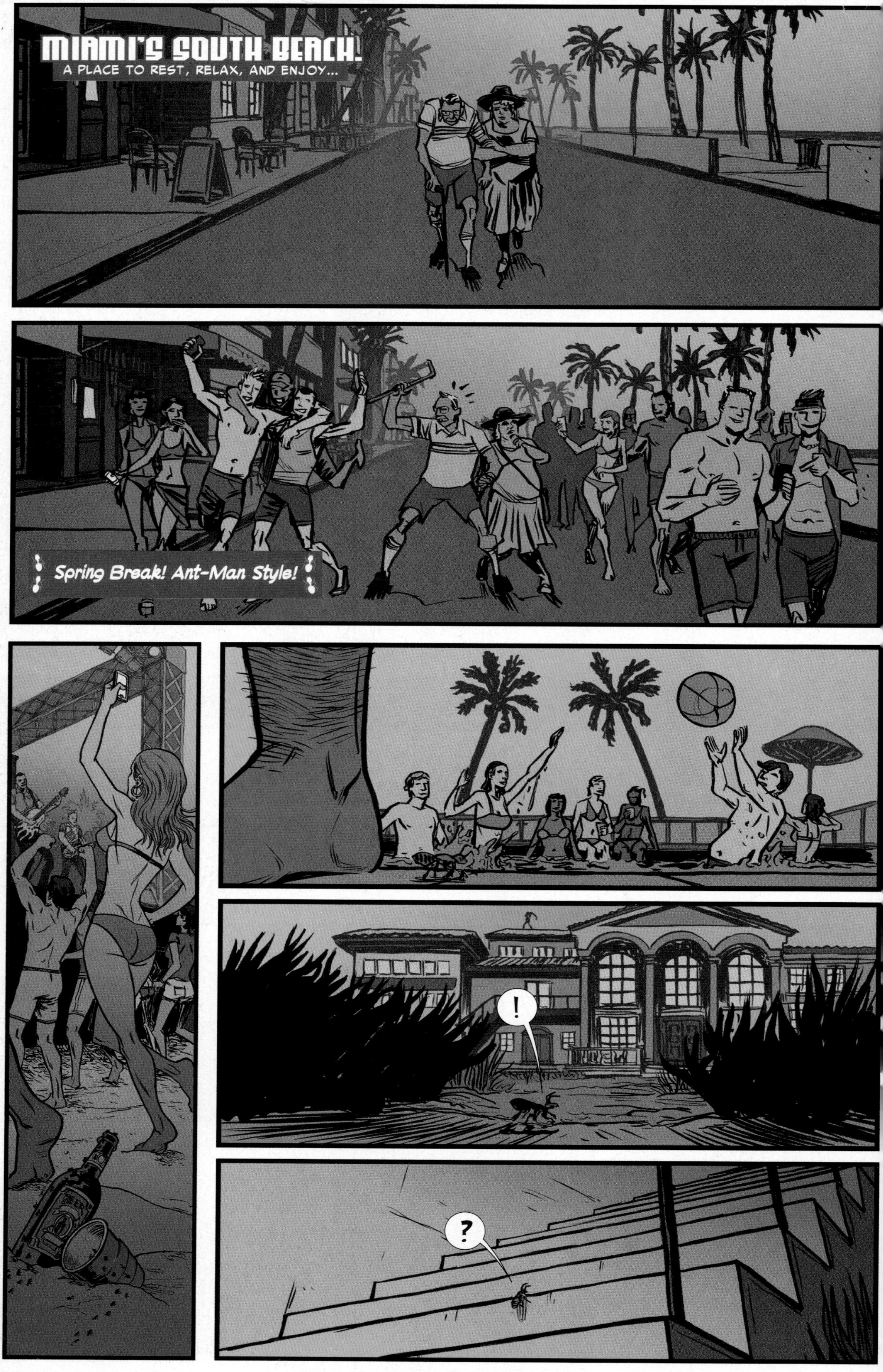
MIAMI'S SOUTH BEACH.
A PLACE TO REST, RELAX, AND ENJOY...
Spring Break! Ant-Man Style!
!
?

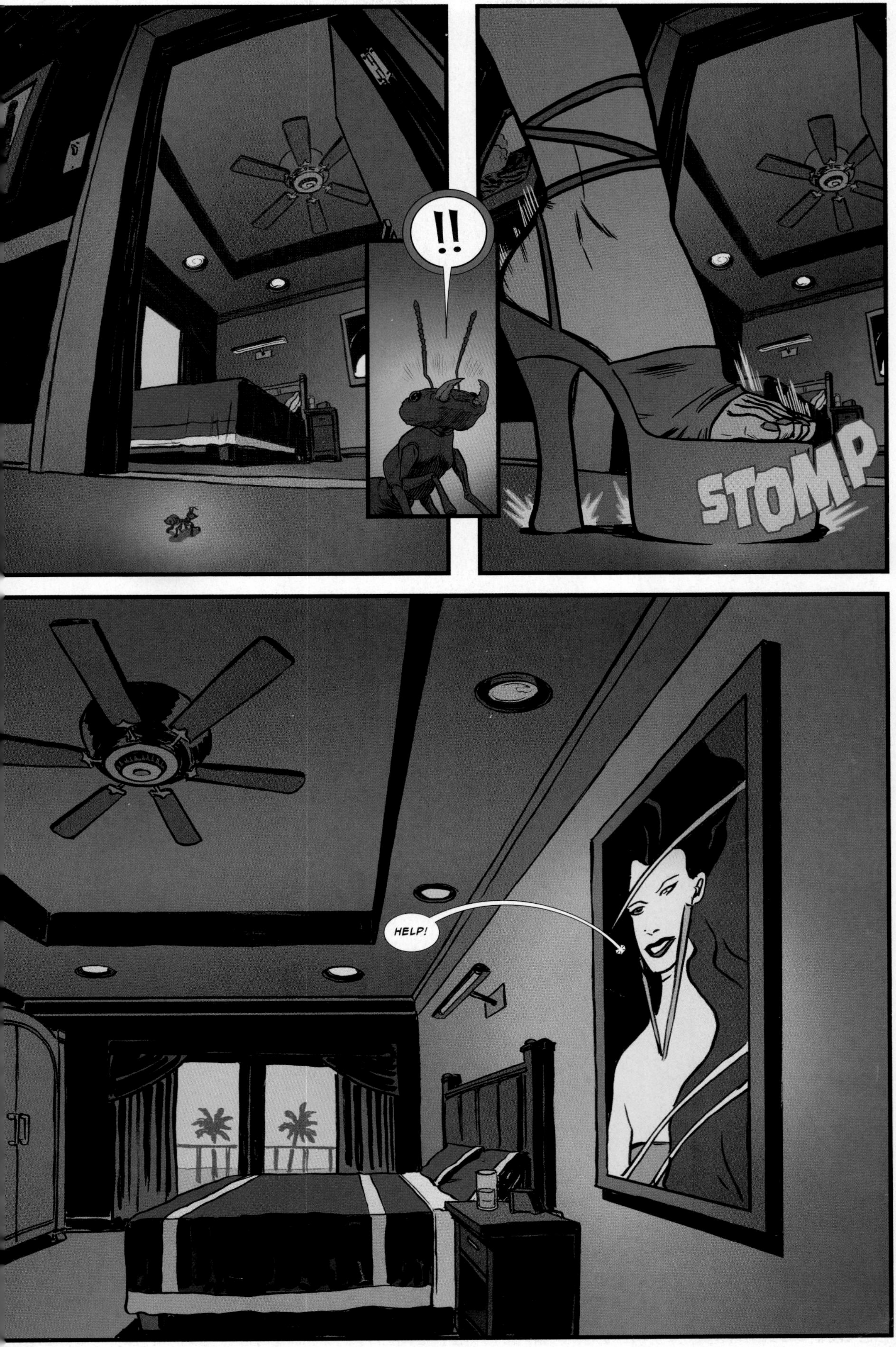
!!
STOMP
HELP!

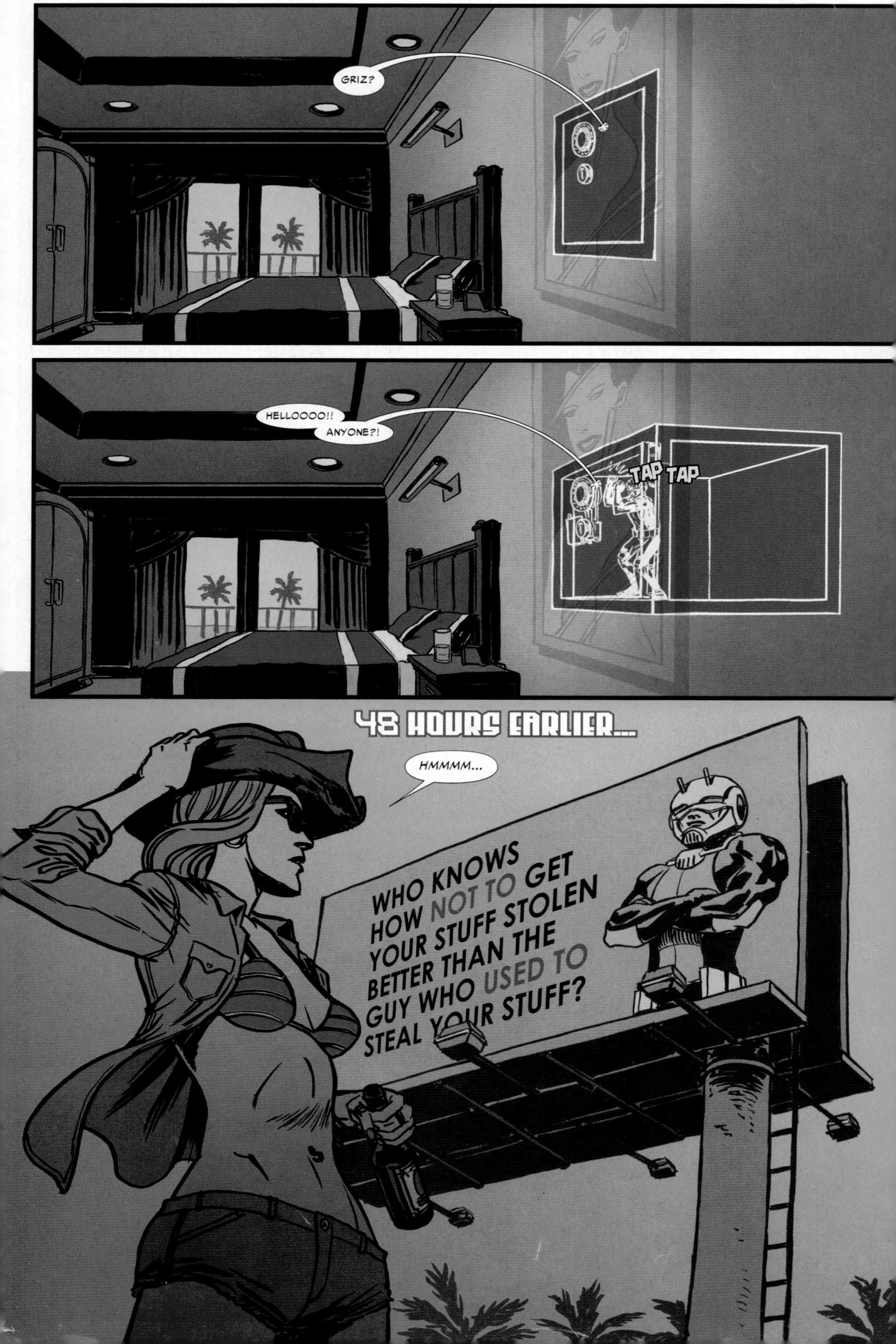

GRIZ?
HELLOOOO!!
ANYONE?!
TAP TAP
48 HOURS EARLIER...
HMMMM...
WHO KNOWS HOW NOT TO GET YOUR STUFF STOLEN BETTER THAN THE GUY WHO USED TO STEAL YOUR STUFF?

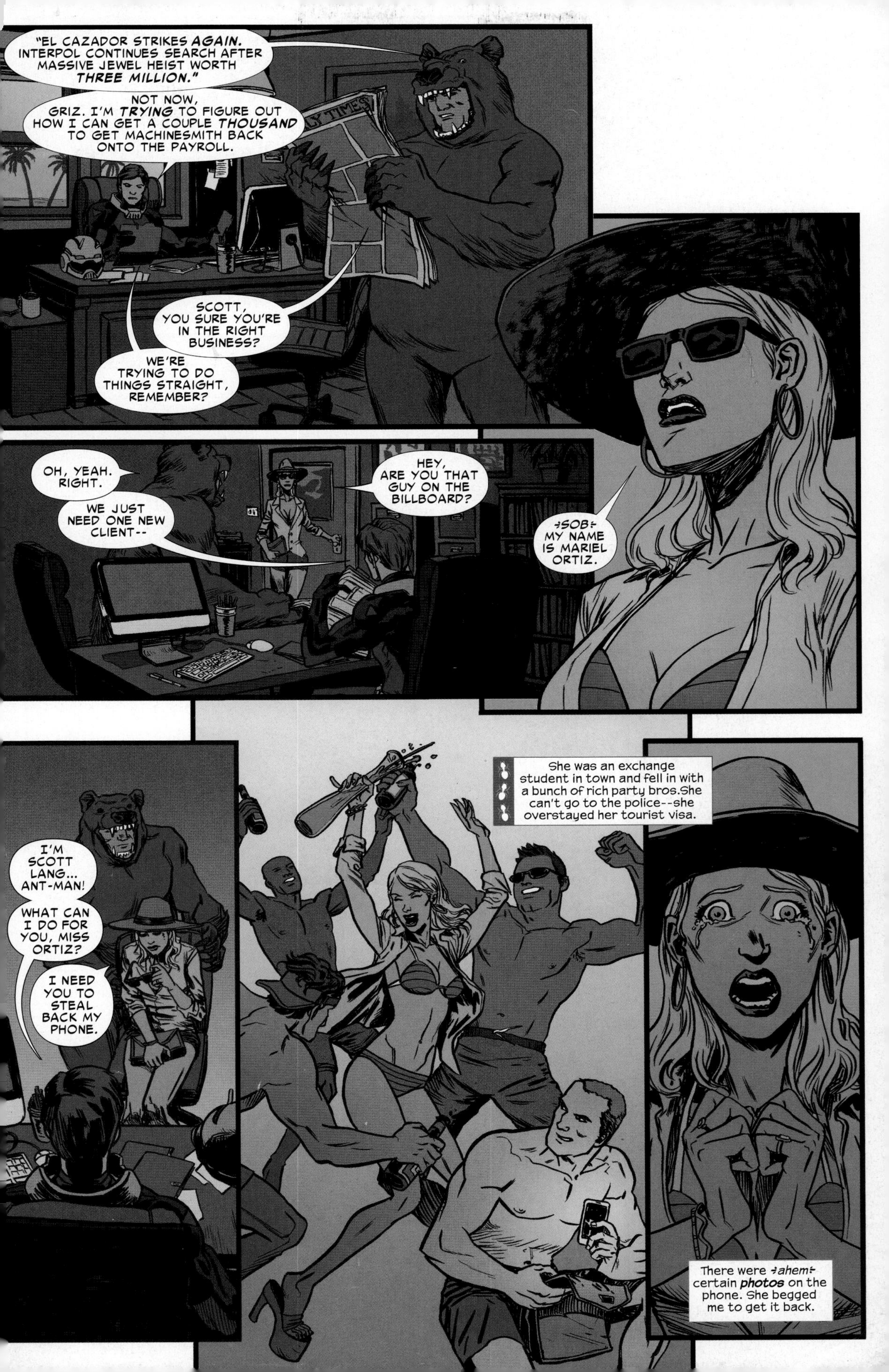
"EL CAZADOR STRIKES AGAIN. INTERPOL CONTINUES SEARCH AFTER MASSIVE JEWEL HEIST WORTH THREE MILLION."
NOT NOW, GRIZ. I'M TRYING TO FIGURE OUT HOW I CAN GET A COUPLE THOUSAND TO GET MACHINESMITH BACK ONTO THE PAYROLL.
SCOTT, YOU SURE YOU'RE IN THE RIGHT BUSINESS?
WE'RE TRYING TO DO THINGS STRAIGHT, REMEMBER?
OH, YEAH. RIGHT.
WE JUST NEED ONE NEW CLIENT--
HEY, ARE YOU THAT GUY ON THE BILLBOARD?
-SOB- MY NAME IS MARIEL ORTIZ.
I'M SCOTT LANG... ANT-MAN!
WHAT CAN I DO FOR YOU, MISS ORTIZ?
I NEED YOU TO STEAL BACK MY PHONE.
She was an exchange student in town and fell in with a bunch of rich party bros. She can't go to the police--she overstayed her tourist visa.
There were -ahem- certain photos on the phone. She begged me to get it back.

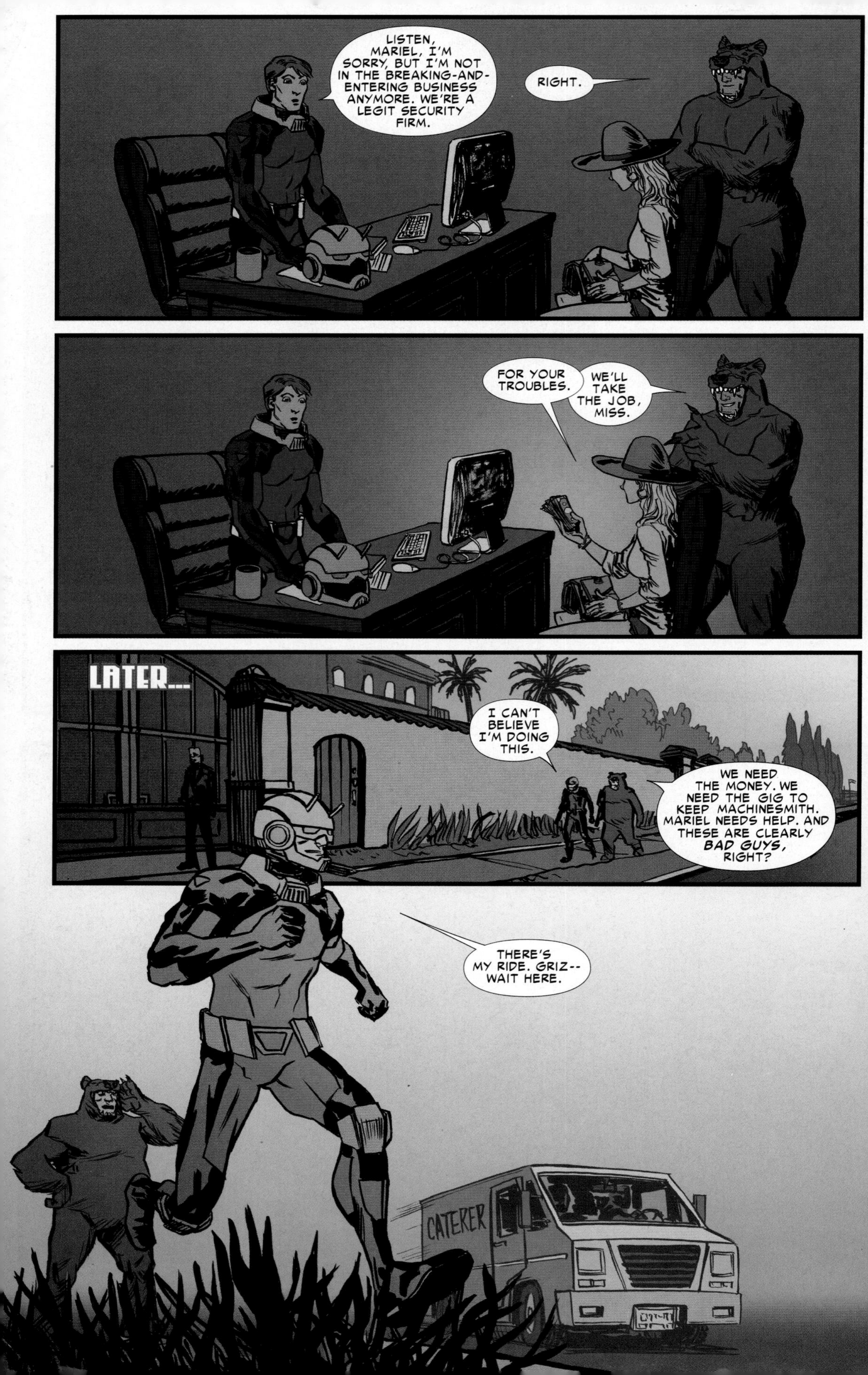
LISTEN, MARIEL, I'M SORRY, BUT I'M NOT IN THE BREAKING-AND-ENTERING BUSINESS ANYMORE. WE'RE A LEGIT SECURITY FIRM.
RIGHT.
FOR YOUR TROUBLES.
WE'LL TAKE THE JOB, MISS.
LATER...
I CAN'T BELIEVE I'M DOING THIS.
WE NEED THE MONEY. WE NEED THE GIG TO KEEP MACHINESMITH. MARIEL NEEDS HELP. AND THESE ARE CLEARLY *BAD GUYS*, RIGHT?
THERE'S MY RIDE. GRIZ-- WAIT HERE.
CATERER

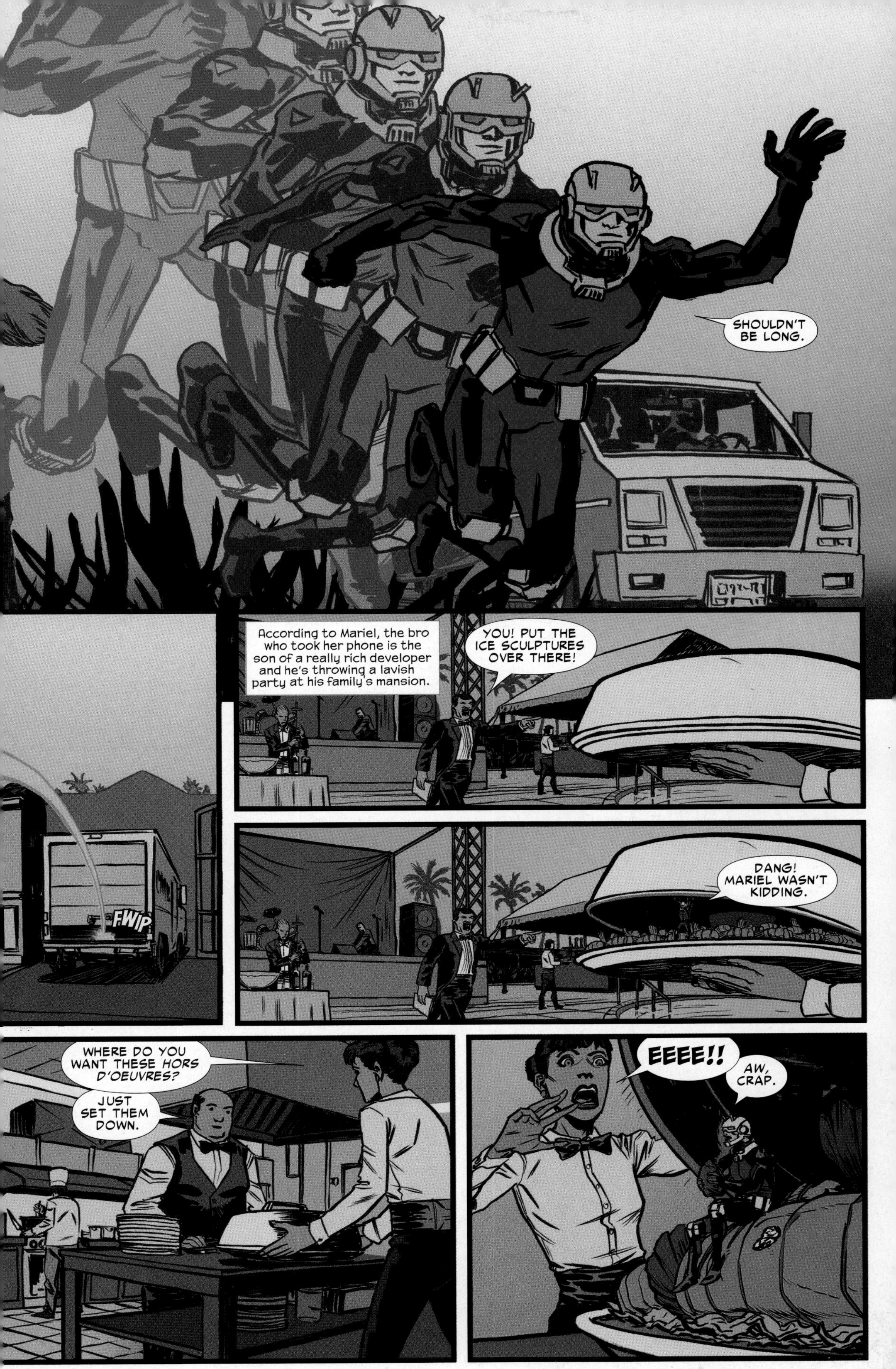
SHOULDN'T BE LONG.
According to Mariel, the bro who took her phone is the son of a really rich developer and he's throwing a lavish party at his family's mansion.
YOU! PUT THE ICE SCULPTURES OVER THERE!
FWIP
DANG! MARIEL WASN'T KIDDING.
WHERE DO YOU WANT THESE HORS D'OEUVRES?
JUST SET THEM DOWN.
EEEE!!
AW, CRAP.

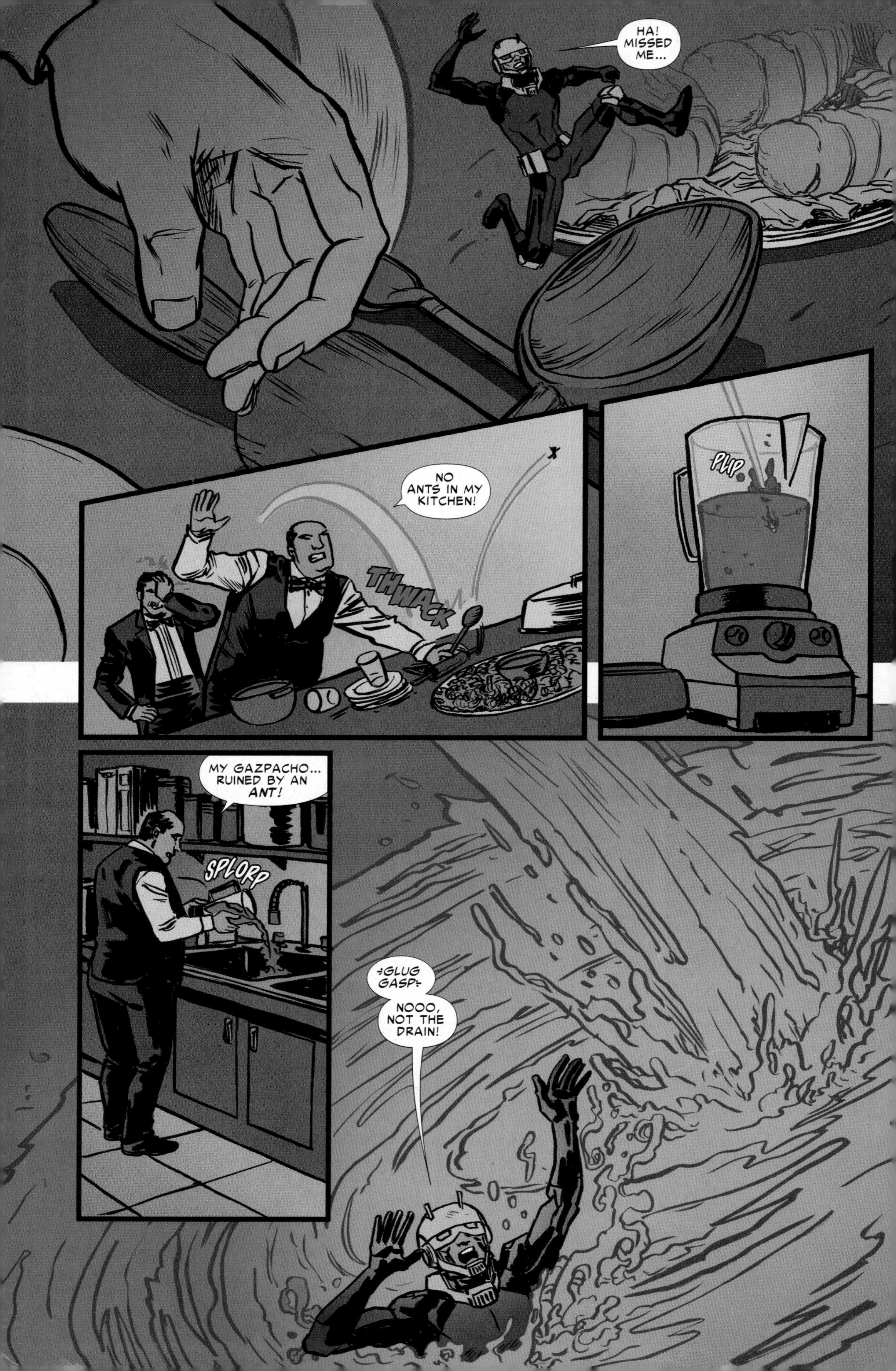
HA! MISSED ME...
NO ANTS IN MY KITCHEN!
THWACK
PLIP
MY GAZPACHO... RUINED BY AN ANT!
SPLORP
GLUG GASP
NOOO, NOT THE DRAIN!

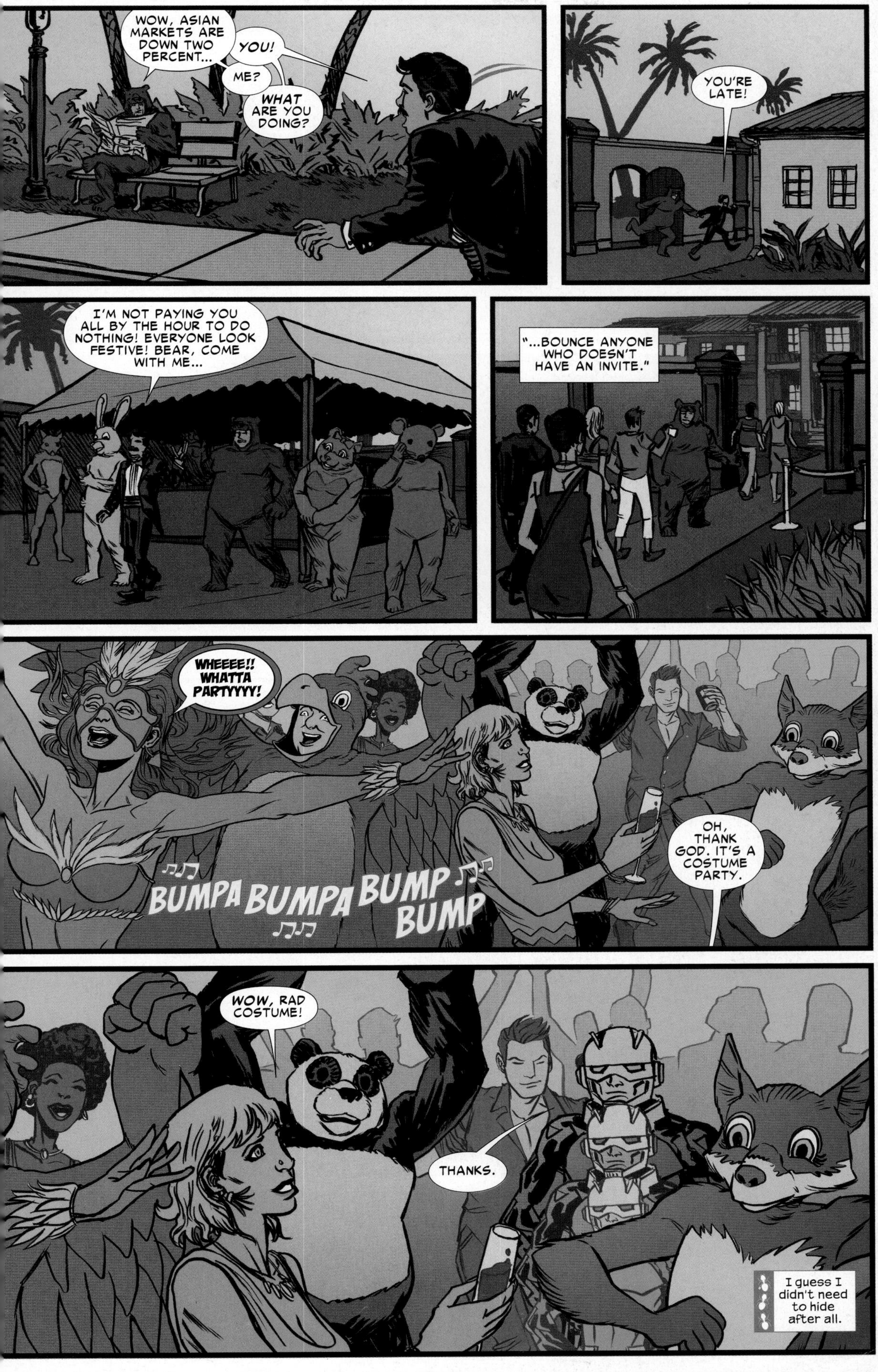

WOW, ASIAN MARKETS ARE DOWN TWO PERCENT...
YOU!
ME?
WHAT ARE YOU DOING?
YOU'RE LATE!
I'M NOT PAYING YOU ALL BY THE HOUR TO DO NOTHING! EVERYONE LOOK FESTIVE! BEAR, COME WITH ME...
"...BOUNCE ANYONE WHO DOESN'T HAVE AN INVITE."
WHEEEE!! WHATTA PARTYYYYY!
BUMPA BUMPA BUMP BUMP
OH, THANK GOD. IT'S A COSTUME PARTY.
WOW, RAD COSTUME!
THANKS.
I guess I didn't need to hide after all.

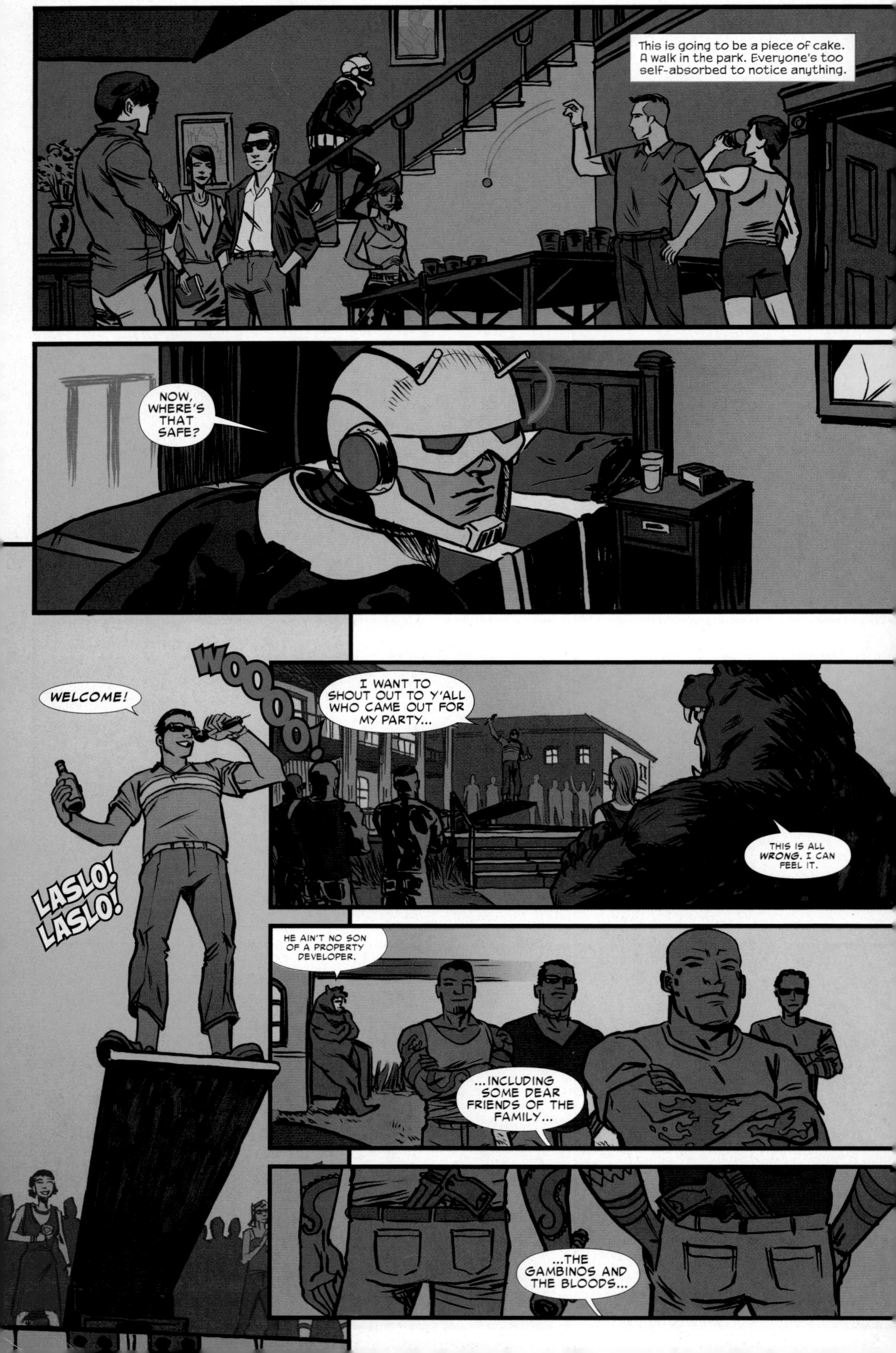
This is going to be a piece of cake. A walk in the park. Everyone's too self-absorbed to notice anything.
NOW, WHERE'S THAT SAFE?
WELCOME!
WOOOOO!
I WANT TO SHOUT OUT TO Y'ALL WHO CAME OUT FOR MY PARTY...
THIS IS ALL WRONG. I CAN FEEL IT.
LASLO! LASLO!
HE AIN'T NO SON OF A PROPERTY DEVELOPER.
...INCLUDING SOME DEAR FRIENDS OF THE FAMILY...
...THE GAMBINOS AND THE BLOODS...

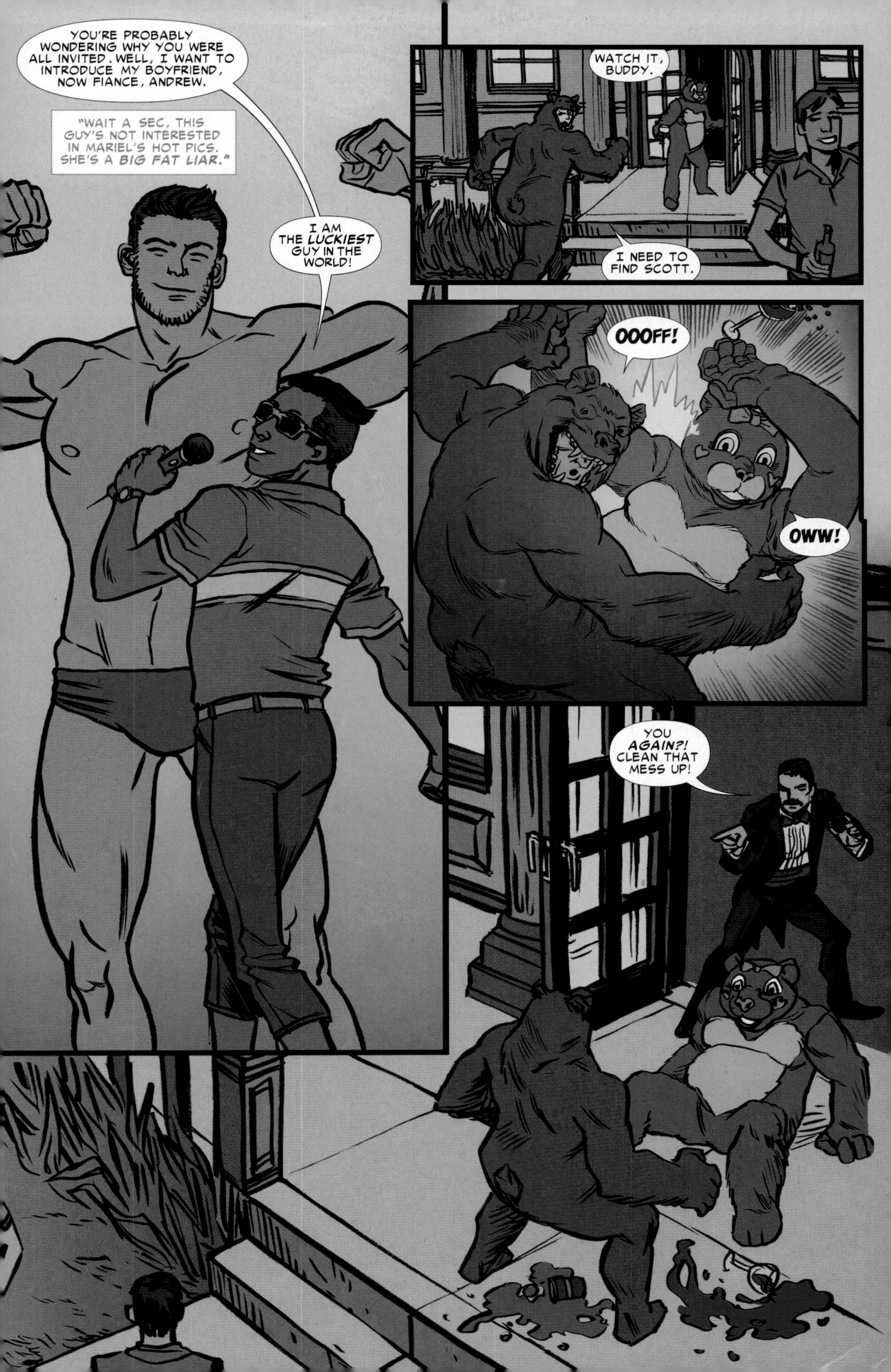
YOU'RE PROBABLY WONDERING WHY YOU WERE ALL INVITED. WELL, I WANT TO INTRODUCE MY BOYFRIEND, NOW FIANCE, ANDREW.
"WAIT A SEC, THIS GUY'S NOT INTERESTED IN MARIEL'S HOT PICS. SHE'S A BIG FAT LIAR."
I AM THE LUCKIEST GUY IN THE WORLD!
WATCH IT, BUDDY.
I NEED TO FIND SCOTT.
OOOFF!
OWW!
YOU AGAIN?! CLEAN THAT MESS UP!

NOW WHERRRE IS IT?

AHA! OBVIOUS.

YEP. I STILL GOT IT.

SNIK

PRESS

...LIKE A WALK...

...IN THE PARK.

CLICK

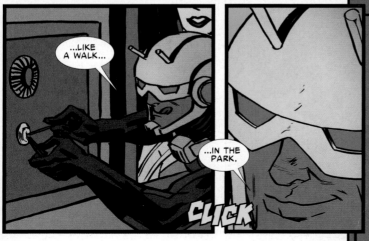

WITH STATE-OF-THE-ART MOT DETECTORS?!

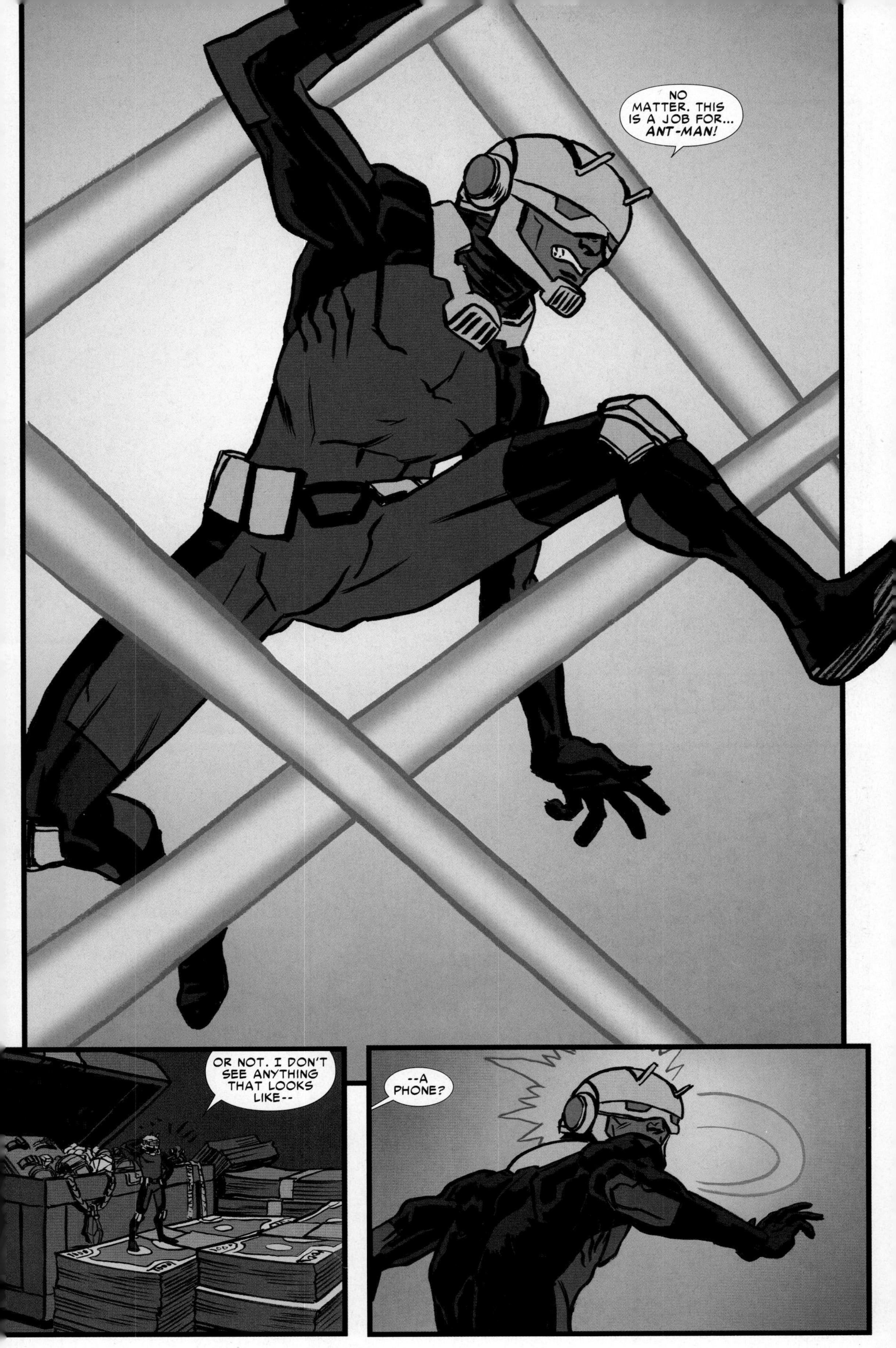
NO MATTER. THIS IS A JOB FOR... ANT-MAN!
OR NOT. I DON'T SEE ANYTHING THAT LOOKS LIKE--
--A PHONE?

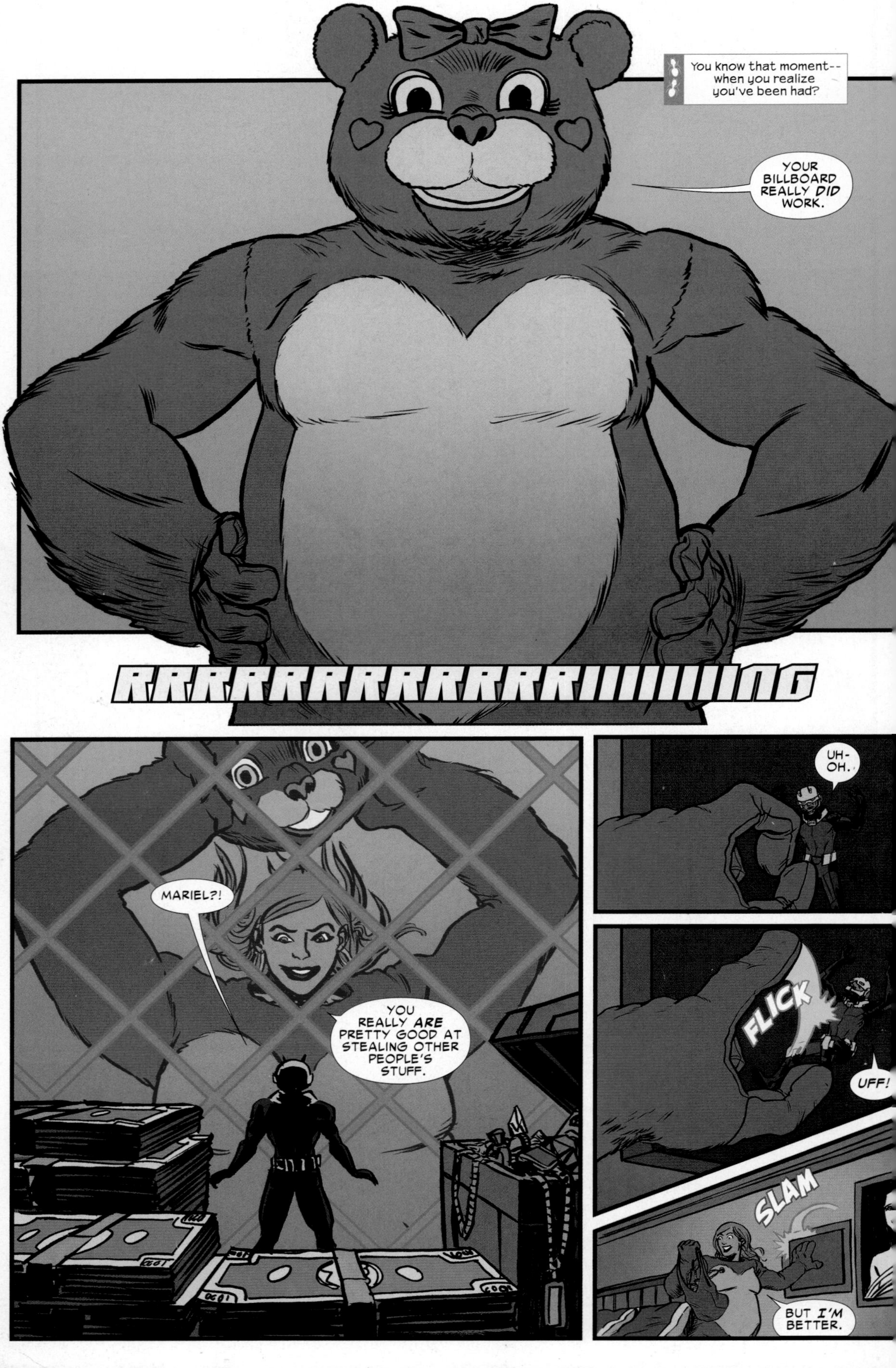

You know that moment-- when you realize you've been had?
YOUR BILLBOARD REALLY DID WORK.
RRRRRRRRRRRRRRRIIIIIIIING
MARIEL?!
YOU REALLY ARE PRETTY GOOD AT STEALING OTHER PEOPLE'S STUFF.
UH-OH.
FLICK
UFF!
SLAM
BUT I'M BETTER.

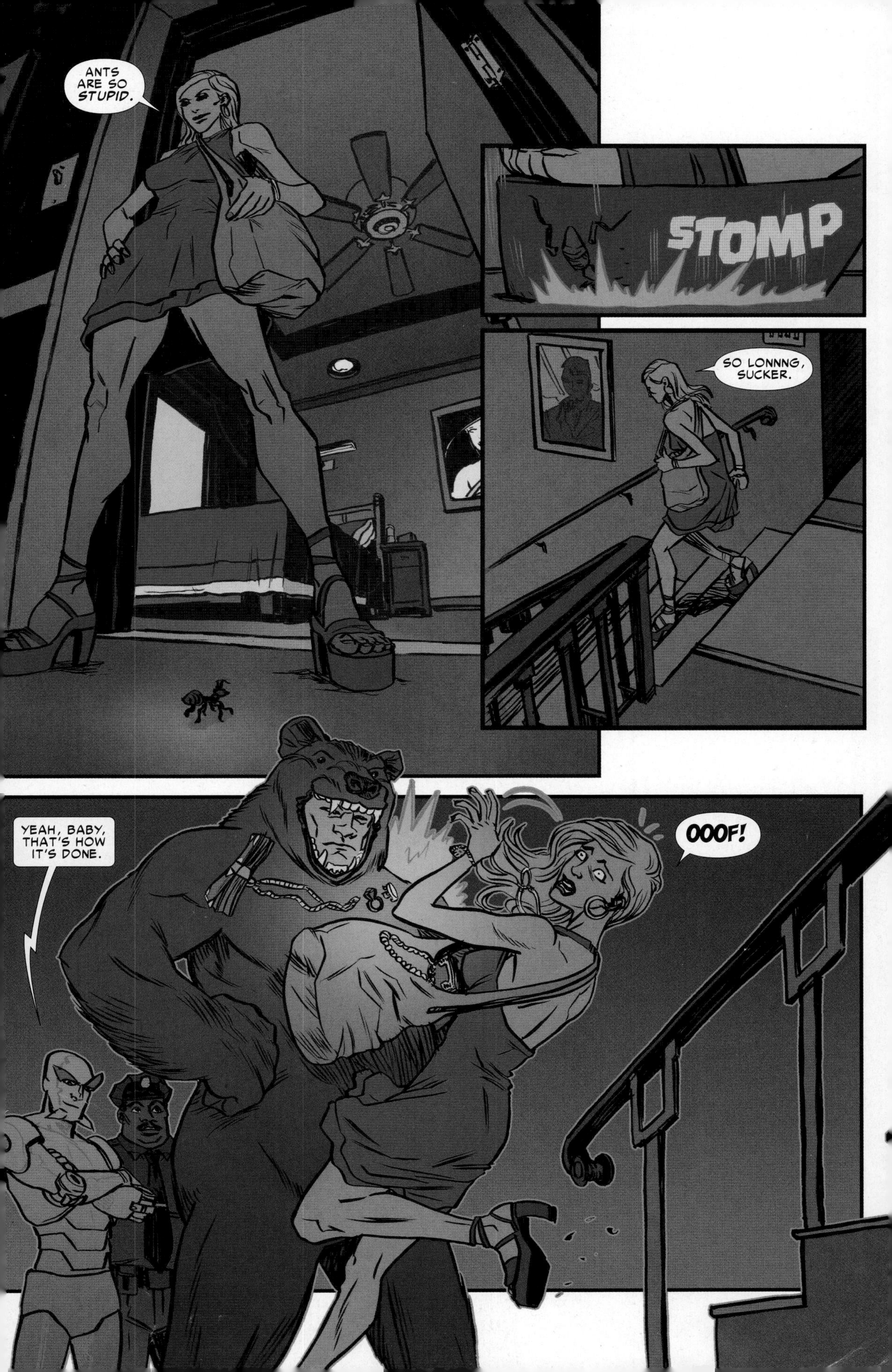
ANTS ARE SO STUPID.
STOMP
SO LONNNG, SUCKER.
YEAH, BABY, THAT'S HOW IT'S DONE.
OOOF!

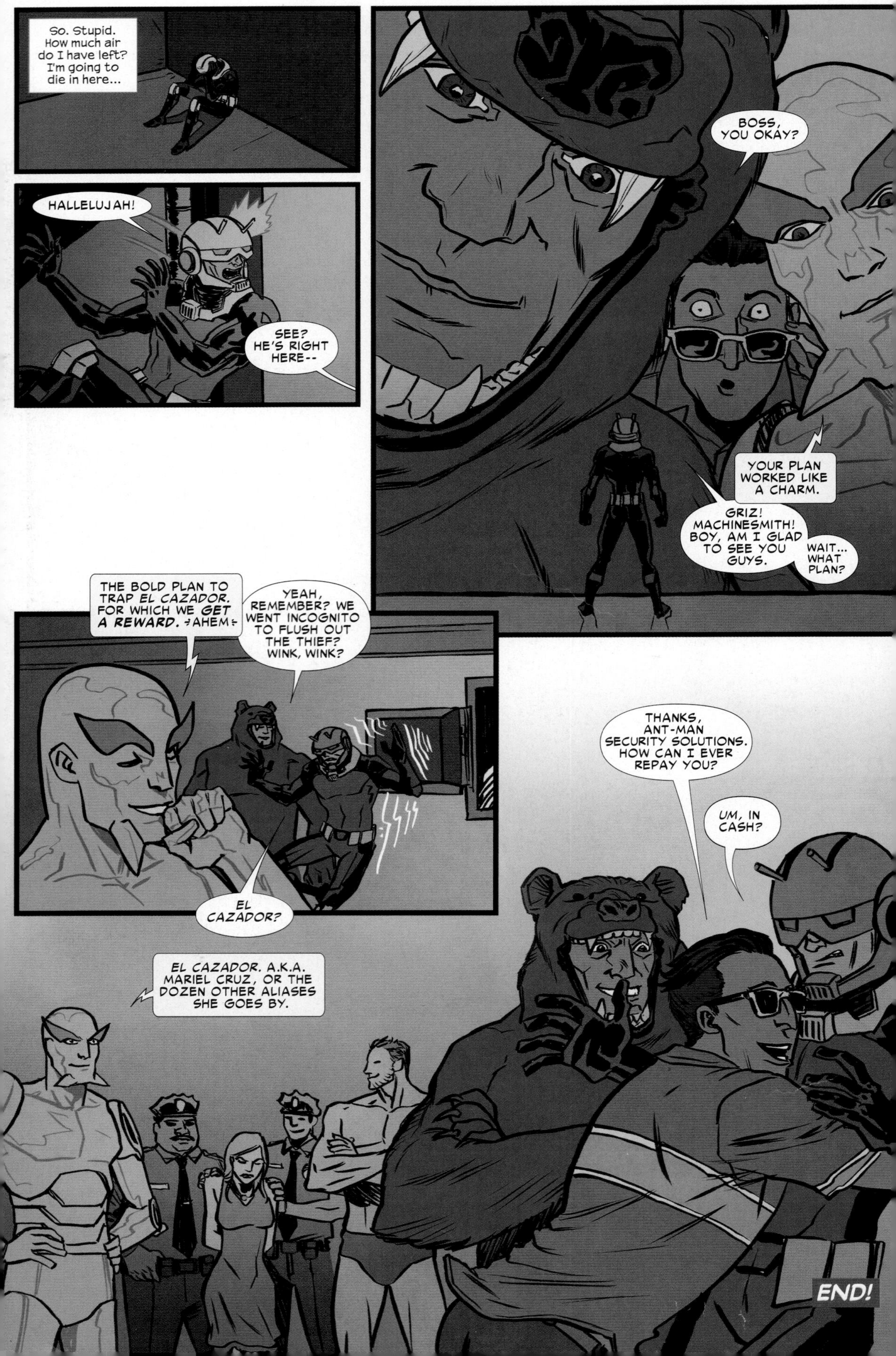
So. Stupid. How much air do I have left? I'm going to die in here...
HALLELUJAH!
SEE? HE'S RIGHT HERE--
BOSS, YOU OKAY?
YOUR PLAN WORKED LIKE A CHARM.
GRIZ! MACHINESMITH! BOY, AM I GLAD TO SEE YOU GUYS.
WAIT... WHAT PLAN?
THE BOLD PLAN TO TRAP EL CAZADOR. FOR WHICH WE GET A REWARD. AHEM
YEAH, REMEMBER? WE WENT INCOGNITO TO FLUSH OUT THE THIEF? WINK, WINK?
EL CAZADOR?
EL CAZADOR. A.K.A. MARIEL CRUZ, OR THE DOZEN OTHER ALIASES SHE GOES BY.
THANKS, ANT-MAN SECURITY SOLUTIONS. HOW CAN I EVER REPAY YOU?
UM, IN CASH?
END!

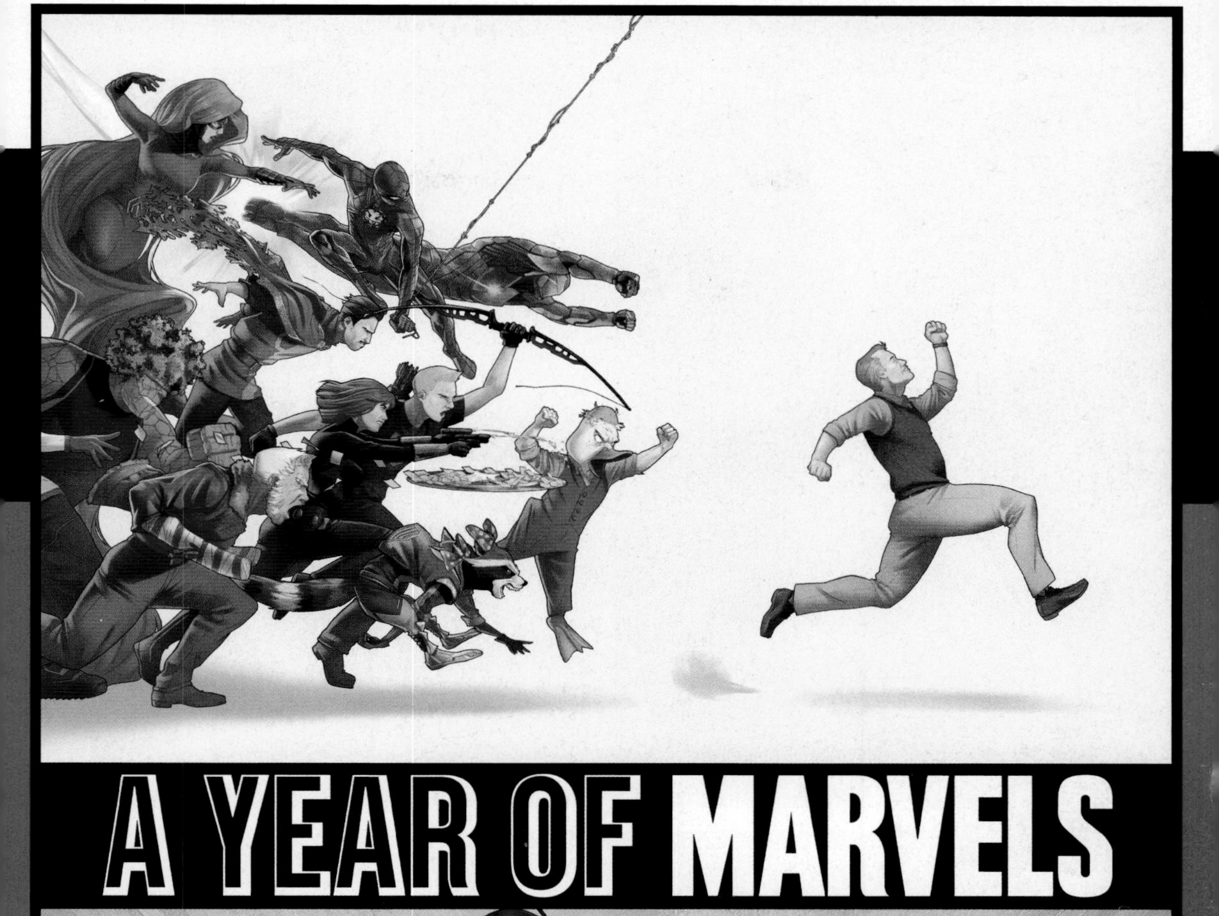

A YEAR OF MARVELS

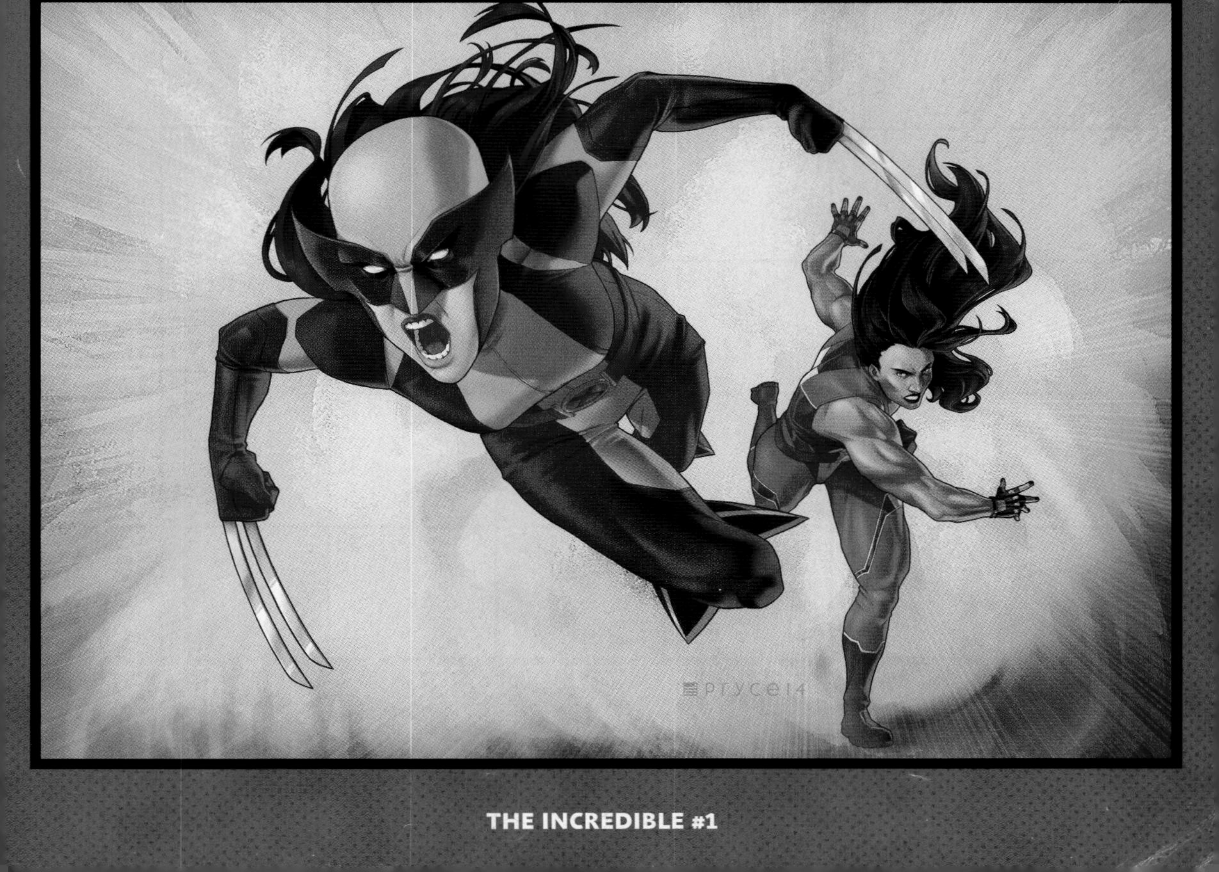
pryce14

THE INCREDIBLE #1

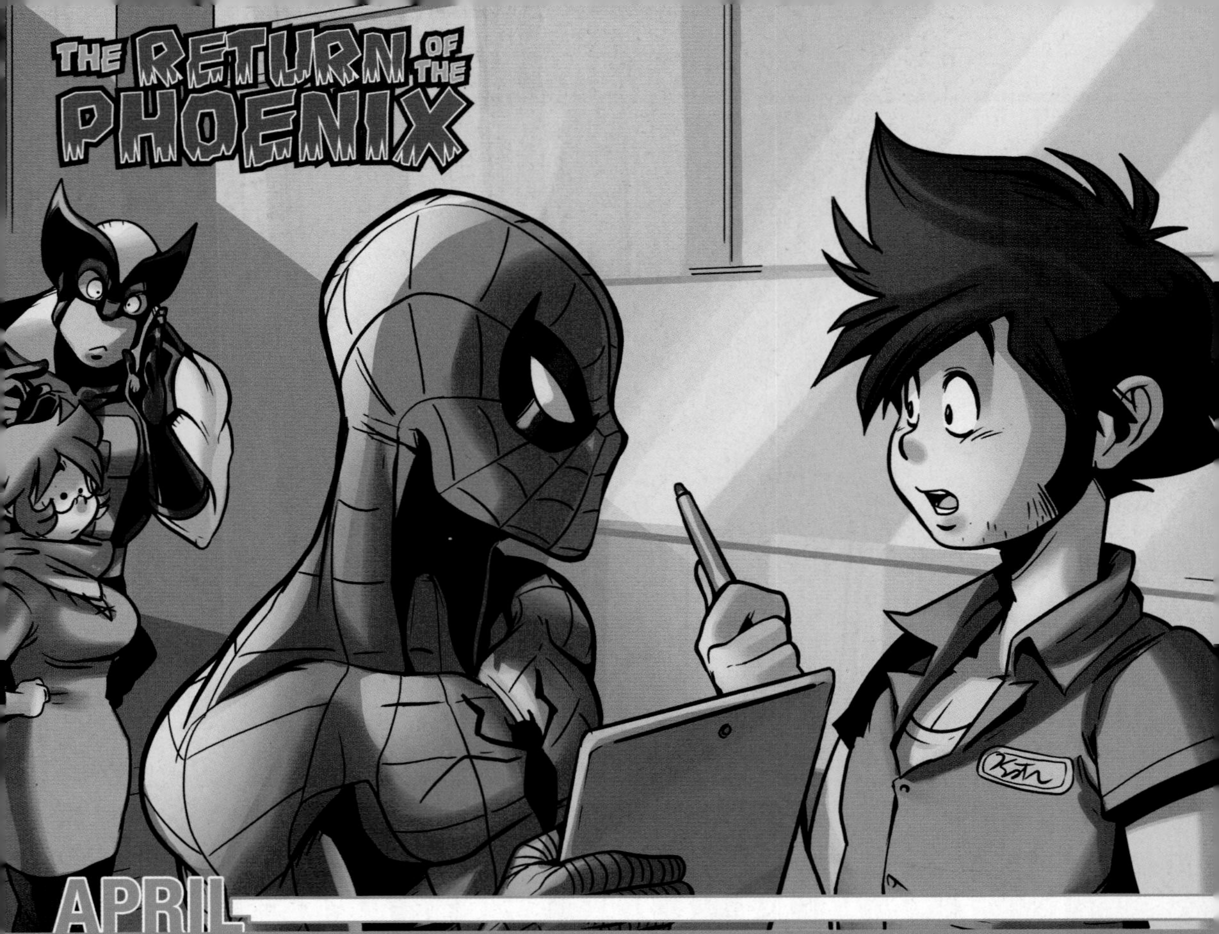
THE RETURN OF THE PHOENIX

APRIL

SUNDAY	MONDAY	TUESDAY	WEDNESDAY	THURSDAY	FRIDAY	SATURDAY
			1 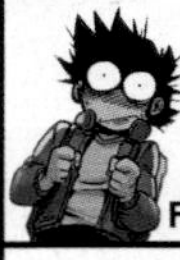 April Fools' Day	2	3	4
5	6	7	8	9	10	11
12	13	14	15	16	17	18
19 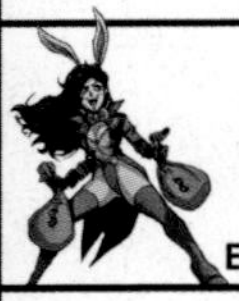 Easter	20	21	22	23	24	25
26	27	28	29	30		

YVES BIGEREL
WRITER & ARTIST

ANDRES MOSSA
COLOR ARTIST

VC'S TRAVIS LANHAM & JOE SABINO
LETTERING

ANNIE CHENG & TIM SMITH 3
PRODUCTION TEAM

CARLOS LAO
PRODUCTION DESIGN

DEVIN LEWIS
EDITOR

JORDAN D. WHITE & NICK LOWE
SUPERVISING EDITORS

EDITOR IN CHIEF AXEL ALONSO CHIEF CREATIVE OFFICER JOE QUESADA PUBLISHER DAN BUCKLEY EXECUTIVE PRODUCER ALAN FINE

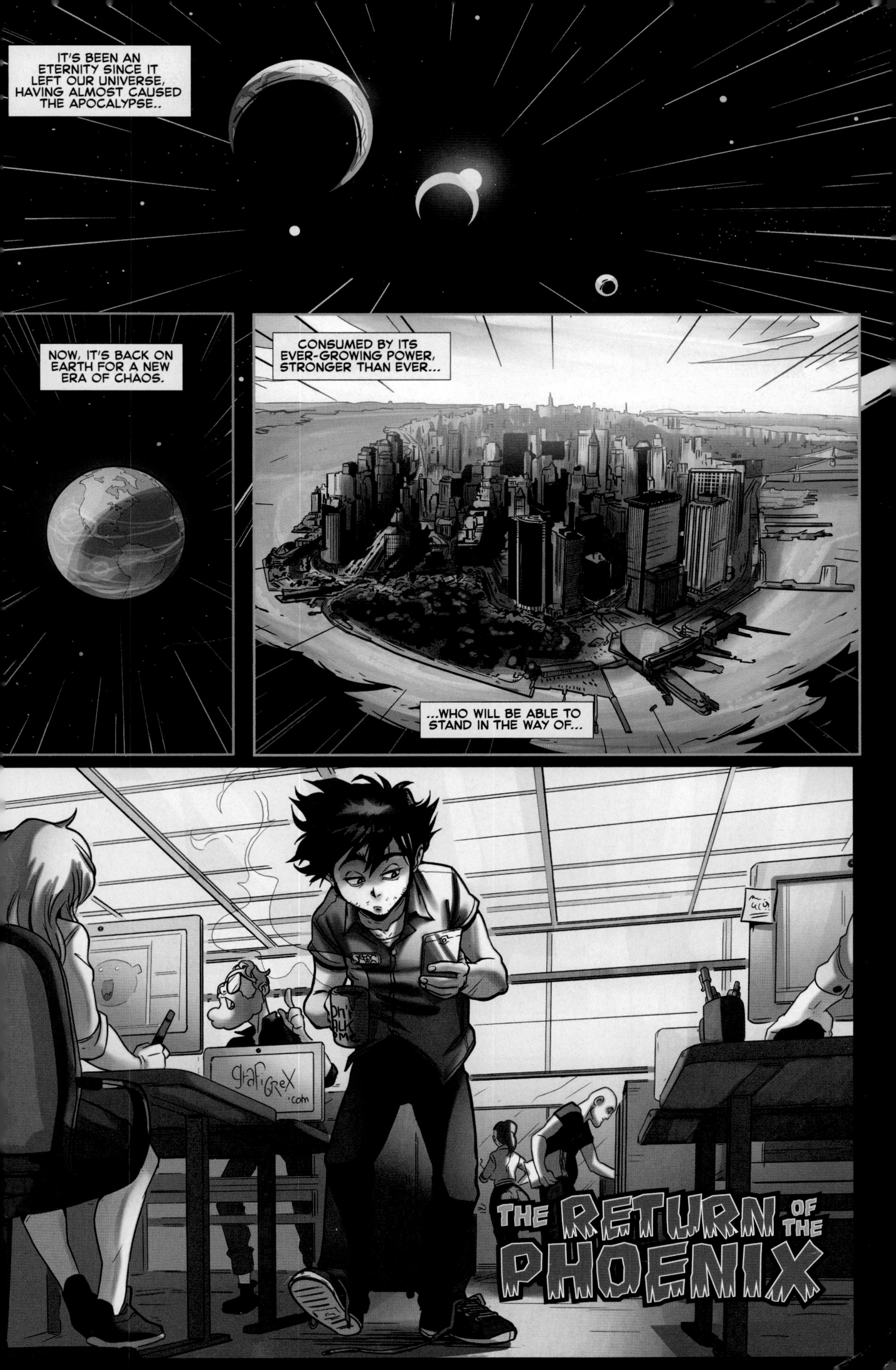
IT'S BEEN AN ETERNITY SINCE IT LEFT OUR UNIVERSE, HAVING ALMOST CAUSED THE APOCALYPSE..
NOW, IT'S BACK ON EARTH FOR A NEW ERA OF CHAOS.
CONSUMED BY ITS EVER-GROWING POWER, STRONGER THAN EVER...
...WHO WILL BE ABLE TO STAND IN THE WAY OF...
grafigrex .com
THE RETURN OF THE PHOENIX

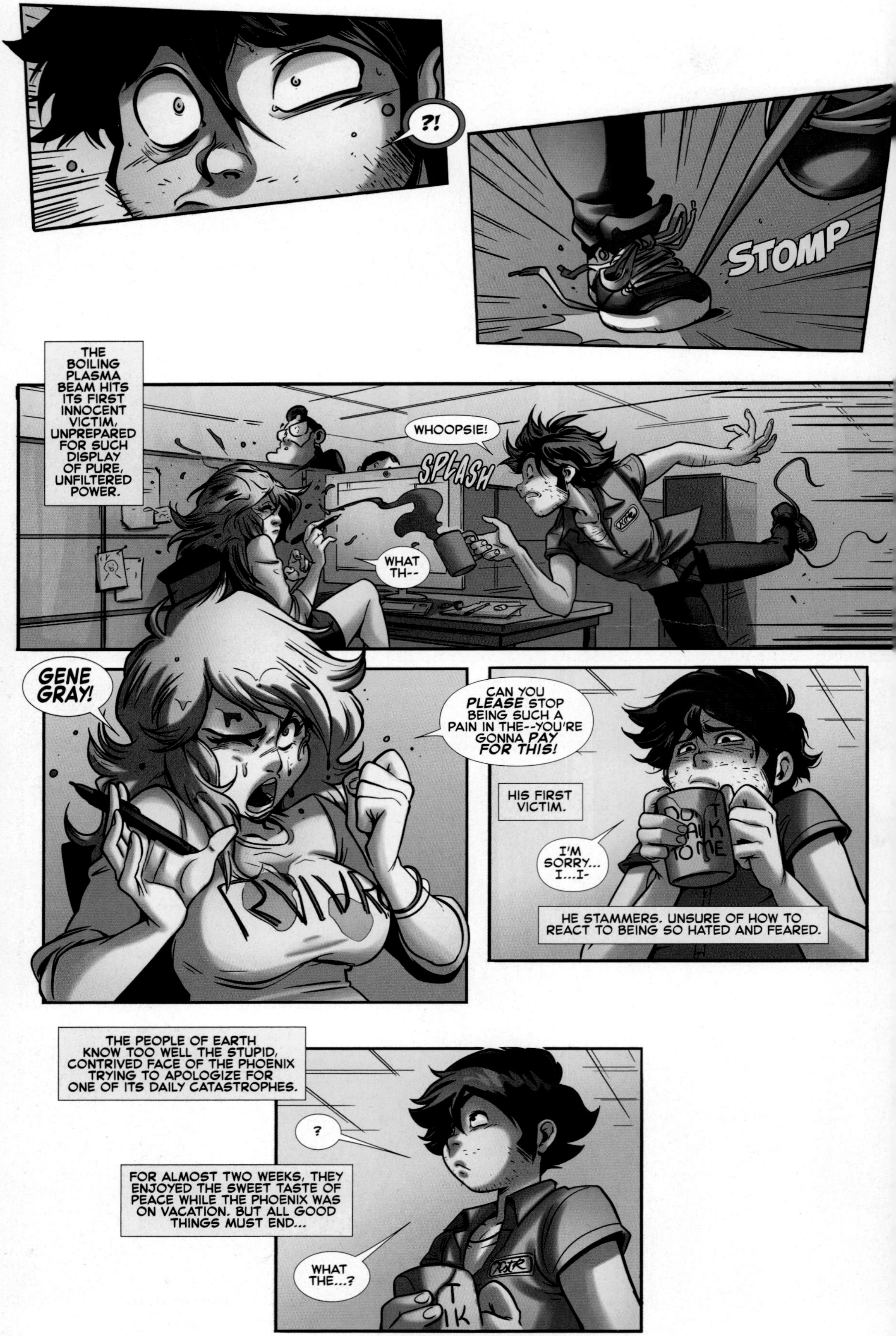
?!
STOMP
THE BOILING PLASMA BEAM HITS ITS FIRST INNOCENT VICTIM, UNPREPARED FOR SUCH DISPLAY OF PURE, UNFILTERED POWER.
WHOOPSIE!
SPLASH
WHAT TH--
GENE GRAY!
CAN YOU PLEASE STOP BEING SUCH A PAIN IN THE--YOU'RE GONNA PAY FOR THIS!
HIS FIRST VICTIM.
I'M SORRY... I...I-
HE STAMMERS. UNSURE OF HOW TO REACT TO BEING SO HATED AND FEARED.
THE PEOPLE OF EARTH KNOW TOO WELL THE STUPID, CONTRIVED FACE OF THE PHOENIX TRYING TO APOLOGIZE FOR ONE OF ITS DAILY CATASTROPHES.
?
FOR ALMOST TWO WEEKS, THEY ENJOYED THE SWEET TASTE OF PEACE WHILE THE PHOENIX WAS ON VACATION. BUT ALL GOOD THINGS MUST END...
WHAT THE...?

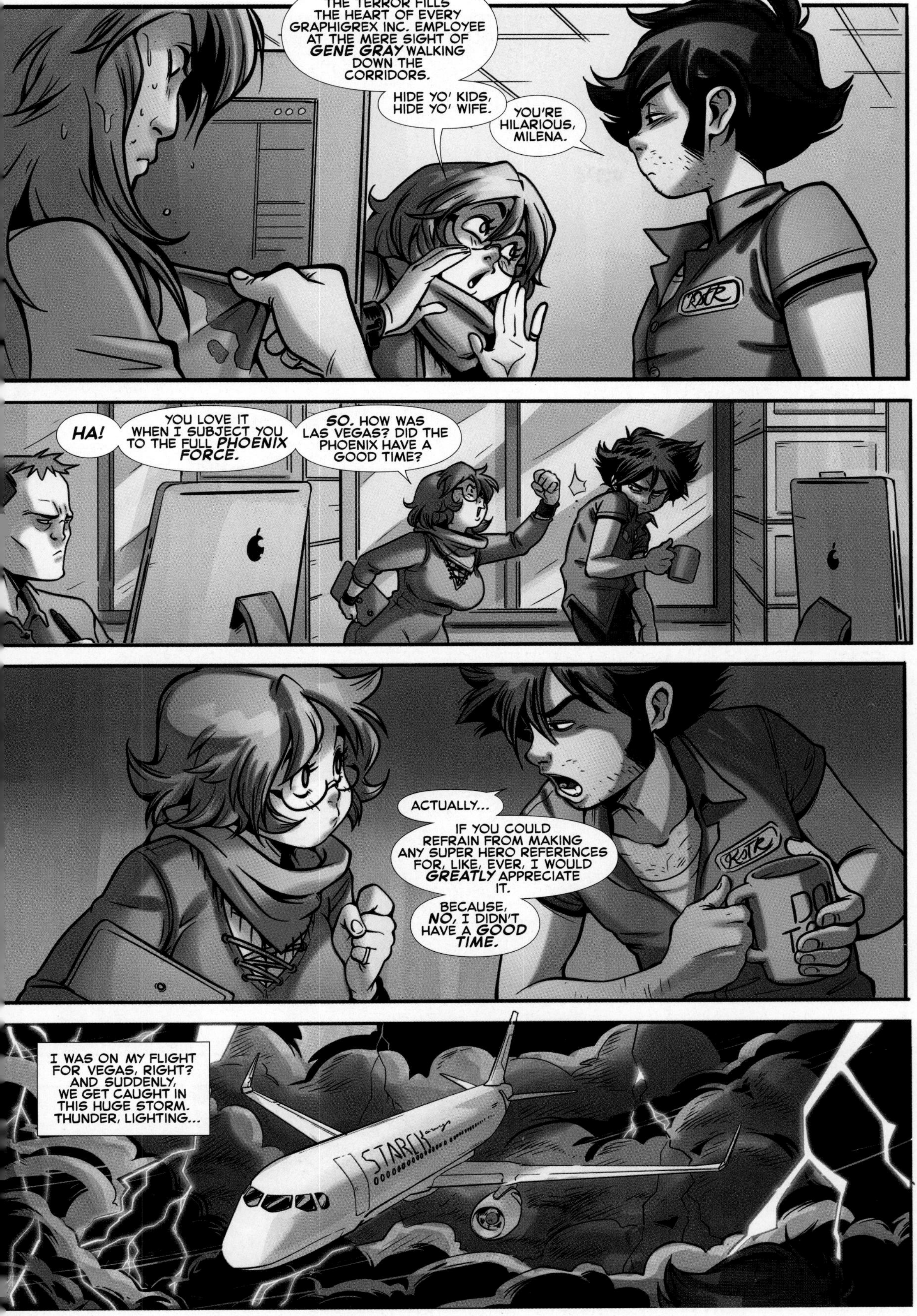
...AND NOW THE TERROR FILLS THE HEART OF EVERY GRAPHIGREX INC. EMPLOYEE AT THE MERE SIGHT OF GENE GRAY WALKING DOWN THE CORRIDORS.
HIDE YO' KIDS, HIDE YO' WIFE.
YOU'RE HILARIOUS, MILENA.
HA!
YOU LOVE IT WHEN I SUBJECT YOU TO THE FULL PHOENIX FORCE.
SO. HOW WAS LAS VEGAS? DID THE PHOENIX HAVE A GOOD TIME?
ACTUALLY...
IF YOU COULD REFRAIN FROM MAKING ANY SUPER HERO REFERENCES FOR, LIKE, EVER, I WOULD GREATLY APPRECIATE IT.
BECAUSE, NO, I DIDN'T HAVE A GOOD TIME.
I WAS ON MY FLIGHT FOR VEGAS, RIGHT? AND SUDDENLY, WE GET CAUGHT IN THIS HUGE STORM. THUNDER, LIGHTING...
STARCK

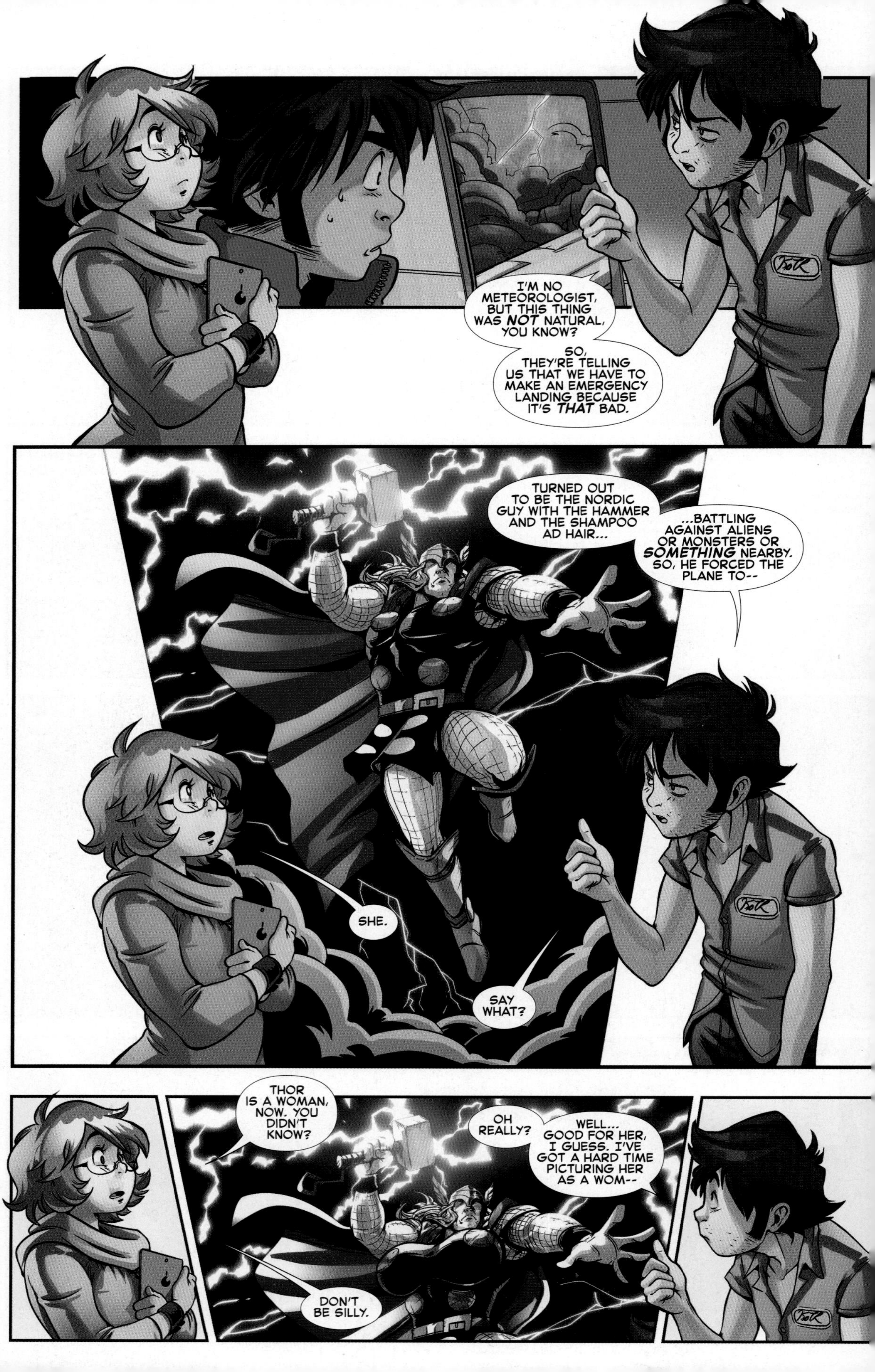
I'M NO METEOROLOGIST, BUT THIS THING WAS *NOT* NATURAL, YOU KNOW?
SO, THEY'RE TELLING US THAT WE HAVE TO MAKE AN EMERGENCY LANDING BECAUSE IT'S *THAT* BAD.
TURNED OUT TO BE THE NORDIC GUY WITH THE HAMMER AND THE SHAMPOO AD HAIR...
...BATTLING AGAINST ALIENS OR MONSTERS OR *SOMETHING* NEARBY. SO, HE FORCED THE PLANE TO--
SHE.
SAY WHAT?
THOR IS A WOMAN, NOW. YOU DIDN'T KNOW?
OH REALLY?
WELL... GOOD FOR HER, I GUESS. I'VE GOT A HARD TIME PICTURING HER AS A WOM--
DON'T BE SILLY.

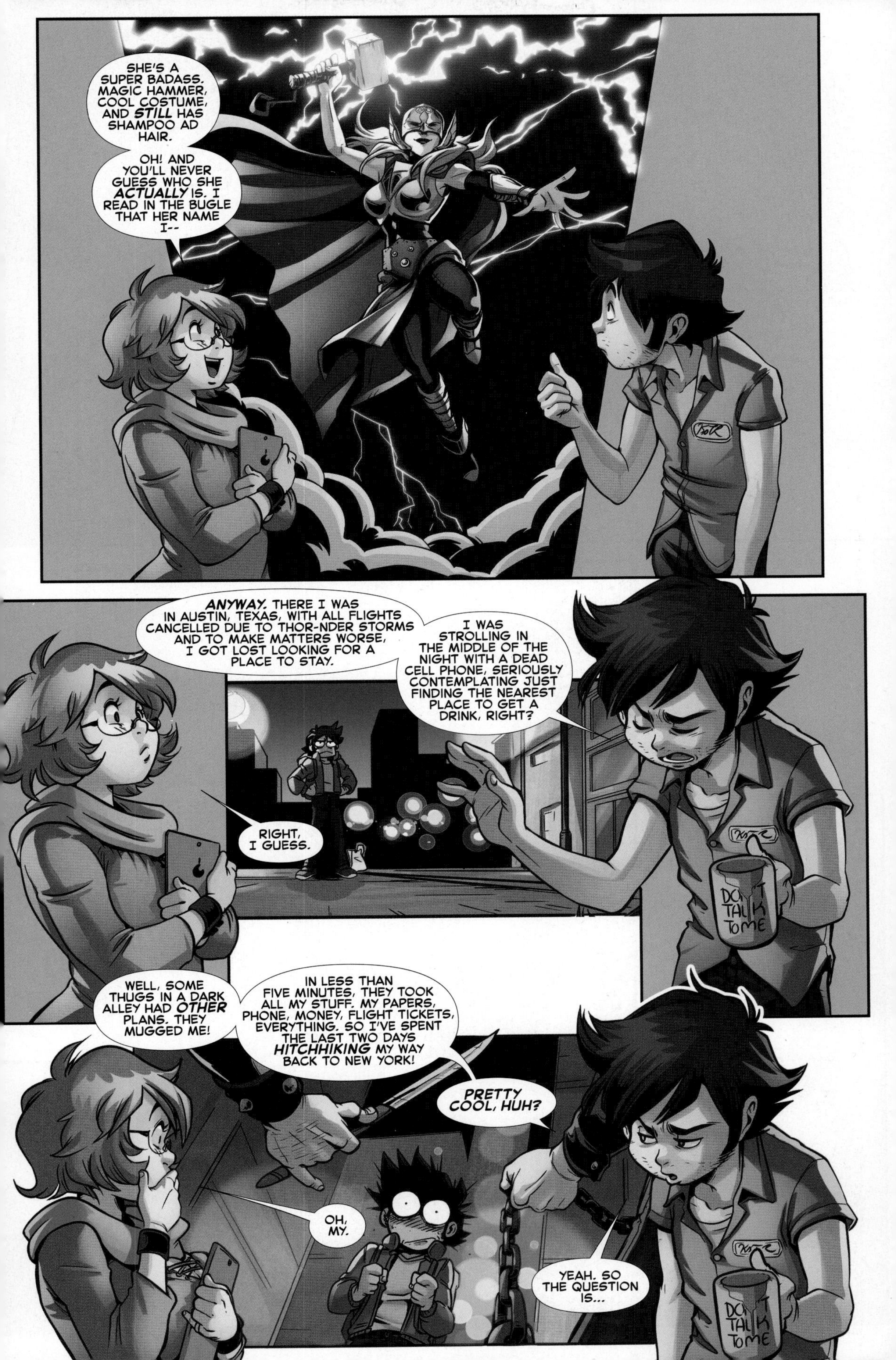
SHE'S A SUPER BADASS. MAGIC HAMMER, COOL COSTUME, AND STILL HAS SHAMPOO AD HAIR.
OH! AND YOU'LL NEVER GUESS WHO SHE ACTUALLY IS. I READ IN THE BUGLE THAT HER NAME I--
ANYWAY. THERE I WAS IN AUSTIN, TEXAS, WITH ALL FLIGHTS CANCELLED DUE TO THOR-NDER STORMS AND TO MAKE MATTERS WORSE, I GOT LOST LOOKING FOR A PLACE TO STAY.
I WAS STROLLING IN THE MIDDLE OF THE NIGHT WITH A DEAD CELL PHONE, SERIOUSLY CONTEMPLATING JUST FINDING THE NEAREST PLACE TO GET A DRINK, RIGHT?
RIGHT, I GUESS.
DON'T TALK TO ME
WELL, SOME THUGS IN A DARK ALLEY HAD OTHER PLANS. THEY MUGGED ME!
IN LESS THAN FIVE MINUTES, THEY TOOK ALL MY STUFF. MY PAPERS, PHONE, MONEY, FLIGHT TICKETS, EVERYTHING. SO I'VE SPENT THE LAST TWO DAYS HITCHHIKING MY WAY BACK TO NEW YORK!
PRETTY COOL, HUH?
OH, MY.
YEAH. SO THE QUESTION IS...
DON'T TALK TO ME

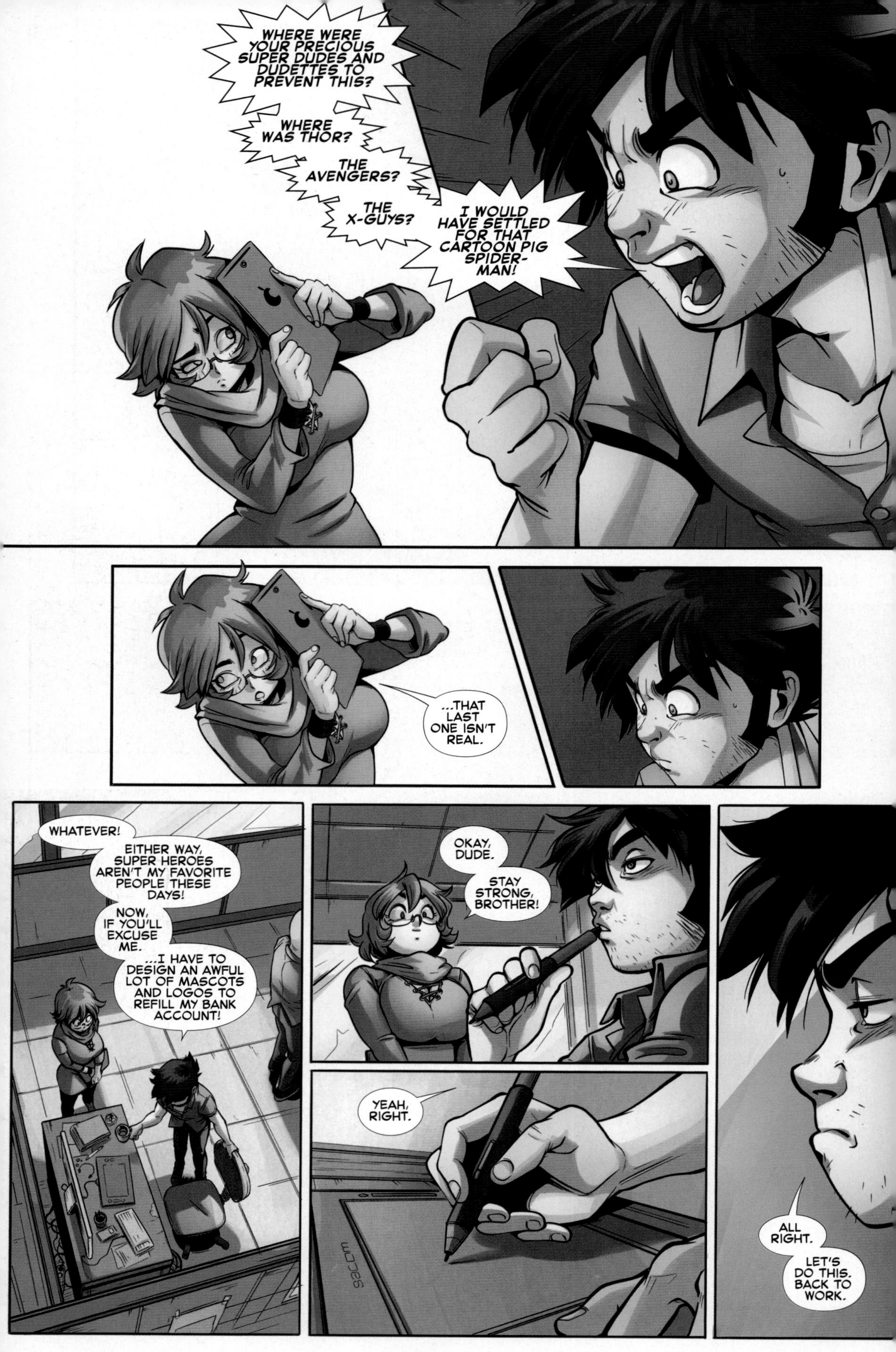
WHERE WERE YOUR PRECIOUS SUPER DUDES AND DUDETTES TO PREVENT THIS?
WHERE WAS THOR?
THE AVENGERS?
THE X-GUYS?
I WOULD HAVE SETTLED FOR THAT CARTOON PIG SPIDER-MAN!
...THAT LAST ONE ISN'T REAL.
WHATEVER!
EITHER WAY, SUPER HEROES AREN'T MY FAVORITE PEOPLE THESE DAYS!
NOW, IF YOU'LL EXCUSE ME.
...I HAVE TO DESIGN AN AWFUL LOT OF MASCOTS AND LOGOS TO REFILL MY BANK ACCOUNT!
OKAY, DUDE.
STAY STRONG, BROTHER!
YEAH, RIGHT.
ALL RIGHT.
LET'S DO THIS. BACK TO WORK.

SHH
SHH SHH
SHH SHH
DAMMIT.
TAK
DELETE
SHH
COME ONCOME ONCOME OOOON
SHHH SHHH SHHH
COME ON, G.
STOP SUCKING.
UUUUGH.
TAK
DELETE
♫

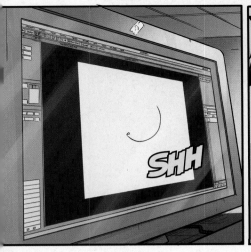

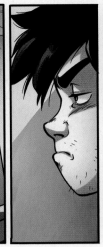

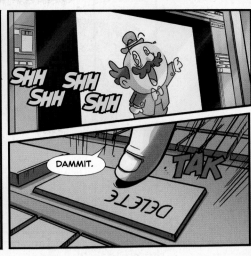

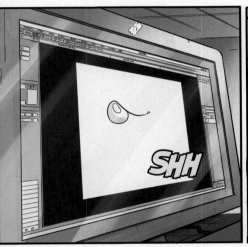

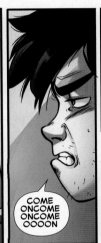

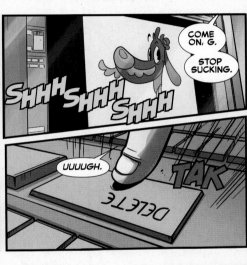

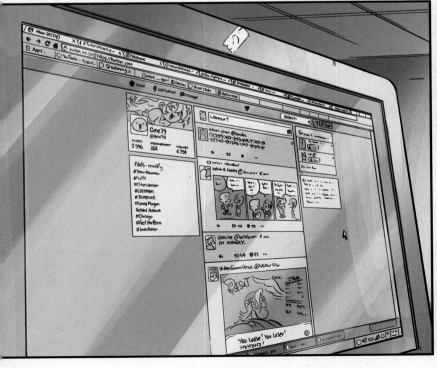

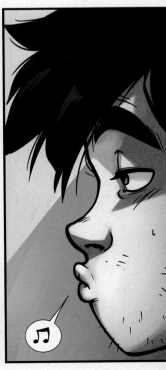

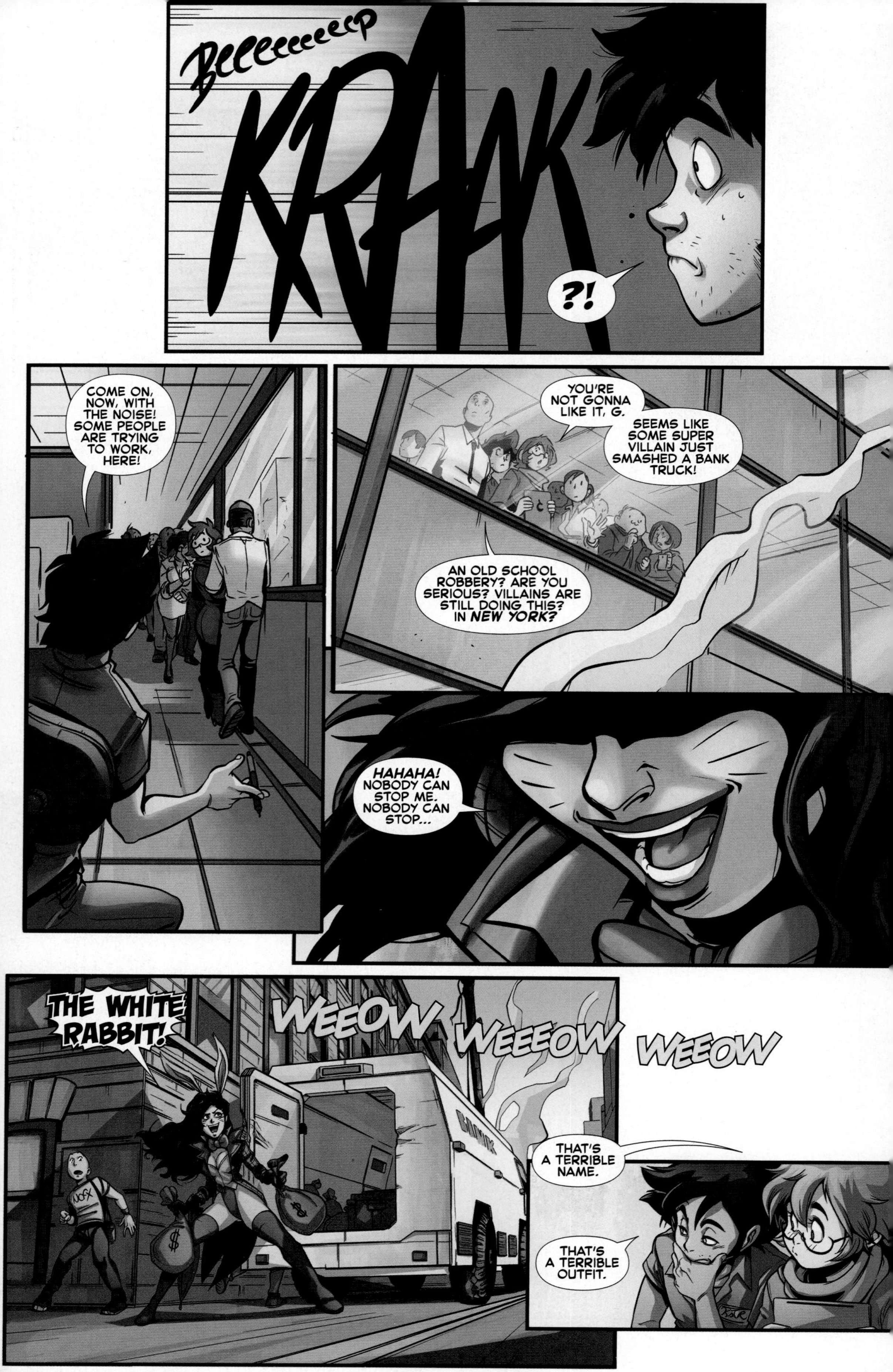

Beeeeeeeep
KRAAK
?!
COME ON, NOW, WITH THE NOISE! SOME PEOPLE ARE TRYING TO WORK, HERE!
YOU'RE NOT GONNA LIKE IT, G.
SEEMS LIKE SOME SUPER VILLAIN JUST SMASHED A BANK TRUCK!
AN OLD SCHOOL ROBBERY? ARE YOU SERIOUS? VILLAINS ARE STILL DOING THIS? IN NEW YORK?
HAHAHA! NOBODY CAN STOP ME. NOBODY CAN STOP...
THE WHITE RABBIT!
WEEOW WEEEOW WEEOW
THAT'S A TERRIBLE NAME.
THAT'S A TERRIBLE OUTFIT.

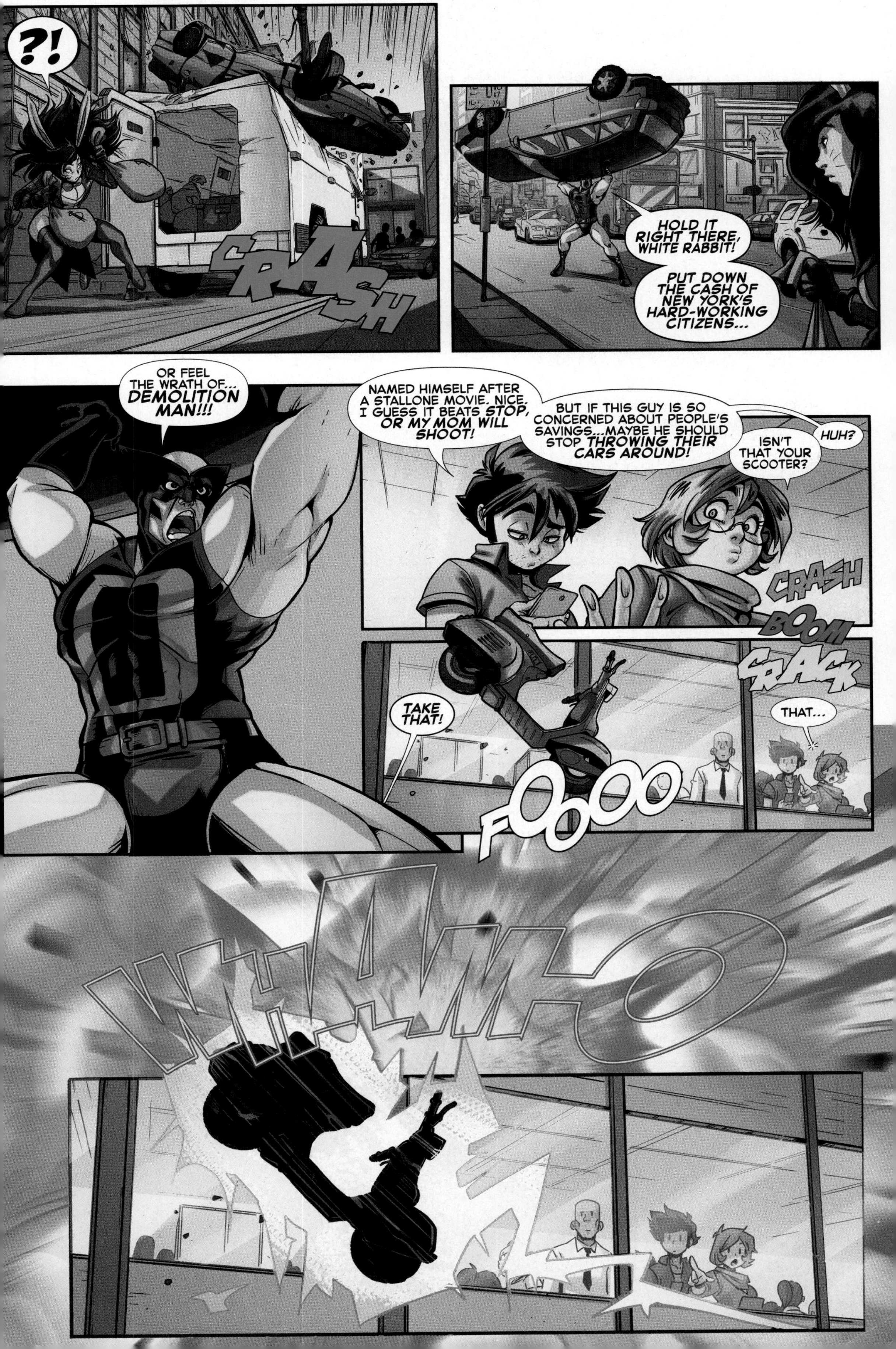

?!
CRASH
HOLD IT RIGHT THERE, WHITE RABBIT!
PUT DOWN THE CASH OF NEW YORK'S HARD-WORKING CITIZENS...
OR FEEL THE WRATH OF... DEMOLITION MAN!!!
NAMED HIMSELF AFTER A STALLONE MOVIE. NICE. I GUESS IT BEATS STOP, OR MY MOM WILL SHOOT!
BUT IF THIS GUY IS SO CONCERNED ABOUT PEOPLE'S SAVINGS...MAYBE HE SHOULD STOP THROWING THEIR CARS AROUND!
HUH?
ISN'T THAT YOUR SCOOTER?
CRASH
BOOM
CRACK
TAKE THAT!
THAT...
FOOOOO
WHAMO

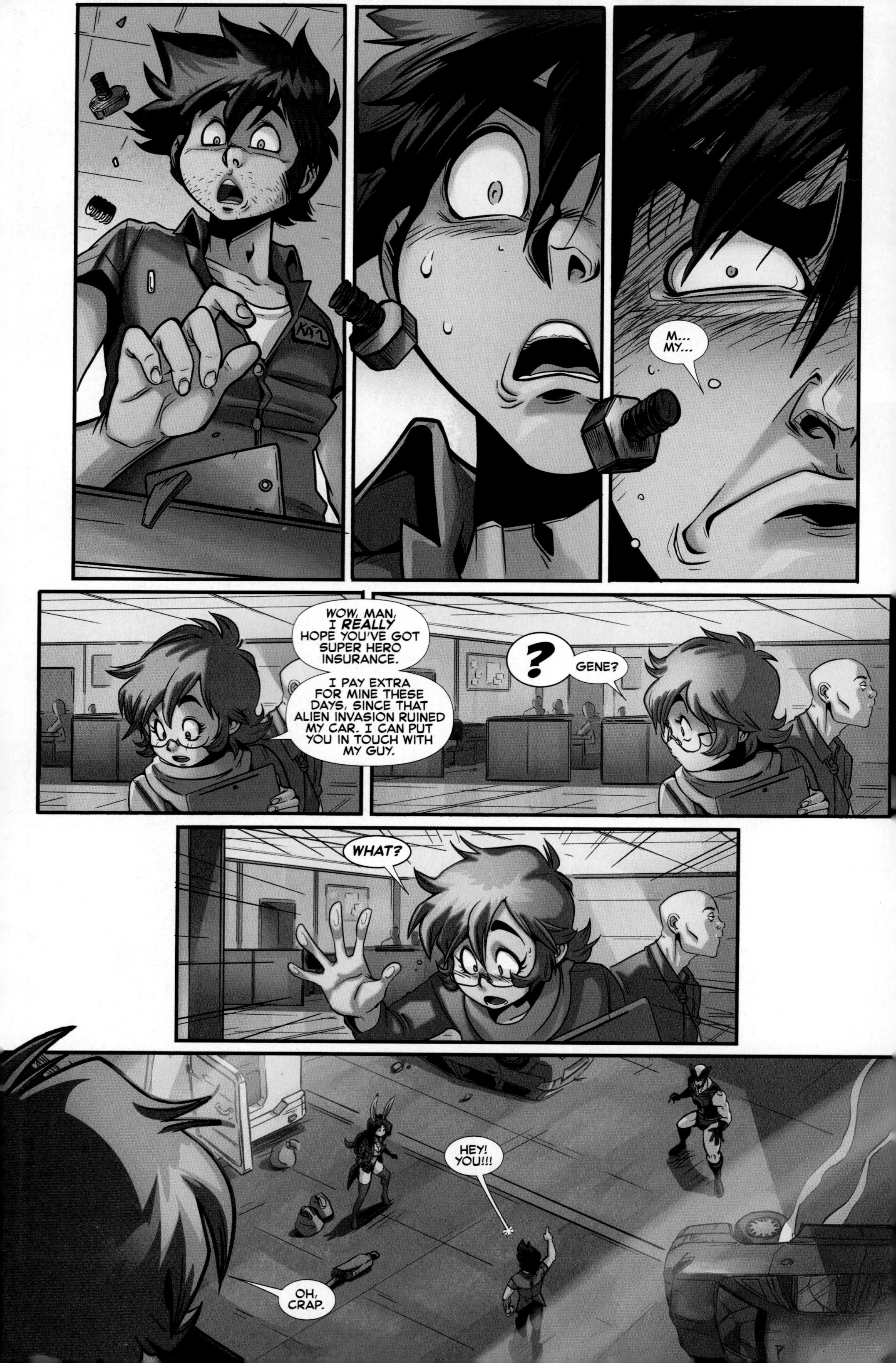
M... MY...
WOW, MAN, I REALLY HOPE YOU'VE GOT SUPER HERO INSURANCE.
I PAY EXTRA FOR MINE THESE DAYS, SINCE THAT ALIEN INVASION RUINED MY CAR. I CAN PUT YOU IN TOUCH WITH MY GUY.
?
GENE?
WHAT?
HEY! YOU!!!
OH, CRAP.

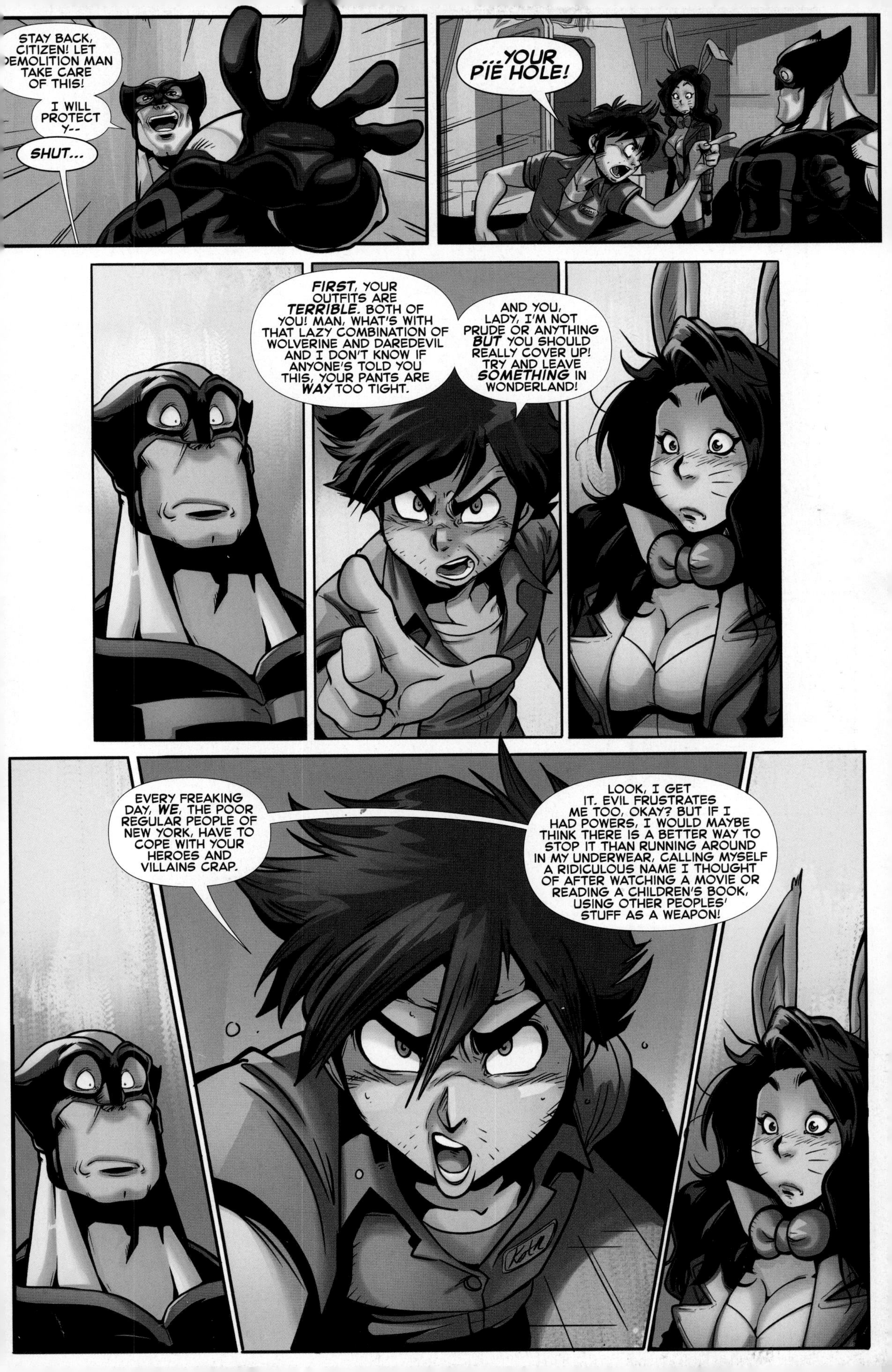
STAY BACK, CITIZEN! LET DEMOLITION MAN TAKE CARE OF THIS!
I WILL PROTECT Y--
SHUT...
...YOUR PIE HOLE!
FIRST, YOUR OUTFITS ARE TERRIBLE. BOTH OF YOU! MAN, WHAT'S WITH THAT LAZY COMBINATION OF WOLVERINE AND DAREDEVIL AND I DON'T KNOW IF ANYONE'S TOLD YOU THIS, YOUR PANTS ARE WAY TOO TIGHT.
AND YOU, LADY, I'M NOT PRUDE OR ANYTHING BUT YOU SHOULD REALLY COVER UP! TRY AND LEAVE SOMETHING IN WONDERLAND!
EVERY FREAKING DAY, WE, THE POOR REGULAR PEOPLE OF NEW YORK, HAVE TO COPE WITH YOUR HEROES AND VILLAINS CRAP.
LOOK, I GET IT. EVIL FRUSTRATES ME TOO, OKAY? BUT IF I HAD POWERS, I WOULD MAYBE THINK THERE IS A BETTER WAY TO STOP IT THAN RUNNING AROUND IN MY UNDERWEAR, CALLING MYSELF A RIDICULOUS NAME I THOUGHT OF AFTER WATCHING A MOVIE OR READING A CHILDREN'S BOOK, USING OTHER PEOPLES' STUFF AS A WEAPON!

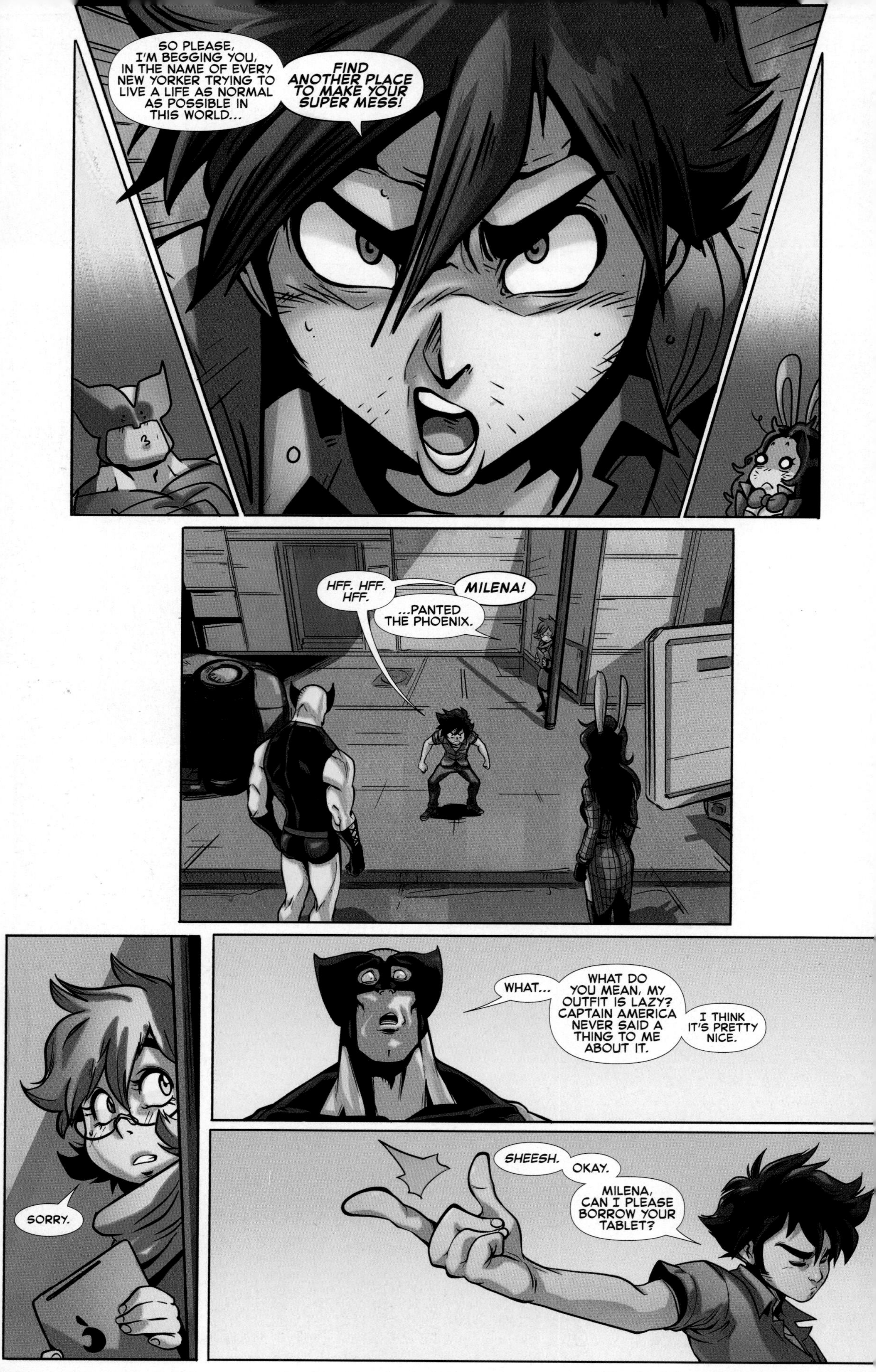

SO PLEASE, I'M BEGGING YOU, IN THE NAME OF EVERY NEW YORKER TRYING TO LIVE A LIFE AS NORMAL AS POSSIBLE IN THIS WORLD...
FIND ANOTHER PLACE TO MAKE YOUR SUPER MESS!
HFF. HFF. HFF.
MILENA!
...PANTED THE PHOENIX.
WHAT...
WHAT DO YOU MEAN, MY OUTFIT IS LAZY? CAPTAIN AMERICA NEVER SAID A THING TO ME ABOUT IT.
I THINK IT'S PRETTY NICE.
SORRY.
SHEESH.
OKAY.
MILENA, CAN I PLEASE BORROW YOUR TABLET?

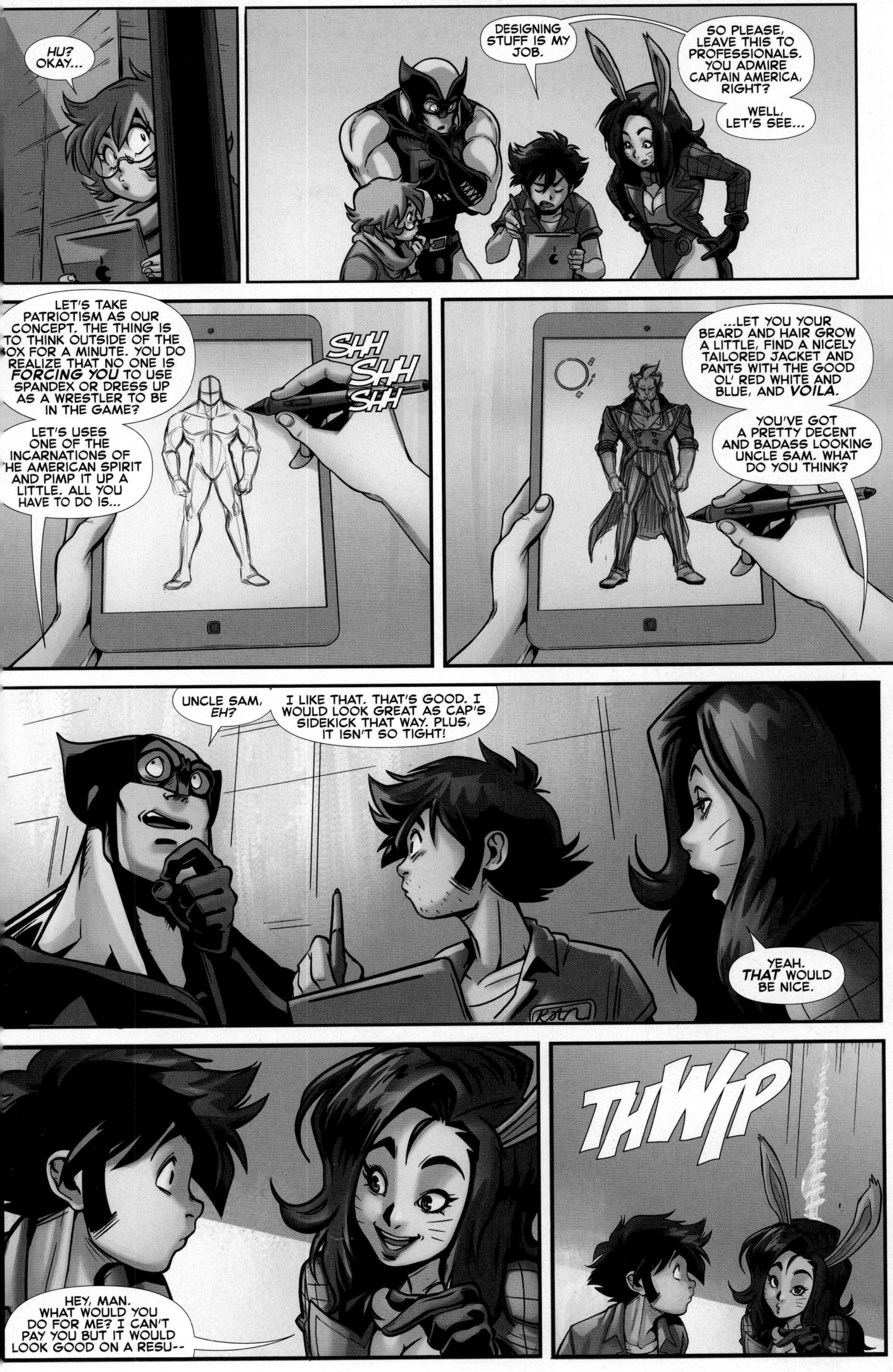
HU? OKAY...
DESIGNING STUFF IS MY JOB.
SO PLEASE, LEAVE THIS TO PROFESSIONALS. YOU ADMIRE CAPTAIN AMERICA, RIGHT?
WELL, LET'S SEE...
LET'S TAKE PATRIOTISM AS OUR CONCEPT. THE THING IS TO THINK OUTSIDE OF THE BOX FOR A MINUTE. YOU DO REALIZE THAT NO ONE IS FORCING YOU TO USE SPANDEX OR DRESS UP AS A WRESTLER TO BE IN THE GAME?
SHH SHH SHH
LET'S USES ONE OF THE INCARNATIONS OF THE AMERICAN SPIRIT AND PIMP IT UP A LITTLE. ALL YOU HAVE TO DO IS...
...LET YOU YOUR BEARD AND HAIR GROW A LITTLE, FIND A NICELY TAILORED JACKET AND PANTS WITH THE GOOD OL' RED WHITE AND BLUE, AND VOILA.
YOU'VE GOT A PRETTY DECENT AND BADASS LOOKING UNCLE SAM. WHAT DO YOU THINK?
UNCLE SAM, EH?
I LIKE THAT. THAT'S GOOD. I WOULD LOOK GREAT AS CAP'S SIDEKICK THAT WAY. PLUS, IT ISN'T SO TIGHT!
YEAH. THAT WOULD BE NICE.
HEY, MAN. WHAT WOULD YOU DO FOR ME? I CAN'T PAY YOU BUT IT WOULD LOOK GOOD ON A RESU--
THWIP

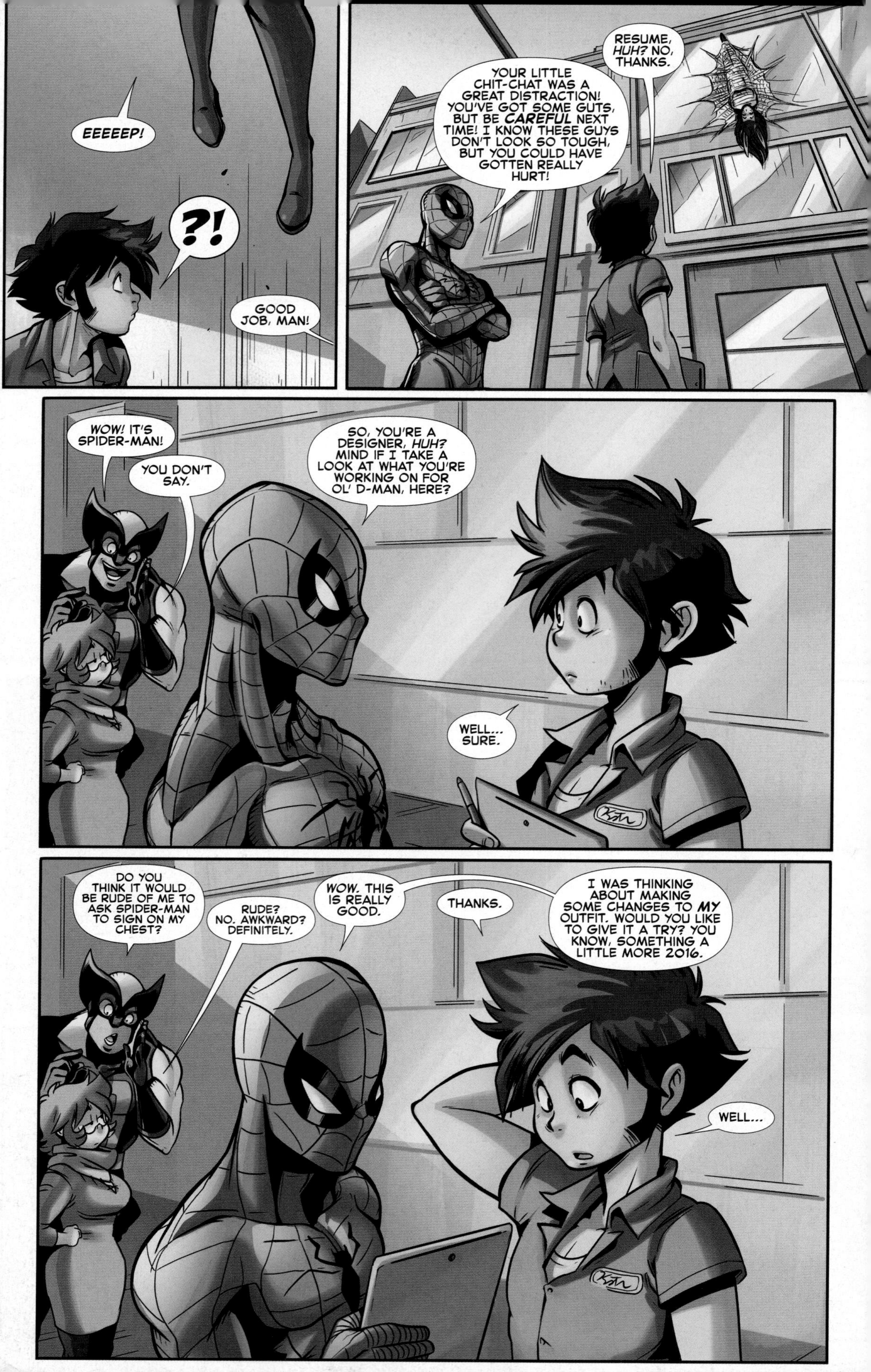
EEEEEP!
?!
GOOD JOB, MAN!
YOUR LITTLE CHIT-CHAT WAS A GREAT DISTRACTION! YOU'VE GOT SOME GUTS, BUT BE CAREFUL NEXT TIME! I KNOW THESE GUYS DON'T LOOK SO TOUGH, BUT YOU COULD HAVE GOTTEN REALLY HURT!
RESUME, HUH? NO, THANKS.
WOW! IT'S SPIDER-MAN!
YOU DON'T SAY.
SO, YOU'RE A DESIGNER, HUH? MIND IF I TAKE A LOOK AT WHAT YOU'RE WORKING ON FOR OL' D-MAN, HERE?
WELL... SURE.
DO YOU THINK IT WOULD BE RUDE OF ME TO ASK SPIDER-MAN TO SIGN ON MY CHEST?
RUDE? NO. AWKWARD? DEFINITELY.
WOW. THIS IS REALLY GOOD.
THANKS.
I WAS THINKING ABOUT MAKING SOME CHANGES TO MY OUTFIT. WOULD YOU LIKE TO GIVE IT A TRY? YOU KNOW, SOMETHING A LITTLE MORE 2016.
WELL...

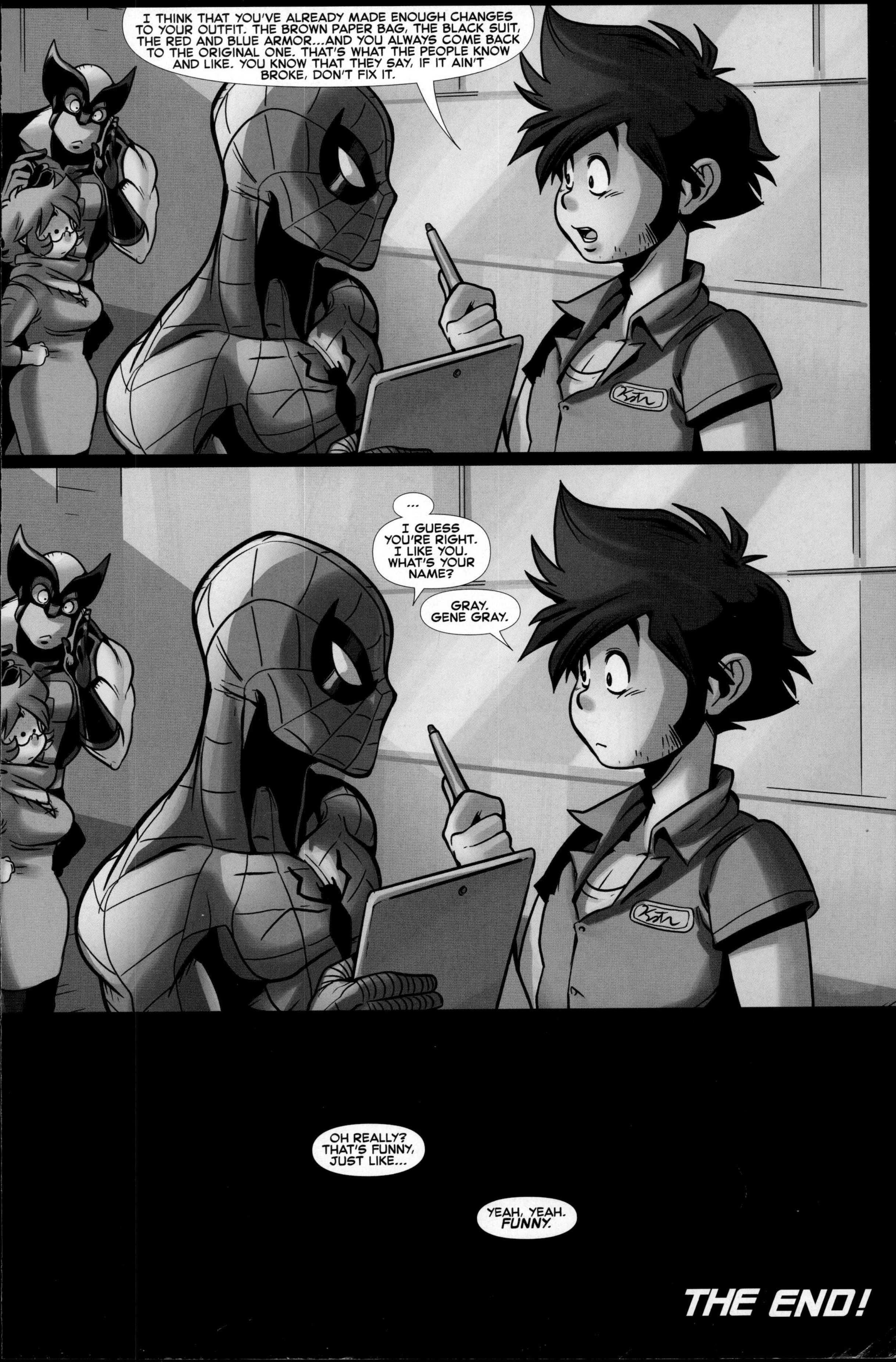
I THINK THAT YOU'VE ALREADY MADE ENOUGH CHANGES TO YOUR OUTFIT. THE BROWN PAPER BAG, THE BLACK SUIT, THE RED AND BLUE ARMOR...AND YOU ALWAYS COME BACK TO THE ORIGINAL ONE. THAT'S WHAT THE PEOPLE KNOW AND LIKE. YOU KNOW THAT THEY SAY, IF IT AIN'T BROKE, DON'T FIX IT.
...
I GUESS YOU'RE RIGHT. I LIKE YOU. WHAT'S YOUR NAME?
GRAY. GENE GRAY.
OH REALLY? THAT'S FUNNY, JUST LIKE...
YEAH, YEAH. FUNNY.
THE END!

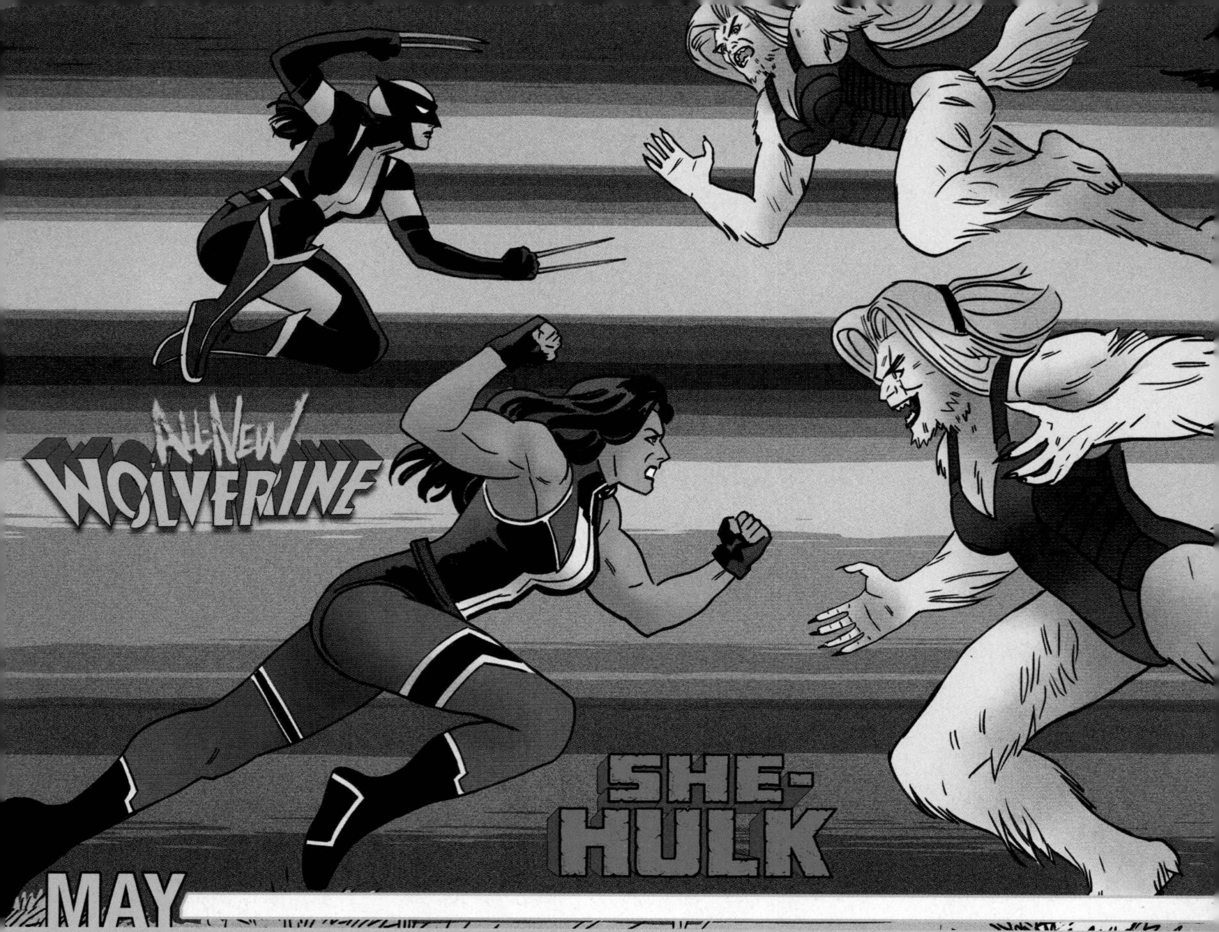
ALL-NEW WOLVERINE
SHE-HULK

MAY

SUNDAY	MONDAY	TUESDAY	WEDNESDAY	THURSDAY	FRIDAY	SATURDAY
					1	2
3	4	5	6	7	8	9
10 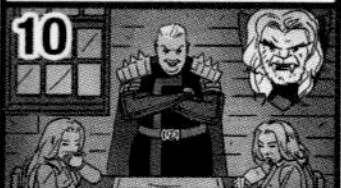 Mother's Day	11	12	13	14	15	16
17	18	19	20	21	22	23
24 / 31	25 Memorial Day	26	27	28	29	30

DENNIS CULVER WRITER
GEOFFO LAYOUTS
LEONARDO ROMERO ARTIST
RUTH REDMOND COLOR ARTIST
VC'S TRAVIS LANHAM LETTERER
JAMAL CAMPBELL COVER ART

ANNIE CHENG & TIM SMITH 3 PRODUCTION TEAM
CARLOS LAO PRODUCTION DESIGN
CHRISTINA HARRINGTON EDITOR
JORDAN D. WHITE & NICK LOWE SUPERVISING EDITORS

EDITOR IN CHIEF AXEL ALONSO CHIEF CREATIVE OFFICER JOE QUESADA PUBLISHER DAN BUCKLEY EXECUTIVE PRODUCER ALAN FINE

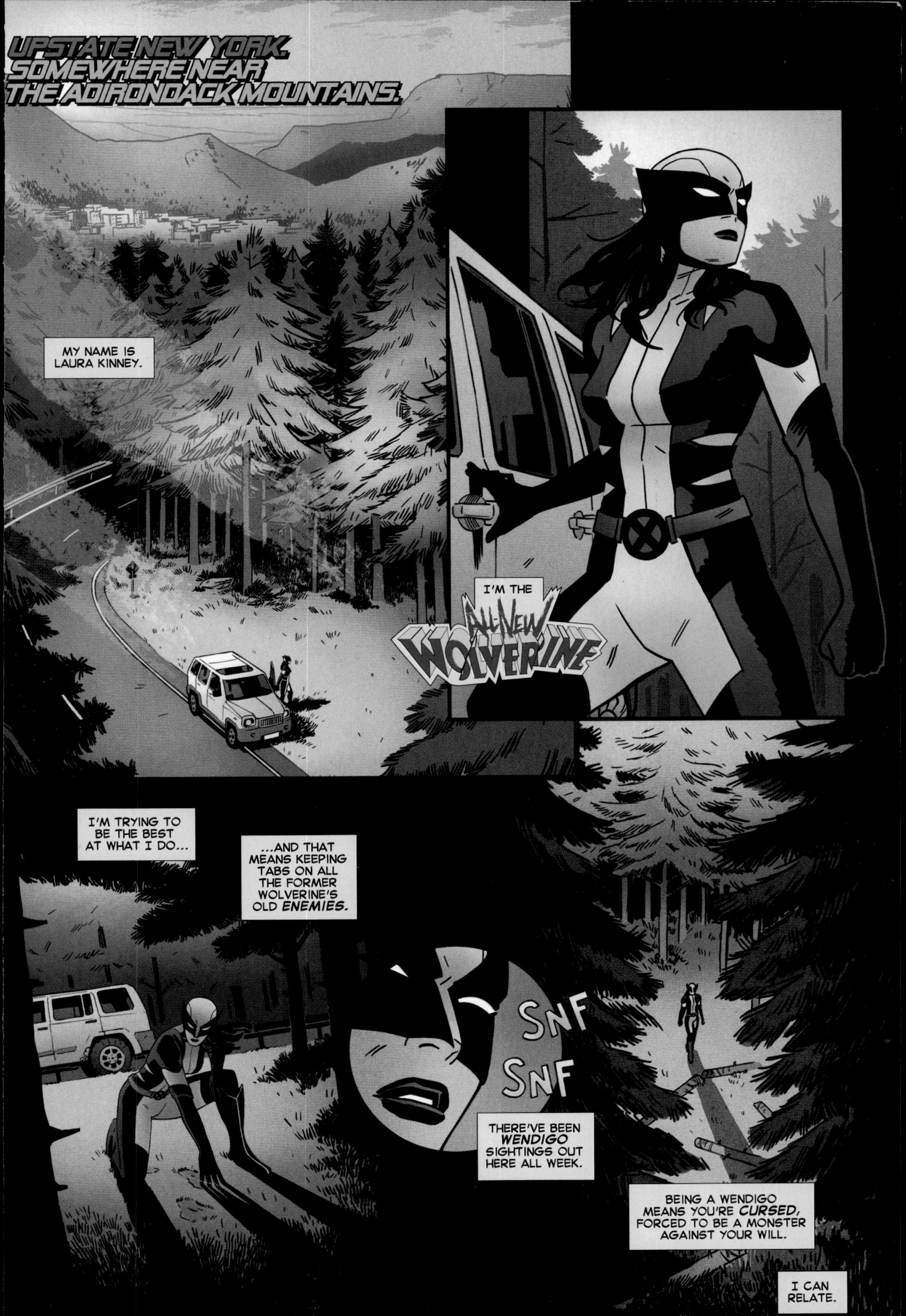
UPSTATE NEW YORK. SOMEWHERE NEAR THE ADIRONDACK MOUNTAINS.
MY NAME IS LAURA KINNEY.
I'M THE
ALL-NEW WOLVERINE
I'M TRYING TO BE THE BEST AT WHAT I DO...
...AND THAT MEANS KEEPING TABS ON ALL THE FORMER WOLVERINE'S OLD ENEMIES.
SNF
SNF
THERE'VE BEEN WENDIGO SIGHTINGS OUT HERE ALL WEEK.
BEING A WENDIGO MEANS YOU'RE CURSED, FORCED TO BE A MONSTER AGAINST YOUR WILL.
I CAN RELATE.

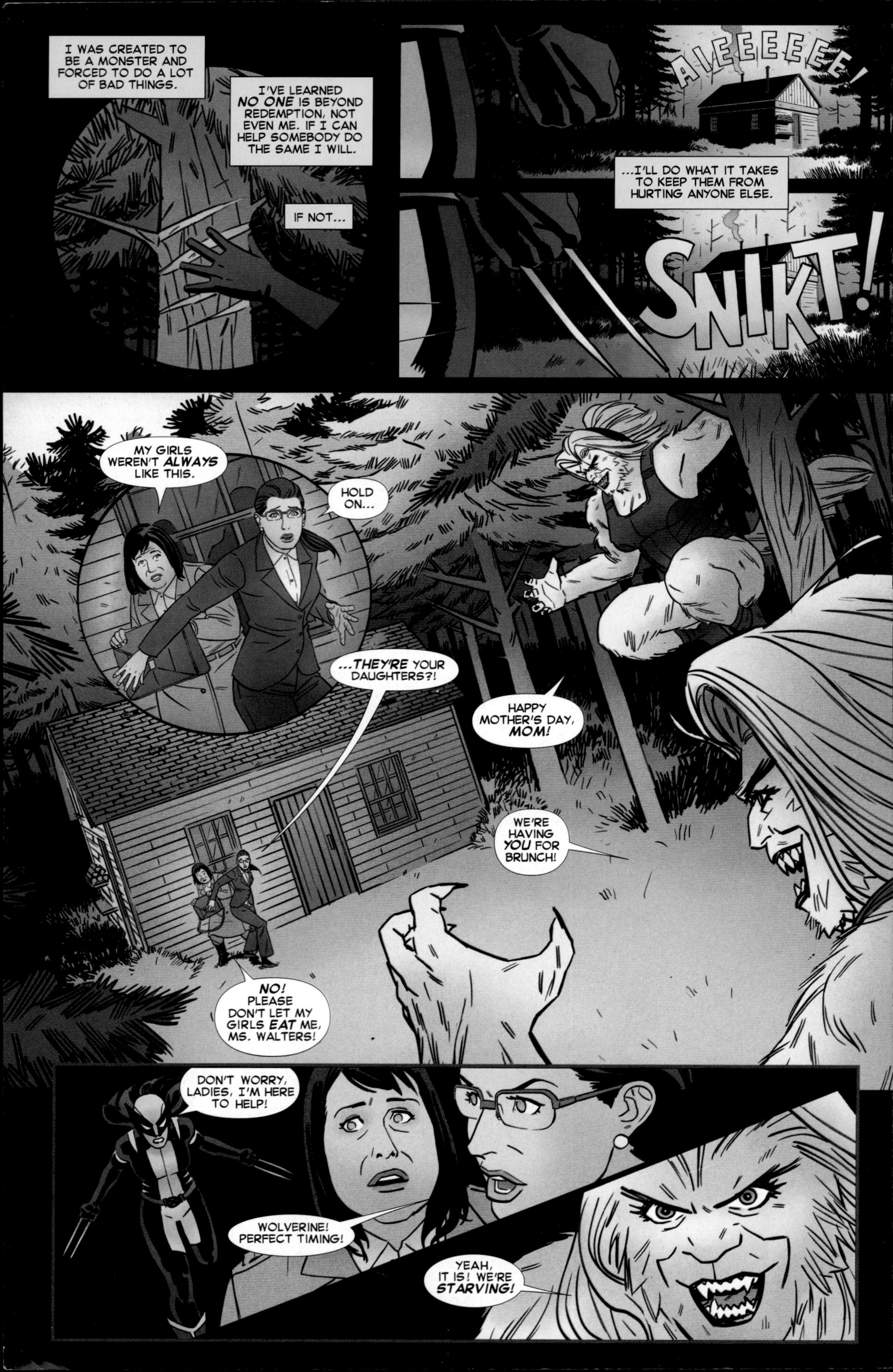

I WAS CREATED TO BE A MONSTER AND FORCED TO DO A LOT OF BAD THINGS.
I'VE LEARNED NO ONE IS BEYOND REDEMPTION, NOT EVEN ME. IF I CAN HELP SOMEBODY DO THE SAME I WILL.
IF NOT...
AIEEEEEE!
...I'LL DO WHAT IT TAKES TO KEEP THEM FROM HURTING ANYONE ELSE.
SNIKT!
MY GIRLS WEREN'T ALWAYS LIKE THIS.
HOLD ON...
...THEY'RE YOUR DAUGHTERS?!
HAPPY MOTHER'S DAY, MOM!
WE'RE HAVING YOU FOR BRUNCH!
NO! PLEASE DON'T LET MY GIRLS EAT ME, MS. WALTERS!
DON'T WORRY, LADIES, I'M HERE TO HELP!
WOLVERINE! PERFECT TIMING!
YEAH, IT IS! WE'RE STARVING!

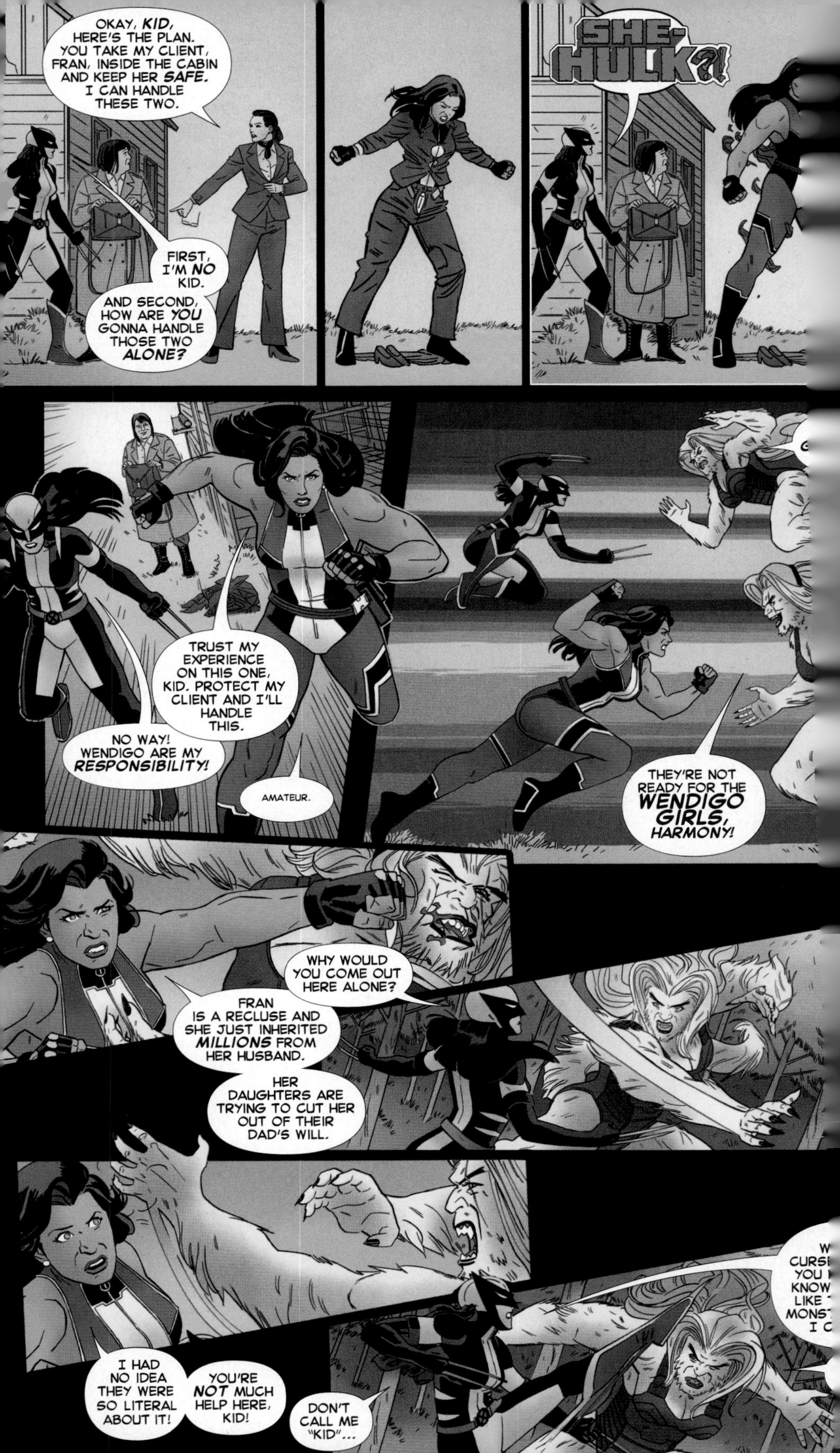
OKAY, KID, HERE'S THE PLAN. YOU TAKE MY CLIENT, FRAN, INSIDE THE CABIN AND KEEP HER SAFE. I CAN HANDLE THESE TWO.
FIRST, I'M NO KID.
AND SECOND, HOW ARE YOU GONNA HANDLE THOSE TWO ALONE?
SHE-HULK?!
TRUST MY EXPERIENCE ON THIS ONE, KID. PROTECT MY CLIENT AND I'LL HANDLE THIS.
NO WAY! WENDIGO ARE MY RESPONSIBILITY!
AMATEUR.
THEY'RE NOT READY FOR THE WENDIGO GIRLS, HARMONY!
WHY WOULD YOU COME OUT HERE ALONE?
FRAN IS A RECLUSE AND SHE JUST INHERITED MILLIONS FROM HER HUSBAND.
HER DAUGHTERS ARE TRYING TO CUT HER OUT OF THEIR DAD'S WILL.
I HAD NO IDEA THEY WERE SO LITERAL ABOUT IT!
YOU'RE NOT MUCH HELP HERE, KID!
DON'T CALL ME "KID"...

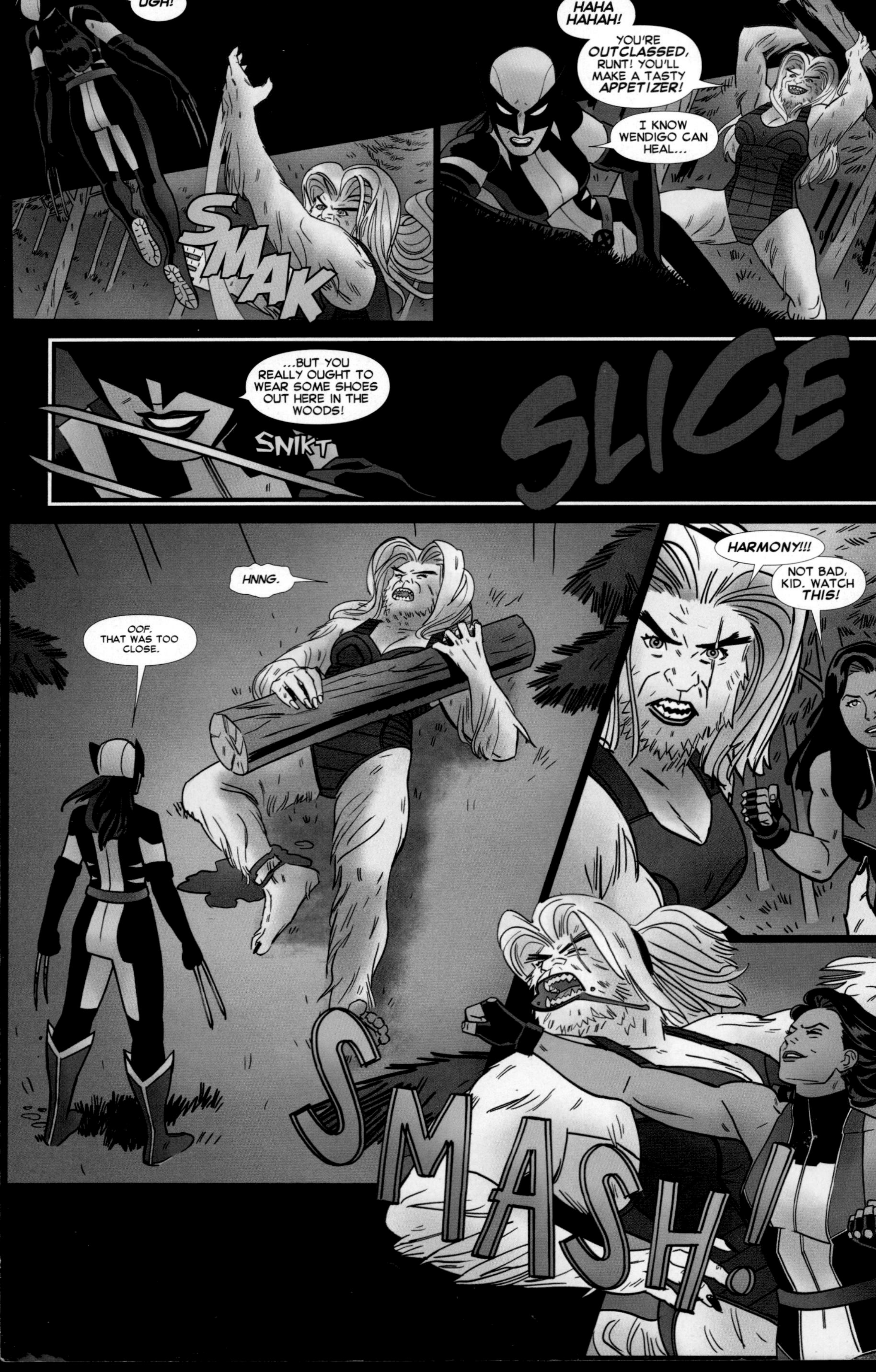
UGH!
SMAK
HAHA HAHAH!
YOU'RE OUTCLASSED, RUNT! YOU'LL MAKE A TASTY APPETIZER!
I KNOW WENDIGO CAN HEAL...
...BUT YOU REALLY OUGHT TO WEAR SOME SHOES OUT HERE IN THE WOODS!
SNIKT
SLICE
HNNG.
OOF. THAT WAS TOO CLOSE.
HARMONY!!!
NOT BAD, KID. WATCH THIS!
SMASH!

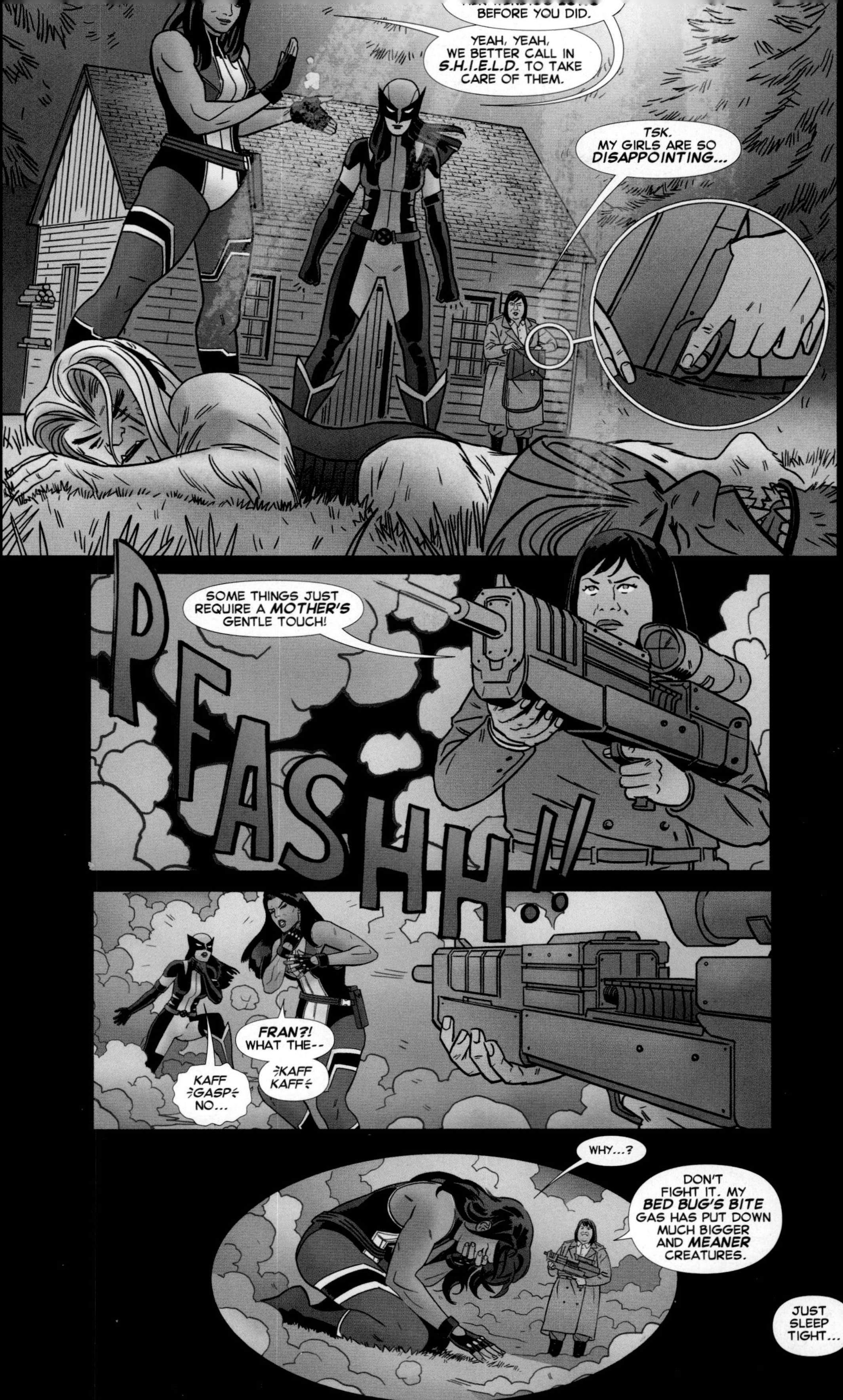
BEFORE YOU DID.
YEAH, YEAH, WE BETTER CALL IN S.H.I.E.L.D. TO TAKE CARE OF THEM.
TSK. MY GIRLS ARE SO DISAPPOINTING...
SOME THINGS JUST REQUIRE A MOTHER'S GENTLE TOUCH!
PFASHH!!
FRAN?! WHAT THE--
KAFF KAFF
KAFF GASP NO...
WHY...?
DON'T FIGHT IT. MY BED BUG'S BITE GAS HAS PUT DOWN MUCH BIGGER AND MEANER CREATURES.
JUST SLEEP TIGHT...

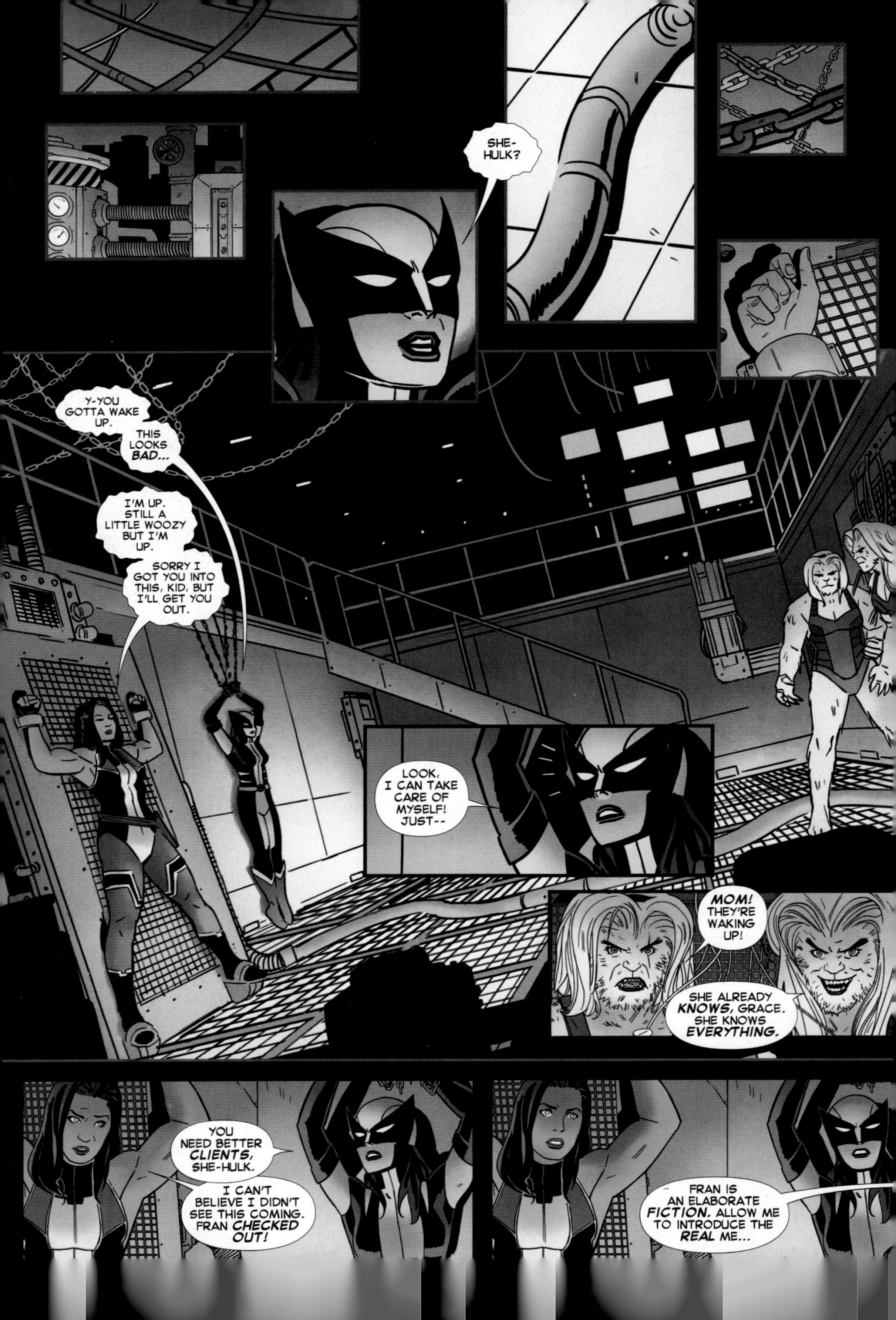

SHE-HULK?
Y-YOU GOTTA WAKE UP.
THIS LOOKS BAD...
I'M UP. STILL A LITTLE WOOZY BUT I'M UP.
SORRY I GOT YOU INTO THIS, KID, BUT I'LL GET YOU OUT.
LOOK, I CAN TAKE CARE OF MYSELF! JUST--
MOM! THEY'RE WAKING UP!
SHE ALREADY KNOWS, GRACE. SHE KNOWS EVERYTHING.
YOU NEED BETTER CLIENTS, SHE-HULK.
I CAN'T BELIEVE I DIDN'T SEE THIS COMING. FRAN CHECKED OUT!
FRAN IS AN ELABORATE FICTION. ALLOW ME TO INTRODUCE THE REAL ME...

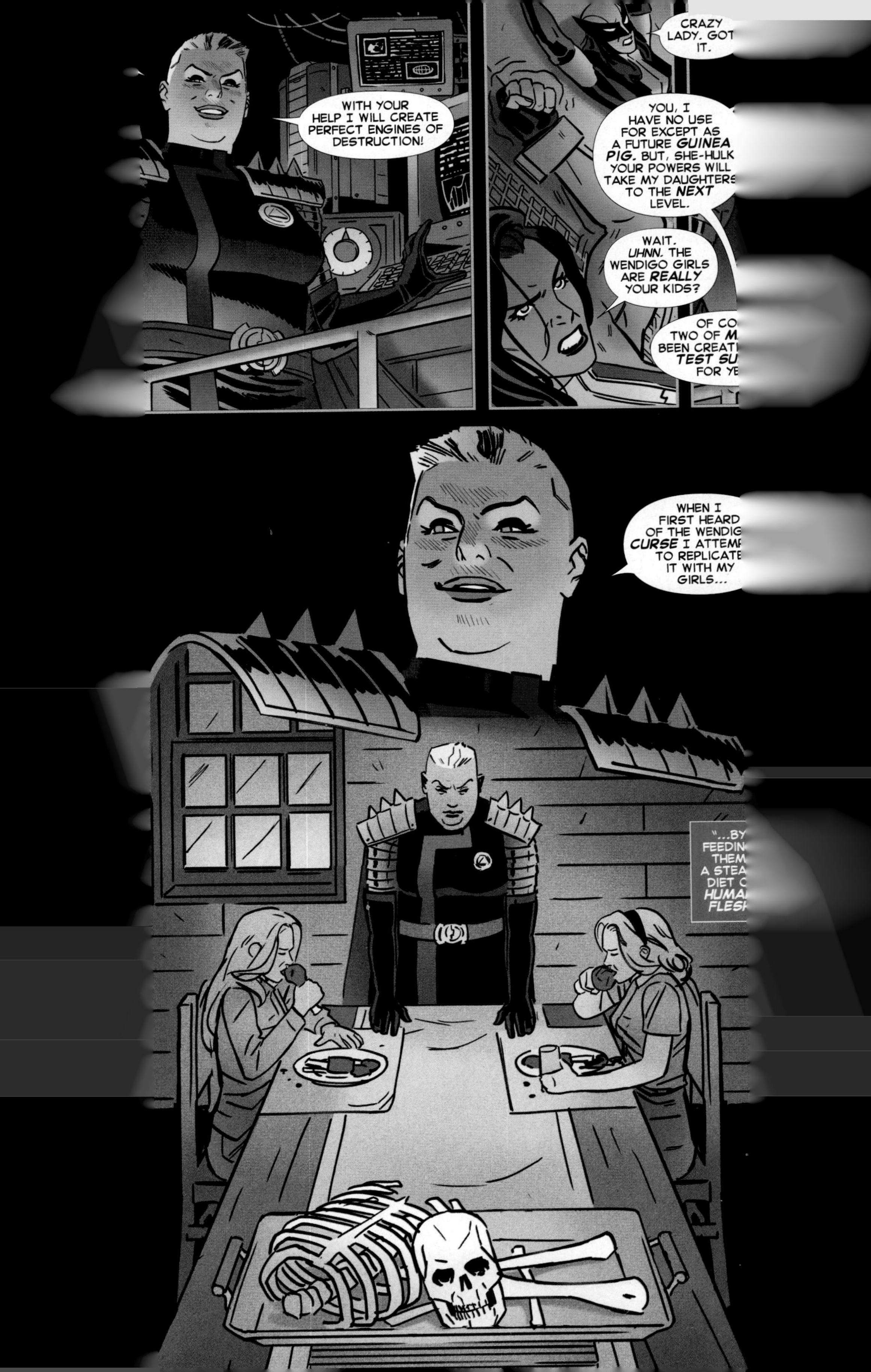
WITH YOUR HELP I WILL CREATE PERFECT ENGINES OF DESTRUCTION!
CRAZY LADY. GOT IT.
YOU, I HAVE NO USE FOR EXCEPT AS A FUTURE GUINEA PIG. BUT, SHE-HULK YOUR POWERS WILL TAKE MY DAUGHTERS TO THE NEXT LEVEL.
WAIT. UHNN. THE WENDIGO GIRLS ARE REALLY YOUR KIDS?
OF CO TWO OF M BEEN CREAT TEST SU FOR YE
WHEN I FIRST HEARD OF THE WENDIG CURSE I ATTEMP TO REPLICATE IT WITH MY GIRLS...
"...BY FEEDIN THEM A STEA DIET O HUMA FLESH

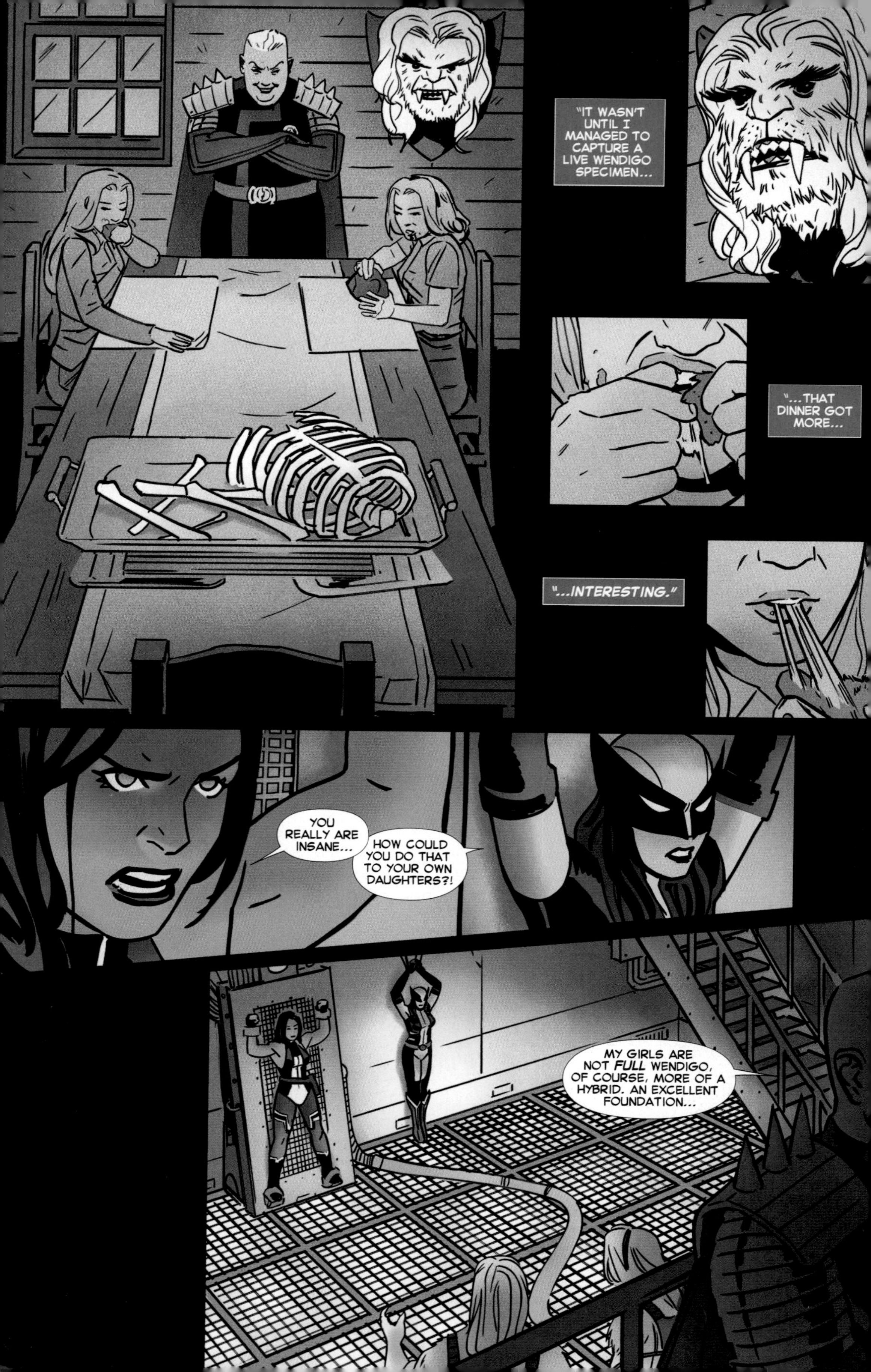

"IT WASN'T UNTIL I MANAGED TO CAPTURE A LIVE WENDIGO SPECIMEN...
"...THAT DINNER GOT MORE...
"...INTERESTING."
YOU REALLY ARE INSANE...
HOW COULD YOU DO THAT TO YOUR OWN DAUGHTERS?!
MY GIRLS ARE NOT *FULL* WENDIGO, OF COURSE, MORE OF A HYBRID. AN EXCELLENT FOUNDATION...

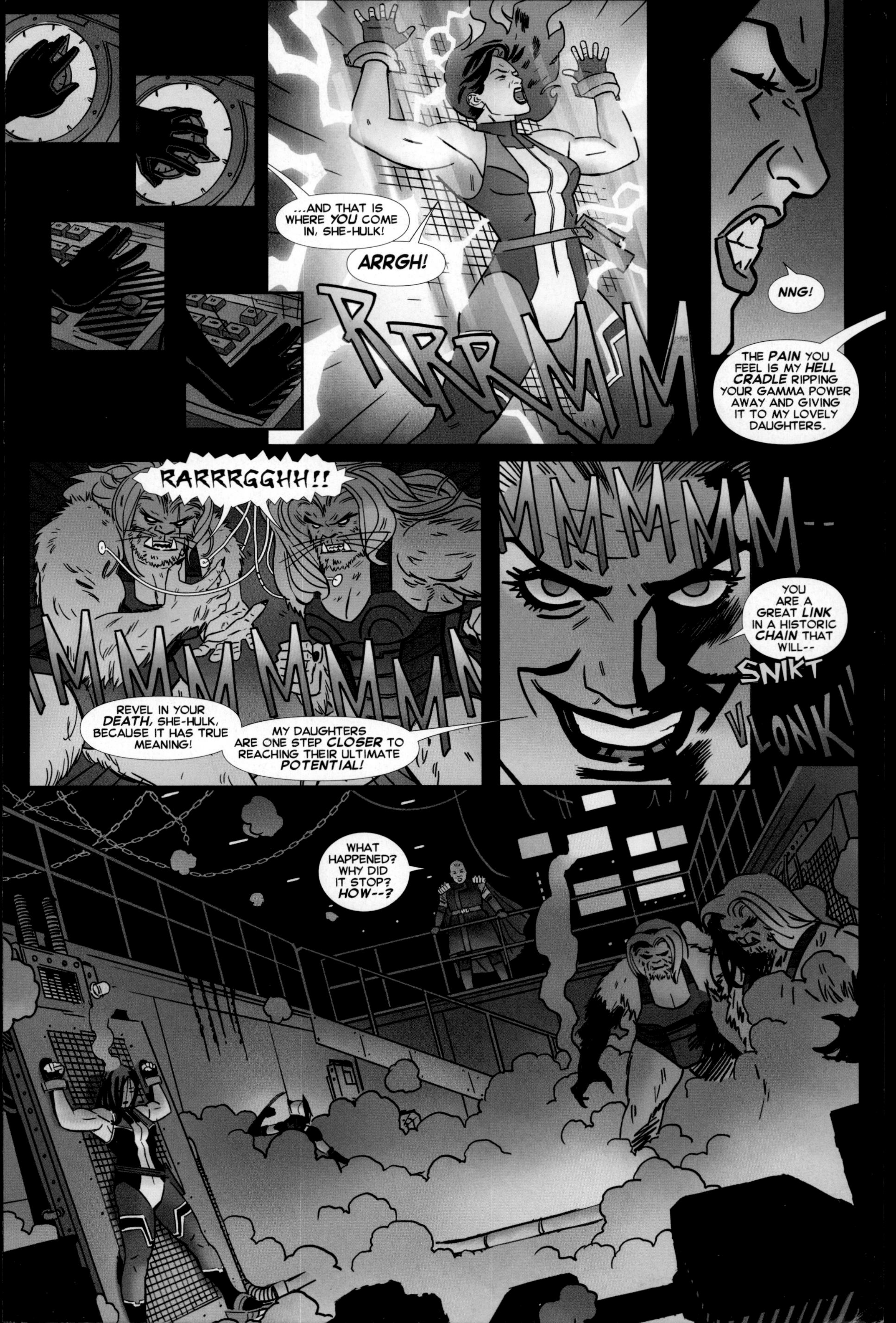
...AND THAT IS WHERE YOU COME IN, SHE-HULK!
ARRGH!
RRRMMM
NNG!
THE PAIN YOU FEEL IS MY HELL CRADLE RIPPING YOUR GAMMA POWER AWAY AND GIVING IT TO MY LOVELY DAUGHTERS.
RARRRGGHH!!
MMMMMMMM
REVEL IN YOUR DEATH, SHE-HULK, BECAUSE IT HAS TRUE MEANING!
MY DAUGHTERS ARE ONE STEP CLOSER TO REACHING THEIR ULTIMATE POTENTIAL!
MMMMMM--
YOU ARE A GREAT LINK IN A HISTORIC CHAIN THAT WILL--
SNIKT
VLONK!
WHAT HAPPENED? WHY DID IT STOP? HOW--?

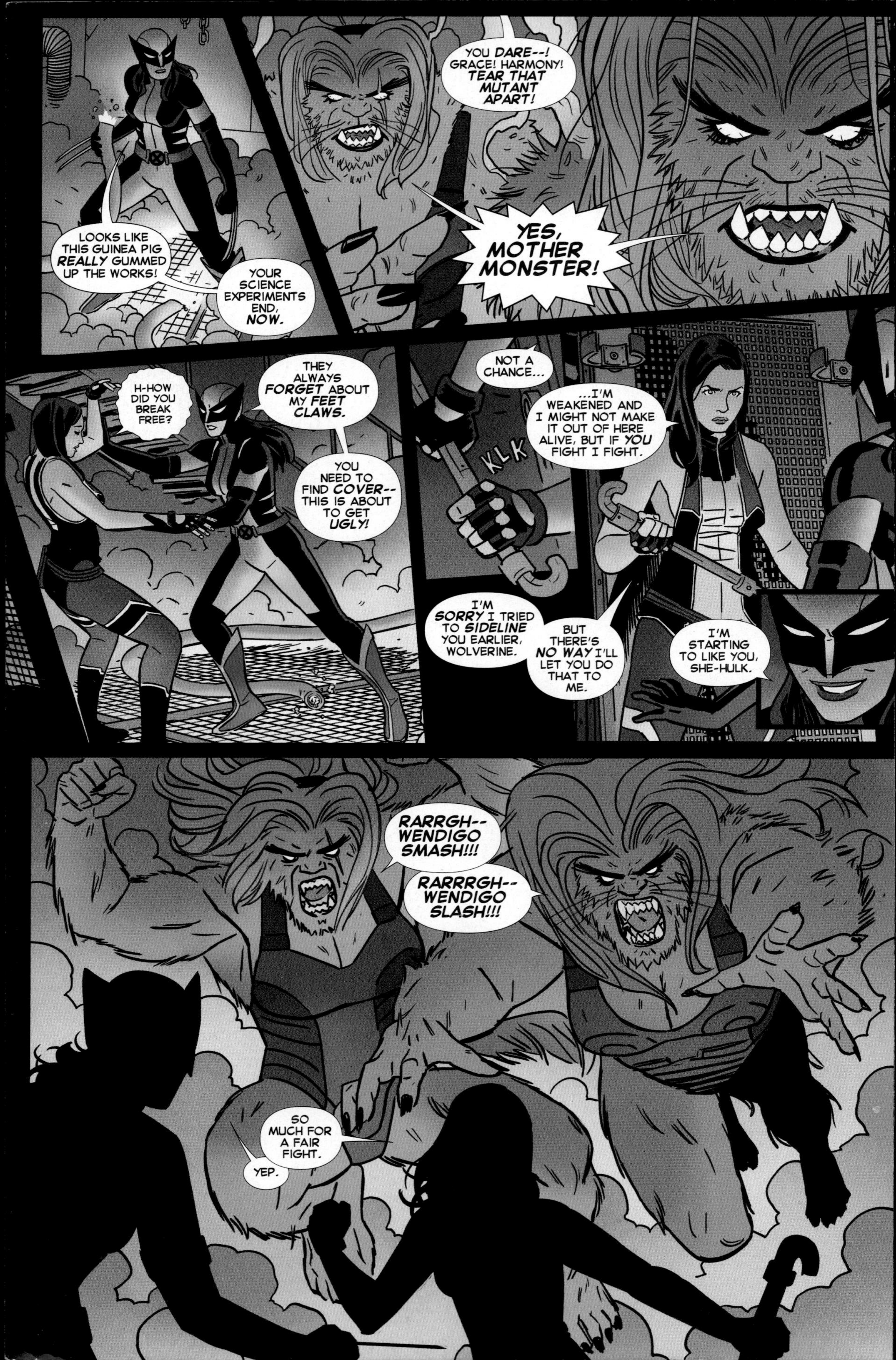
LOOKS LIKE THIS GUINEA PIG REALLY GUMMED UP THE WORKS!
YOUR SCIENCE EXPERIMENTS END, NOW.
YOU DARE--! GRACE! HARMONY! TEAR THAT MUTANT APART!
YES, MOTHER MONSTER!
H-HOW DID YOU BREAK FREE?
THEY ALWAYS FORGET ABOUT MY FEET CLAWS.
YOU NEED TO FIND COVER-- THIS IS ABOUT TO GET UGLY!
NOT A CHANCE...
...I'M WEAKENED AND I MIGHT NOT MAKE IT OUT OF HERE ALIVE, BUT IF YOU FIGHT I FIGHT.
KLK
I'M SORRY I TRIED TO SIDELINE YOU EARLIER, WOLVERINE.
BUT THERE'S NO WAY I'LL LET YOU DO THAT TO ME.
I'M STARTING TO LIKE YOU, SHE-HULK.
RARRGH-- WENDIGO SMASH!!!
RARRRGH-- WENDIGO SLASH!!!
SO MUCH FOR A FAIR FIGHT.
YEP.

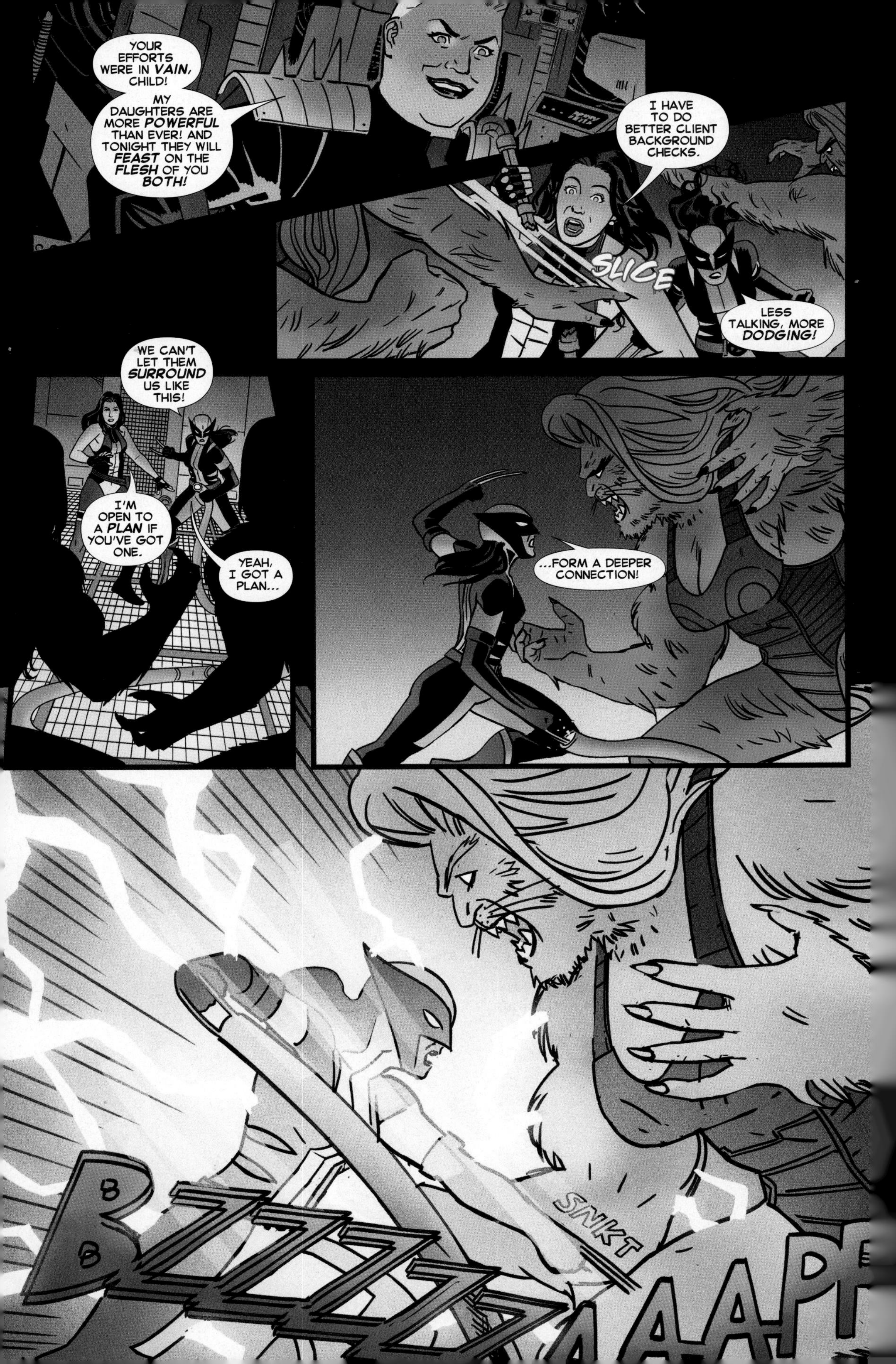
YOUR EFFORTS WERE IN VAIN, CHILD!
MY DAUGHTERS ARE MORE POWERFUL THAN EVER! AND TONIGHT THEY WILL FEAST ON THE FLESH OF YOU BOTH!
I HAVE TO DO BETTER CLIENT BACKGROUND CHECKS.
SLICE
LESS TALKING, MORE DODGING!
WE CAN'T LET THEM SURROUND US LIKE THIS!
I'M OPEN TO A PLAN IF YOU'VE GOT ONE.
YEAH, I GOT A PLAN...
...FORM A DEEPER CONNECTION!
SNKT
BBZZZZZAAAP

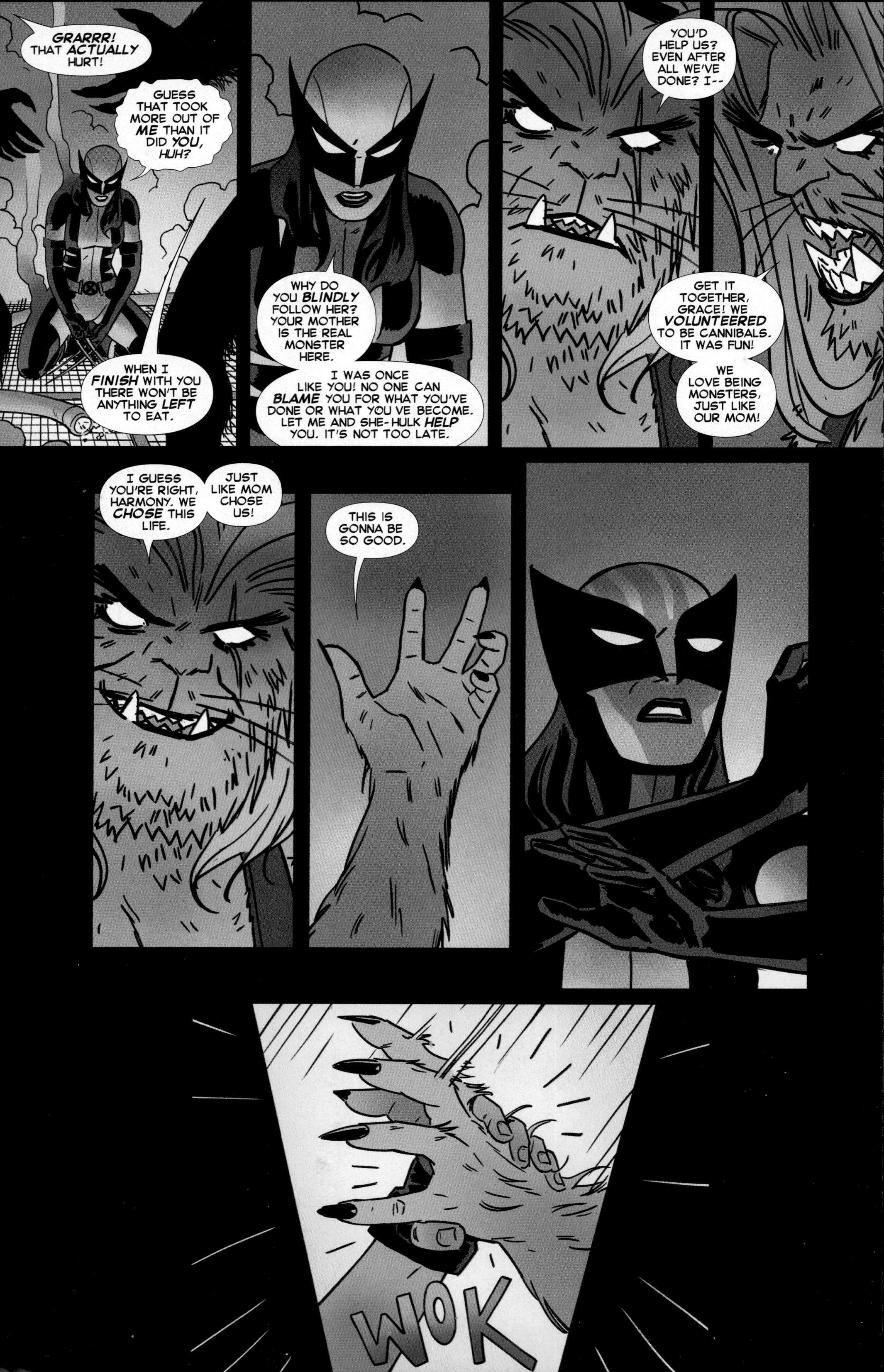
GRARRR! THAT ACTUALLY HURT!
GUESS THAT TOOK MORE OUT OF ME THAN IT DID YOU, HUH?
WHEN I FINISH WITH YOU THERE WON'T BE ANYTHING LEFT TO EAT.
WHY DO YOU BLINDLY FOLLOW HER? YOUR MOTHER IS THE REAL MONSTER HERE.
I WAS ONCE LIKE YOU! NO ONE CAN BLAME YOU FOR WHAT YOU'VE DONE OR WHAT YOU'VE BECOME. LET ME AND SHE-HULK HELP YOU. IT'S NOT TOO LATE.
YOU'D HELP US? EVEN AFTER ALL WE'VE DONE? I--
GET IT TOGETHER, GRACE! WE VOLUNTEERED TO BE CANNIBALS. IT WAS FUN!
WE LOVE BEING MONSTERS, JUST LIKE OUR MOM!
I GUESS YOU'RE RIGHT, HARMONY. WE CHOSE THIS LIFE.
JUST LIKE MOM CHOSE US!
THIS IS GONNA BE SO GOOD.
WOK

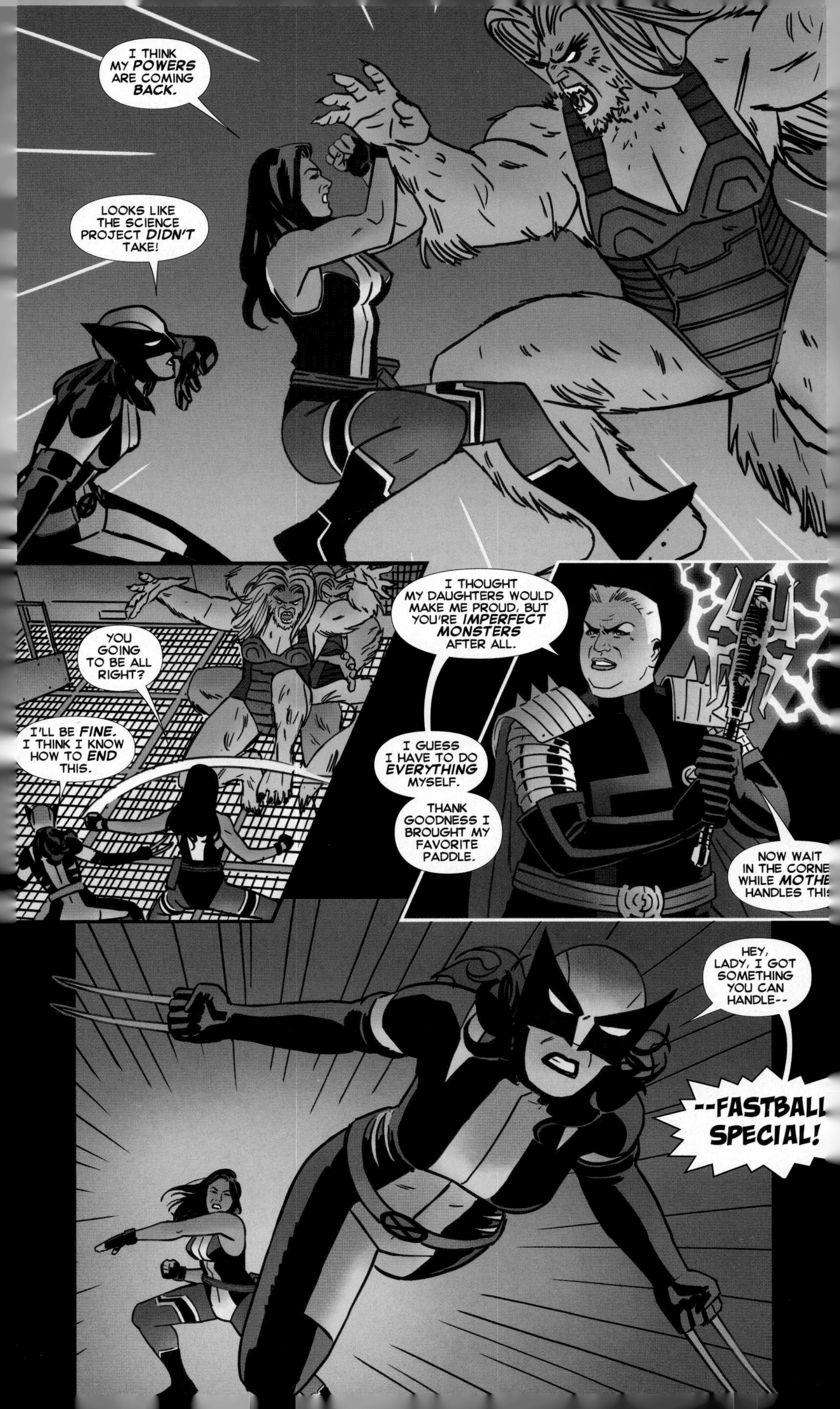

I THINK MY POWERS ARE COMING BACK.
LOOKS LIKE THE SCIENCE PROJECT DIDN'T TAKE!
YOU GOING TO BE ALL RIGHT?
I'LL BE FINE. I THINK I KNOW HOW TO END THIS.
I THOUGHT MY DAUGHTERS WOULD MAKE ME PROUD, BUT YOU'RE IMPERFECT MONSTERS AFTER ALL.
I GUESS I HAVE TO DO EVERYTHING MYSELF.
THANK GOODNESS I BROUGHT MY FAVORITE PADDLE.
NOW WAIT IN THE CORNE WHILE MOTHE HANDLES THIS
HEY, LADY, I GOT SOMETHING YOU CAN HANDLE--
--FASTBALL SPECIAL!

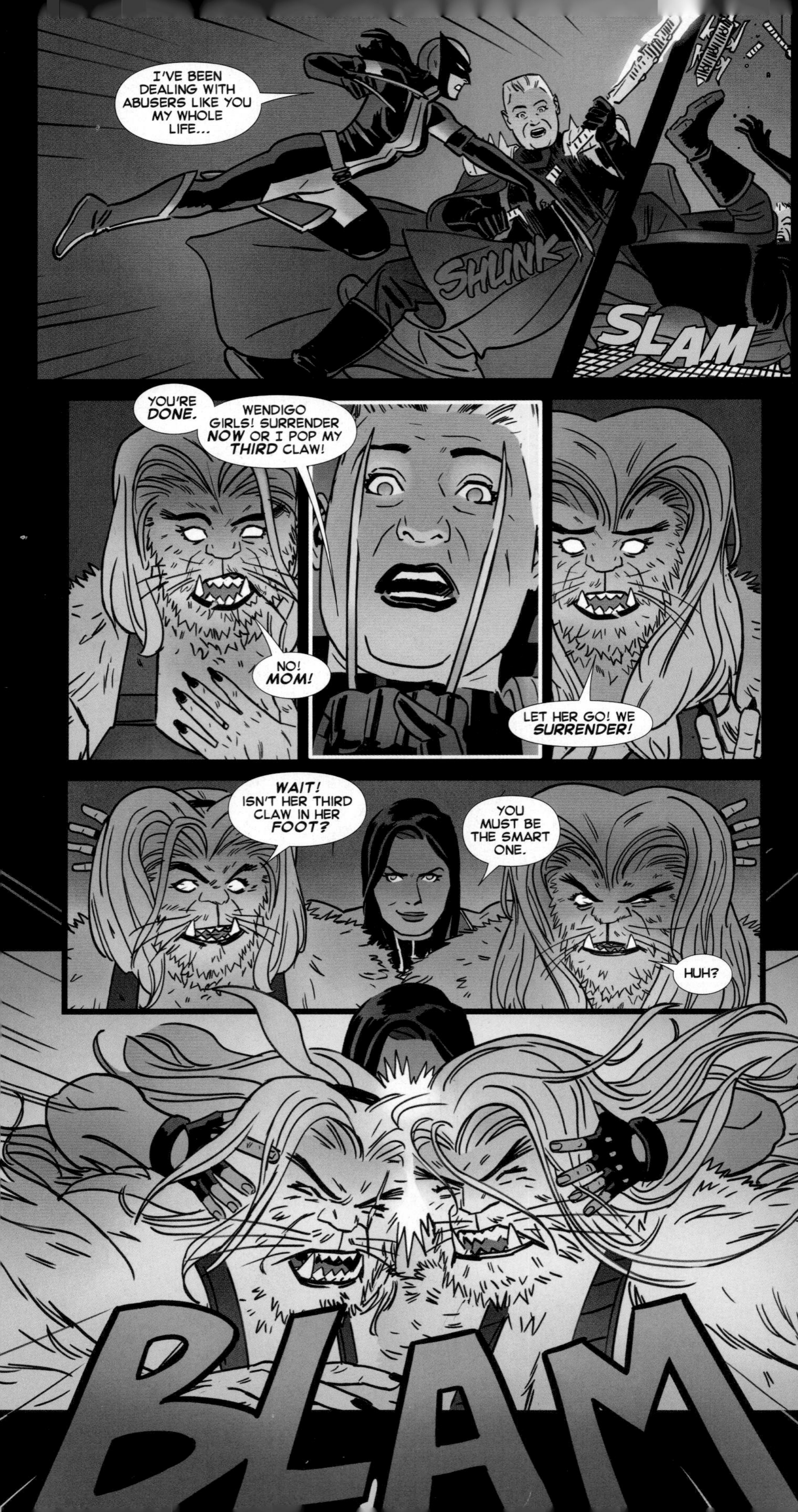
I'VE BEEN DEALING WITH ABUSERS LIKE YOU MY WHOLE LIFE...
SHUNK
SLAM
YOU'RE DONE.
WENDIGO GIRLS! SURRENDER NOW OR I POP MY THIRD CLAW!
NO! MOM!
LET HER GO! WE SURRENDER!
WAIT! ISN'T HER THIRD CLAW IN HER FOOT?
YOU MUST BE THE SMART ONE.
HUH?
BLAM

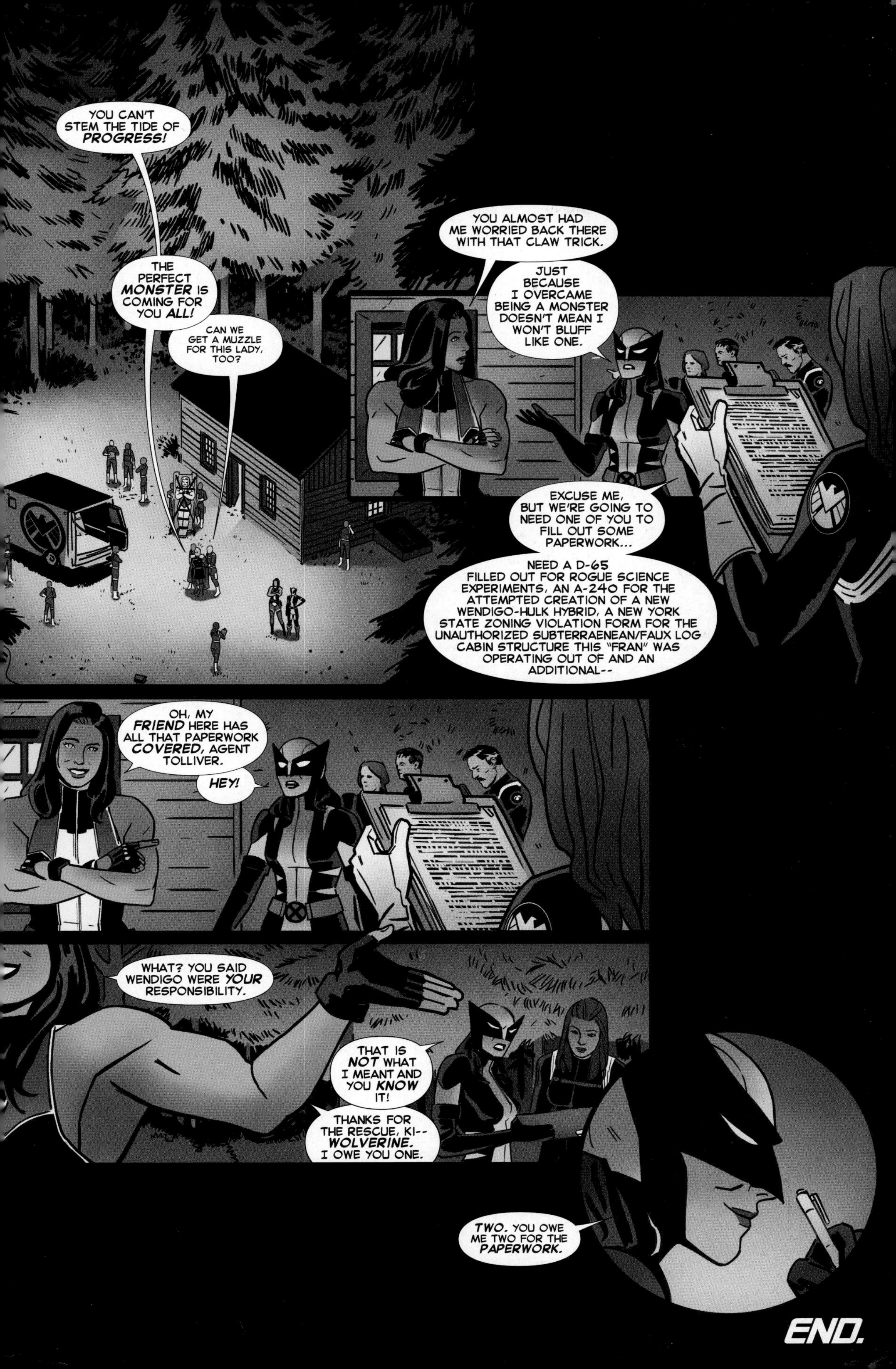

YOU CAN'T STEM THE TIDE OF PROGRESS!
THE PERFECT MONSTER IS COMING FOR YOU ALL!
CAN WE GET A MUZZLE FOR THIS LADY, TOO?
YOU ALMOST HAD ME WORRIED BACK THERE WITH THAT CLAW TRICK.
JUST BECAUSE I OVERCAME BEING A MONSTER DOESN'T MEAN I WON'T BLUFF LIKE ONE.
EXCUSE ME, BUT WE'RE GOING TO NEED ONE OF YOU TO FILL OUT SOME PAPERWORK...
NEED A D-65 FILLED OUT FOR ROGUE SCIENCE EXPERIMENTS, AN A-240 FOR THE ATTEMPTED CREATION OF A NEW WENDIGO-HULK HYBRID, A NEW YORK STATE ZONING VIOLATION FORM FOR THE UNAUTHORIZED SUBTERRAENEAN/FAUX LOG CABIN STRUCTURE THIS "FRAN" WAS OPERATING OUT OF AND AN ADDITIONAL--
OH, MY FRIEND HERE HAS ALL THAT PAPERWORK COVERED, AGENT TOLLIVER.
HEY!
WHAT? YOU SAID WENDIGO WERE YOUR RESPONSIBILITY.
THAT IS NOT WHAT I MEANT AND YOU KNOW IT!
THANKS FOR THE RESCUE, KI-- WOLVERINE. I OWE YOU ONE.
TWO. YOU OWE ME TWO FOR THE PAPERWORK.
END.

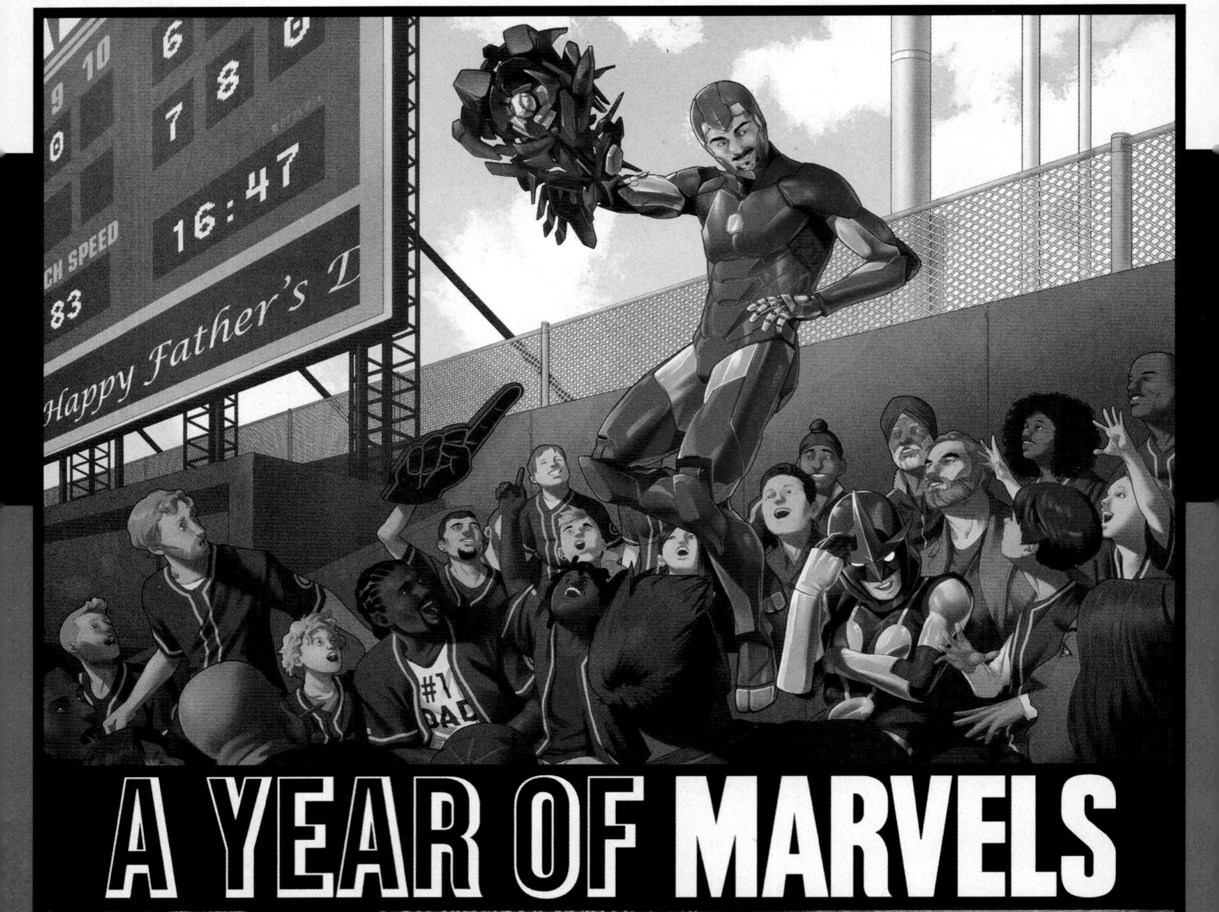
CH SPEED
83
16:47
Happy Father's D
#1
DAD

A YEAR OF MARVELS

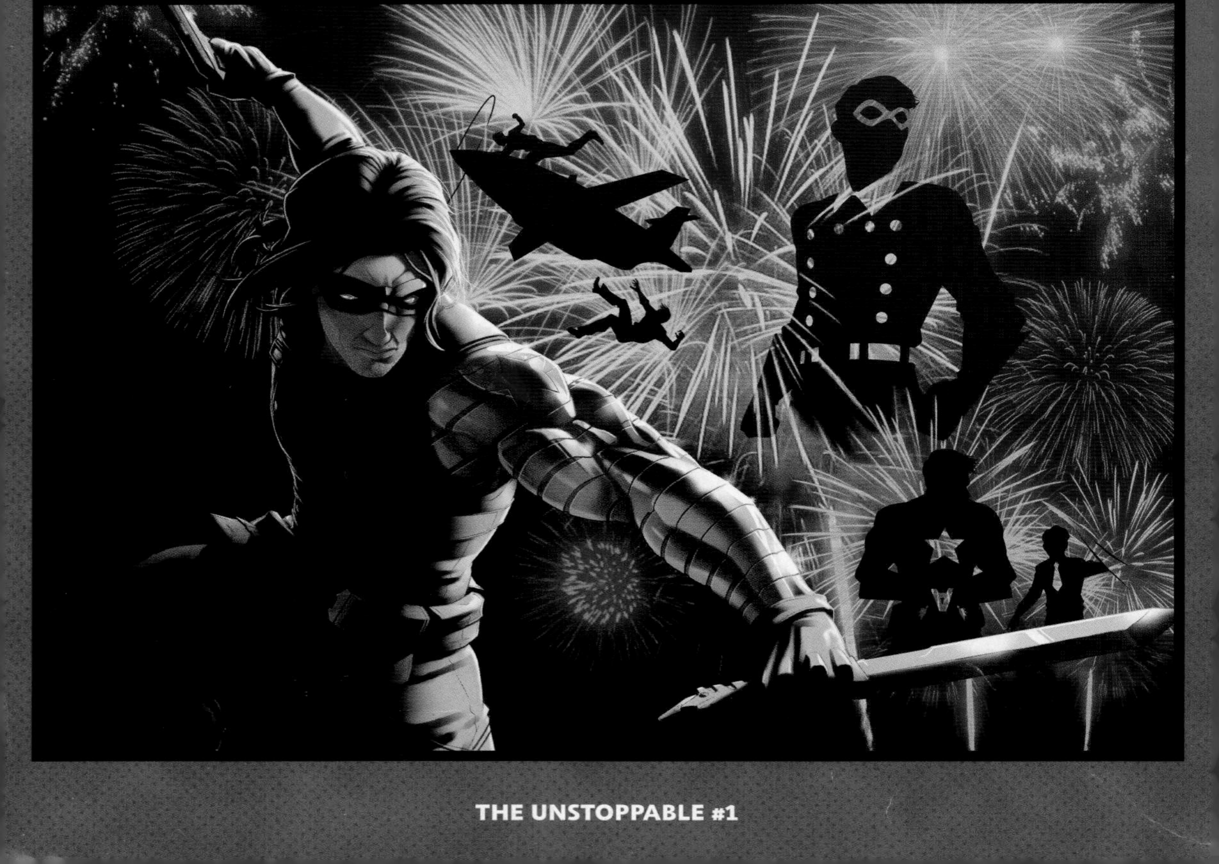

NOVA & INVINCIBLE IRON MAN

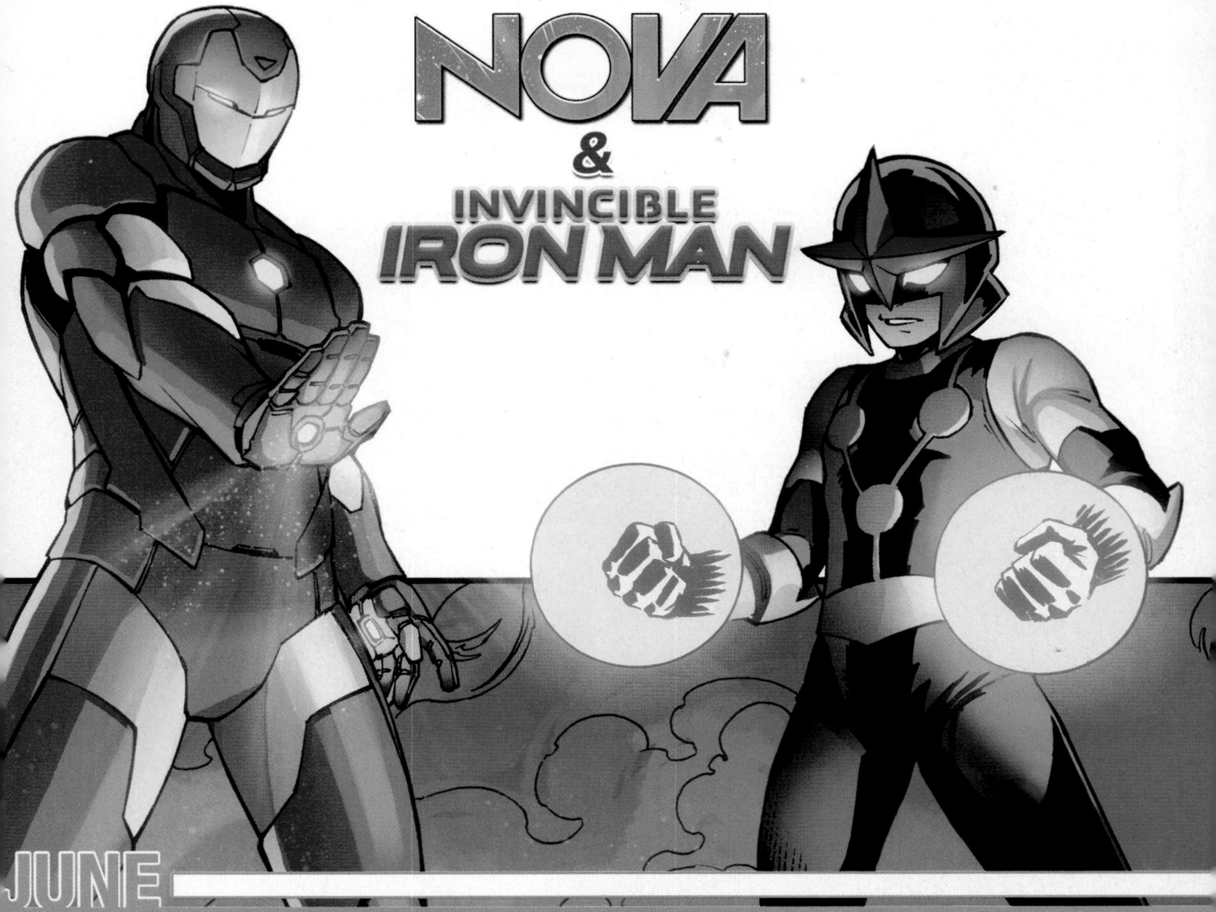

JUNE

SUNDAY	MONDAY	TUESDAY	WEDNESDAY	THURSDAY	FRIDAY	SATURDAY
	1	2	3	4	5 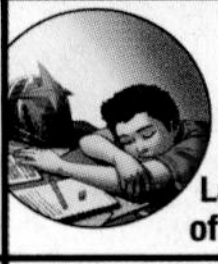 Last Day of School	6
7	8	10	11	12	13	14
15	16	17	18	19	20	21 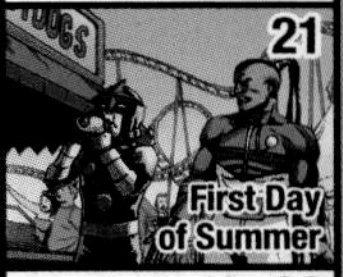 First Day of Summer
22 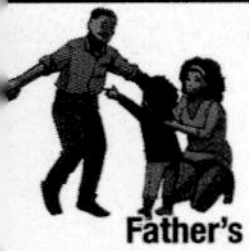 Father's Day	23	24	25	26	27	28
29	30	31				

AUL ALLOR WRITER · DIEGO OLORTEGUI ARTIST · RACHELLE ROSENBERG COLOR ARTIST · GEOFFO STORYBOARD ARTIST · VC'S TRAVIS LANHAM LETTERING
NNIE CHENG & TIM SMITH 3 PRODUCTION TEAM · CARLOS LAO PRODUCTION DESIGN · CHARLES BEACHAM EDITOR · JORDAN D. WHITE & NICK LOWE SUPERVISING EDITORS
EDITOR IN CHIEF AXEL ALONSO CHIEF CREATIVE OFFICER JOE QUESADA PUBLISHER DAN BUCKLEY EXECUTIVE PRODUCER ALAN FINE

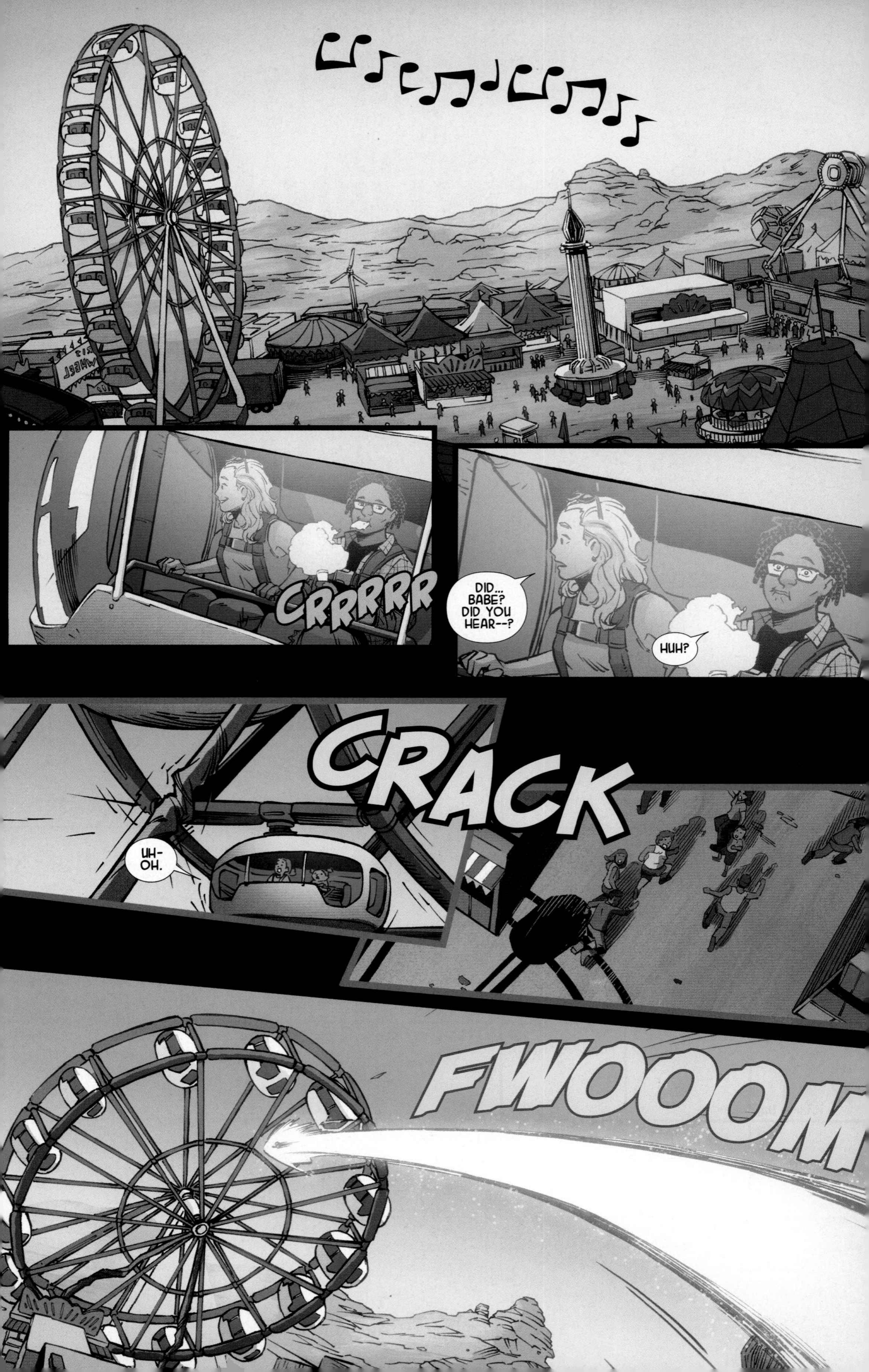
CRRRRR
DID... BABE? DID YOU HEAR--?
HUH?
CRACK
UH-OH.
FWOOOM

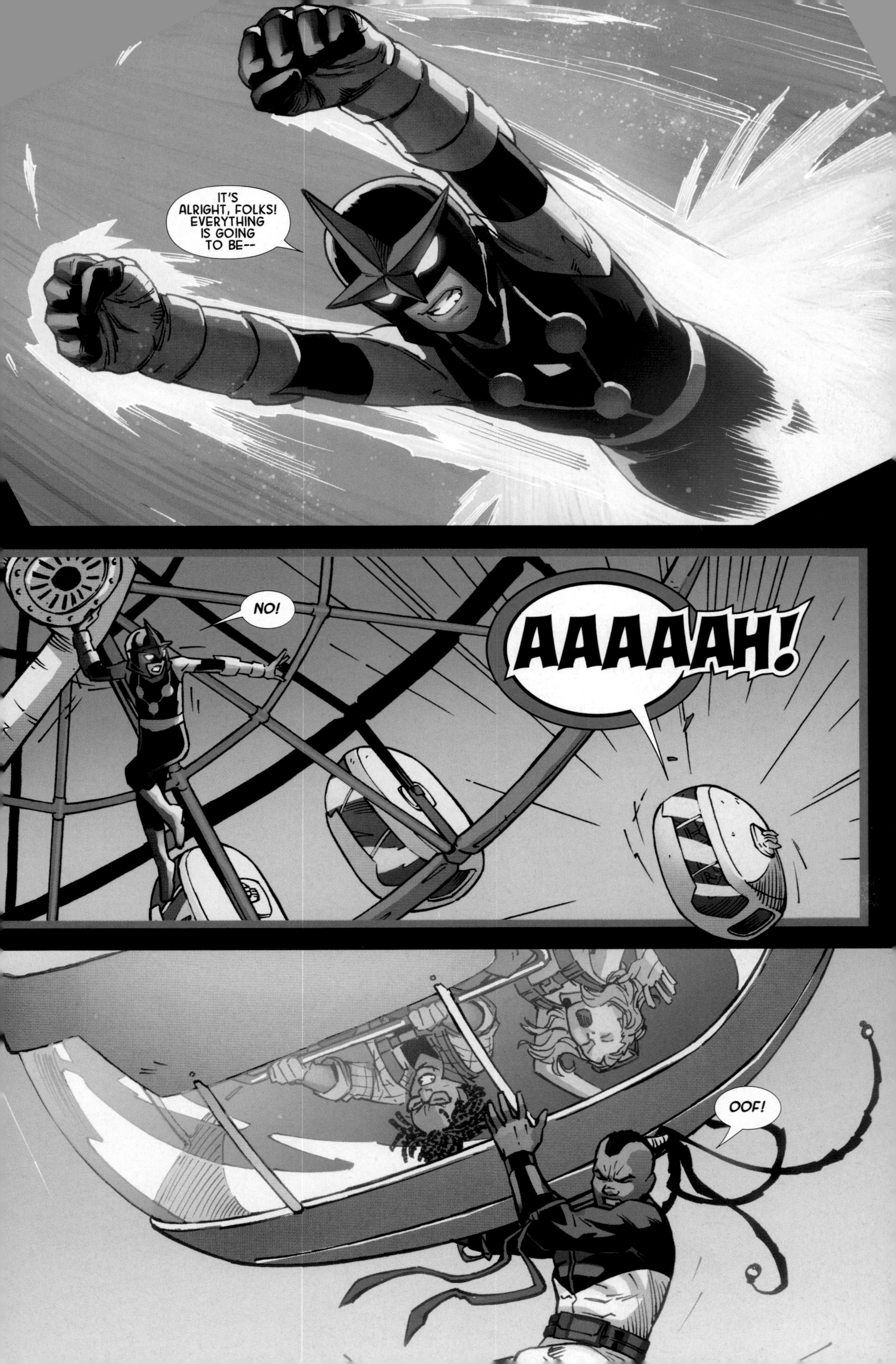
IT'S ALRIGHT, FOLKS! EVERYTHING IS GOING TO BE--
NO!
AAAAAH!
OOF!

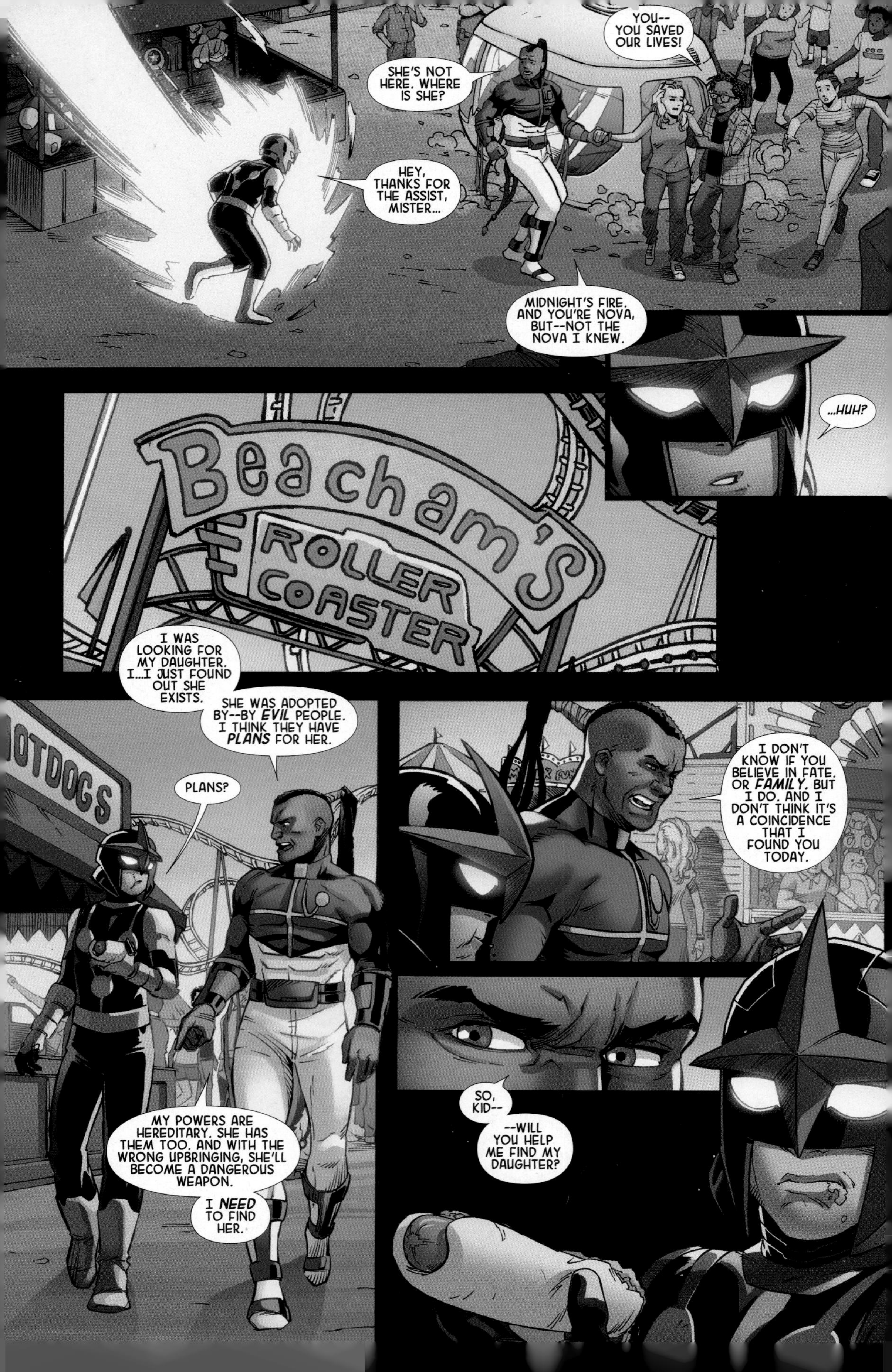
YOU-- YOU SAVED OUR LIVES!
SHE'S NOT HERE. WHERE IS SHE?
HEY, THANKS FOR THE ASSIST, MISTER...
MIDNIGHT'S FIRE. AND YOU'RE NOVA, BUT--NOT THE NOVA I KNEW.
...HUH?
Beacham's ROLLER COASTER
I WAS LOOKING FOR MY DAUGHTER. I...I JUST FOUND OUT SHE EXISTS.
SHE WAS ADOPTED BY--BY EVIL PEOPLE. I THINK THEY HAVE PLANS FOR HER.
PLANS?
HOTDOGS
MY POWERS ARE HEREDITARY. SHE HAS THEM TOO. AND WITH THE WRONG UPBRINGING, SHE'LL BECOME A DANGEROUS WEAPON.
I NEED TO FIND HER.
I DON'T KNOW IF YOU BELIEVE IN FATE, OR FAMILY. BUT I DO. AND I DON'T THINK IT'S A COINCIDENCE THAT I FOUND YOU TODAY.
SO, KID--
--WILL YOU HELP ME FIND MY DAUGHTER?

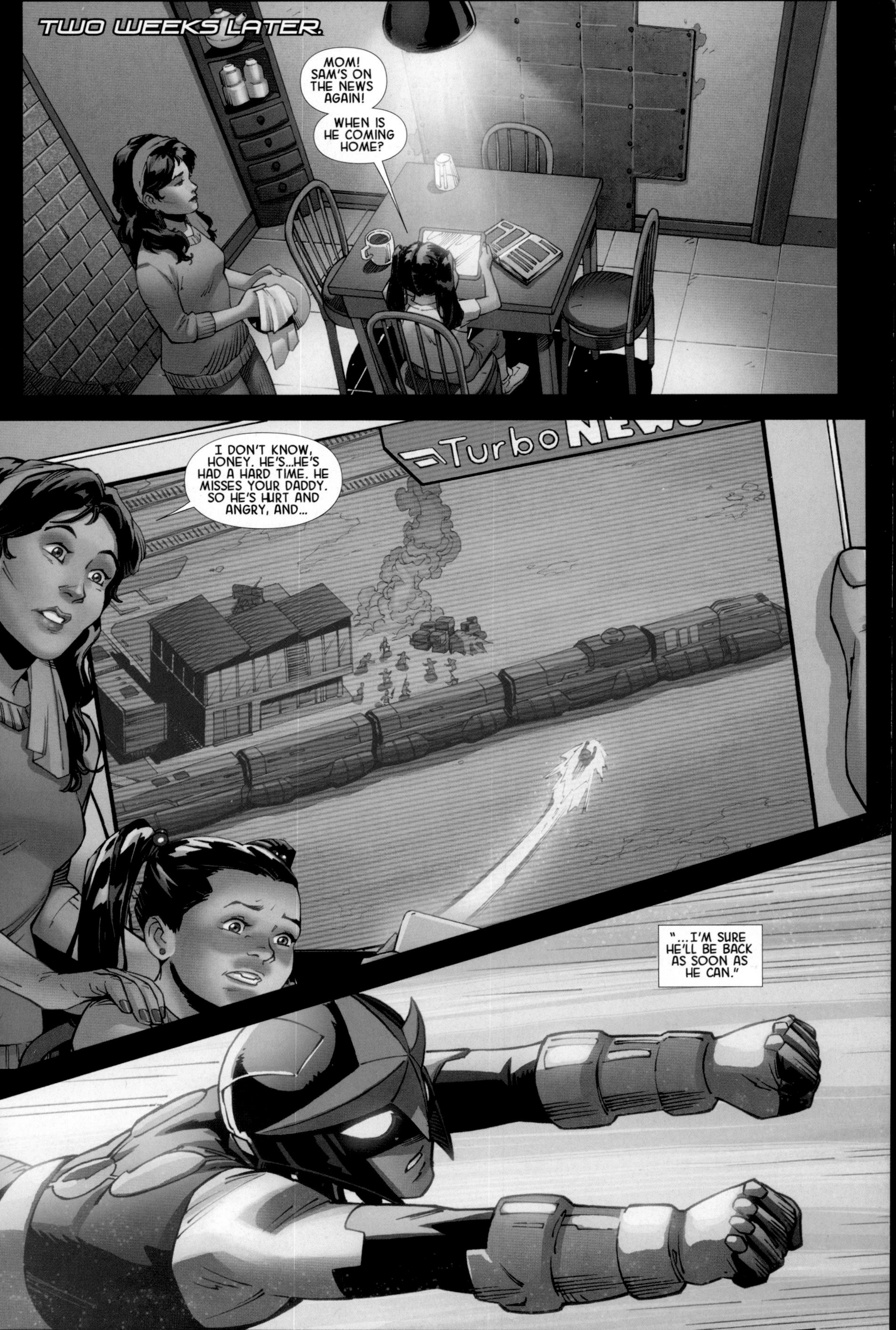
TWO WEEKS LATER.
MOM! SAM'S ON THE NEWS AGAIN!
WHEN IS HE COMING HOME?
TurboNEWS
I DON'T KNOW, HONEY. HE'S...HE'S HAD A HARD TIME. HE MISSES YOUR DADDY. SO HE'S HURT AND ANGRY, AND...
"...I'M SURE HE'LL BE BACK AS SOON AS HE CAN."

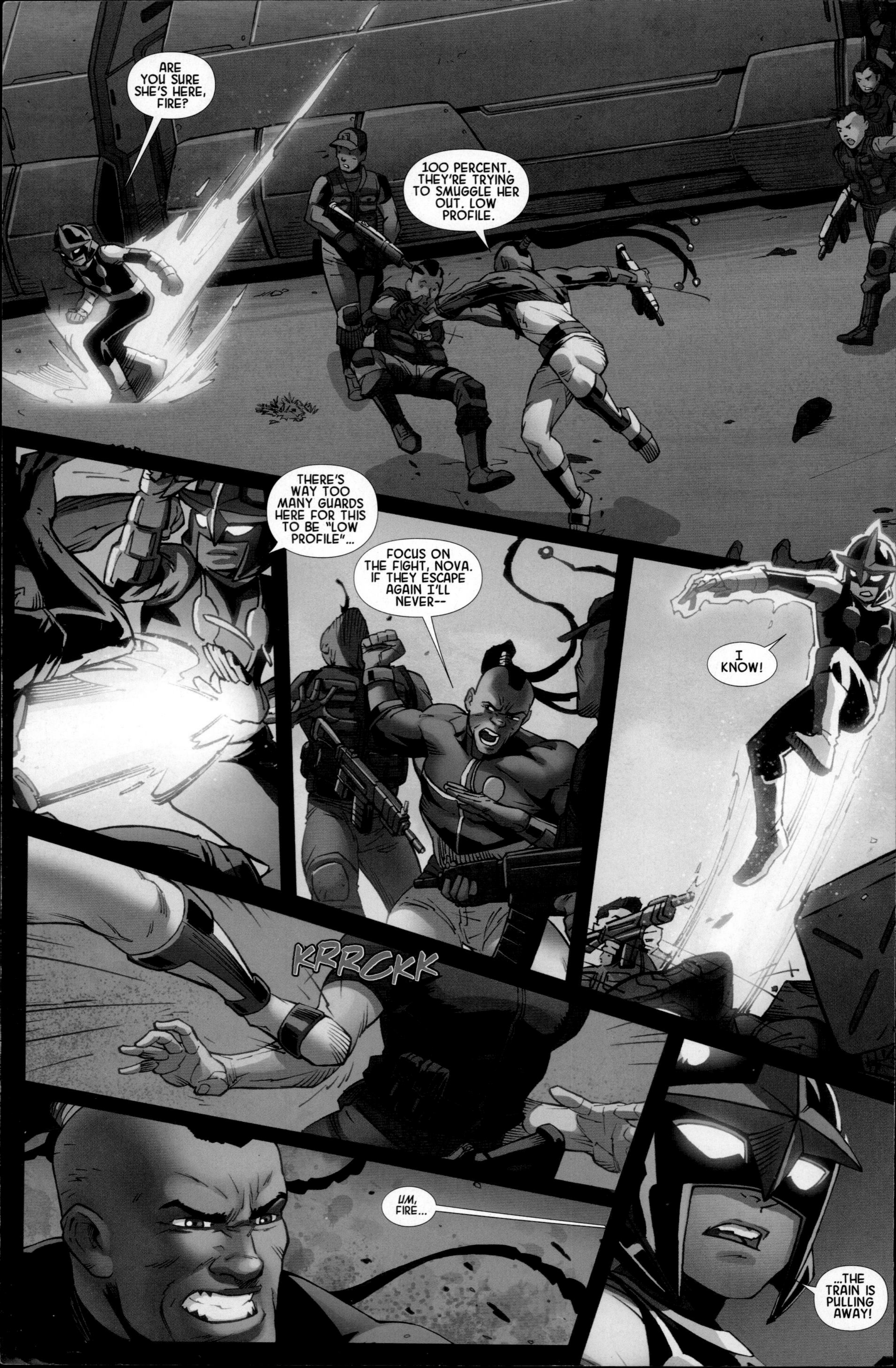

ARE YOU SURE SHE'S HERE, FIRE?
100 PERCENT. THEY'RE TRYING TO SMUGGLE HER OUT. LOW PROFILE.
THERE'S WAY TOO MANY GUARDS HERE FOR THIS TO BE "LOW PROFILE"...
FOCUS ON THE FIGHT, NOVA. IF THEY ESCAPE AGAIN I'LL NEVER--
I KNOW!
KRRCKK
UM, FIRE...
...THE TRAIN IS PULLING AWAY!

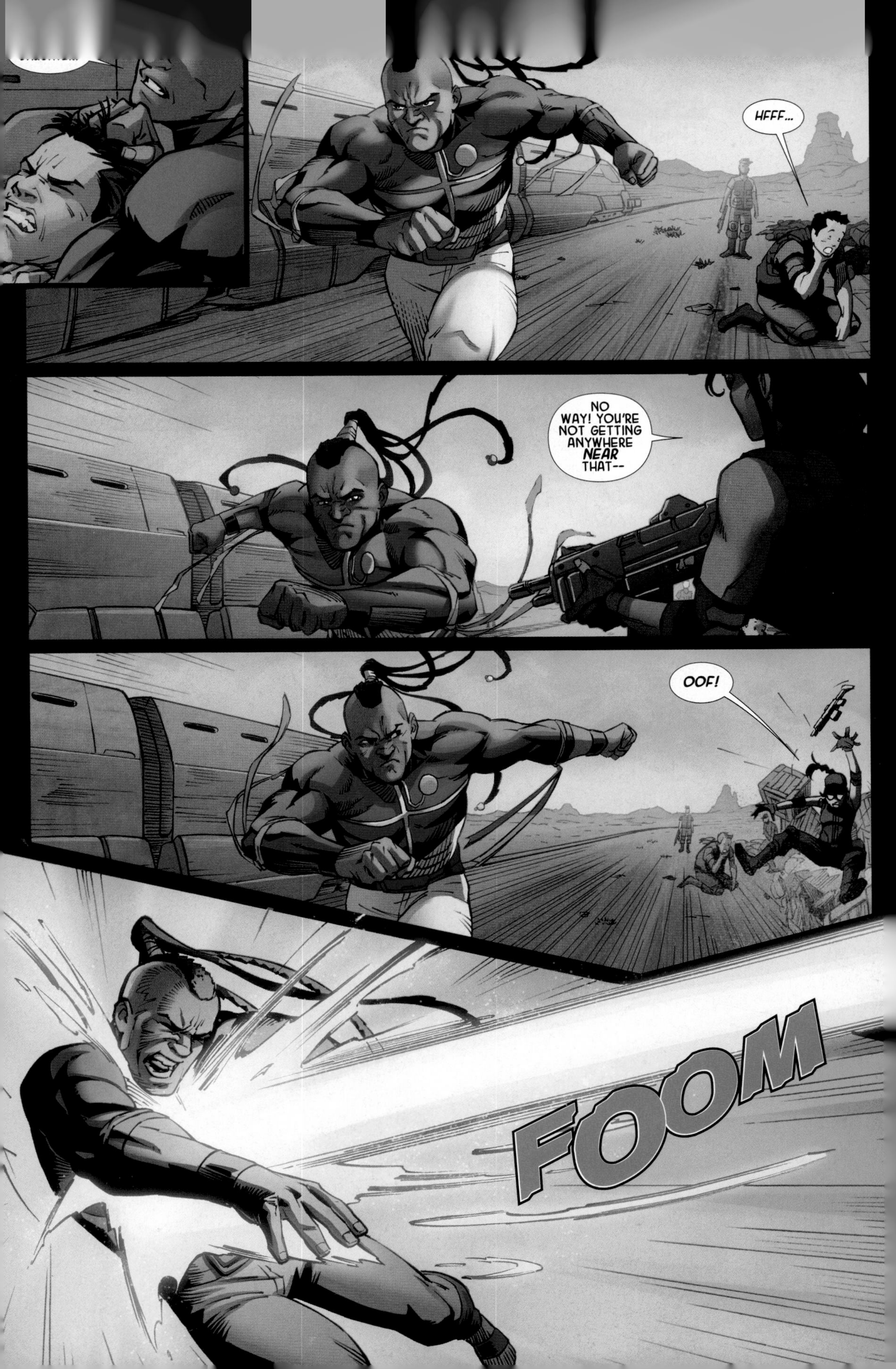
HFFF...
NO WAY! YOU'RE NOT GETTING ANYWHERE NEAR THAT--
OOF!
FOOM

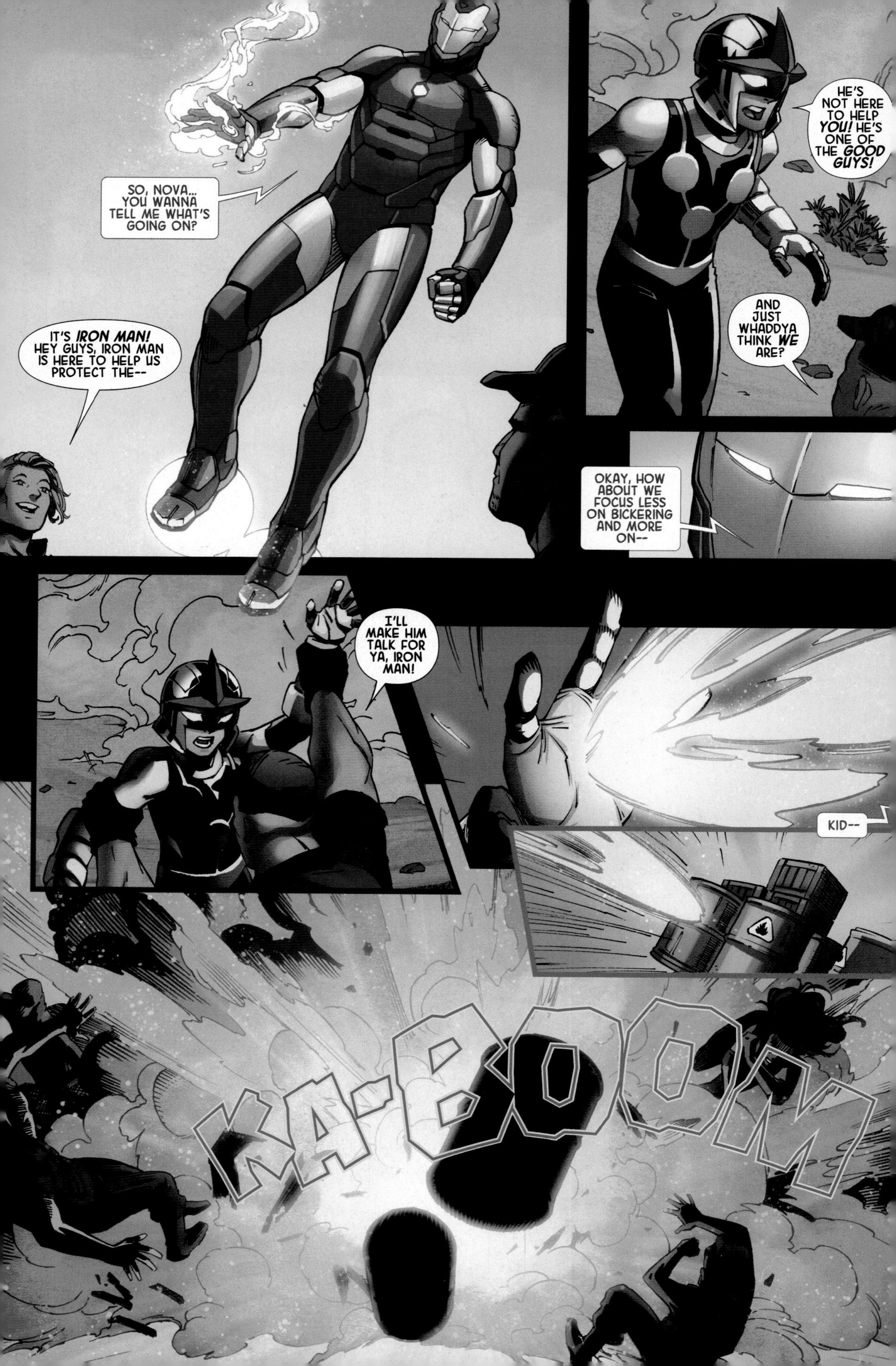

SO, NOVA... YOU WANNA TELL ME WHAT'S GOING ON?
IT'S IRON MAN! HEY GUYS, IRON MAN IS HERE TO HELP US PROTECT THE--
HE'S NOT HERE TO HELP YOU! HE'S ONE OF THE GOOD GUYS!
AND JUST WHADDYA THINK WE ARE?
OKAY, HOW ABOUT WE FOCUS LESS ON BICKERING AND MORE ON--
I'LL MAKE HIM TALK FOR YA, IRON MAN!
KID--
KA-BOOM

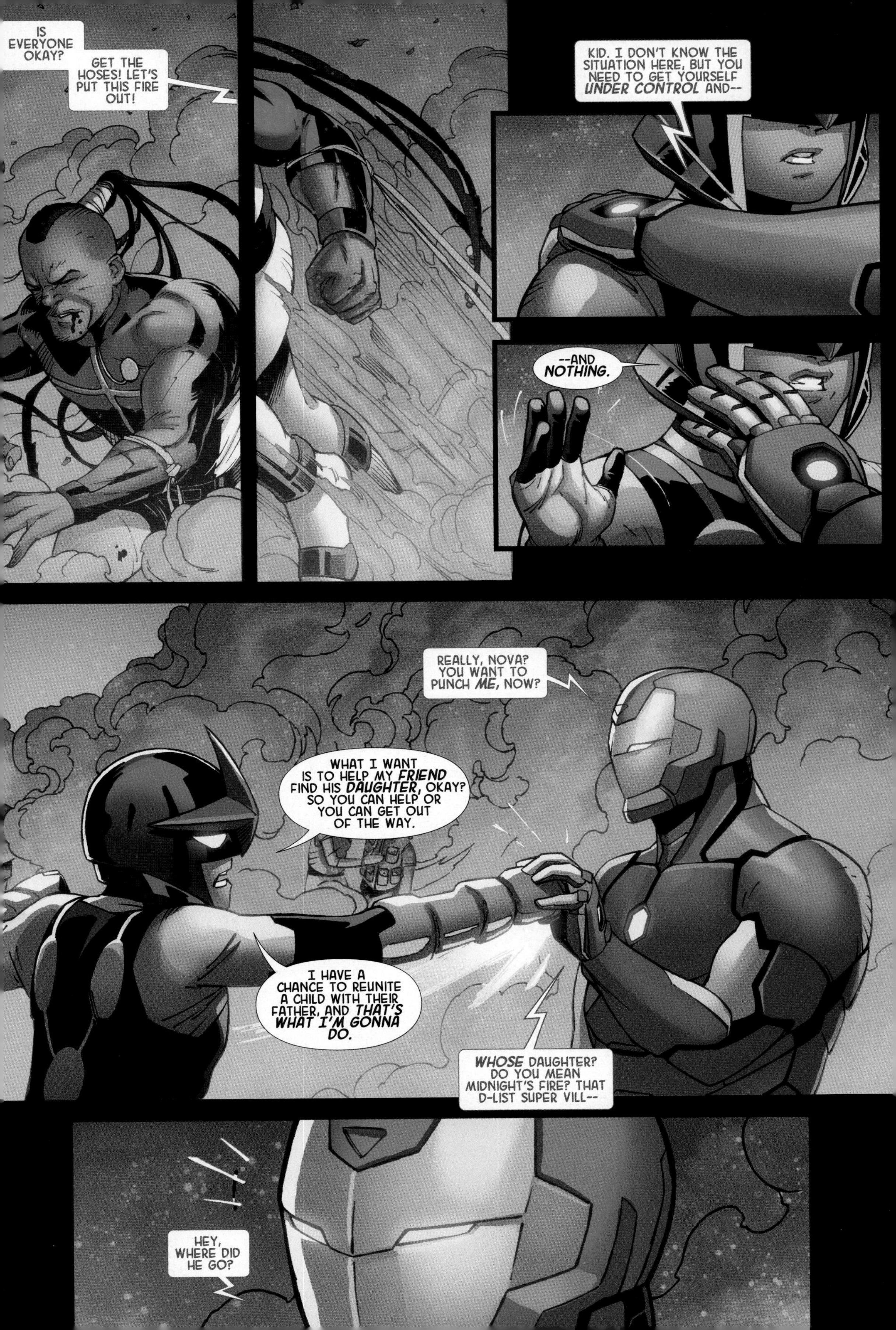
IS EVERYONE OKAY?
GET THE HOSES! LET'S PUT THIS FIRE OUT!
KID. I DON'T KNOW THE SITUATION HERE, BUT YOU NEED TO GET YOURSELF UNDER CONTROL AND--
--AND NOTHING.
REALLY, NOVA? YOU WANT TO PUNCH ME, NOW?
WHAT I WANT IS TO HELP MY FRIEND FIND HIS DAUGHTER, OKAY? SO YOU CAN HELP OR YOU CAN GET OUT OF THE WAY.
I HAVE A CHANCE TO REUNITE A CHILD WITH THEIR FATHER, AND THAT'S WHAT I'M GONNA DO.
WHOSE DAUGHTER? DO YOU MEAN MIDNIGHT'S FIRE? THAT D-LIST SUPER VILL--
HEY, WHERE DID HE GO?

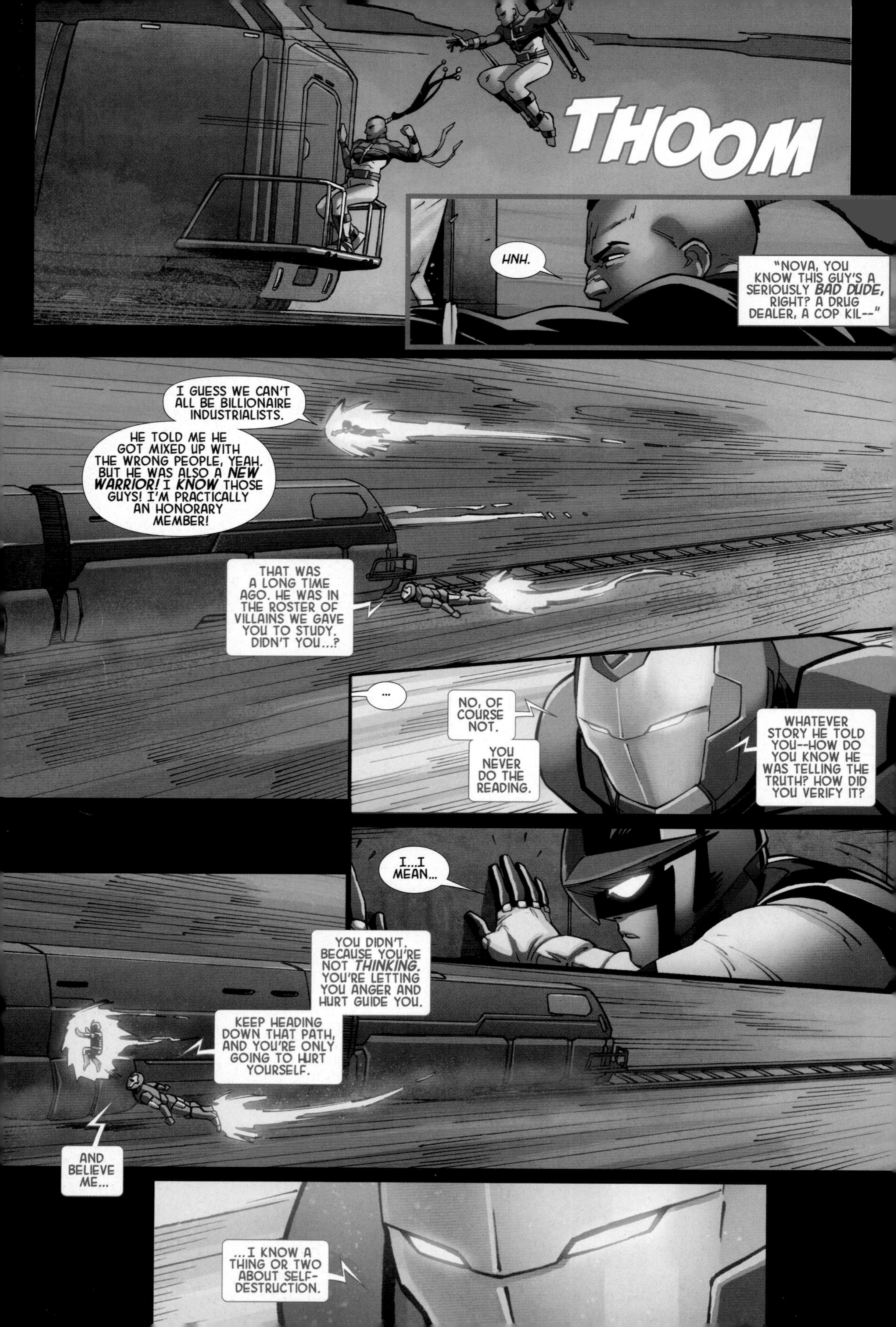
THOOM
HNH.
"NOVA, YOU KNOW THIS GUY'S A SERIOUSLY BAD DUDE, RIGHT? A DRUG DEALER, A COP KIL--"
I GUESS WE CAN'T ALL BE BILLIONAIRE INDUSTRIALISTS.
HE TOLD ME HE GOT MIXED UP WITH THE WRONG PEOPLE, YEAH. BUT HE WAS ALSO A NEW WARRIOR! I KNOW THOSE GUYS! I'M PRACTICALLY AN HONORARY MEMBER!
THAT WAS A LONG TIME AGO. HE WAS IN THE ROSTER OF VILLAINS WE GAVE YOU TO STUDY. DIDN'T YOU...?
...
NO, OF COURSE NOT.
YOU NEVER DO THE READING.
WHATEVER STORY HE TOLD YOU--HOW DO YOU KNOW HE WAS TELLING THE TRUTH? HOW DID YOU VERIFY IT?
I...I MEAN...
YOU DIDN'T, BECAUSE YOU'RE NOT THINKING. YOU'RE LETTING YOU ANGER AND HURT GUIDE YOU.
KEEP HEADING DOWN THAT PATH, AND YOU'RE ONLY GOING TO HURT YOURSELF.
AND BELIEVE ME...
...I KNOW A THING OR TWO ABOUT SELF-DESTRUCTION.

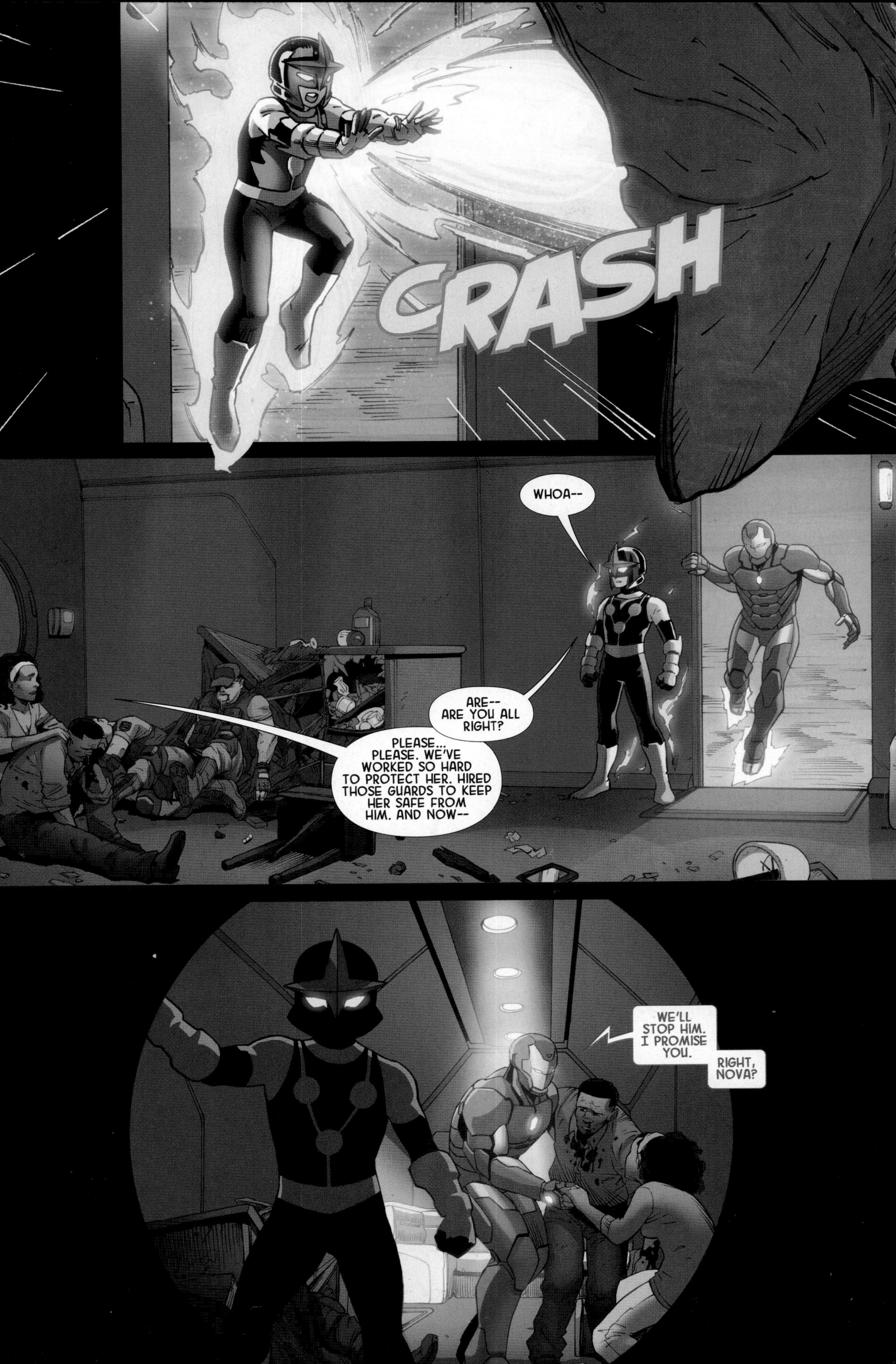
CRASH
WHOA--
ARE-- ARE YOU ALL RIGHT?
PLEASE... PLEASE. WE'VE WORKED SO HARD TO PROTECT HER. HIRED THOSE GUARDS TO KEEP HER SAFE FROM HIM. AND NOW--
WE'LL STOP HIM. I PROMISE YOU.
RIGHT, NOVA?

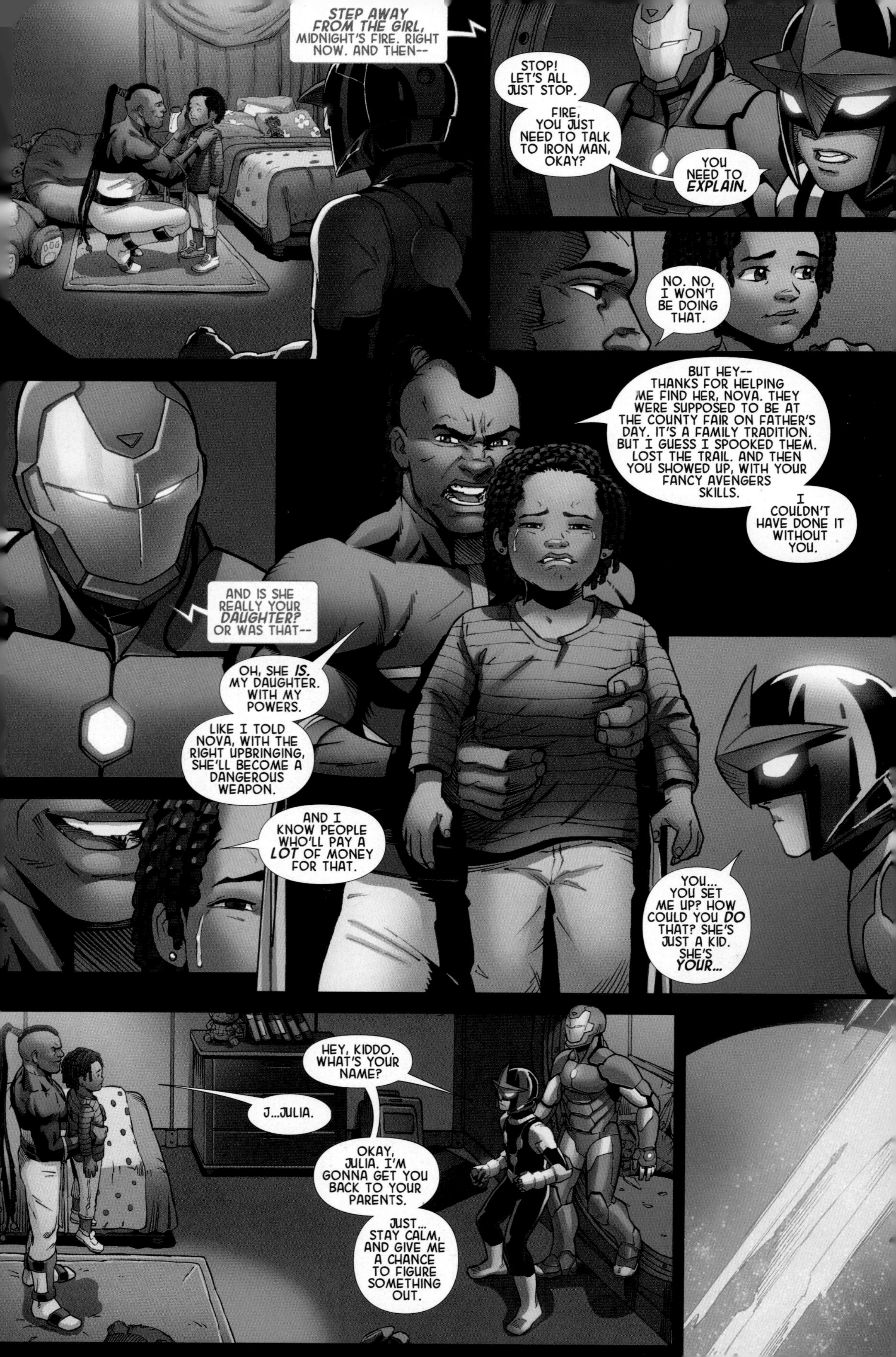
STEP AWAY FROM THE GIRL, MIDNIGHT'S FIRE. RIGHT NOW. AND THEN--
STOP! LET'S ALL JUST STOP.
FIRE, YOU JUST NEED TO TALK TO IRON MAN, OKAY?
YOU NEED TO EXPLAIN.
NO. NO, I WON'T BE DOING THAT.
BUT HEY-- THANKS FOR HELPING ME FIND HER, NOVA. THEY WERE SUPPOSED TO BE AT THE COUNTY FAIR ON FATHER'S DAY. IT'S A FAMILY TRADITION. BUT I GUESS I SPOOKED THEM. LOST THE TRAIL. AND THEN YOU SHOWED UP, WITH YOUR FANCY AVENGERS SKILLS.
I COULDN'T HAVE DONE IT WITHOUT YOU.
AND IS SHE REALLY YOUR DAUGHTER? OR WAS THAT--
OH, SHE IS. MY DAUGHTER. WITH MY POWERS.
LIKE I TOLD NOVA, WITH THE RIGHT UPBRINGING, SHE'LL BECOME A DANGEROUS WEAPON.
AND I KNOW PEOPLE WHO'LL PAY A LOT OF MONEY FOR THAT.
YOU... YOU SET ME UP? HOW COULD YOU DO THAT? SHE'S JUST A KID. SHE'S YOUR...
HEY, KIDDO. WHAT'S YOUR NAME?
J...JULIA.
OKAY, JULIA. I'M GONNA GET YOU BACK TO YOUR PARENTS.
JUST... STAY CALM, AND GIVE ME A CHANCE TO FIGURE SOMETHING OUT.

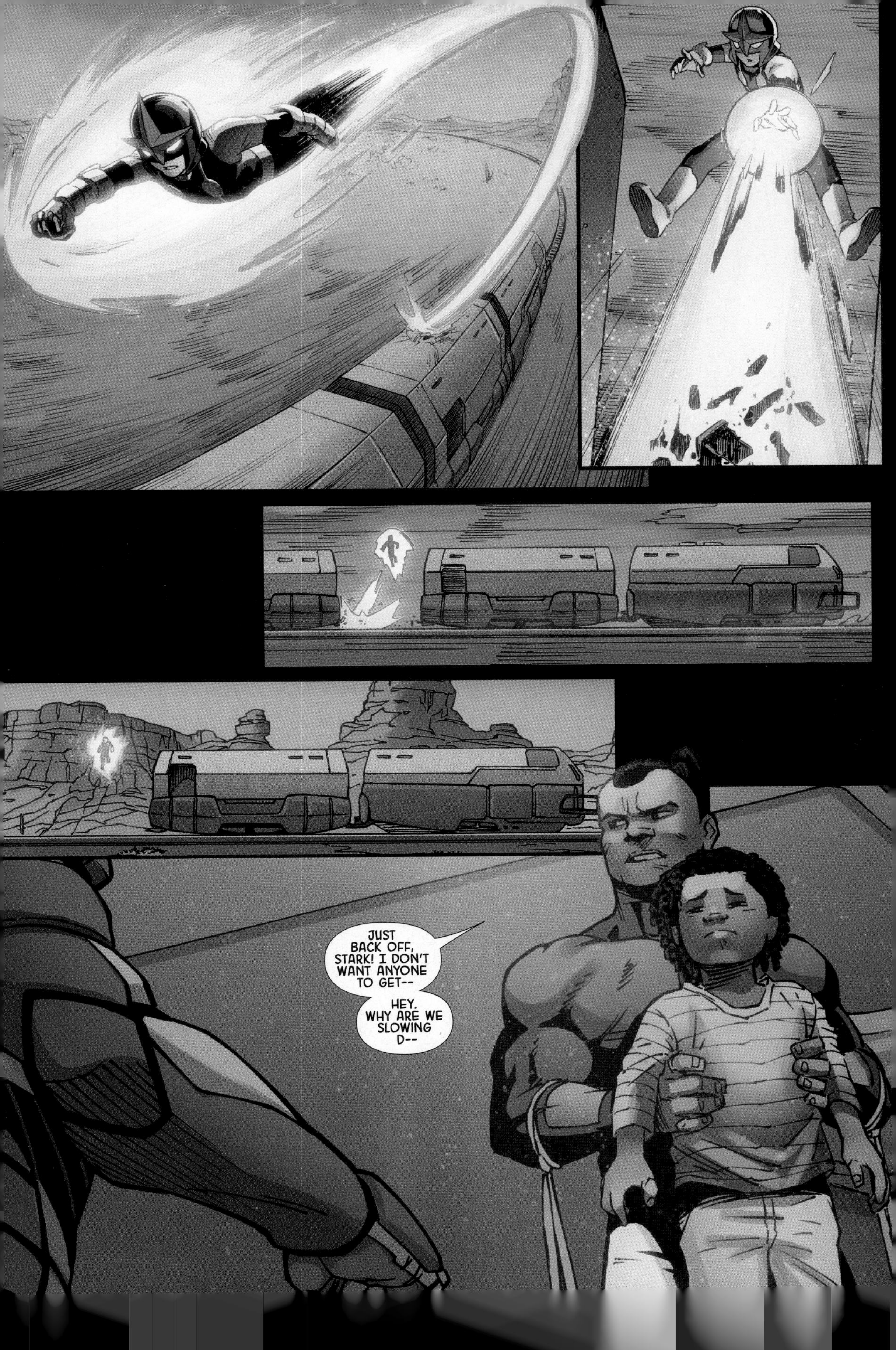
JUST BACK OFF, STARK! I DON'T WANT ANYONE TO GET--
HEY. WHY ARE WE SLOWING D--

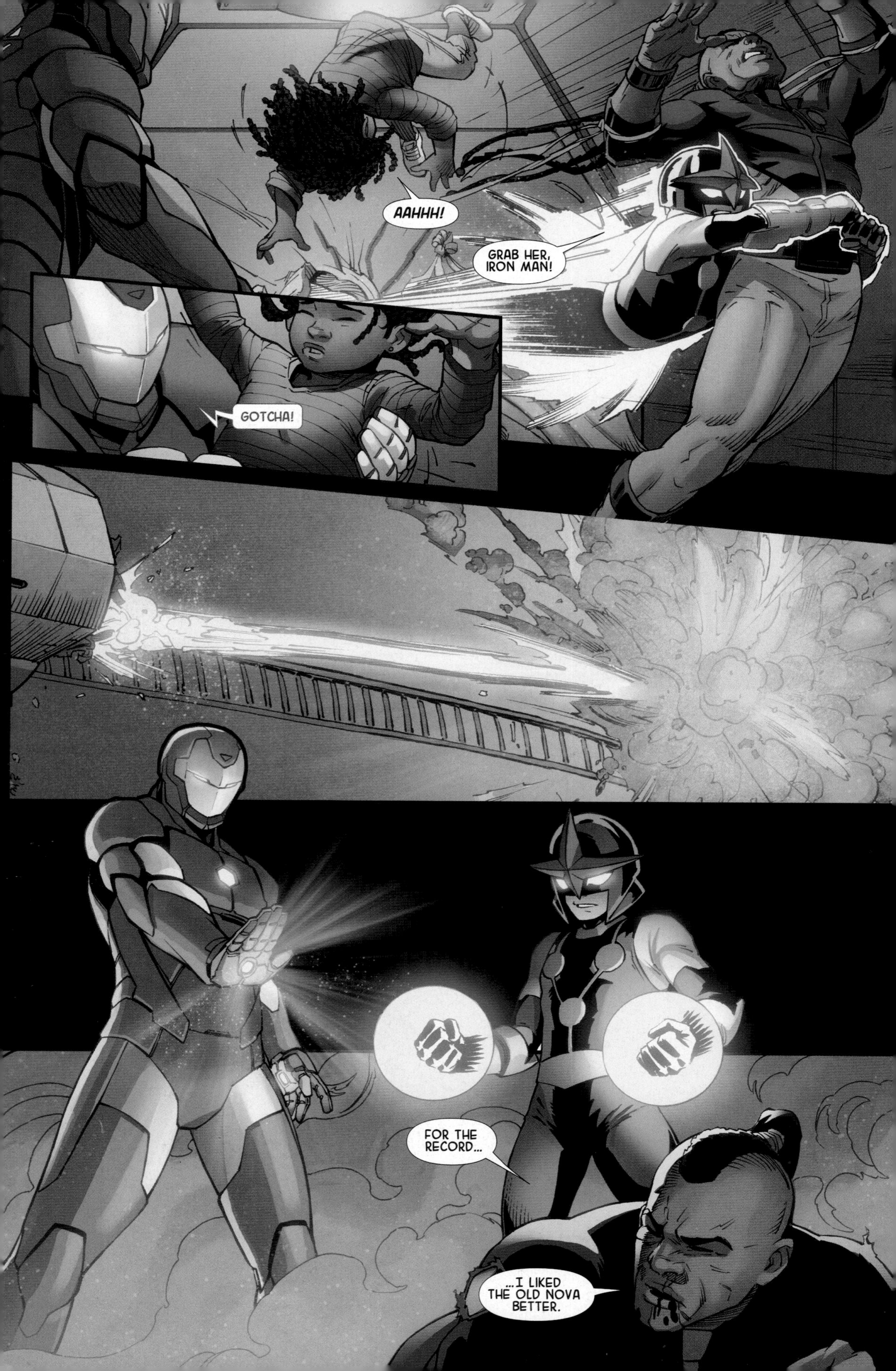
AAHHH!
GRAB HER, IRON MAN!
GOTCHA!
FOR THE RECORD...
...I LIKED THE OLD NOVA BETTER.

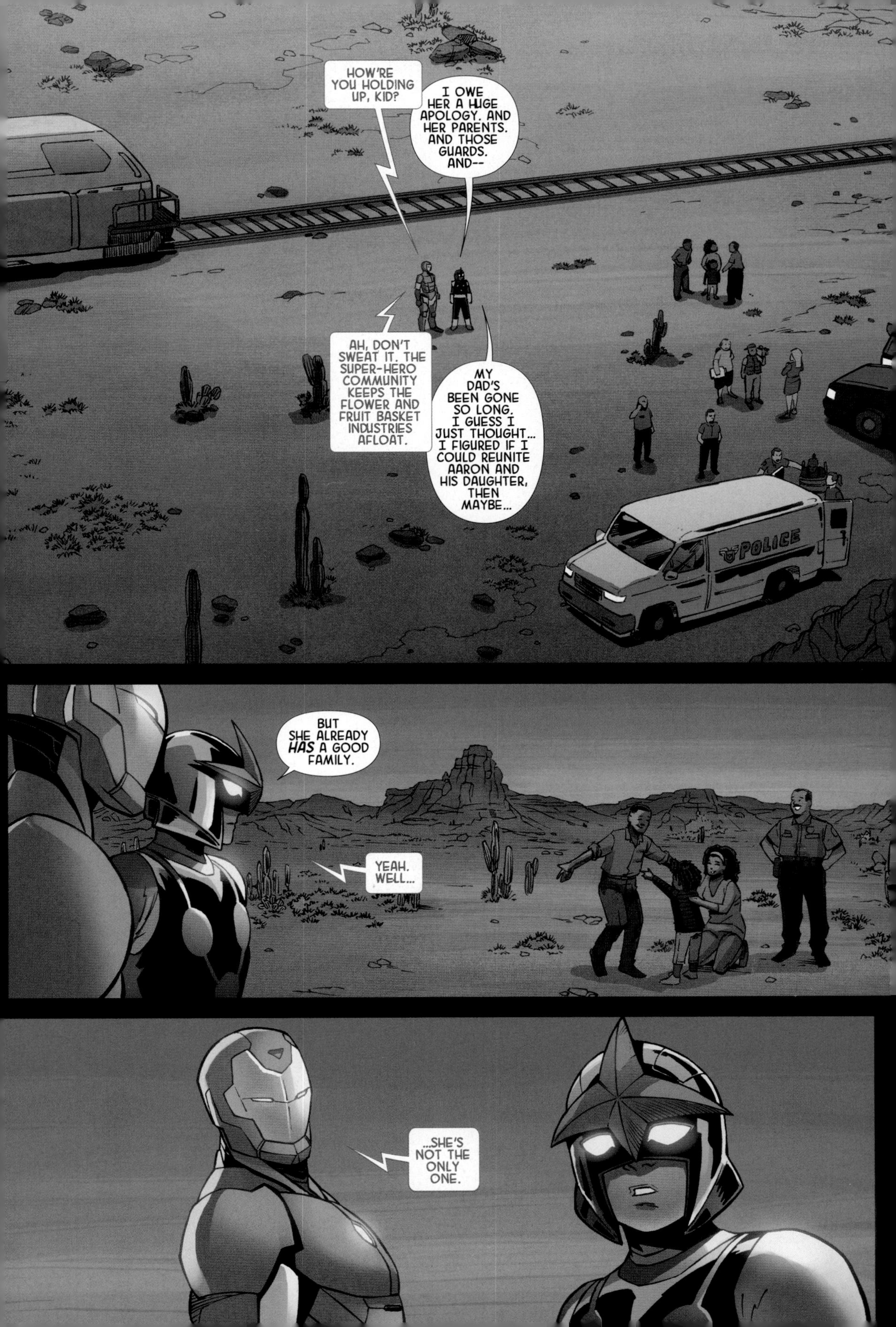

HOW'RE YOU HOLDING UP, KID?
I OWE HER A HUGE APOLOGY. AND HER PARENTS. AND THOSE GUARDS. AND--
AH, DON'T SWEAT IT. THE SUPER-HERO COMMUNITY KEEPS THE FLOWER AND FRUIT BASKET INDUSTRIES AFLOAT.
MY DAD'S BEEN GONE SO LONG. I GUESS I JUST THOUGHT... I FIGURED IF I COULD REUNITE AARON AND HIS DAUGHTER, THEN MAYBE...
POLICE
BUT SHE ALREADY HAS A GOOD FAMILY.
YEAH. WELL...
...SHE'S NOT THE ONLY ONE.

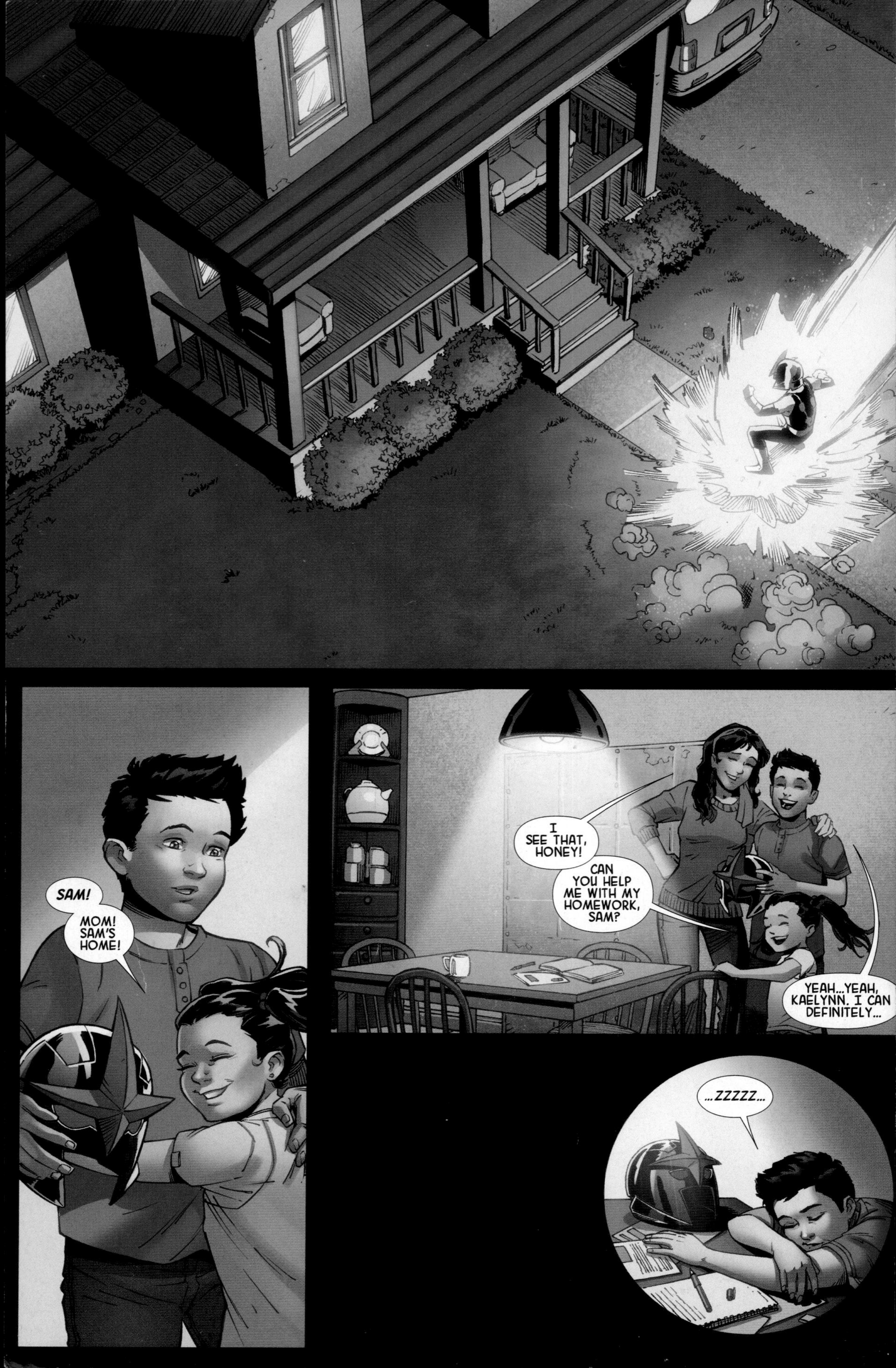
SAM!
MOM! SAM'S HOME!
I SEE THAT, HONEY!
CAN YOU HELP ME WITH MY HOMEWORK, SAM?
YEAH...YEAH, KAELYNN. I CAN DEFINITELY...
...ZZZZZ...

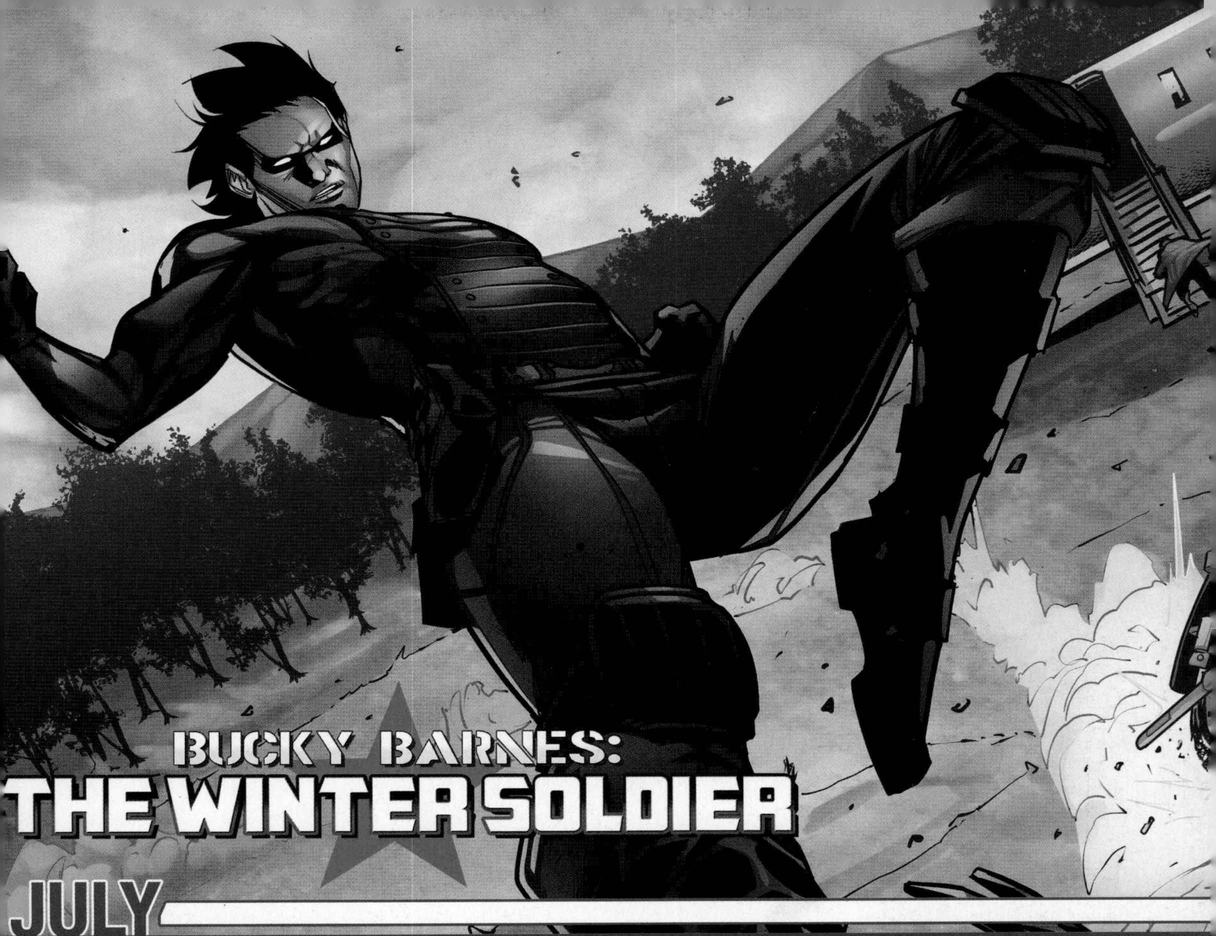
BUCKY BARNES:
THE WINTER SOLDIER

JULY

SUNDAY	MONDAY	TUESDAY	WEDNESDAY	THURSDAY	FRIDAY	SATURDAY
			1	2	3	4 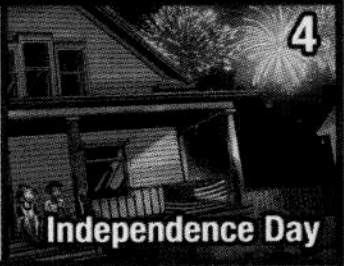 Independence Day
5	6	7	8	9	10	11
12	13	14	15	16	17	18
19	20	21	22	23	24	25
26	27	28	29	30	31	

CHUCK WENDIG WRITER
GEOFFO LAYOUTS
JUANAN RAMÍREZ ARTIST
JESUS ABURTOV COLOR ARTIST
VC'S TRAVIS LANHAM LETTERER
JAMAL CAMPBELL COVER ART
ANNIE CHENG & TIM SMITH 3 PRODUCTION TEAM
CARLOS LAO PRODUCTION DESIGN
ALANNA SMITH EDITOR
JORDAN D. WHITE & NICK LOWE SUPERVISING EDITORS
EDITOR IN CHIEF AXEL ALONSO CHIEF CREATIVE OFFICER JOE QUESADA PUBLISHER DAN BUCKLEY EXECUTIVE PRODUCER ALAN FINE

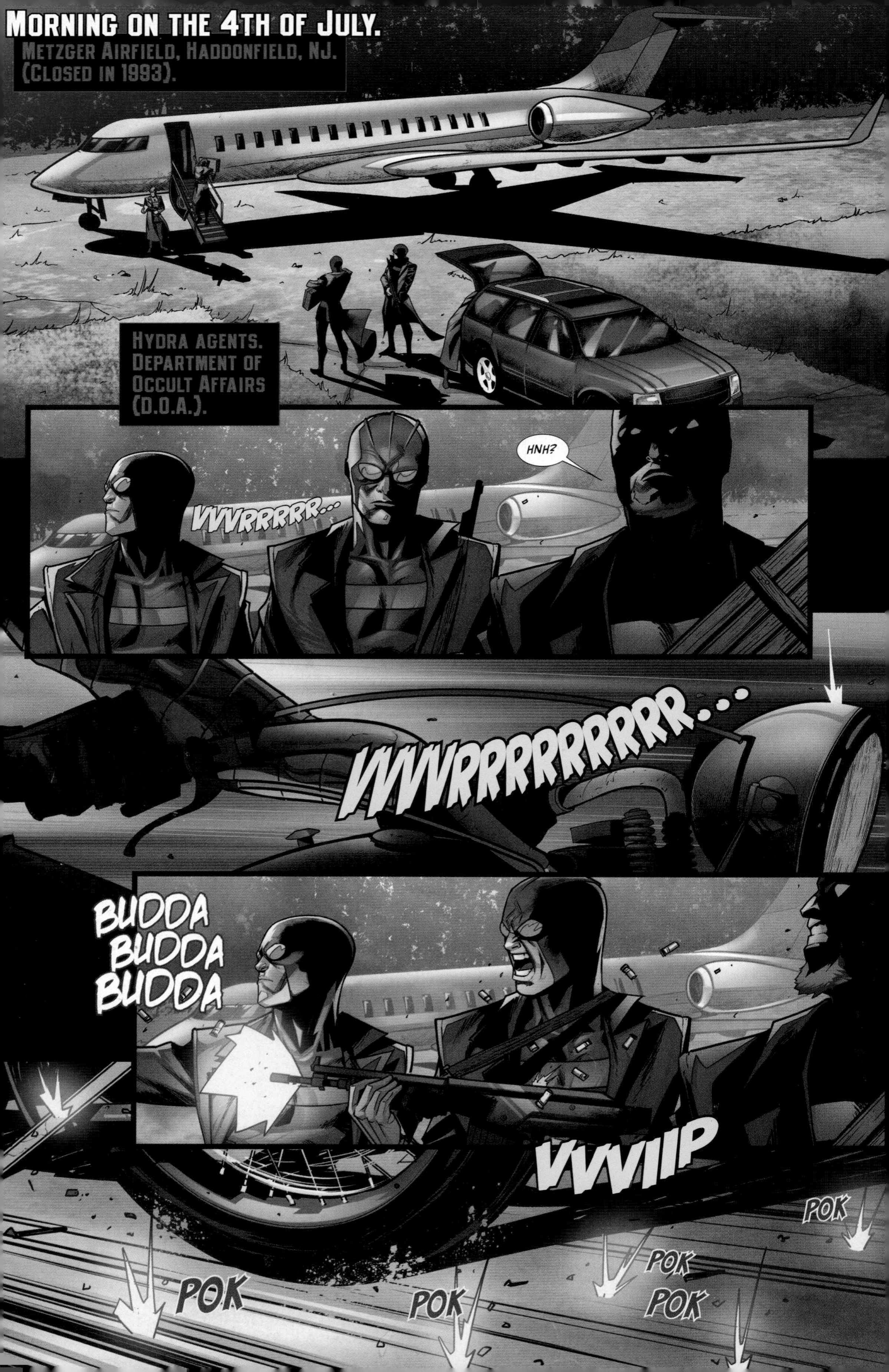
Morning on the 4th of July.
Metzger Airfield, Haddonfield, NJ.
(Closed in 1993).
Hydra agents. Department of Occult Affairs (D.O.A.).
HNH?
VVVRRRRR...
VVVVRRRRRRRRR...
BUDDA BUDDA BUDDA
VVVIIP
POK
POK
POK
POK
POK

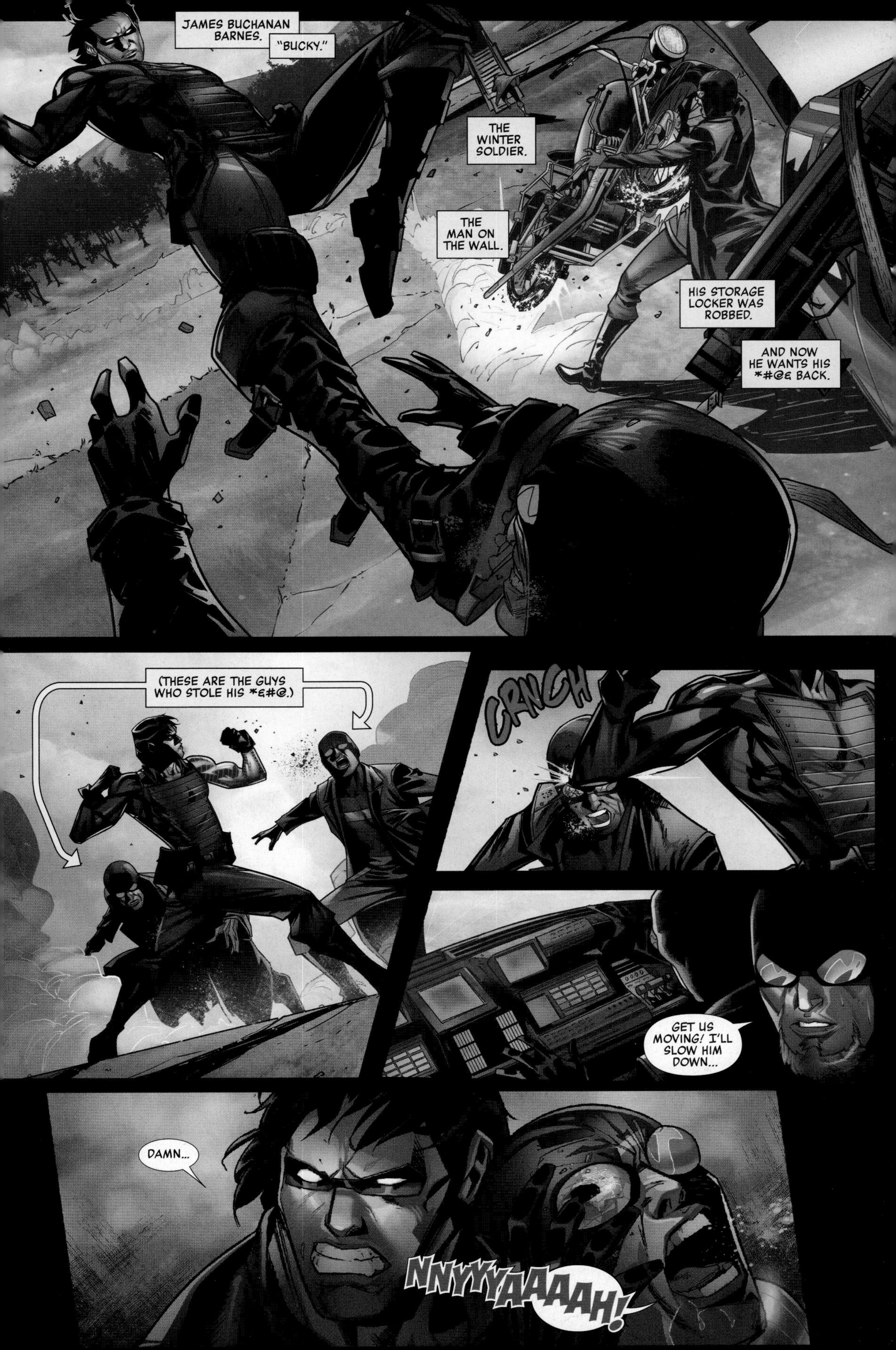
JAMES BUCHANAN BARNES.
"BUCKY."
THE WINTER SOLDIER.
THE MAN ON THE WALL.
HIS STORAGE LOCKER WAS ROBBED.
AND NOW HE WANTS HIS *#@& BACK.
(THESE ARE THE GUYS WHO STOLE HIS *&#@.)
CRNCH
GET US MOVING! I'LL SLOW HIM DOWN...
DAMN...
NNYYYAAAAH!

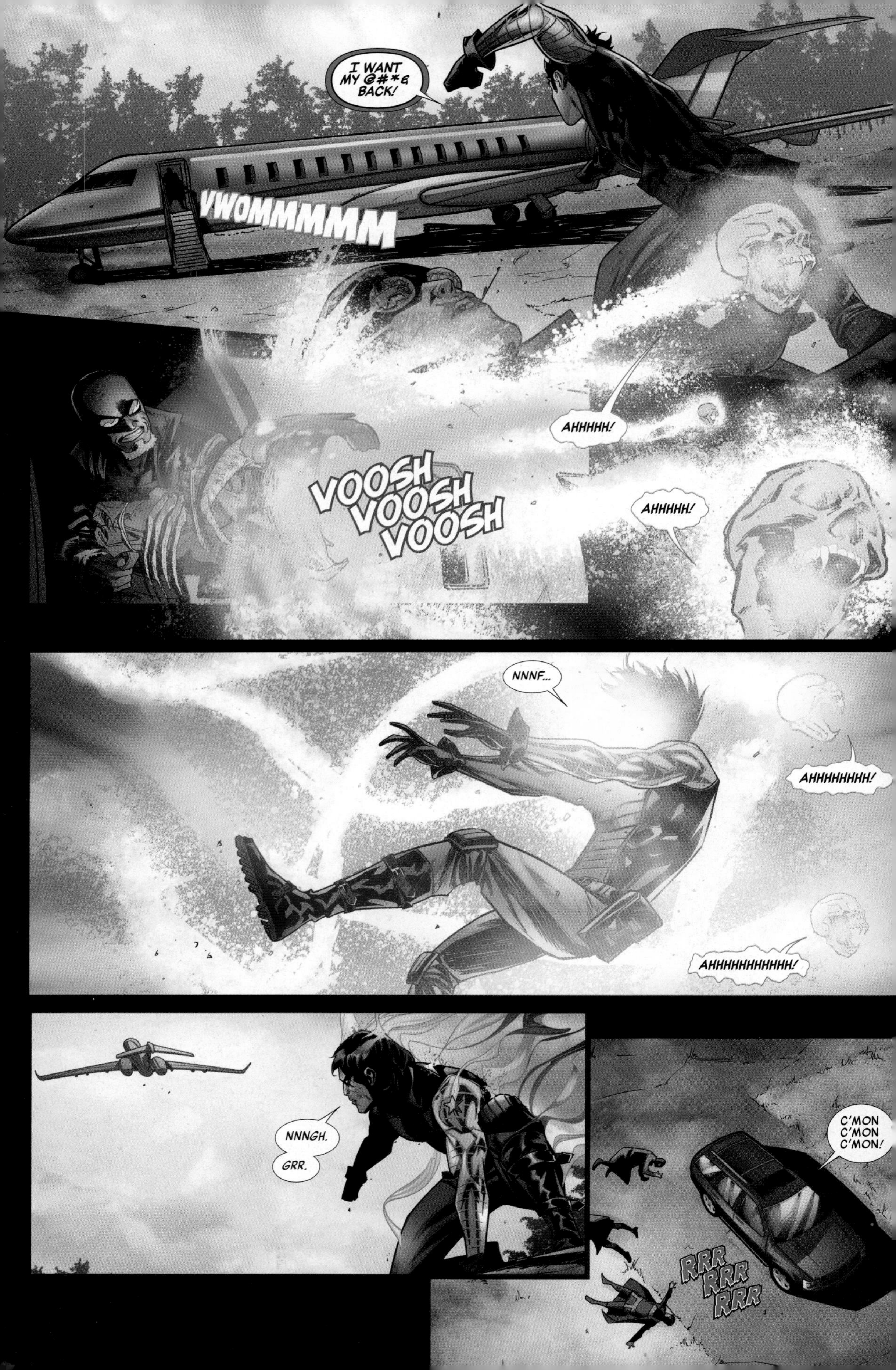
I WANT MY @#*& BACK!
VWOMMMMM
AHHHHH!
VOOSH VOOSH VOOSH
AHHHHH!
NNNF...
AHHHHHHHH!
AHHHHHHHHHHH!
NNNGH.
GRR.
C'MON C'MON C'MON!
RRR RRR RRR

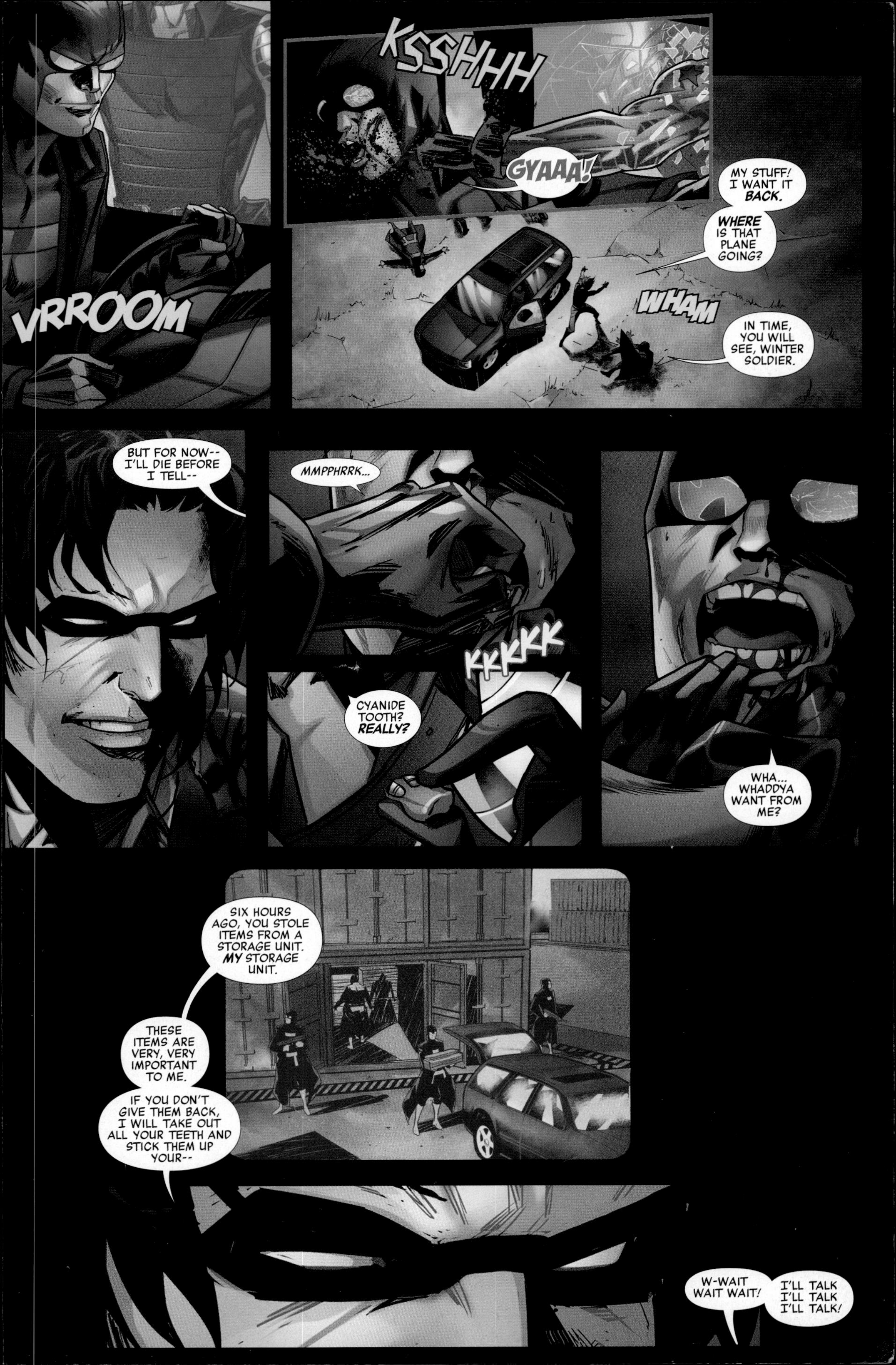
VRROOM
KSSHHH
GYAAA!
MY STUFF! I WANT IT BACK.
WHERE IS THAT PLANE GOING?
WHAM
IN TIME, YOU WILL SEE, WINTER SOLDIER.
BUT FOR NOW-- I'LL DIE BEFORE I TELL--
MMPPHRRK...
KKKKK
CYANIDE TOOTH? REALLY?
WHA... WHADDYA WANT FROM ME?
SIX HOURS AGO, YOU STOLE ITEMS FROM A STORAGE UNIT. MY STORAGE UNIT.
THESE ITEMS ARE VERY, VERY IMPORTANT TO ME.
IF YOU DON'T GIVE THEM BACK, I WILL TAKE OUT ALL YOUR TEETH AND STICK THEM UP YOUR--
W-WAIT WAIT WAIT!
I'LL TALK I'LL TALK I'LL TALK!

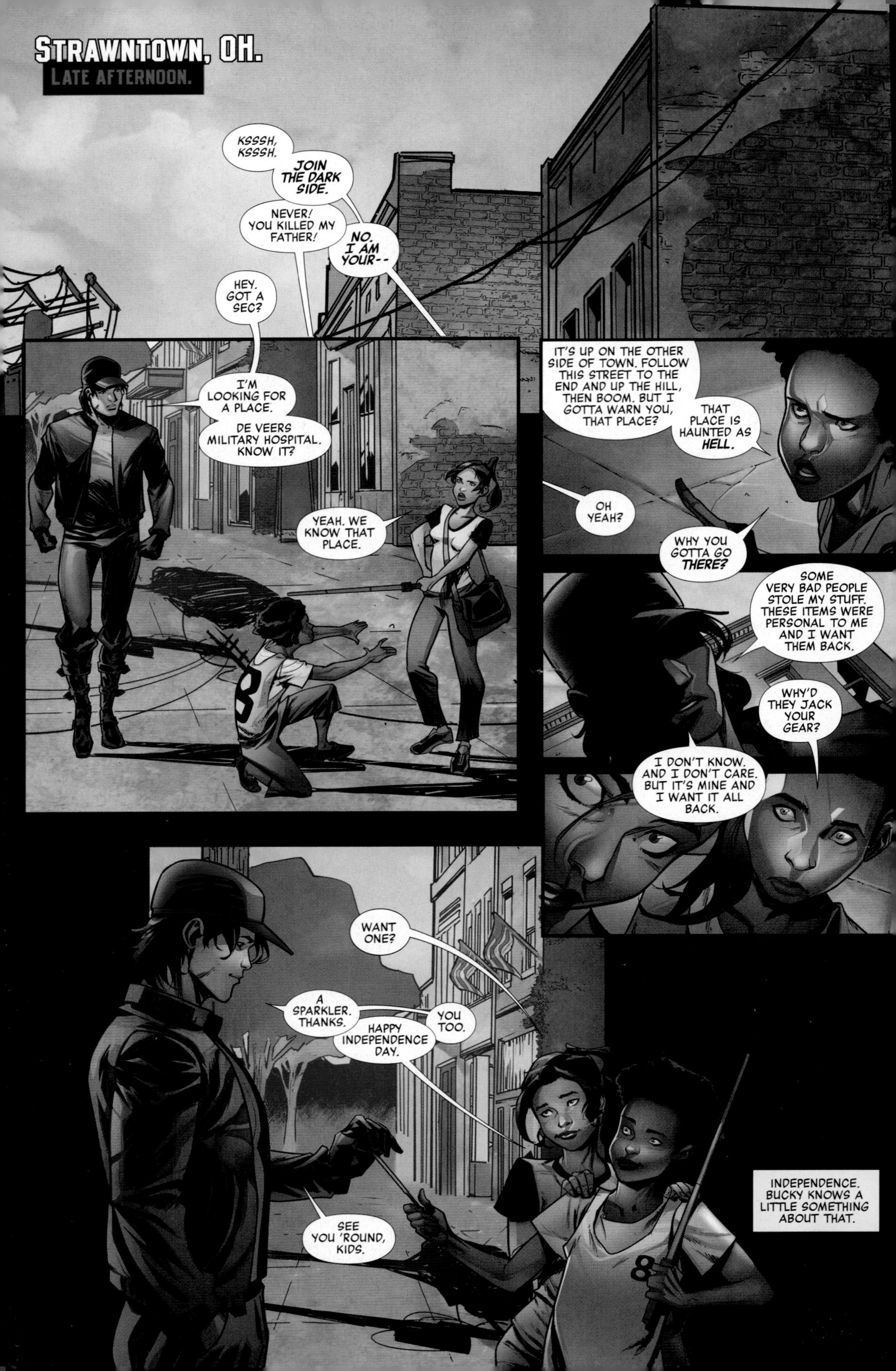

STRAWNTOWN, OH.
LATE AFTERNOON.
KSSSH, KSSSH.
JOIN THE DARK SIDE.
NEVER! YOU KILLED MY FATHER!
NO. I AM YOUR--
HEY. GOT A SEC?
I'M LOOKING FOR A PLACE.
DE VEERS MILITARY HOSPITAL. KNOW IT?
YEAH. WE KNOW THAT PLACE.
IT'S UP ON THE OTHER SIDE OF TOWN. FOLLOW THIS STREET TO THE END AND UP THE HILL, THEN BOOM. BUT I GOTTA WARN YOU, THAT PLACE?
THAT PLACE IS HAUNTED AS HELL.
OH YEAH?
WHY YOU GOTTA GO THERE?
SOME VERY BAD PEOPLE STOLE MY STUFF. THESE ITEMS WERE PERSONAL TO ME AND I WANT THEM BACK.
WHY'D THEY JACK YOUR GEAR?
I DON'T KNOW. AND I DON'T CARE. BUT IT'S MINE AND I WANT IT ALL BACK.
WANT ONE?
A SPARKLER. THANKS.
YOU TOO.
HAPPY INDEPENDENCE DAY.
SEE YOU 'ROUND, KIDS.
INDEPENDENCE. BUCKY KNOWS A LITTLE SOMETHING ABOUT THAT.

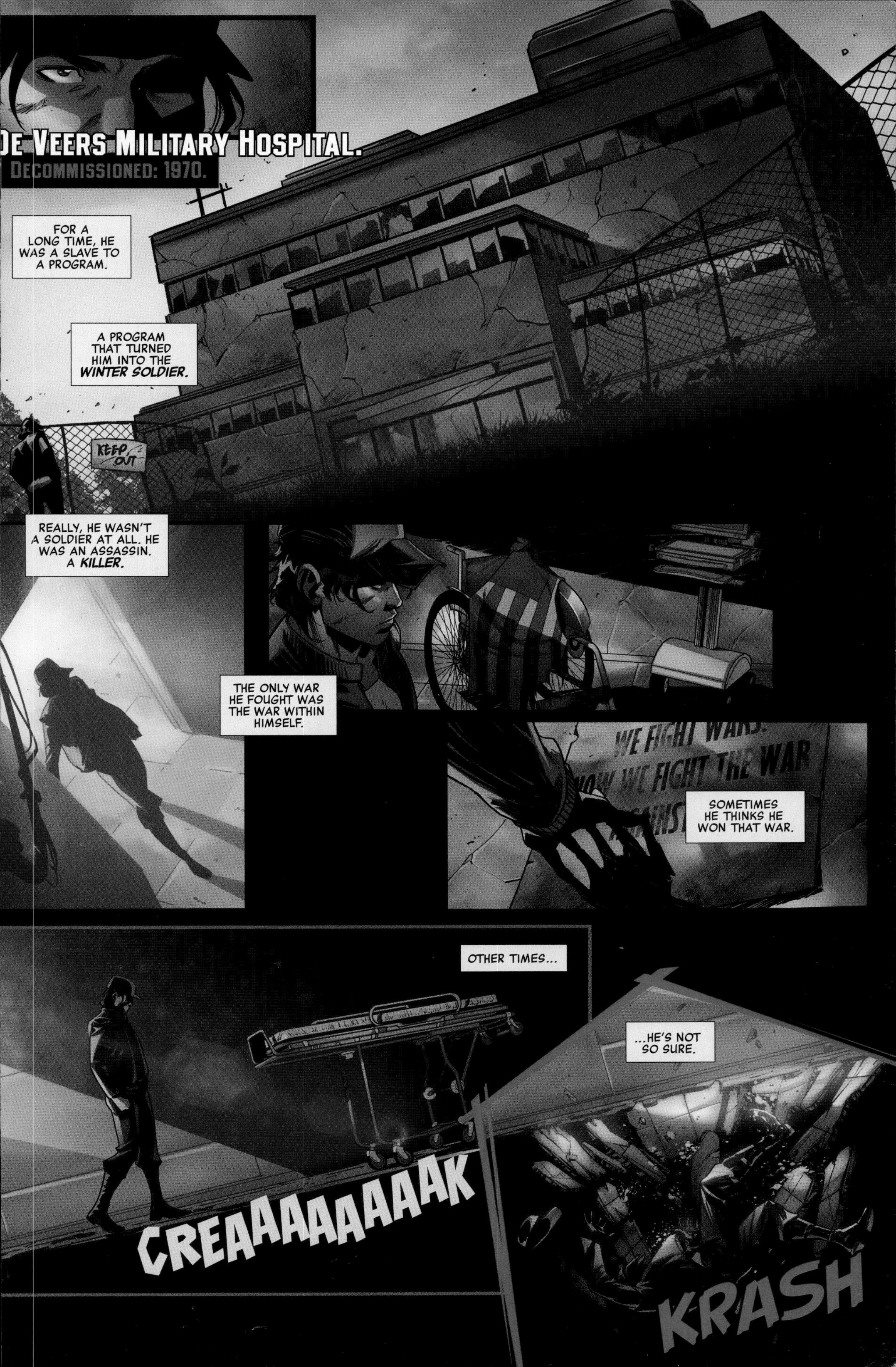

DE VEERS MILITARY HOSPITAL.
DECOMMISSIONED: 1970.
FOR A LONG TIME, HE WAS A SLAVE TO A PROGRAM.
A PROGRAM THAT TURNED HIM INTO THE *WINTER SOLDIER*.
KEEP OUT
REALLY, HE WASN'T A SOLDIER AT ALL. HE WAS AN ASSASSIN. A *KILLER*.
THE ONLY WAR HE FOUGHT WAS THE WAR WITHIN HIMSELF.
SOMETIMES HE THINKS HE WON THAT WAR.
OTHER TIMES...
...HE'S NOT SO SURE.
CREAAAAAAAAK
KRASH

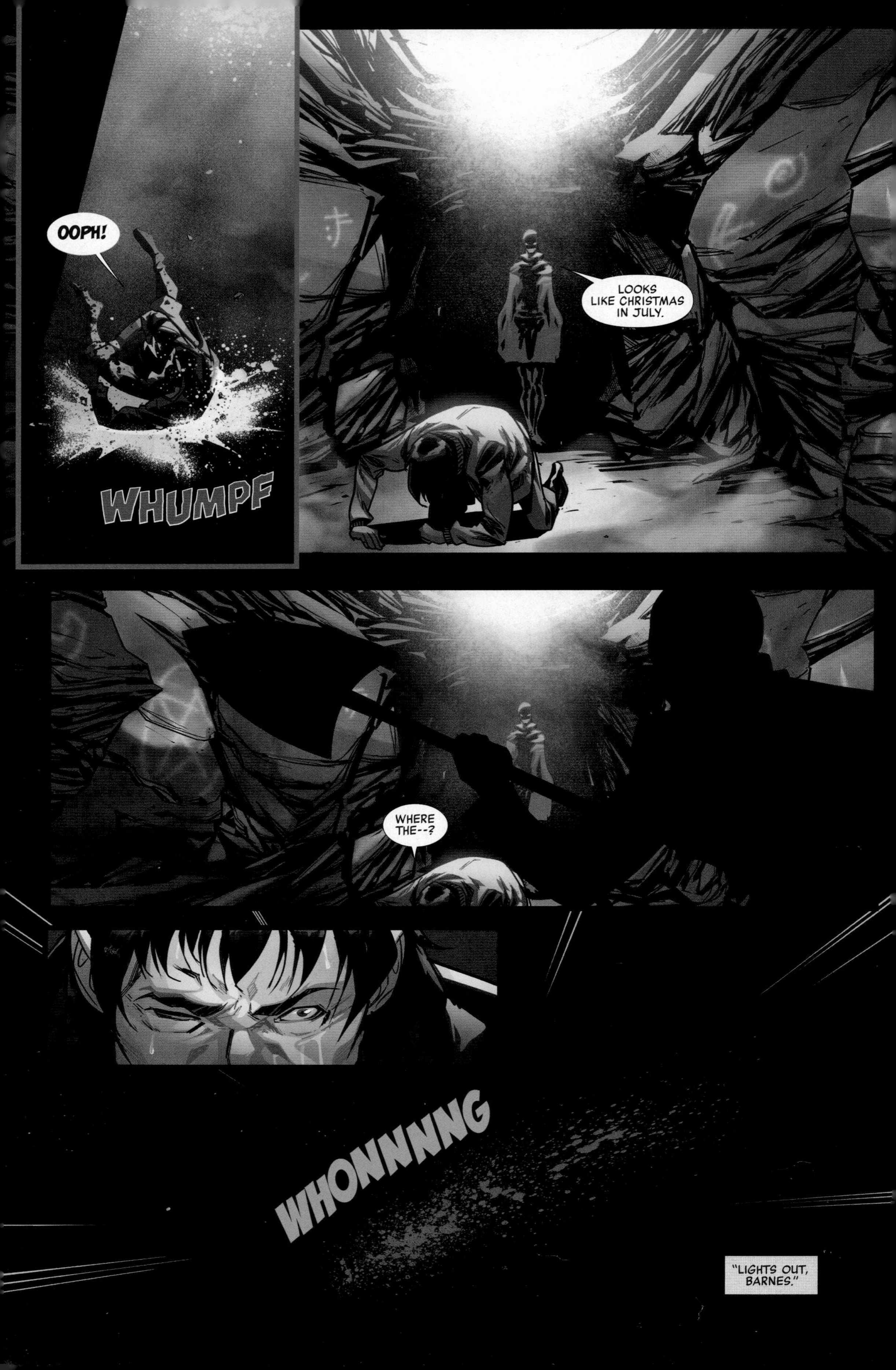
OOPH!
WHUMPF
LOOKS LIKE CHRISTMAS IN JULY.
WHERE THE--?
WHONNNNG
"LIGHTS OUT, BARNES."

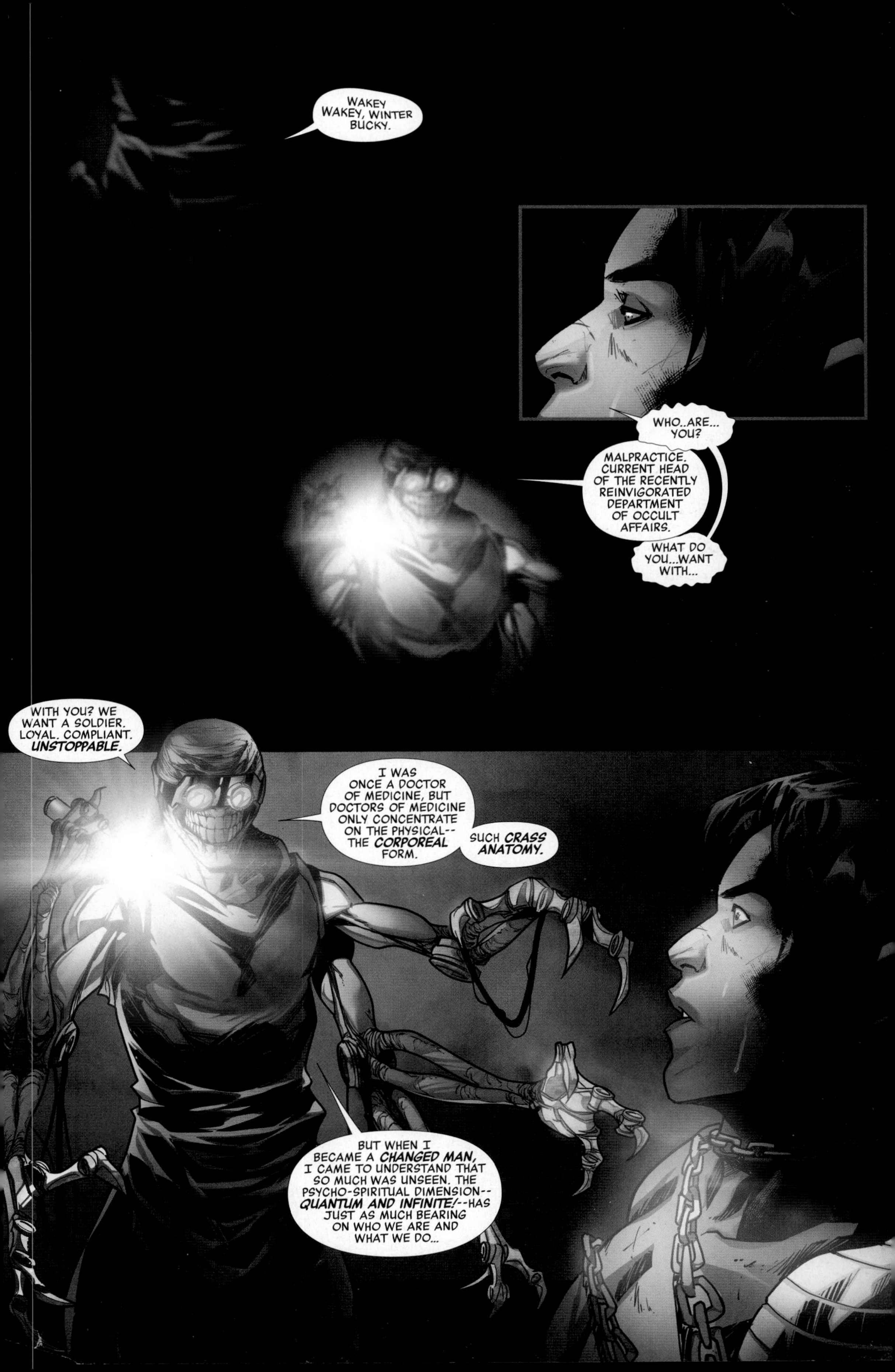

WAKEY WAKEY, WINTER BUCKY.
WHO..ARE... YOU?
MALPRACTICE. CURRENT HEAD OF THE RECENTLY REINVIGORATED DEPARTMENT OF OCCULT AFFAIRS.
WHAT DO YOU...WANT WITH...
WITH YOU? WE WANT A SOLDIER. LOYAL. COMPLIANT. **UNSTOPPABLE.**
I WAS ONCE A DOCTOR OF MEDICINE, BUT DOCTORS OF MEDICINE ONLY CONCENTRATE ON THE PHYSICAL-- THE ***CORPOREAL*** FORM.
SUCH ***CRASS ANATOMY.***
BUT WHEN I BECAME A ***CHANGED MAN,*** I CAME TO UNDERSTAND THAT SO MUCH WAS UNSEEN. THE PSYCHO-SPIRITUAL DIMENSION-- ***QUANTUM AND INFINITE!***--HAS JUST AS MUCH BEARING ON WHO WE ARE AND WHAT WE DO...

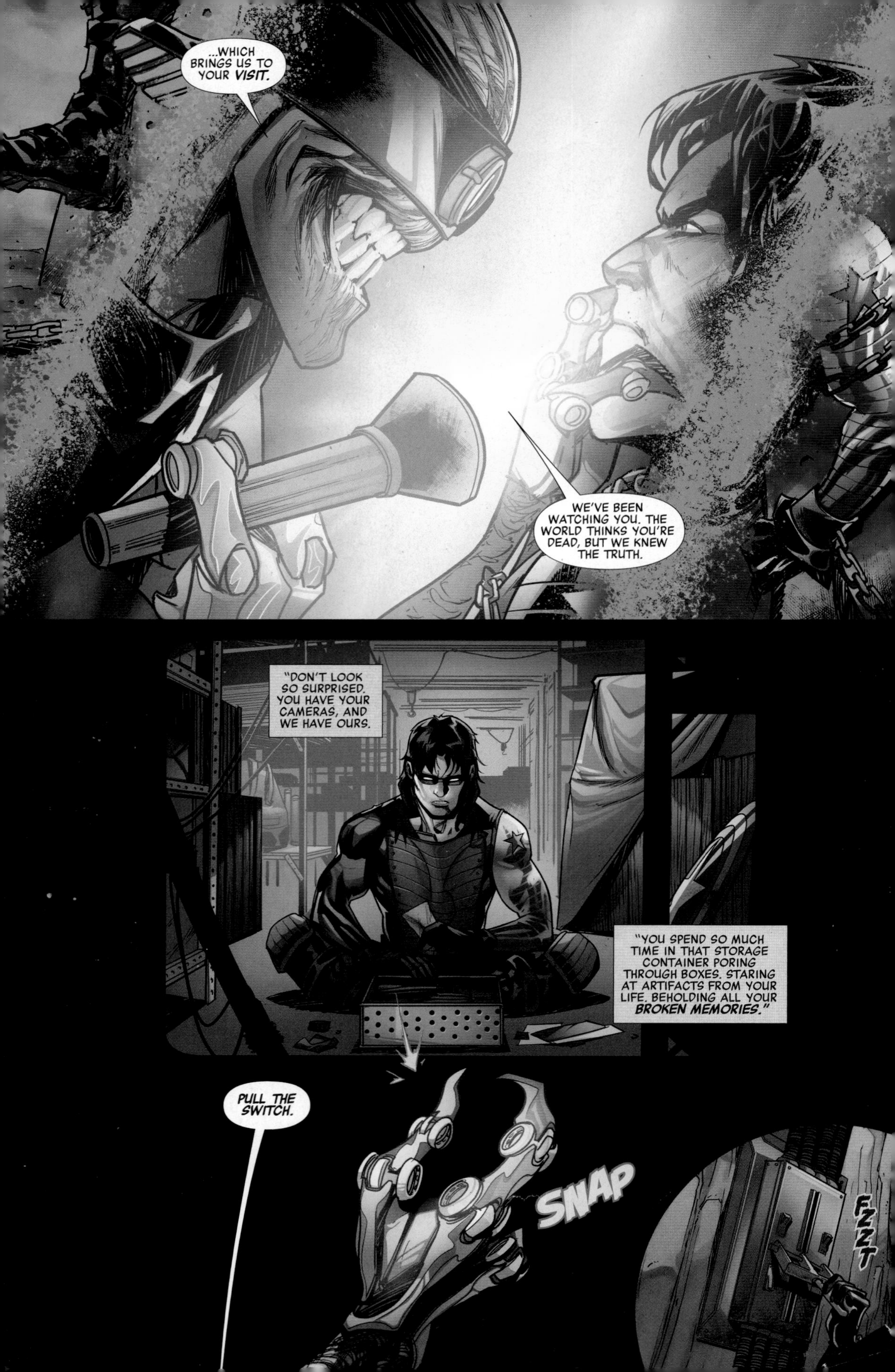
...WHICH BRINGS US TO YOUR VISIT.
WE'VE BEEN WATCHING YOU. THE WORLD THINKS YOU'RE DEAD, BUT WE KNEW THE TRUTH.
"DON'T LOOK SO SURPRISED. YOU HAVE YOUR CAMERAS, AND WE HAVE OURS.
"YOU SPEND SO MUCH TIME IN THAT STORAGE CONTAINER PORING THROUGH BOXES. STARING AT ARTIFACTS FROM YOUR LIFE. BEHOLDING ALL YOUR BROKEN MEMORIES."
PULL THE SWITCH.
SNAP
FZZT

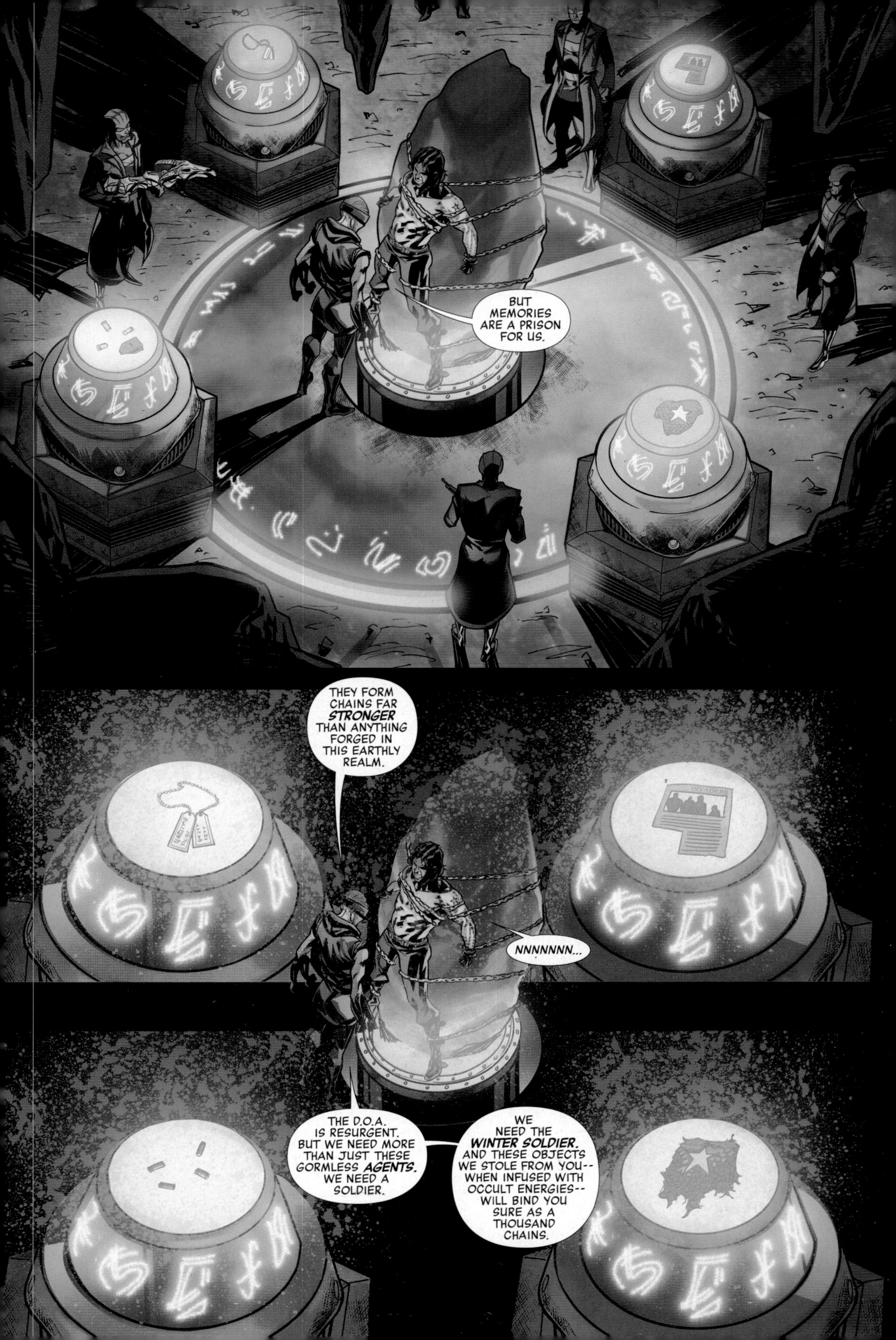
BUT MEMORIES ARE A PRISON FOR US.
THEY FORM CHAINS FAR STRONGER THAN ANYTHING FORGED IN THIS EARTHLY REALM.
INVADERS
NNNNNNN...
THE D.O.A. IS RESURGENT. BUT WE NEED MORE THAN JUST THESE GORMLESS AGENTS. WE NEED A SOLDIER.
WE NEED THE WINTER SOLDIER. AND THESE OBJECTS WE STOLE FROM YOU-- WHEN INFUSED WITH OCCULT ENERGIES-- WILL BIND YOU SURE AS A THOUSAND CHAINS.

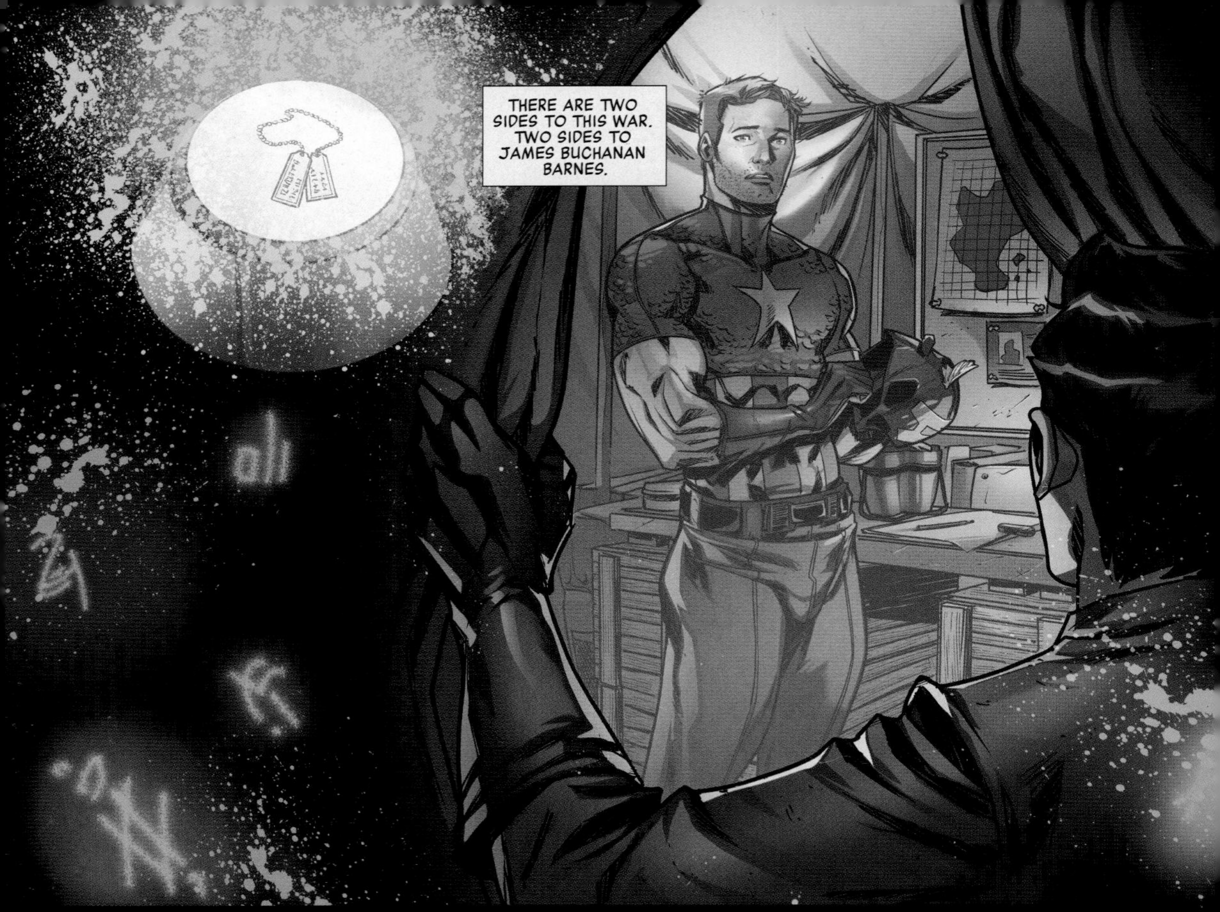
THERE ARE TWO SIDES TO THIS WAR. TWO SIDES TO JAMES BUCHANAN BARNES.

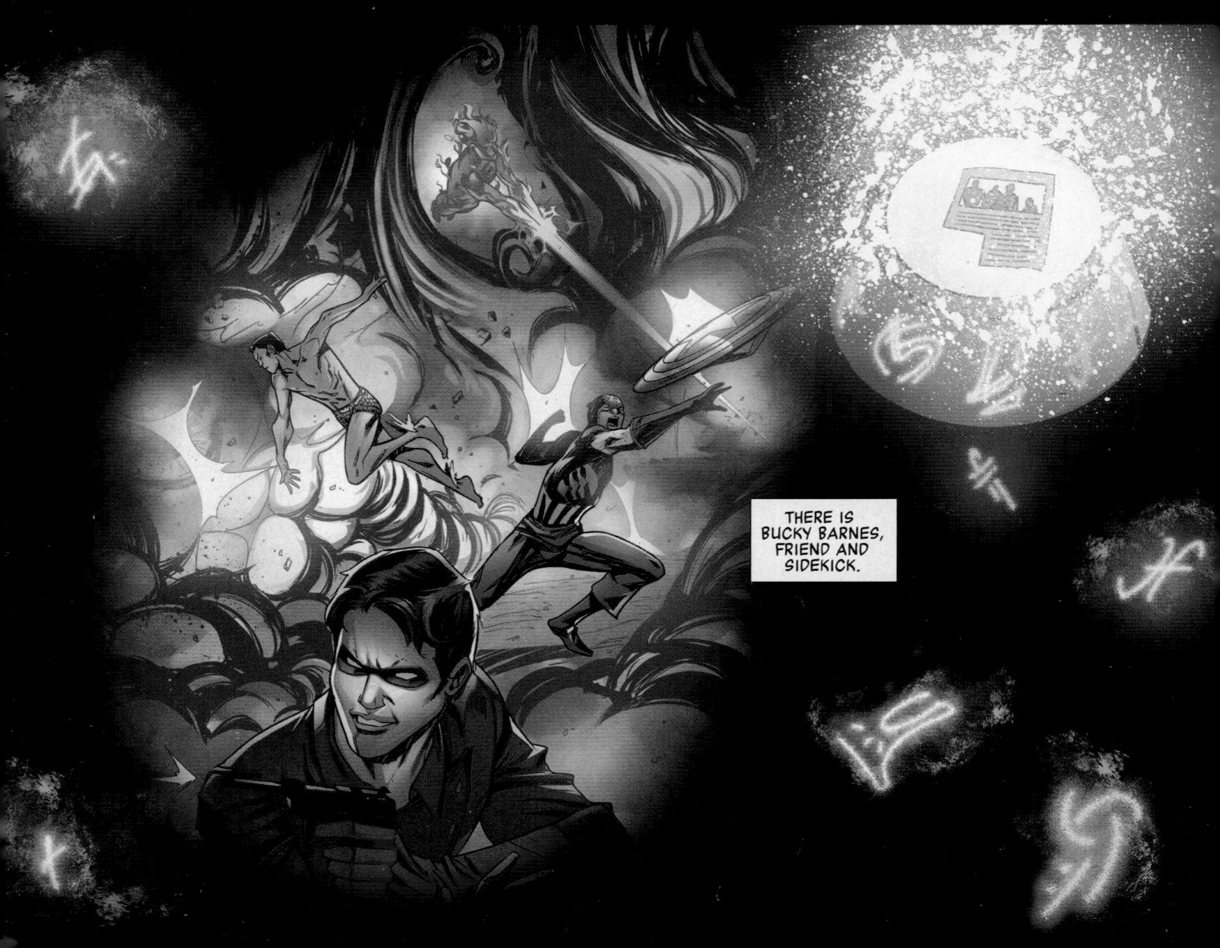
THERE IS BUCKY BARNES, FRIEND AND SIDEKICK.

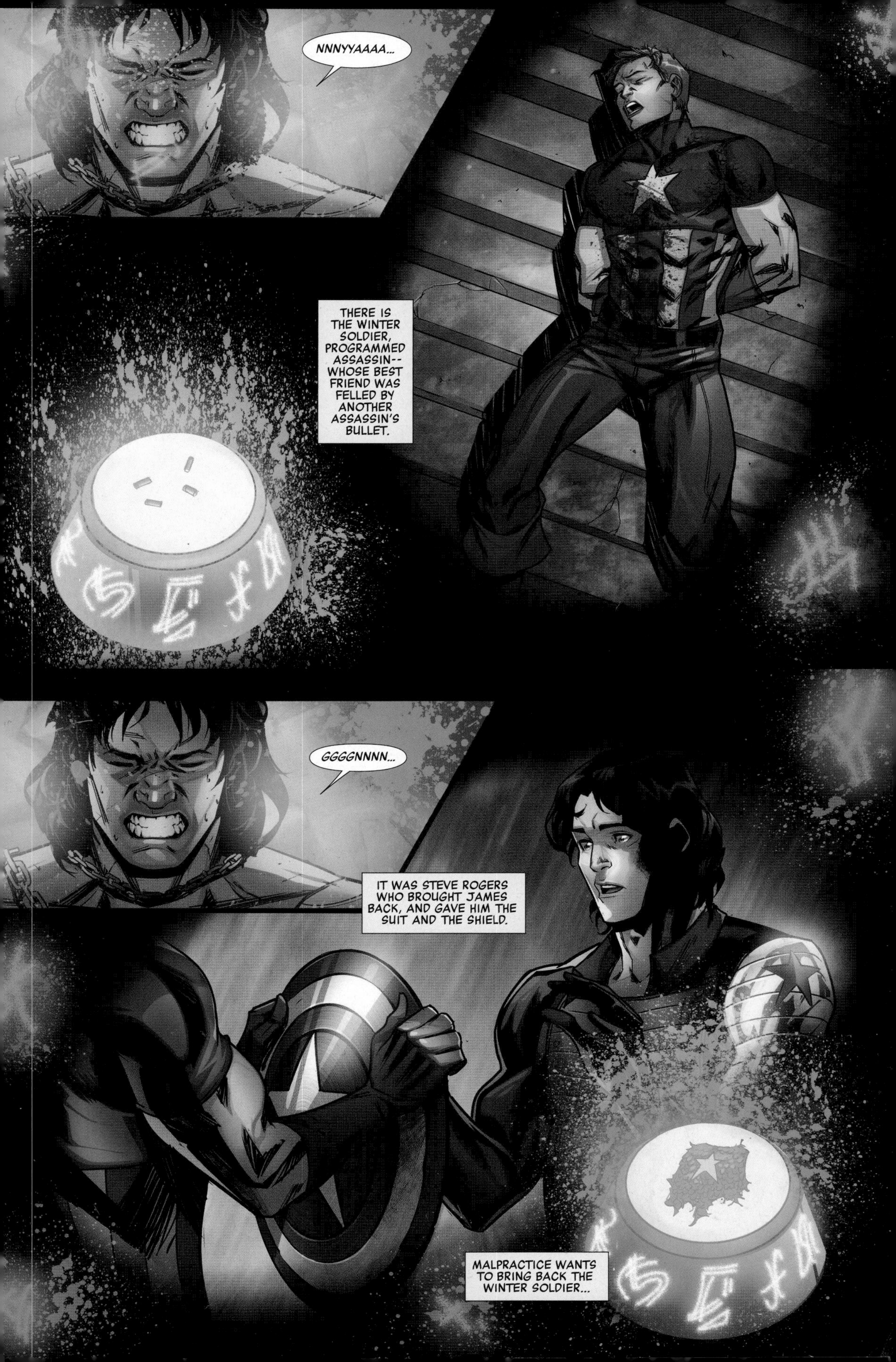
NNNYYAAAA...
THERE IS THE WINTER SOLDIER, PROGRAMMED ASSASSIN-- WHOSE BEST FRIEND WAS FELLED BY ANOTHER ASSASSIN'S BULLET.
GGGGNNNN...
IT WAS STEVE ROGERS WHO BROUGHT JAMES BACK, AND GAVE HIM THE SUIT AND THE SHIELD.
MALPRACTICE WANTS TO BRING BACK THE WINTER SOLDIER...

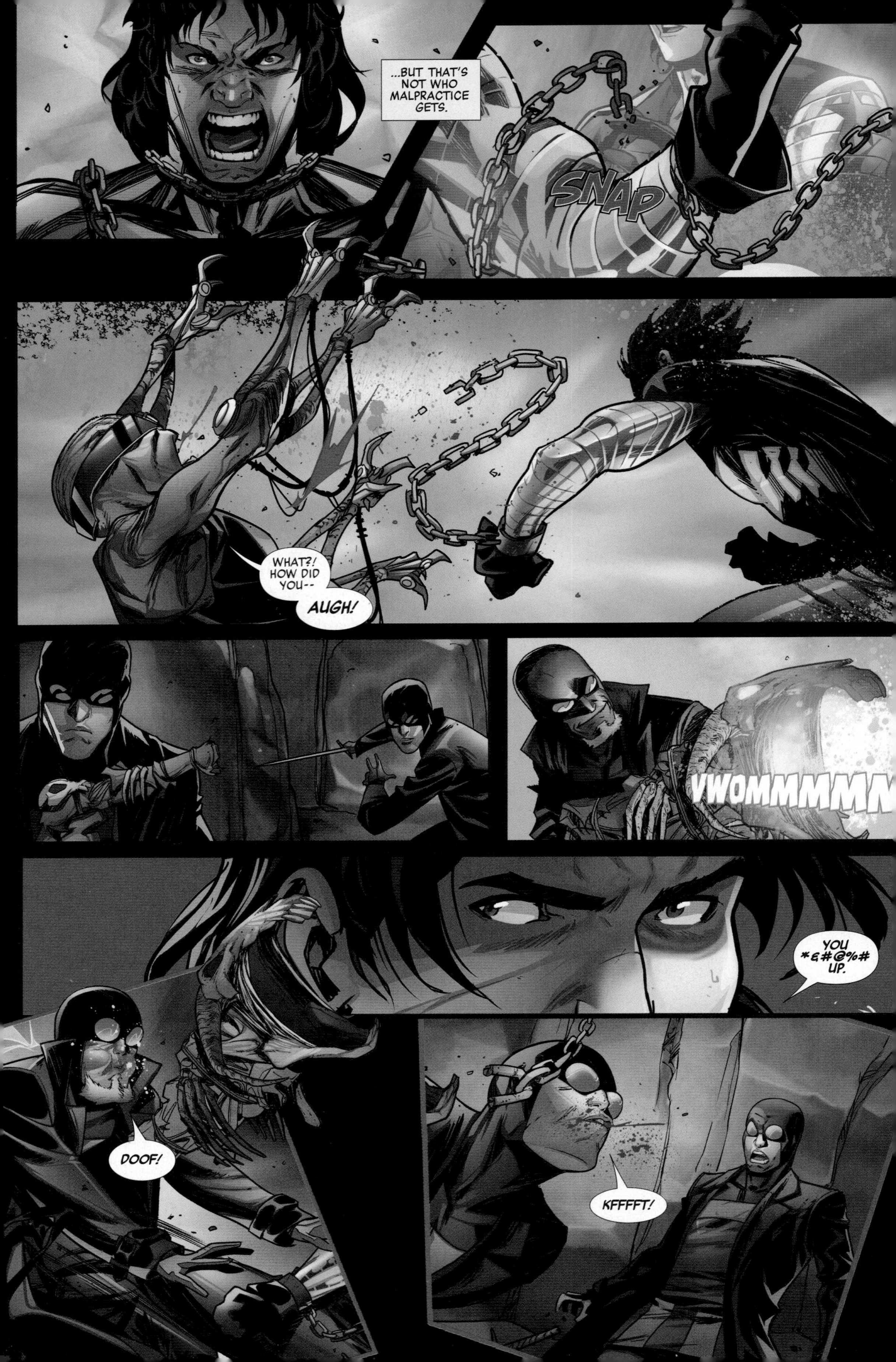
...BUT THAT'S NOT WHO MALPRACTICE GETS.
SNAP
WHAT?! HOW DID YOU--
AUGH!
VWOMMMMN
YOU *&#@%# UP.
DOOF!
KFFFFT!

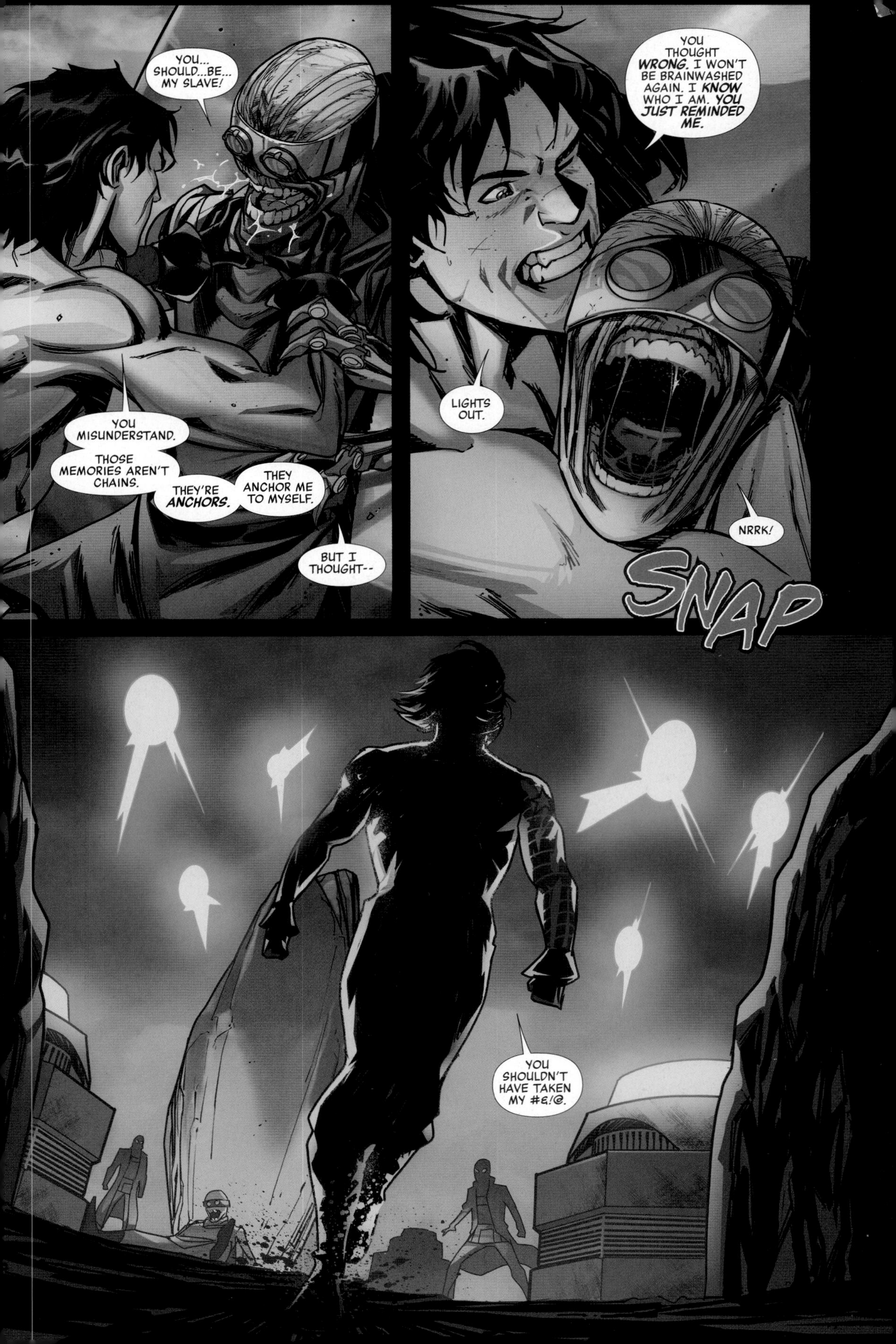
YOU... SHOULD...BE... MY SLAVE!
YOU MISUNDERSTAND.
THOSE MEMORIES AREN'T CHAINS.
THEY'RE ANCHORS.
THEY ANCHOR ME TO MYSELF.
BUT I THOUGHT--
YOU THOUGHT WRONG. I WON'T BE BRAINWASHED AGAIN. I KNOW WHO I AM. YOU JUST REMINDED ME.
LIGHTS OUT.
NRRK!
SNAP
YOU SHOULDN'T HAVE TAKEN MY #€!@.

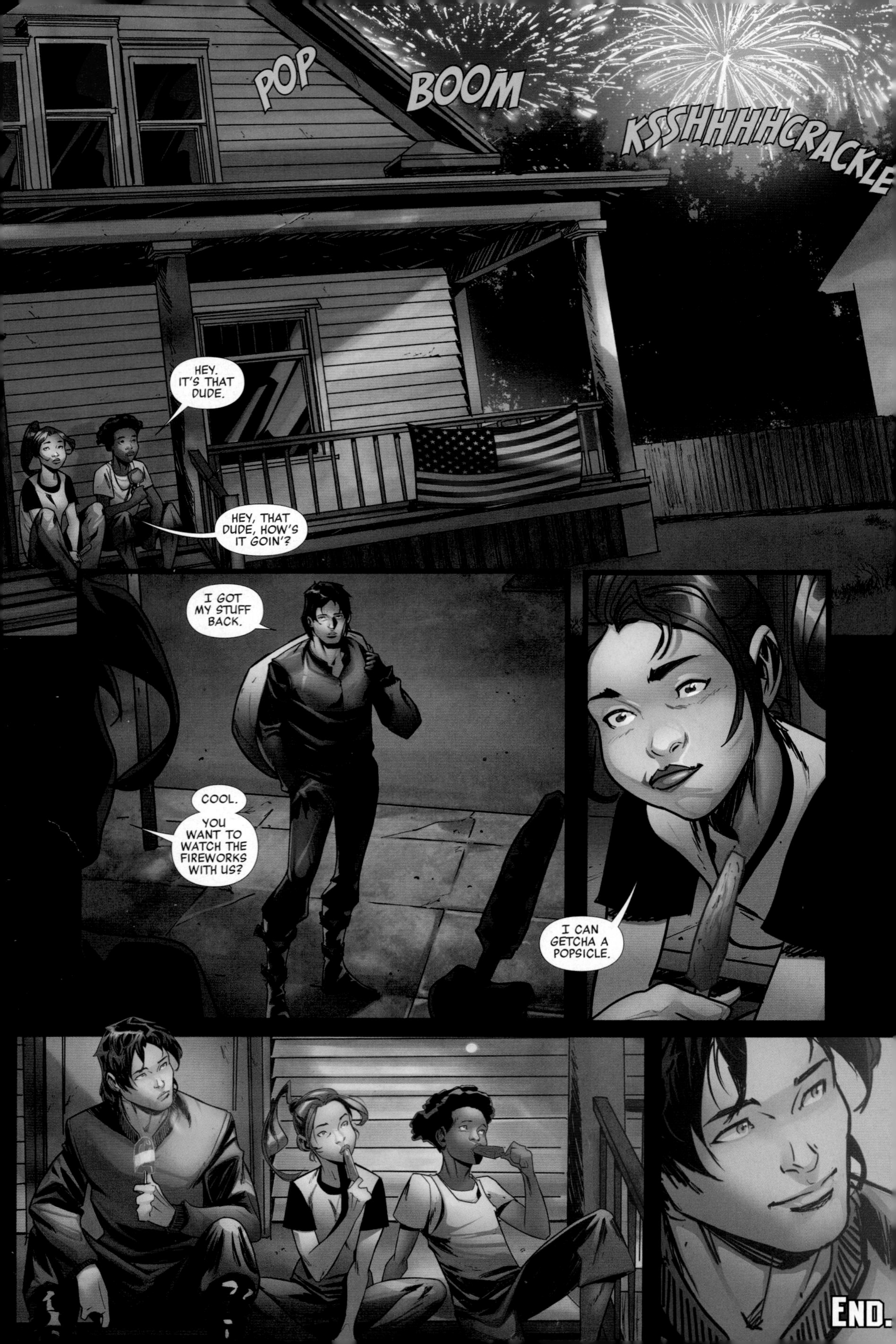
POP
BOOM
KSSHHHHCRACKLE
HEY. IT'S THAT DUDE.
HEY, THAT DUDE, HOW'S IT GOIN'?
I GOT MY STUFF BACK.
COOL.
YOU WANT TO WATCH THE FIREWORKS WITH US?
I CAN GETCHA A POPSICLE.
END.

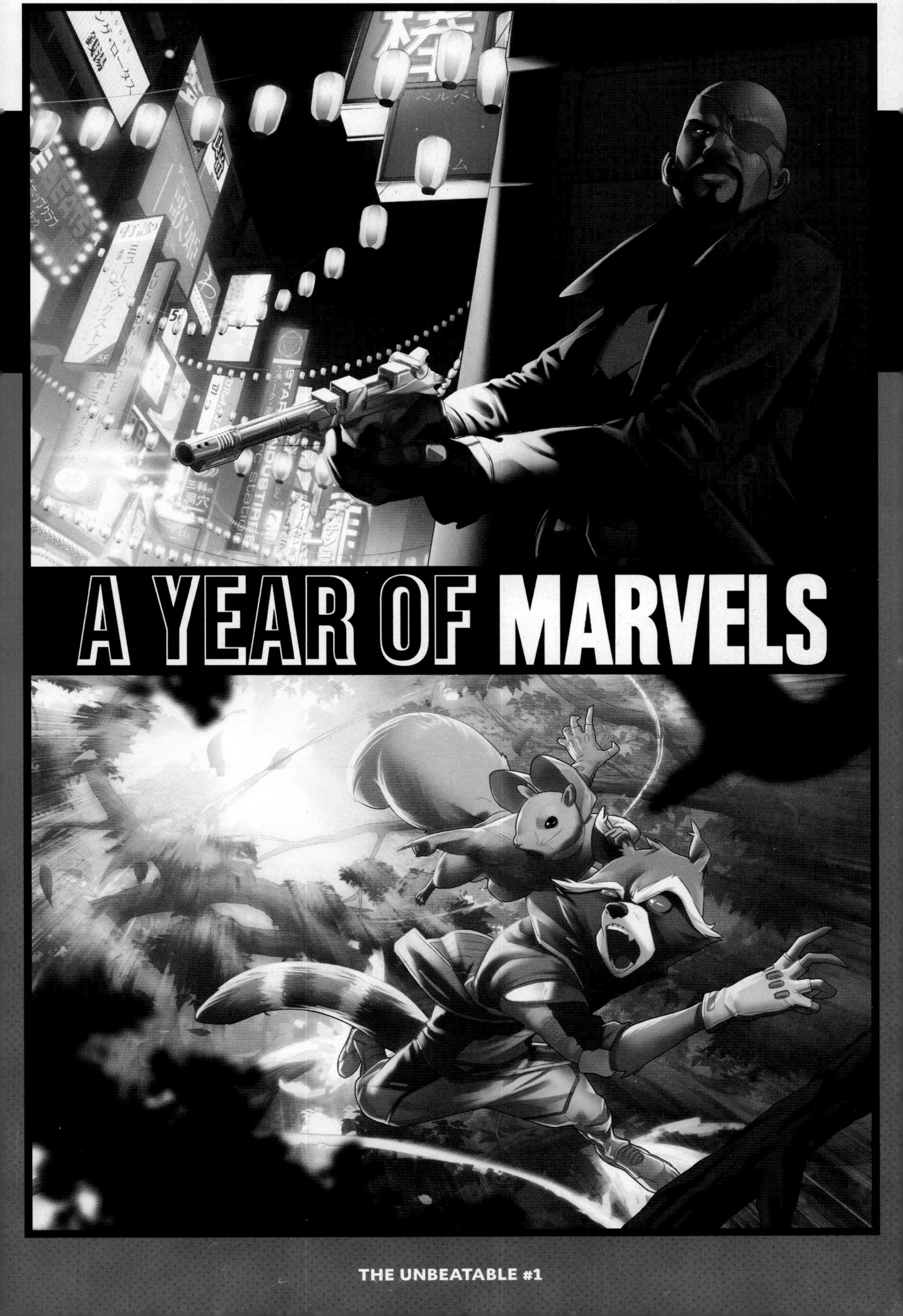
A YEAR OF MARVELS

THE UNBEATABLE #1

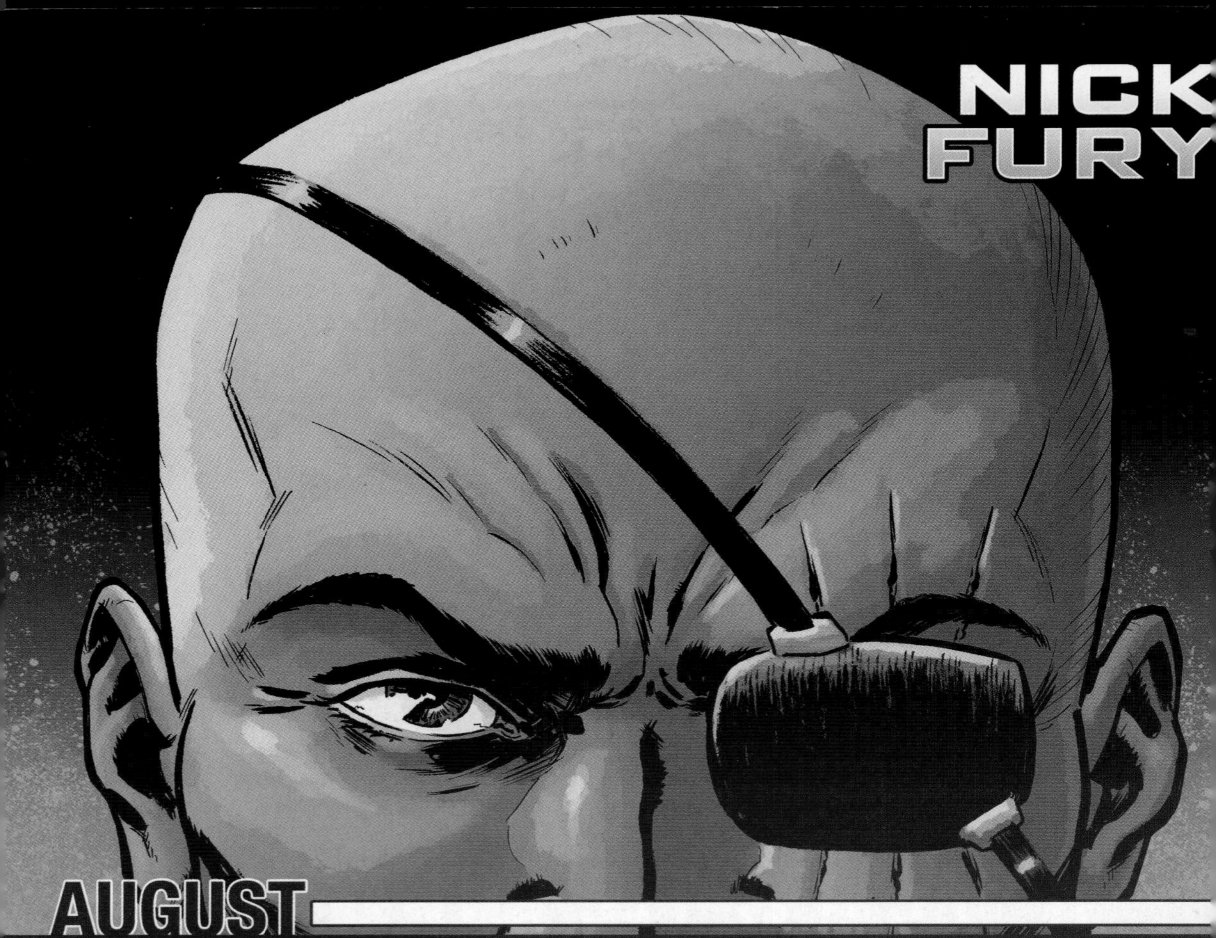
NICK FURY
AUGUST

SUNDAY	MONDAY	TUESDAY	WEDNESDAY	THURSDAY	FRIDAY	SATURDAY
						1
2	3	4	5	6	7	8
9	10	11	12	13 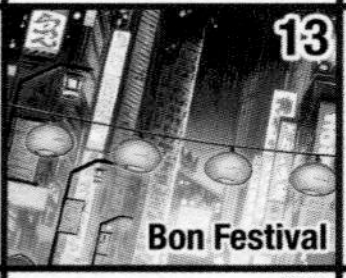 Bon Festival	14	15
16	17	18	19	20	21	22
23 / 27	24 / 28	25 / 29	23 / 30	24 / 31	25	26

CHAD BOWERS & CHRIS SIMS — WRITERS
GEOFFO — STORYBOARD ARTIST
BRIAN LEVEL — ARTIST
JORDAN BOYD — COLOR ARTIST
VC'S TRAVIS LANHAM — LETTERING
JAMAL CAMPBELL — COVER
ANNIE CHENG & TIM SMITH 3 — PRODUCTION TEAM
CARLOS LAO — PRODUCTION DESIGN
DARREN SHAN — EDITOR
JORDAN D. WHITE & NICK LOWE — SUPERVISING EDITORS
EDITOR IN CHIEF AXEL ALONSO CHIEF CREATIVE OFFICER JOE QUESADA PUBLISHER DAN BUCKLEY EXECUTIVE PRODUCER ALAN FINE

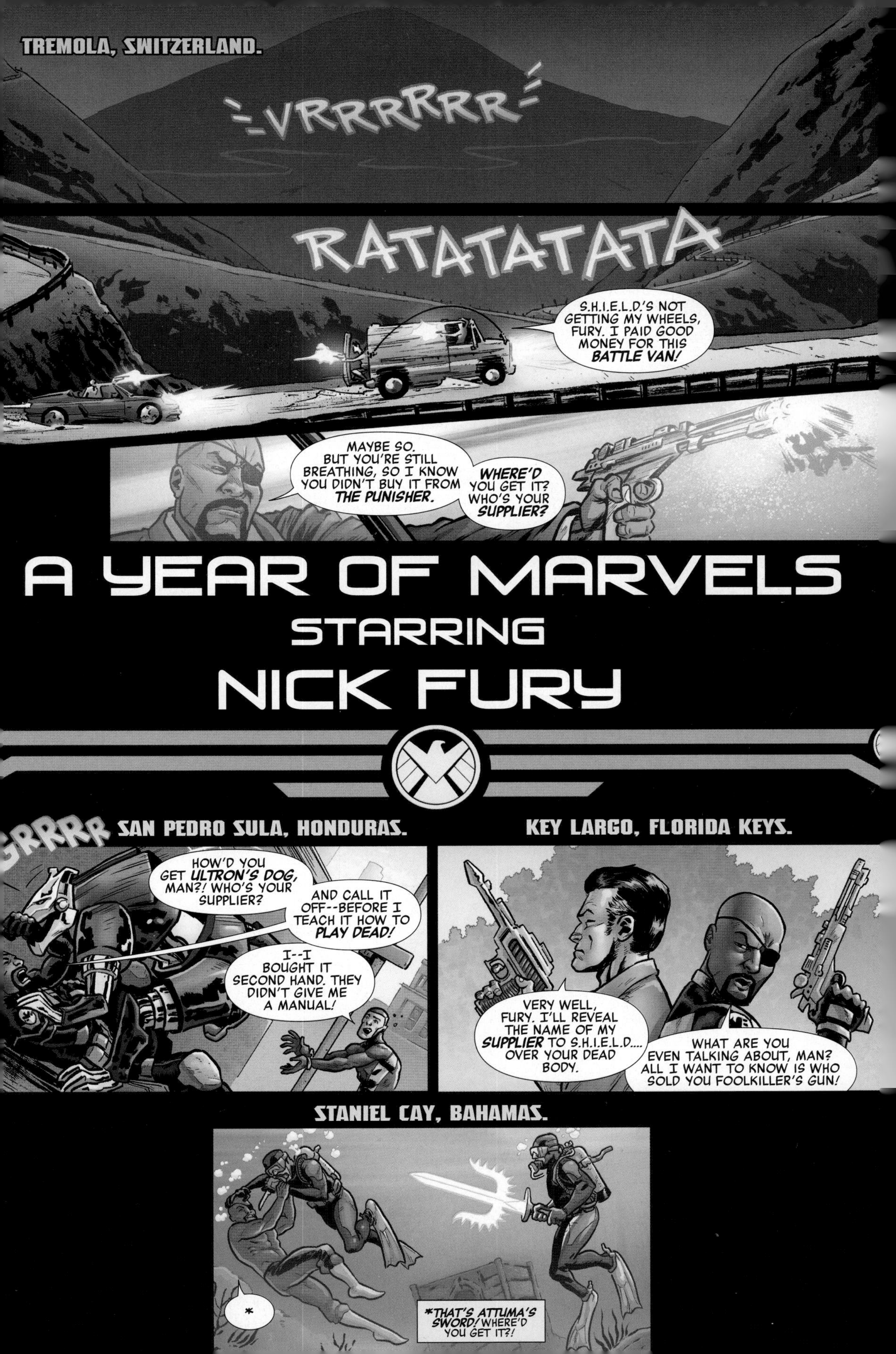
TREMOLA, SWITZERLAND.
VRRRRRR
RATATATATA
S.H.I.E.L.D.'S NOT GETTING MY WHEELS, FURY. I PAID GOOD MONEY FOR THIS BATTLE VAN!
MAYBE SO. BUT YOU'RE STILL BREATHING, SO I KNOW YOU DIDN'T BUY IT FROM THE PUNISHER.
WHERE'D YOU GET IT? WHO'S YOUR SUPPLIER?
A YEAR OF MARVELS
STARRING
NICK FURY
GRRRR
SAN PEDRO SULA, HONDURAS.
HOW'D YOU GET ULTRON'S DOG, MAN?! WHO'S YOUR SUPPLIER?
AND CALL IT OFF--BEFORE I TEACH IT HOW TO PLAY DEAD!
I--I BOUGHT IT SECOND HAND. THEY DIDN'T GIVE ME A MANUAL!
KEY LARGO, FLORIDA KEYS.
VERY WELL, FURY. I'LL REVEAL THE NAME OF MY SUPPLIER TO S.H.I.E.L.D.... OVER YOUR DEAD BODY.
WHAT ARE YOU EVEN TALKING ABOUT, MAN? ALL I WANT TO KNOW IS WHO SOLD YOU FOOLKILLER'S GUN!
STANIEL CAY, BAHAMAS.
*
*THAT'S ATTUMA'S SWORD! WHERE'D YOU GET IT?!

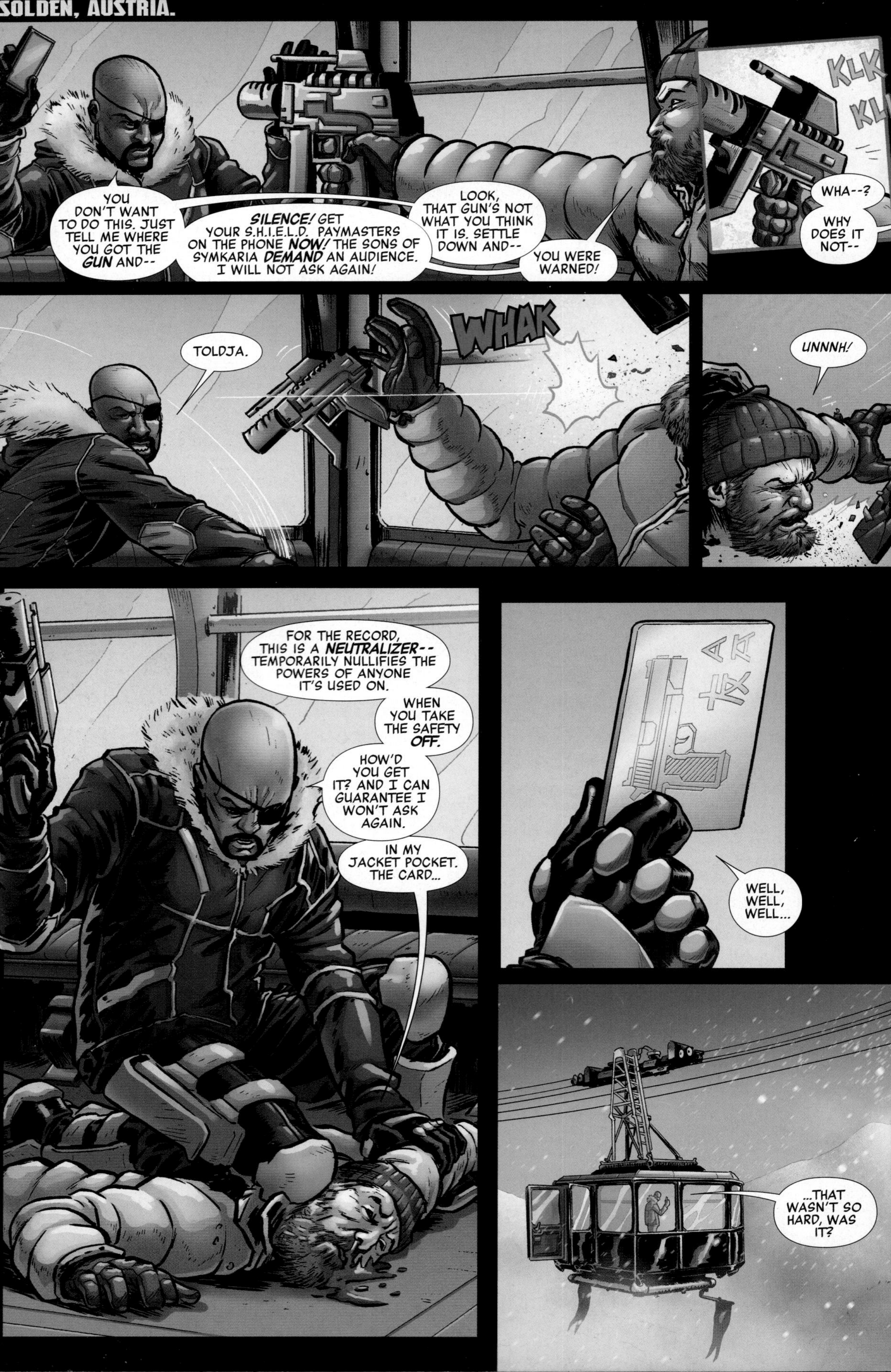
SOLDEN, AUSTRIA.
YOU DON'T WANT TO DO THIS. JUST TELL ME WHERE YOU GOT THE GUN AND--
SILENCE! GET YOUR S.H.I.E.L.D. PAYMASTERS ON THE PHONE NOW! THE SONS OF SYMKARIA DEMAND AN AUDIENCE. I WILL NOT ASK AGAIN!
LOOK, THAT GUN'S NOT WHAT YOU THINK IT IS. SETTLE DOWN AND--
YOU WERE WARNED!
KLK KLK
WHA--?
WHY DOES IT NOT--
TOLDJA.
WHAK
UNNNH!
FOR THE RECORD, THIS IS A NEUTRALIZER-- TEMPORARILY NULLIFIES THE POWERS OF ANYONE IT'S USED ON.
WHEN YOU TAKE THE SAFETY OFF.
HOW'D YOU GET IT? AND I CAN GUARANTEE I WON'T ASK AGAIN.
IN MY JACKET POCKET. THE CARD...
WELL, WELL, WELL...
...THAT WASN'T SO HARD, WAS IT?

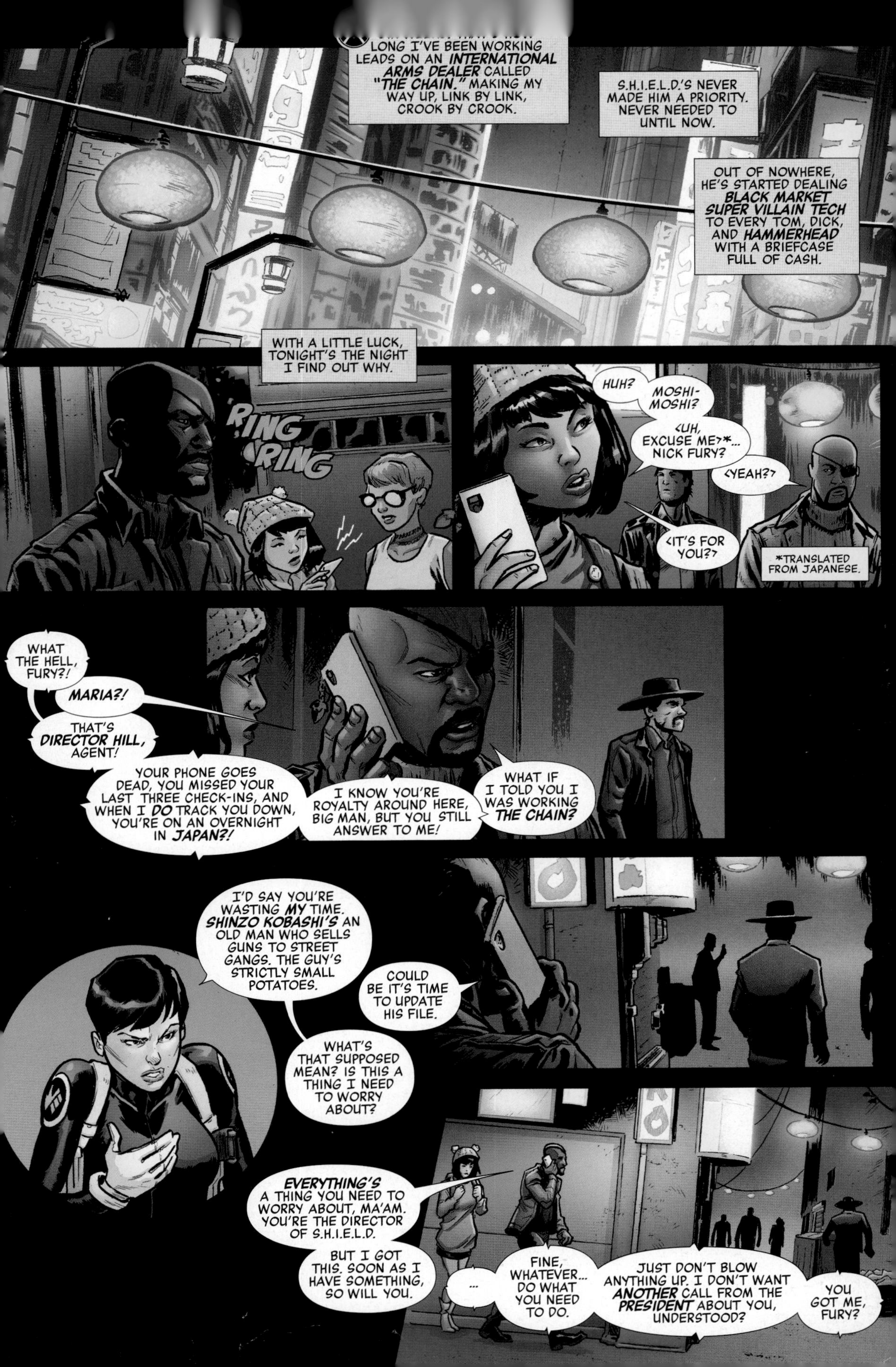
LONG I'VE BEEN WORKING LEADS ON AN INTERNATIONAL ARMS DEALER CALLED "THE CHAIN." MAKING MY WAY UP, LINK BY LINK, CROOK BY CROOK.
S.H.I.E.L.D.'S NEVER MADE HIM A PRIORITY. NEVER NEEDED TO UNTIL NOW.
OUT OF NOWHERE, HE'S STARTED DEALING BLACK MARKET SUPER VILLAIN TECH TO EVERY TOM, DICK, AND HAMMERHEAD WITH A BRIEFCASE FULL OF CASH.
WITH A LITTLE LUCK, TONIGHT'S THE NIGHT I FIND OUT WHY.
RING RING
HUH?
MOSHI-MOSHI?
<UH, EXCUSE ME>*... NICK FURY?
<YEAH?>
<IT'S FOR YOU?>
*TRANSLATED FROM JAPANESE.
WHAT THE HELL, FURY?!
MARIA?!
THAT'S DIRECTOR HILL, AGENT!
YOUR PHONE GOES DEAD, YOU MISSED YOUR LAST THREE CHECK-INS, AND WHEN I DO TRACK YOU DOWN, YOU'RE ON AN OVERNIGHT IN JAPAN?!
I KNOW YOU'RE ROYALTY AROUND HERE, BIG MAN, BUT YOU STILL ANSWER TO ME!
WHAT IF I TOLD YOU I WAS WORKING THE CHAIN?
I'D SAY YOU'RE WASTING MY TIME. SHINZO KOBASHI'S AN OLD MAN WHO SELLS GUNS TO STREET GANGS. THE GUY'S STRICTLY SMALL POTATOES.
COULD BE IT'S TIME TO UPDATE HIS FILE.
WHAT'S THAT SUPPOSED MEAN? IS THIS A THING I NEED TO WORRY ABOUT?
EVERYTHING'S A THING YOU NEED TO WORRY ABOUT, MA'AM. YOU'RE THE DIRECTOR OF S.H.I.E.L.D.
BUT I GOT THIS. SOON AS I HAVE SOMETHING, SO WILL YOU.
...
FINE, WHATEVER... DO WHAT YOU NEED TO DO.
JUST DON'T BLOW ANYTHING UP. I DON'T WANT ANOTHER CALL FROM THE PRESIDENT ABOUT YOU, UNDERSTOOD?
YOU GOT ME, FURY?

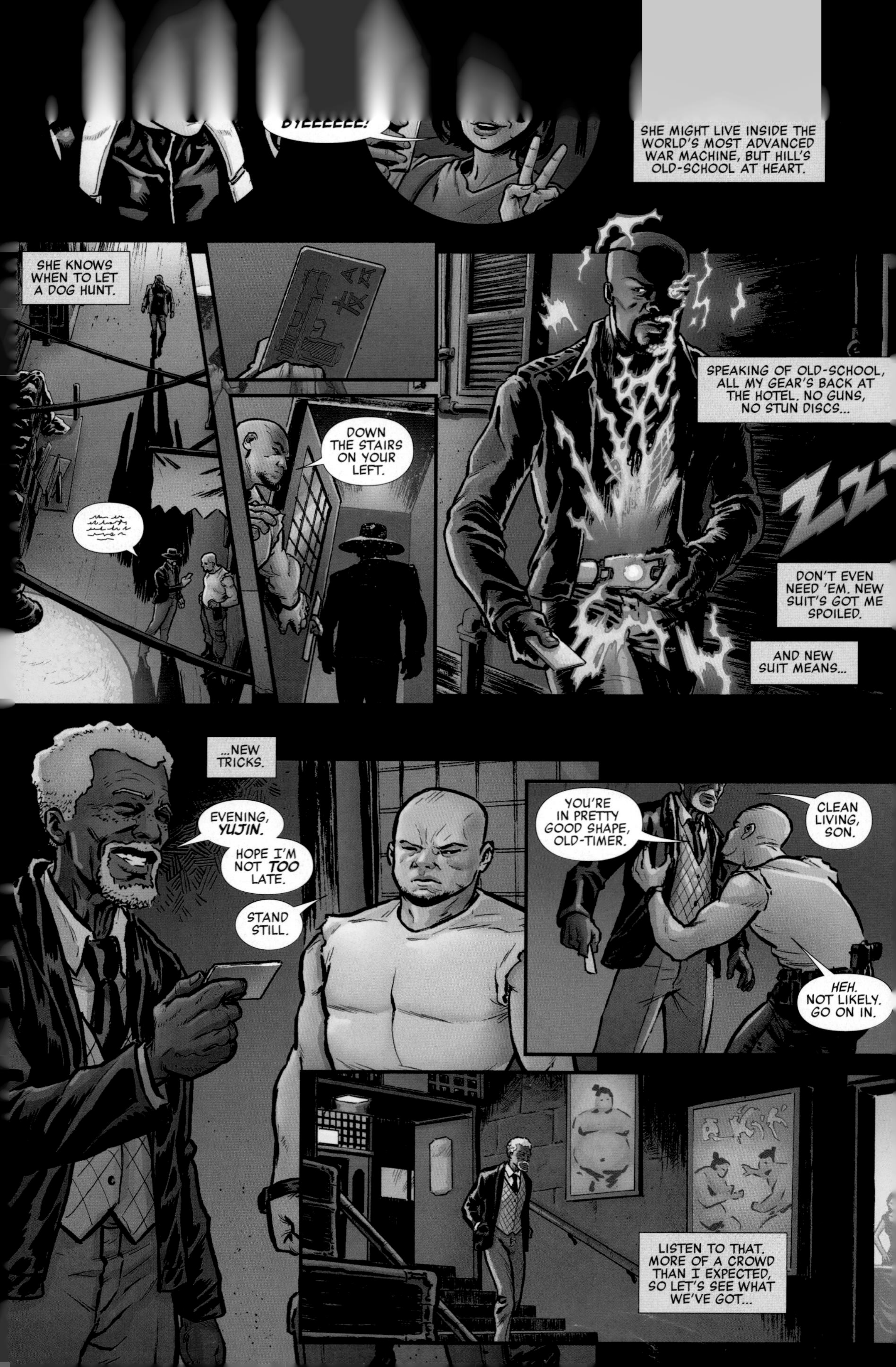
BYEEEEEE!
SHE MIGHT LIVE INSIDE THE WORLD'S MOST ADVANCED WAR MACHINE, BUT HILL'S OLD-SCHOOL AT HEART.
SHE KNOWS WHEN TO LET A DOG HUNT.
DOWN THE STAIRS ON YOUR LEFT.
SPEAKING OF OLD-SCHOOL, ALL MY GEAR'S BACK AT THE HOTEL. NO GUNS, NO STUN DISCS...
DON'T EVEN NEED 'EM. NEW SUIT'S GOT ME SPOILED.
AND NEW SUIT MEANS...
...NEW TRICKS.
EVENING, YUJIN.
HOPE I'M NOT TOO LATE.
STAND STILL.
YOU'RE IN PRETTY GOOD SHAPE, OLD-TIMER.
CLEAN LIVING, SON.
HEH. NOT LIKELY. GO ON IN.
LISTEN TO THAT. MORE OF A CROWD THAN I EXPECTED, SO LET'S SEE WHAT WE'VE GOT...

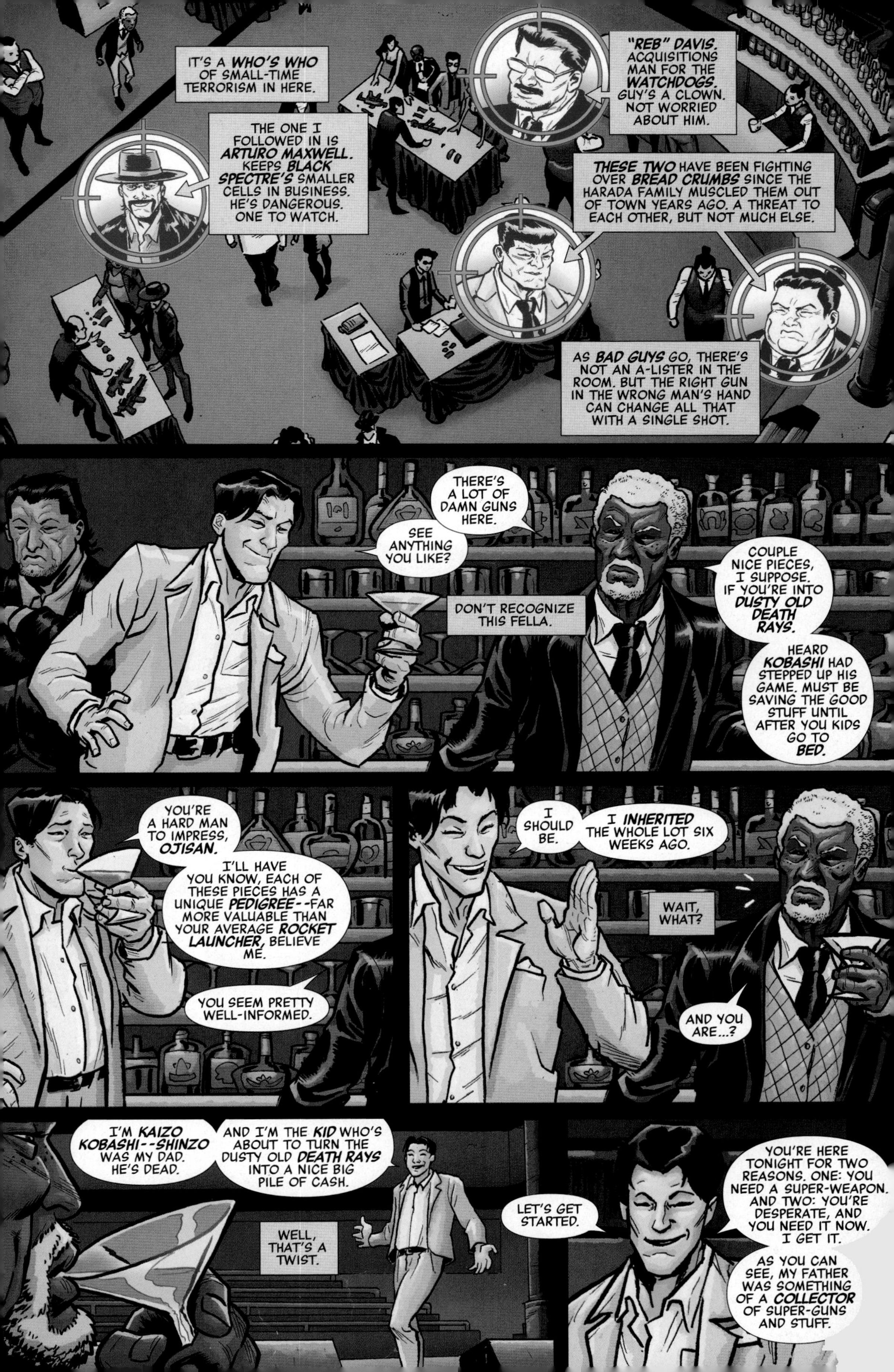
IT'S A WHO'S WHO OF SMALL-TIME TERRORISM IN HERE.
THE ONE I FOLLOWED IN IS ARTURO MAXWELL. KEEPS BLACK SPECTRE'S SMALLER CELLS IN BUSINESS. HE'S DANGEROUS. ONE TO WATCH.
"REB" DAVIS. ACQUISITIONS MAN FOR THE WATCHDOGS. GUY'S A CLOWN. NOT WORRIED ABOUT HIM.
THESE TWO HAVE BEEN FIGHTING OVER BREAD CRUMBS SINCE THE HARADA FAMILY MUSCLED THEM OUT OF TOWN YEARS AGO. A THREAT TO EACH OTHER, BUT NOT MUCH ELSE.
AS BAD GUYS GO, THERE'S NOT AN A-LISTER IN THE ROOM. BUT THE RIGHT GUN IN THE WRONG MAN'S HAND CAN CHANGE ALL THAT WITH A SINGLE SHOT.
THERE'S A LOT OF DAMN GUNS HERE.
SEE ANYTHING YOU LIKE?
DON'T RECOGNIZE THIS FELLA.
COUPLE NICE PIECES, I SUPPOSE. IF YOU'RE INTO DUSTY OLD DEATH RAYS.
HEARD KOBASHI HAD STEPPED UP HIS GAME. MUST BE SAVING THE GOOD STUFF UNTIL AFTER YOU KIDS GO TO BED.
YOU'RE A HARD MAN TO IMPRESS, OJISAN.
I'LL HAVE YOU KNOW, EACH OF THESE PIECES HAS A UNIQUE PEDIGREE--FAR MORE VALUABLE THAN YOUR AVERAGE ROCKET LAUNCHER, BELIEVE ME.
YOU SEEM PRETTY WELL-INFORMED.
I SHOULD BE.
I INHERITED THE WHOLE LOT SIX WEEKS AGO.
WAIT, WHAT?
AND YOU ARE...?
I'M KAIZO KOBASHI--SHINZO WAS MY DAD. HE'S DEAD.
AND I'M THE KID WHO'S ABOUT TO TURN THE DUSTY OLD DEATH RAYS INTO A NICE BIG PILE OF CASH.
WELL, THAT'S A TWIST.
LET'S GET STARTED.
YOU'RE HERE TONIGHT FOR TWO REASONS. ONE: YOU NEED A SUPER-WEAPON. AND TWO: YOU'RE DESPERATE, AND YOU NEED IT NOW. I GET IT.
AS YOU CAN SEE, MY FATHER WAS SOMETHING OF A COLLECTOR OF SUPER-GUNS AND STUFF.

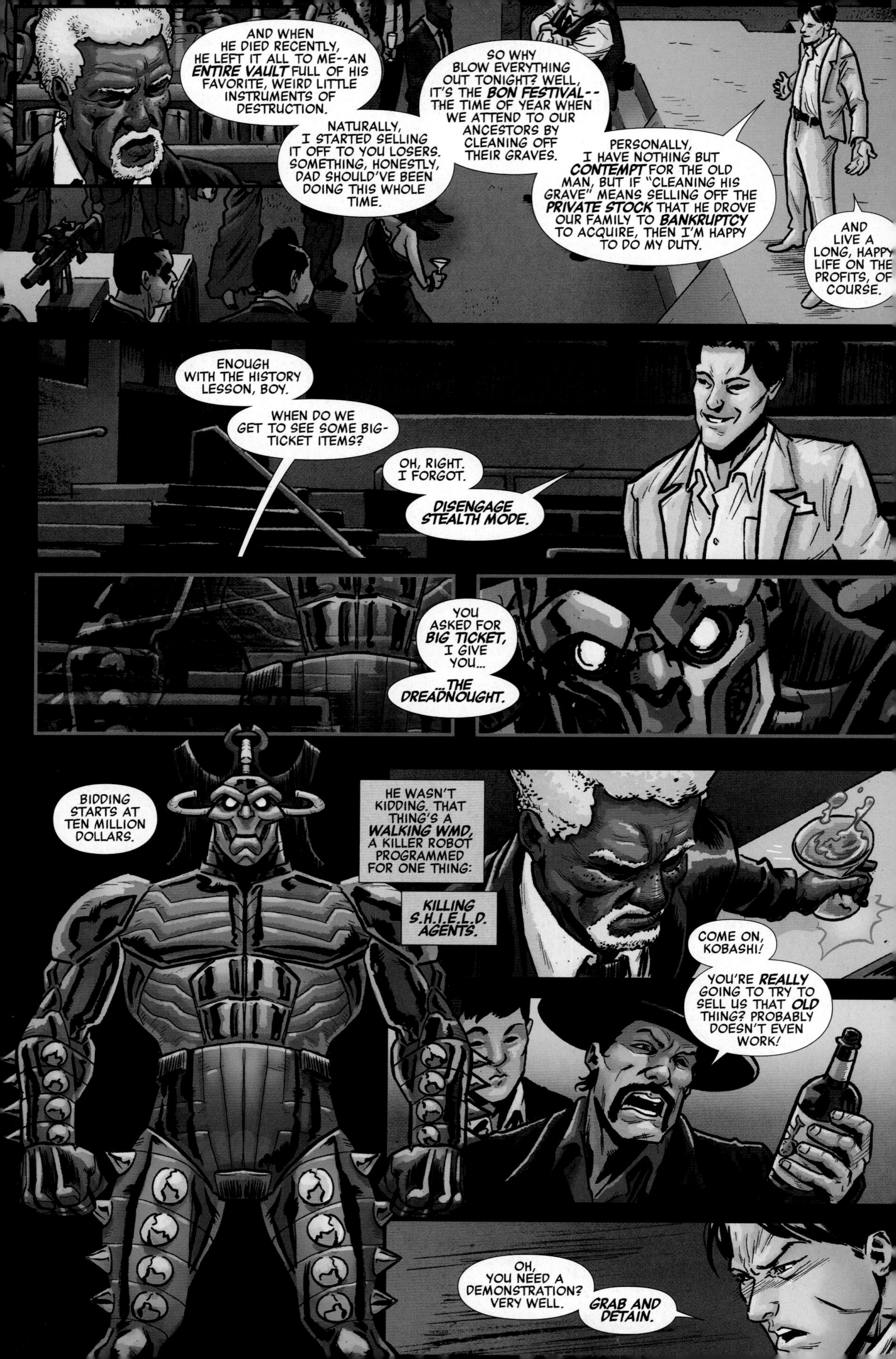
AND WHEN HE DIED RECENTLY, HE LEFT IT ALL TO ME--AN ENTIRE VAULT FULL OF HIS FAVORITE, WEIRD LITTLE INSTRUMENTS OF DESTRUCTION.
NATURALLY, I STARTED SELLING IT OFF TO YOU LOSERS. SOMETHING, HONESTLY, DAD SHOULD'VE BEEN DOING THIS WHOLE TIME.
SO WHY BLOW EVERYTHING OUT TONIGHT? WELL, IT'S THE BON FESTIVAL-- THE TIME OF YEAR WHEN WE ATTEND TO OUR ANCESTORS BY CLEANING OFF THEIR GRAVES.
PERSONALLY, I HAVE NOTHING BUT CONTEMPT FOR THE OLD MAN, BUT IF "CLEANING HIS GRAVE" MEANS SELLING OFF THE PRIVATE STOCK THAT HE DROVE OUR FAMILY TO BANKRUPTCY TO ACQUIRE, THEN I'M HAPPY TO DO MY DUTY.
AND LIVE A LONG, HAPPY LIFE ON THE PROFITS, OF COURSE.
ENOUGH WITH THE HISTORY LESSON, BOY.
WHEN DO WE GET TO SEE SOME BIG-TICKET ITEMS?
OH, RIGHT. I FORGOT.
DISENGAGE STEALTH MODE.
YOU ASKED FOR BIG TICKET, I GIVE YOU...
...THE DREADNOUGHT.
BIDDING STARTS AT TEN MILLION DOLLARS.
HE WASN'T KIDDING. THAT THING'S A WALKING WMD, A KILLER ROBOT PROGRAMMED FOR ONE THING:
KILLING S.H.I.E.L.D. AGENTS.
COME ON, KOBASHI!
YOU'RE REALLY GOING TO TRY TO SELL US THAT OLD THING? PROBABLY DOESN'T EVEN WORK!
OH, YOU NEED A DEMONSTRATION? VERY WELL.
GRAB AND DETAIN.

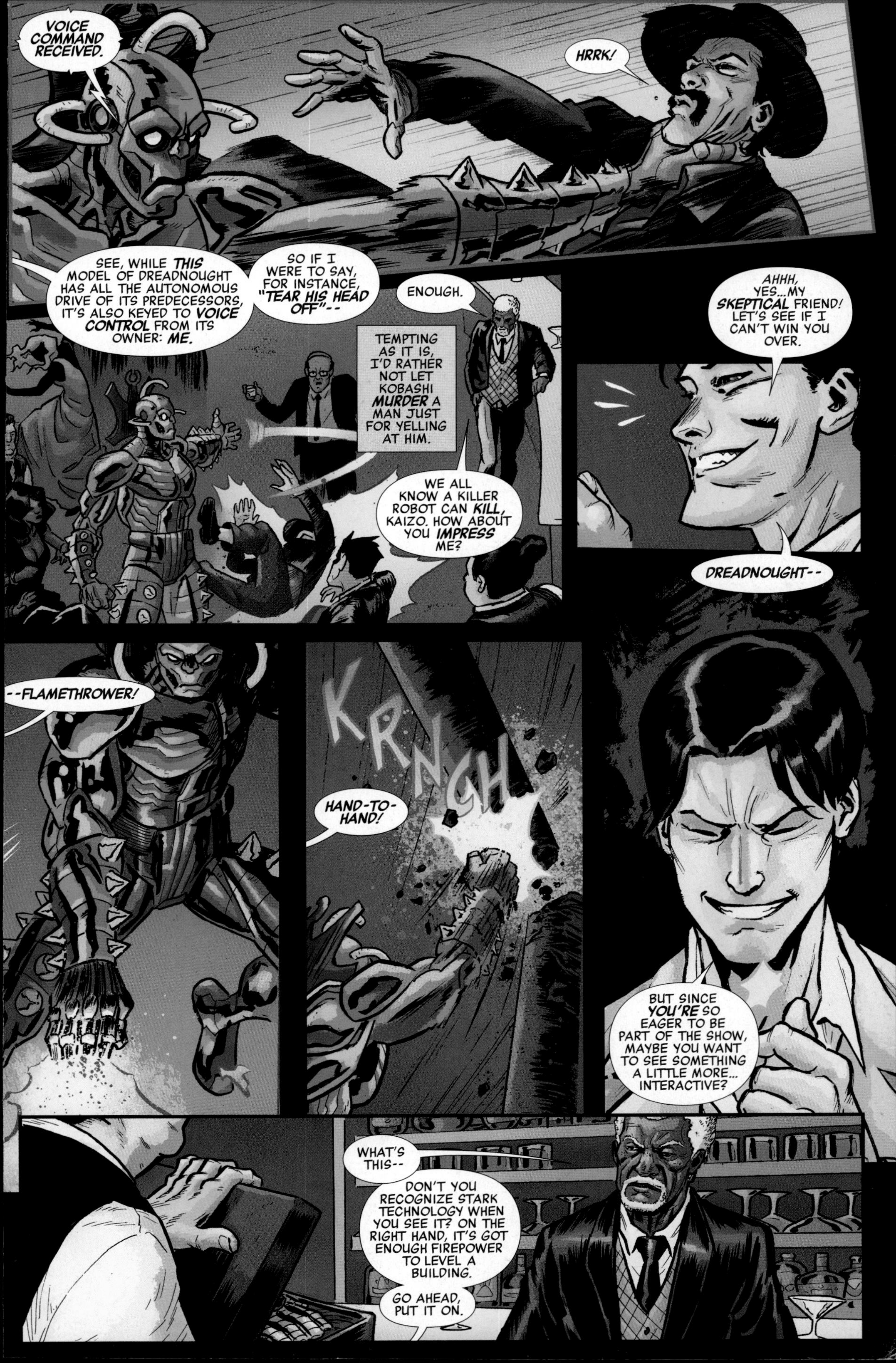
VOICE COMMAND RECEIVED.
HRRK!
SEE, WHILE THIS MODEL OF DREADNOUGHT HAS ALL THE AUTONOMOUS DRIVE OF ITS PREDECESSORS, IT'S ALSO KEYED TO VOICE CONTROL FROM ITS OWNER: ME.
SO IF I WERE TO SAY, FOR INSTANCE, "TEAR HIS HEAD OFF"--
ENOUGH.
TEMPTING AS IT IS, I'D RATHER NOT LET KOBASHI MURDER A MAN JUST FOR YELLING AT HIM.
WE ALL KNOW A KILLER ROBOT CAN KILL, KAIZO. HOW ABOUT YOU IMPRESS ME?
AHHH, YES...MY SKEPTICAL FRIEND! LET'S SEE IF I CAN'T WIN YOU OVER.
DREADNOUGHT--
--FLAMETHROWER!
KRNCH
HAND-TO-HAND!
BUT SINCE YOU'RE SO EAGER TO BE PART OF THE SHOW, MAYBE YOU WANT TO SEE SOMETHING A LITTLE MORE... INTERACTIVE?
WHAT'S THIS--
DON'T YOU RECOGNIZE STARK TECHNOLOGY WHEN YOU SEE IT? ON THE RIGHT HAND, IT'S GOT ENOUGH FIREPOWER TO LEVEL A BUILDING.
GO AHEAD, PUT IT ON.

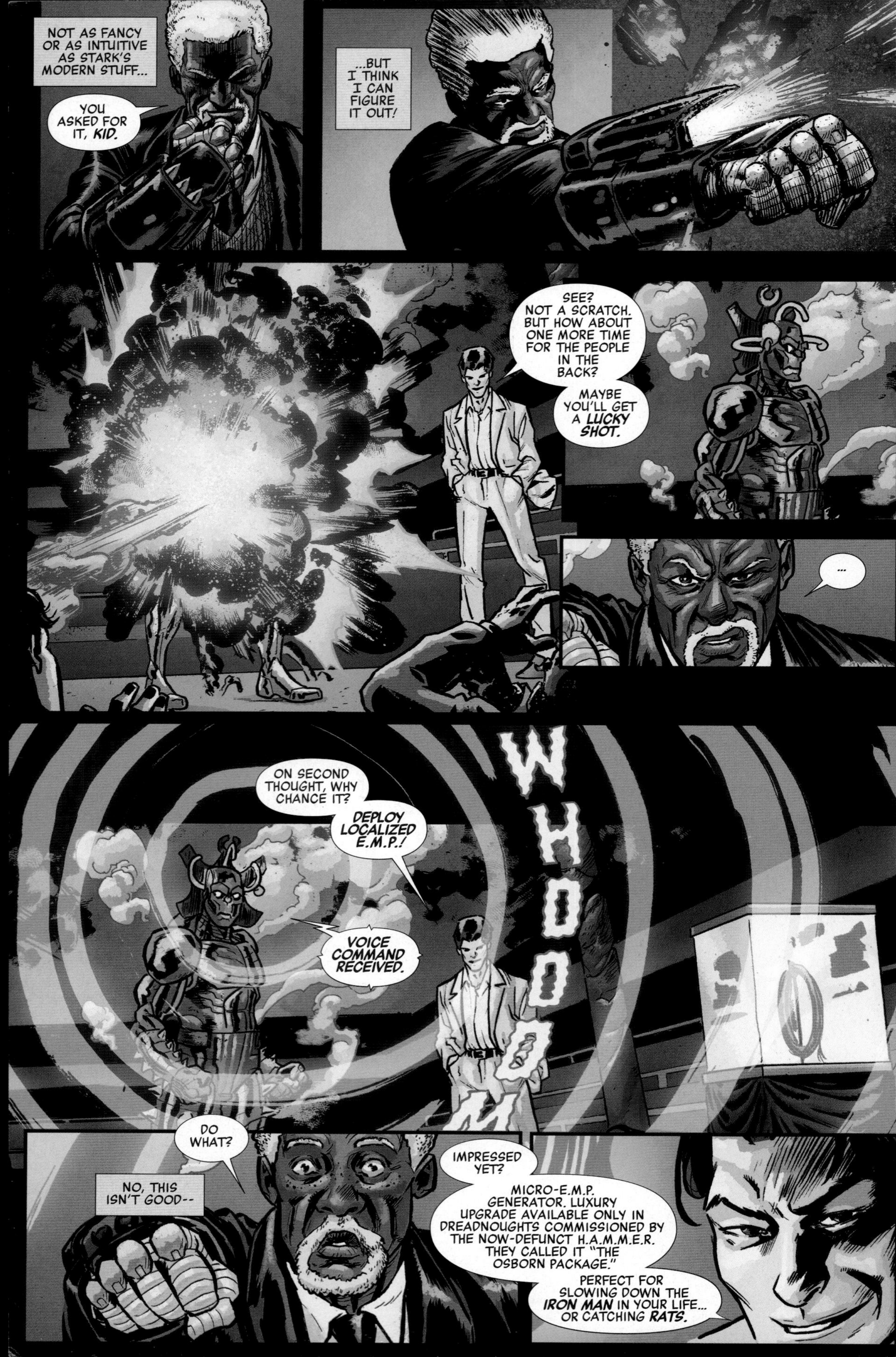

NOT AS FANCY OR AS INTUITIVE AS STARK'S MODERN STUFF...
YOU ASKED FOR IT, KID.
...BUT I THINK I CAN FIGURE IT OUT!
SEE? NOT A SCRATCH. BUT HOW ABOUT ONE MORE TIME FOR THE PEOPLE IN THE BACK?
MAYBE YOU'LL GET A LUCKY SHOT.
...
ON SECOND THOUGHT, WHY CHANCE IT?
DEPLOY LOCALIZED E.M.P.!
VOICE COMMAND RECEIVED.
WHOOOM
DO WHAT?
NO, THIS ISN'T GOOD--
IMPRESSED YET?
MICRO-E.M.P. GENERATOR. LUXURY UPGRADE AVAILABLE ONLY IN DREADNOUGHTS COMMISSIONED BY THE NOW-DEFUNCT H.A.M.M.E.R. THEY CALLED IT "THE OSBORN PACKAGE."
PERFECT FOR SLOWING DOWN THE IRON MAN IN YOUR LIFE... OR CATCHING RATS.

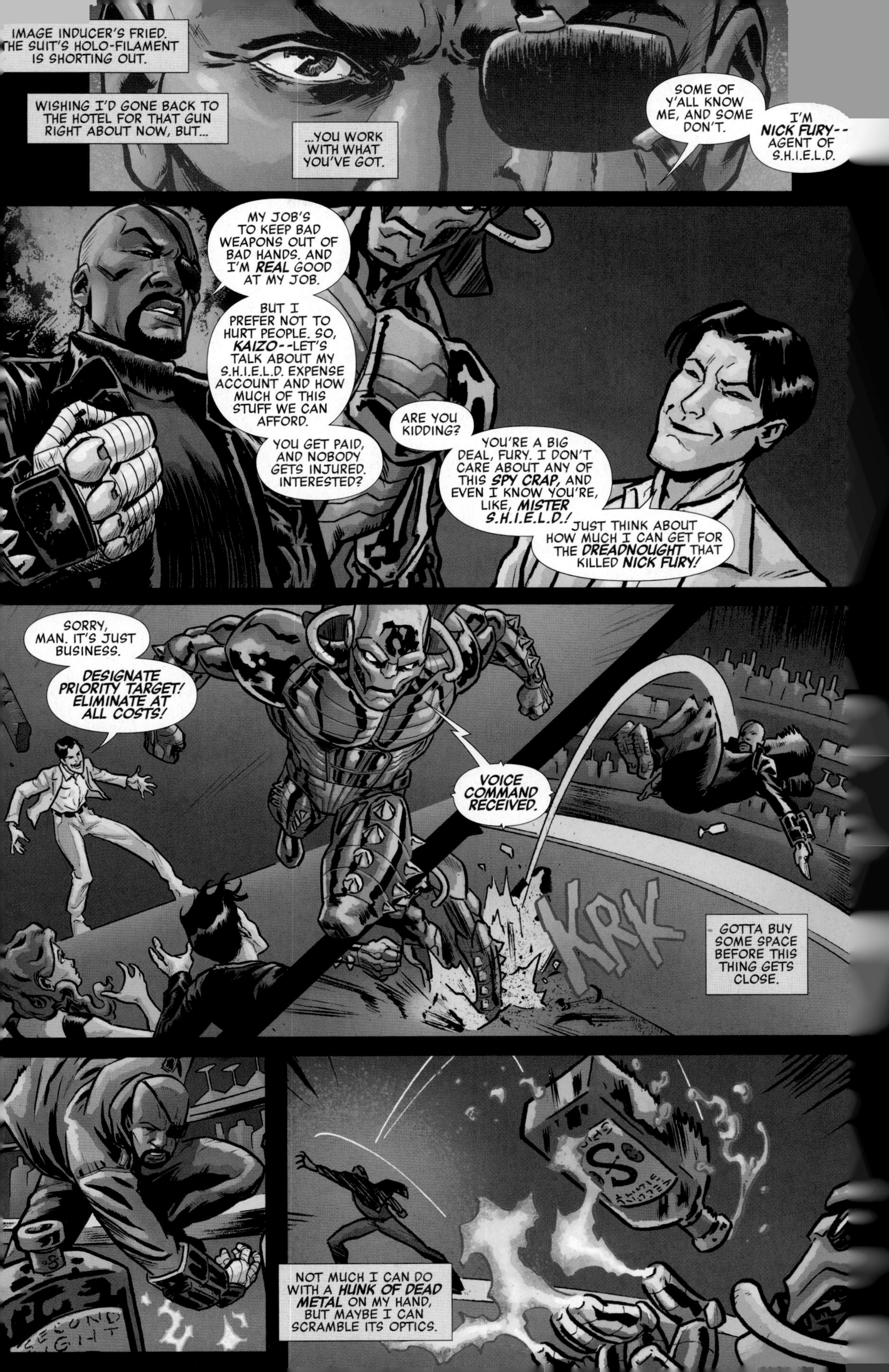
IMAGE INDUCER'S FRIED. THE SUIT'S HOLO-FILAMENT IS SHORTING OUT.
WISHING I'D GONE BACK TO THE HOTEL FOR THAT GUN RIGHT ABOUT NOW, BUT...
...YOU WORK WITH WHAT YOU'VE GOT.
SOME OF Y'ALL KNOW ME, AND SOME DON'T.
I'M NICK FURY-- AGENT OF S.H.I.E.L.D.
MY JOB'S TO KEEP BAD WEAPONS OUT OF BAD HANDS. AND I'M REAL GOOD AT MY JOB.
BUT I PREFER NOT TO HURT PEOPLE. SO, KAIZO--LET'S TALK ABOUT MY S.H.I.E.L.D. EXPENSE ACCOUNT AND HOW MUCH OF THIS STUFF WE CAN AFFORD.
YOU GET PAID, AND NOBODY GETS INJURED. INTERESTED?
ARE YOU KIDDING?
YOU'RE A BIG DEAL, FURY. I DON'T CARE ABOUT ANY OF THIS SPY CRAP, AND EVEN I KNOW YOU'RE, LIKE, MISTER S.H.I.E.L.D.!
JUST THINK ABOUT HOW MUCH I CAN GET FOR THE DREADNOUGHT THAT KILLED NICK FURY!
SORRY, MAN. IT'S JUST BUSINESS.
DESIGNATE PRIORITY TARGET! ELIMINATE AT ALL COSTS!
VOICE COMMAND RECEIVED.
KRK
GOTTA BUY SOME SPACE BEFORE THIS THING GETS CLOSE.
SECOND SIGHT
NOT MUCH I CAN DO WITH A HUNK OF DEAD METAL ON MY HAND, BUT MAYBE I CAN SCRAMBLE ITS OPTICS.

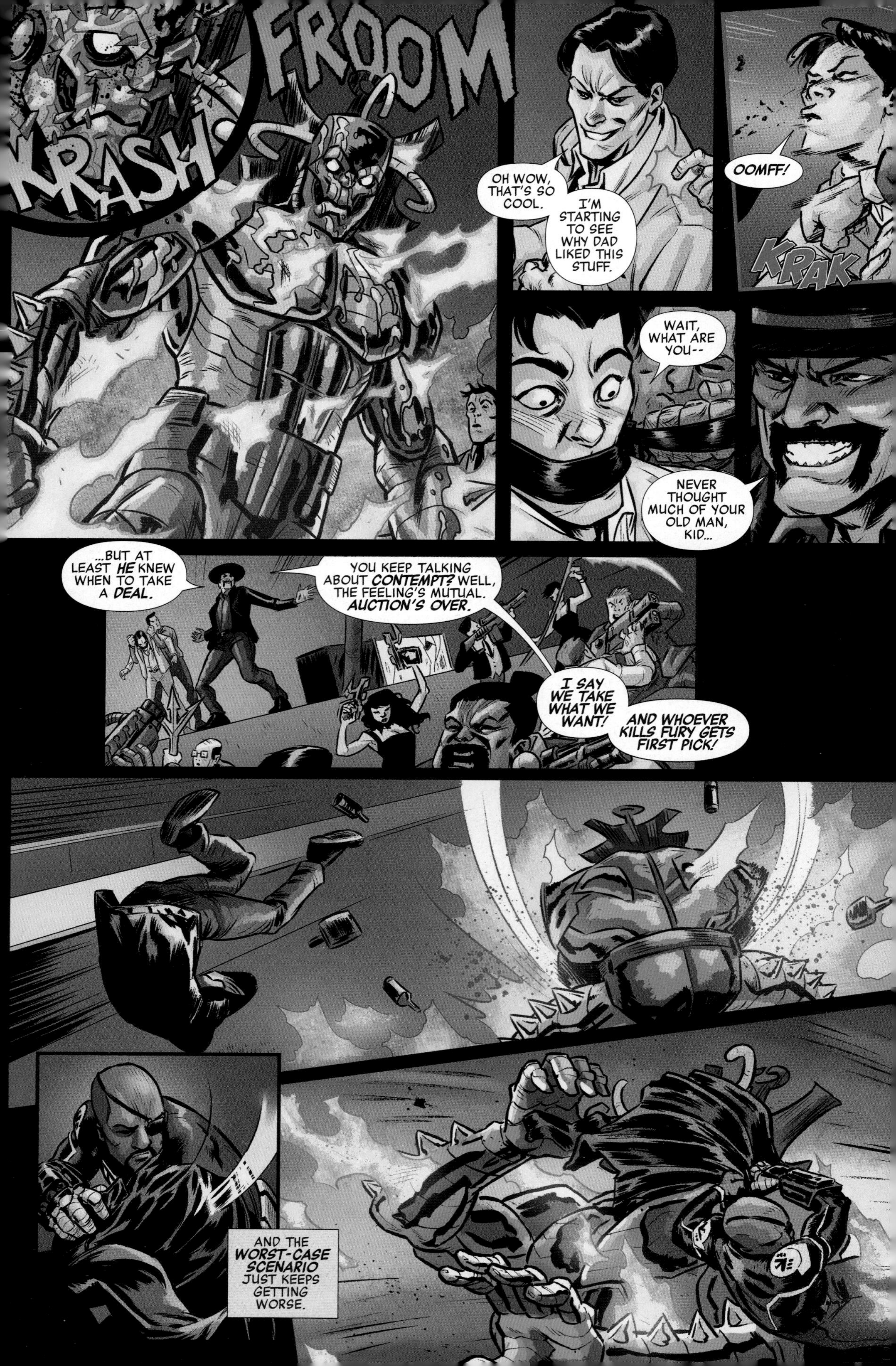
KRASH
FROOM
OH WOW, THAT'S SO COOL.
I'M STARTING TO SEE WHY DAD LIKED THIS STUFF.
OOMFF!
KRAK
WAIT, WHAT ARE YOU--
NEVER THOUGHT MUCH OF YOUR OLD MAN, KID...
...BUT AT LEAST HE KNEW WHEN TO TAKE A DEAL.
YOU KEEP TALKING ABOUT CONTEMPT? WELL, THE FEELING'S MUTUAL. AUCTION'S OVER.
I SAY WE TAKE WHAT WE WANT!
AND WHOEVER KILLS FURY GETS FIRST PICK!
AND THE WORST-CASE SCENARIO JUST KEEPS GETTING WORSE.

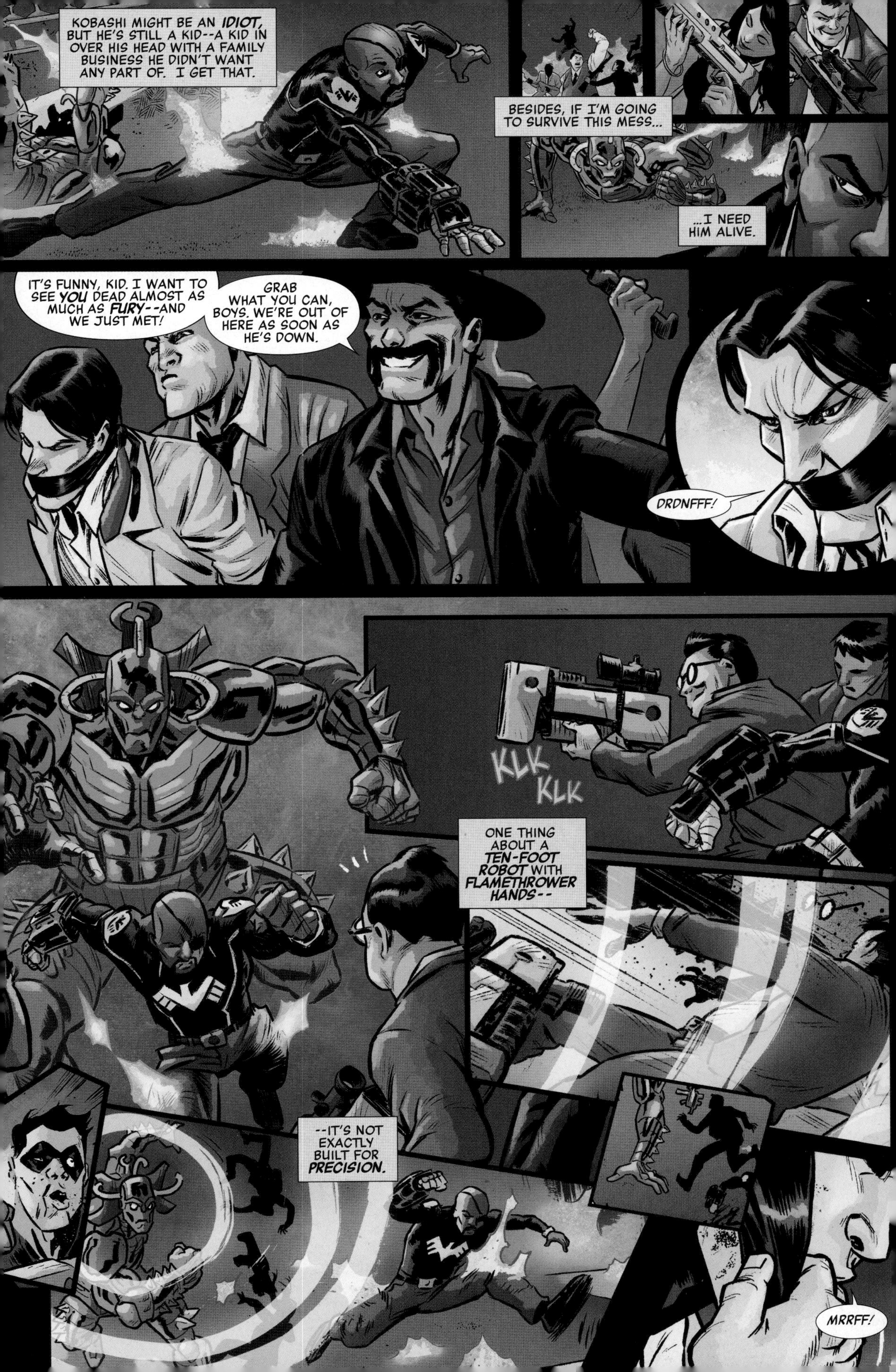
KOBASHI MIGHT BE AN IDIOT, BUT HE'S STILL A KID--A KID IN OVER HIS HEAD WITH A FAMILY BUSINESS HE DIDN'T WANT ANY PART OF. I GET THAT.
BESIDES, IF I'M GOING TO SURVIVE THIS MESS...
...I NEED HIM ALIVE.
IT'S FUNNY, KID. I WANT TO SEE YOU DEAD ALMOST AS MUCH AS FURY--AND WE JUST MET!
GRAB WHAT YOU CAN, BOYS. WE'RE OUT OF HERE AS SOON AS HE'S DOWN.
DRDNFFF!
KLK KLK
ONE THING ABOUT A TEN-FOOT ROBOT WITH FLAMETHROWER HANDS--
--IT'S NOT EXACTLY BUILT FOR PRECISION.
MRRFF!

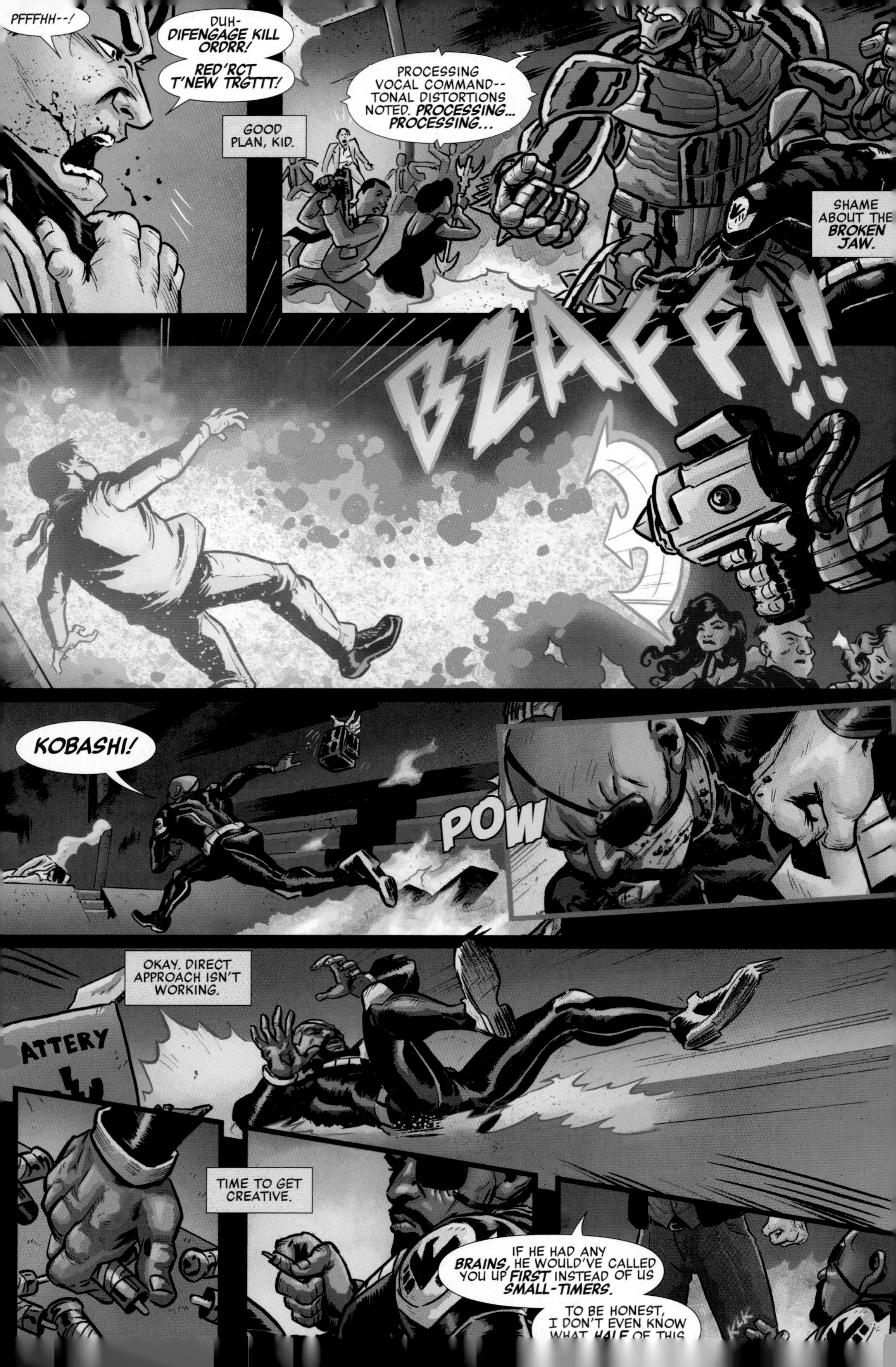
PFFFHH--!
DUH-DIFENGAGE KILL ORDRR!
RED'RCT T'NEW TRGTTT!
GOOD PLAN, KID.
PROCESSING VOCAL COMMAND-- TONAL DISTORTIONS NOTED. PROCESSING... PROCESSING...
SHAME ABOUT THE BROKEN JAW.
BZAFF!!
KOBASHI!
POW
OKAY. DIRECT APPROACH ISN'T WORKING.
ATTERY
TIME TO GET CREATIVE.
IF HE HAD ANY BRAINS, HE WOULD'VE CALLED YOU UP FIRST INSTEAD OF US SMALL-TIMERS.
TO BE HONEST, I DON'T EVEN KNOW WHAT HALF OF THIS

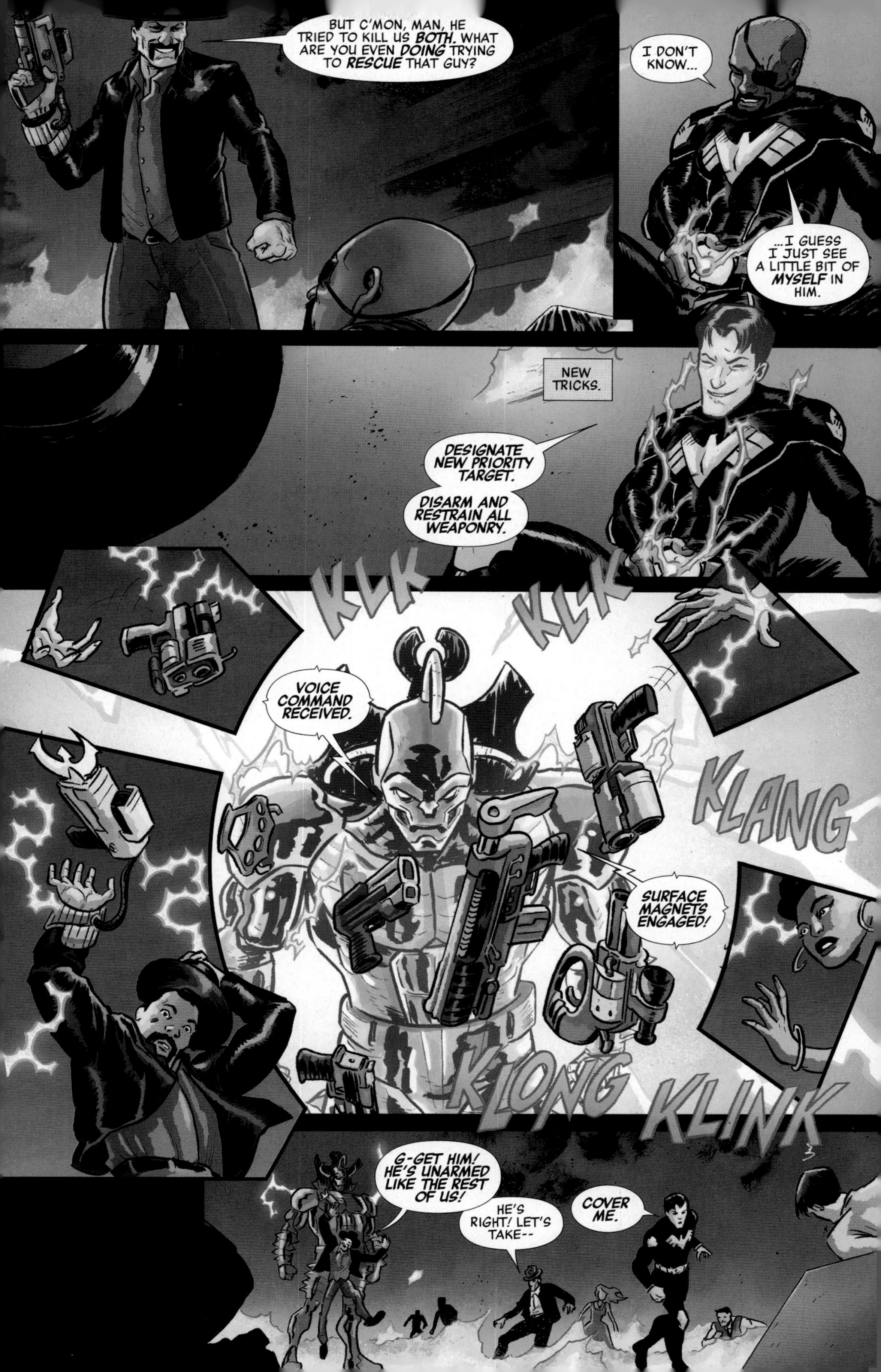
BUT C'MON, MAN, HE TRIED TO KILL US BOTH. WHAT ARE YOU EVEN DOING TRYING TO RESCUE THAT GUY?
I DON'T KNOW...
...I GUESS I JUST SEE A LITTLE BIT OF MYSELF IN HIM.
NEW TRICKS.
DESIGNATE NEW PRIORITY TARGET.
DISARM AND RESTRAIN ALL WEAPONRY.
KLK
KLK
VOICE COMMAND RECEIVED.
KLANG
SURFACE MAGNETS ENGAGED!
KLONG
KLINK
G-GET HIM! HE'S UNARMED LIKE THE REST OF US!
HE'S RIGHT! LET'S TAKE--
COVER ME.

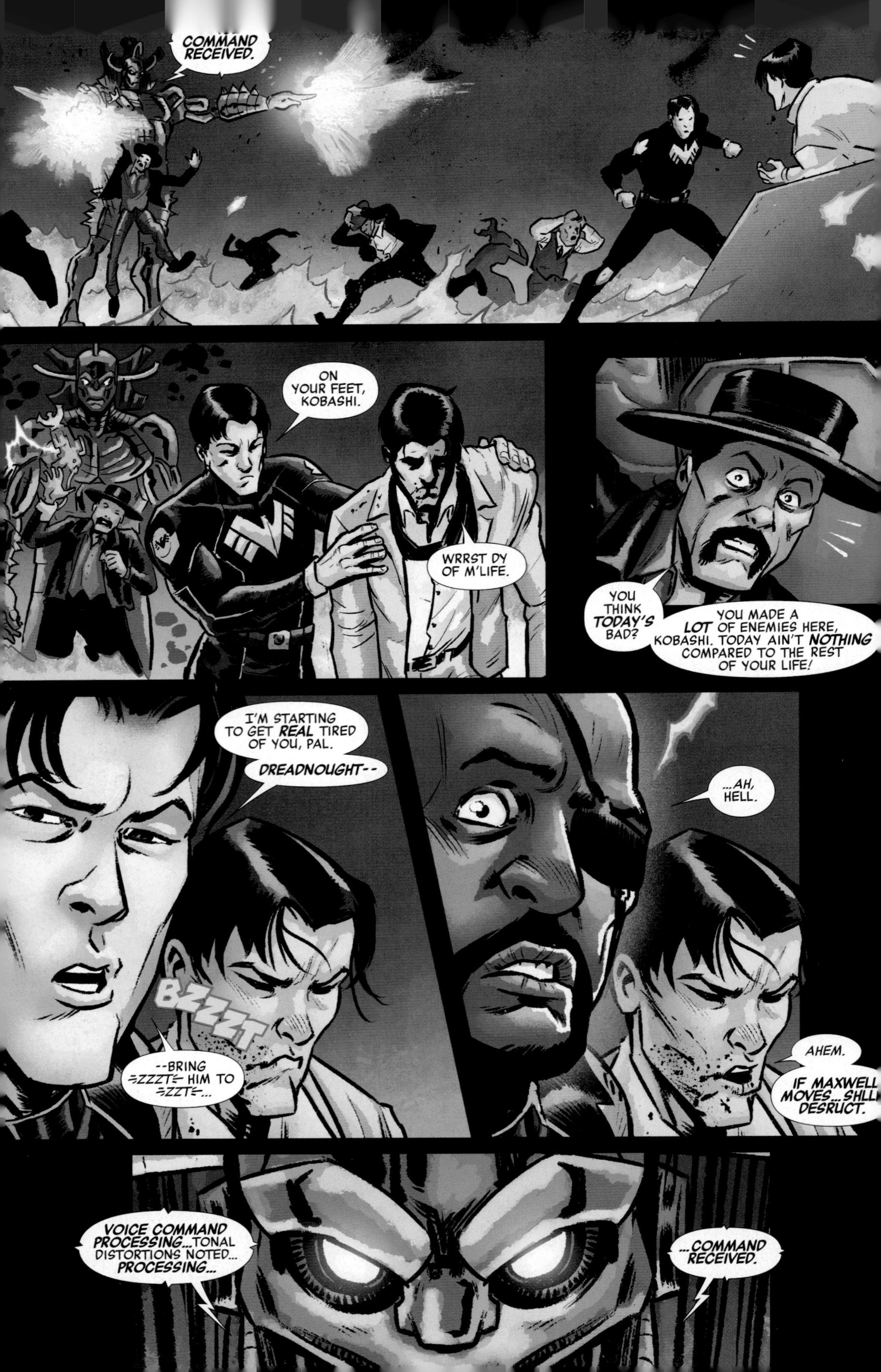
COMMAND RECEIVED.
ON YOUR FEET, KOBASHI.
WRRST DY OF M'LIFE.
YOU THINK TODAY'S BAD?
YOU MADE A LOT OF ENEMIES HERE, KOBASHI. TODAY AIN'T NOTHING COMPARED TO THE REST OF YOUR LIFE!
I'M STARTING TO GET REAL TIRED OF YOU, PAL.
DREADNOUGHT--
BZZZT
--BRING =ZZZT= HIM TO =ZZT=...
...AH, HELL.
AHEM.
IF MAXWELL MOVES...SHLL DESRUCT.
VOICE COMMAND PROCESSING...TONAL DISTORTIONS NOTED... PROCESSING...
...COMMAND RECEIVED.

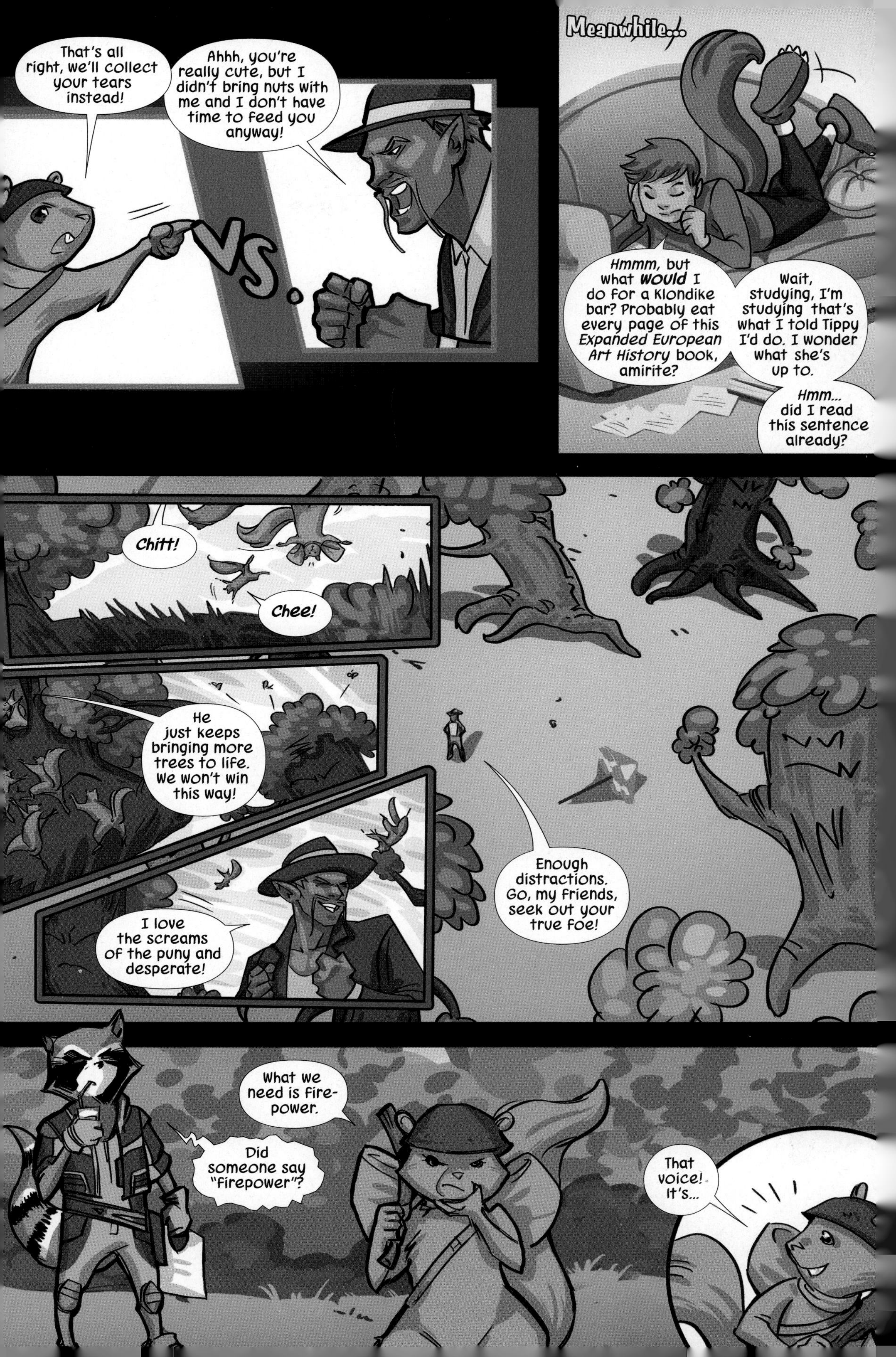

That's all right, we'll collect your tears instead!
Ahhh, you're really cute, but I didn't bring nuts with me and I don't have time to feed you anyway!
VS.
Meanwhile...
Hmmm, but what WOULD I do for a Klondike bar? Probably eat every page of this Expanded European Art History book, amirite?
Wait, studying, I'm studying that's what I told Tippy I'd do. I wonder what she's up to.
Hmm... did I read this sentence already?
Chitt!
Chee!
He just keeps bringing more trees to life. We won't win this way!
I love the screams of the puny and desperate!
Enough distractions. Go, my friends, seek out your true foe!
What we need is fire-power.
Did someone say "Firepower"?
That voice! It's...

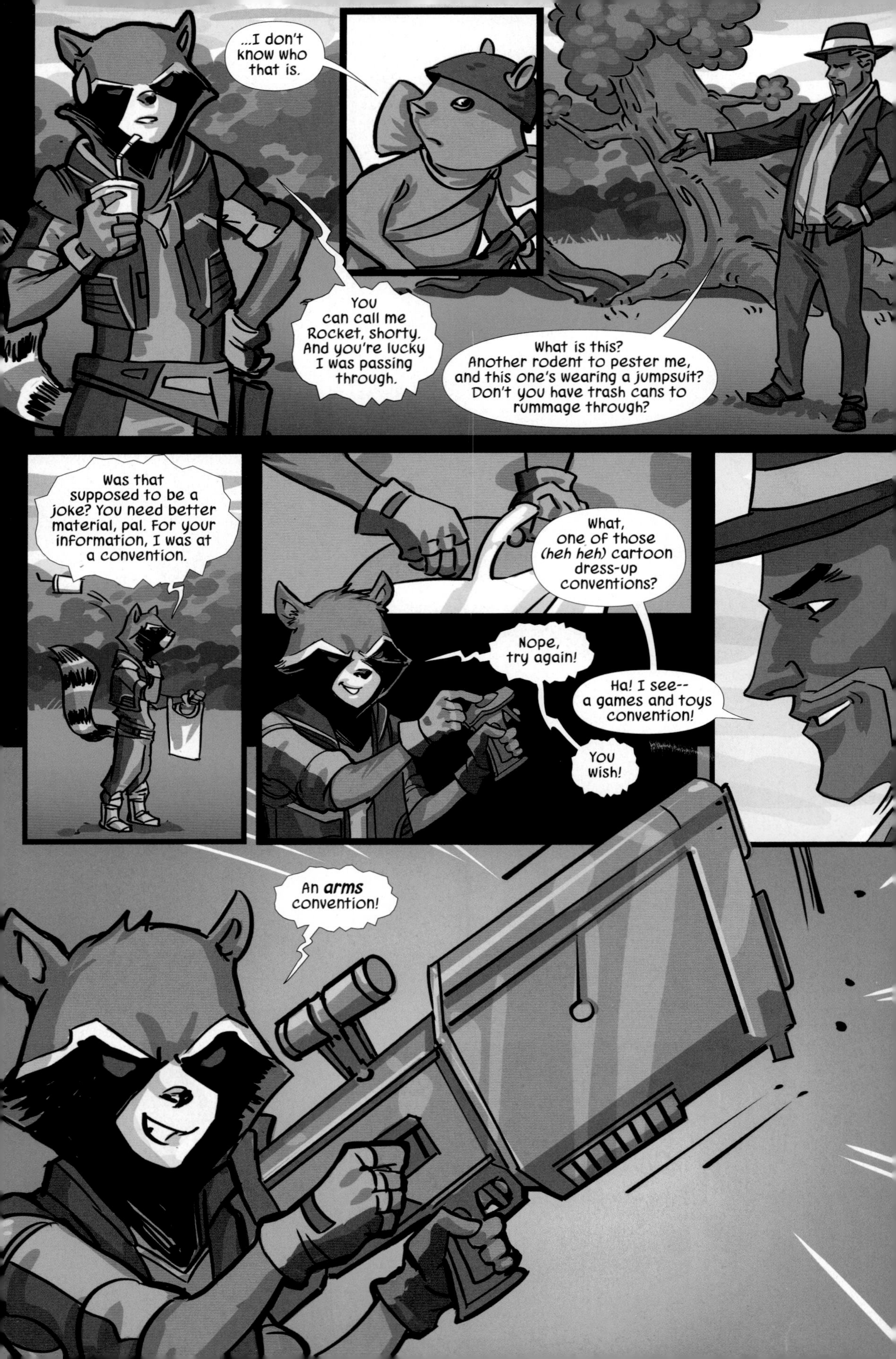
...I don't know who that is.
You can call me Rocket, shorty. And you're lucky I was passing through.
What is this? Another rodent to pester me, and this one's wearing a jumpsuit? Don't you have trash cans to rummage through?
Was that supposed to be a joke? You need better material, pal. For your information, I was at a convention.
What, one of those (heh heh) cartoon dress-up conventions?
Nope, try again!
Ha! I see-- a games and toys convention!
You wish!
An arms convention!

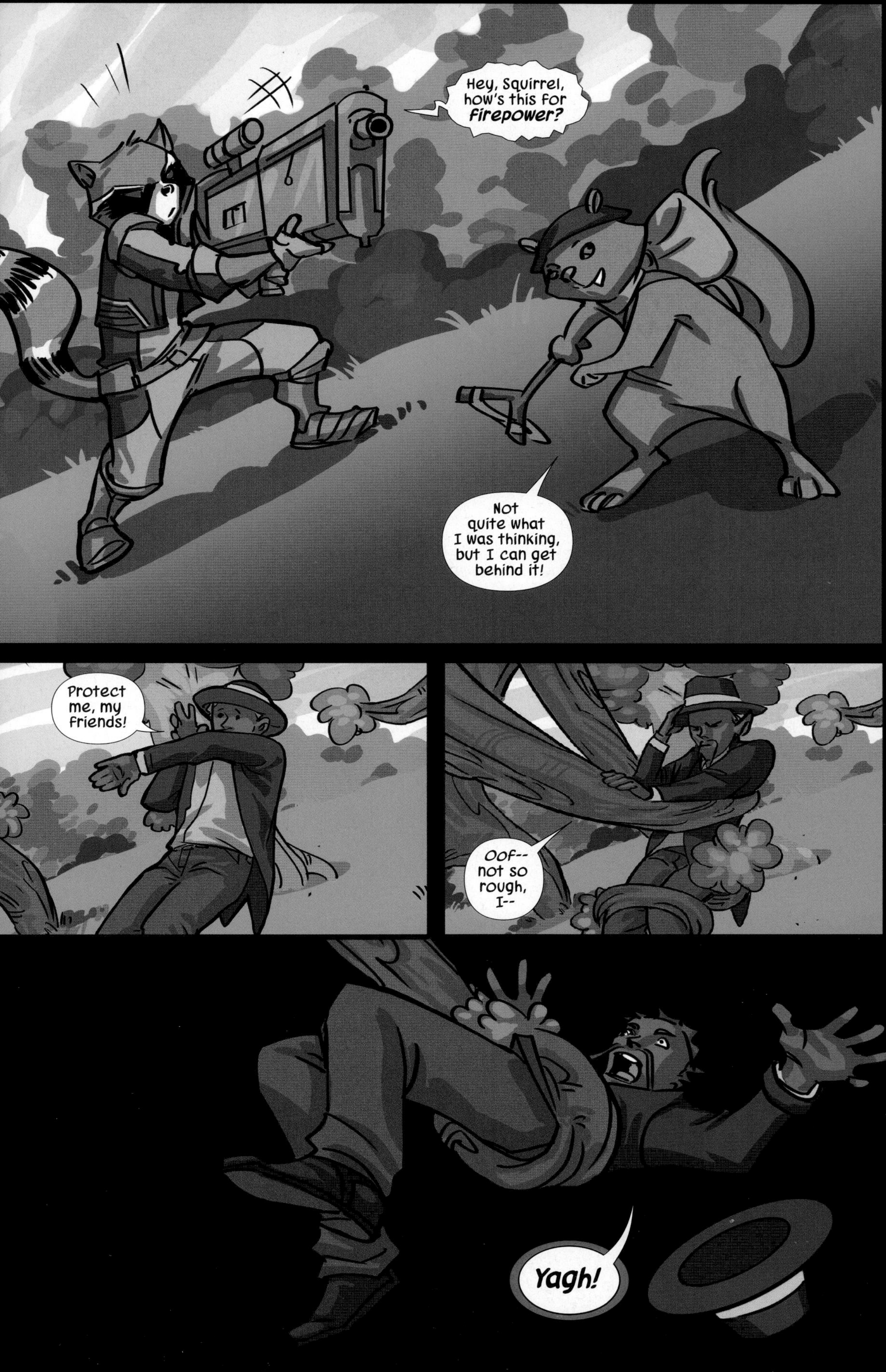
Hey, Squirrel, how's this for firepower?
Not quite what I was thinking, but I can get behind it!
Protect me, my friends!
Oof-- not so rough, I--
Yagh!

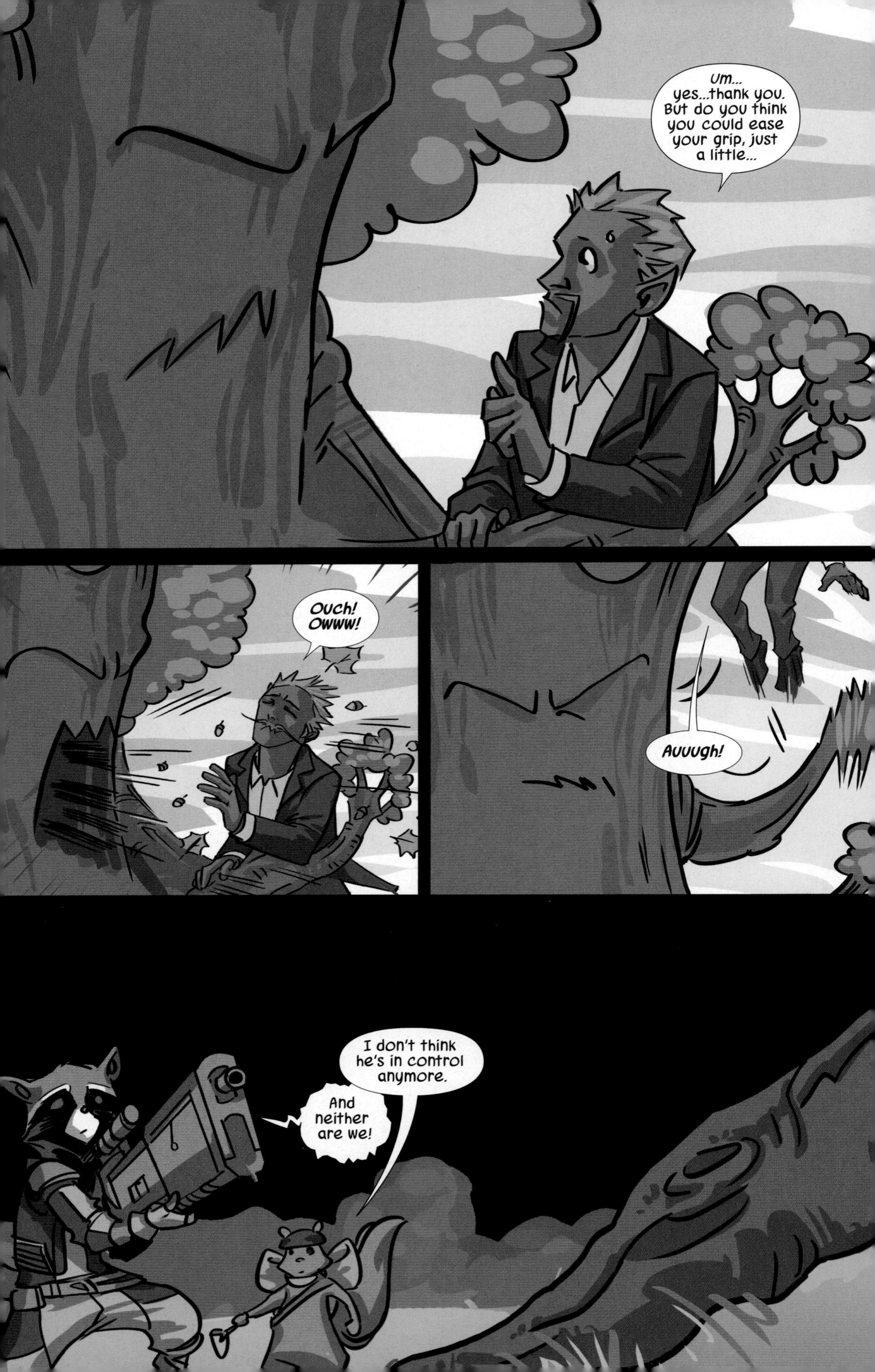
Um... yes...thank you. But do you think you could ease your grip, just a little...
Ouch! OWWW!
Auuugh!
I don't think he's in control anymore.
And neither are we!

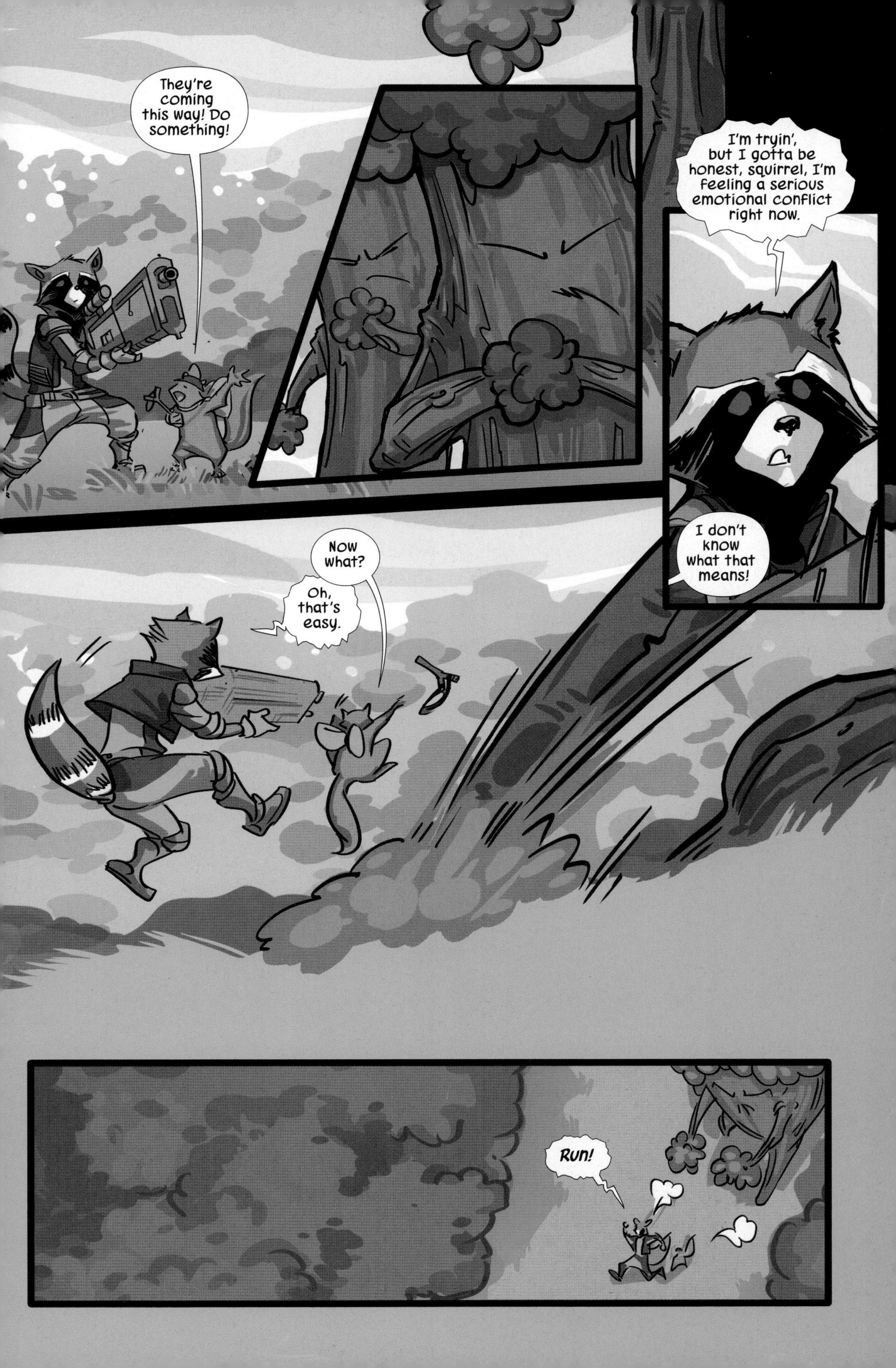
They're coming this way! Do something!
I'm tryin', but I gotta be honest, squirrel, I'm feeling a serious emotional conflict right now.
I don't know what that means!
Now what?
Oh, that's easy.
Run!

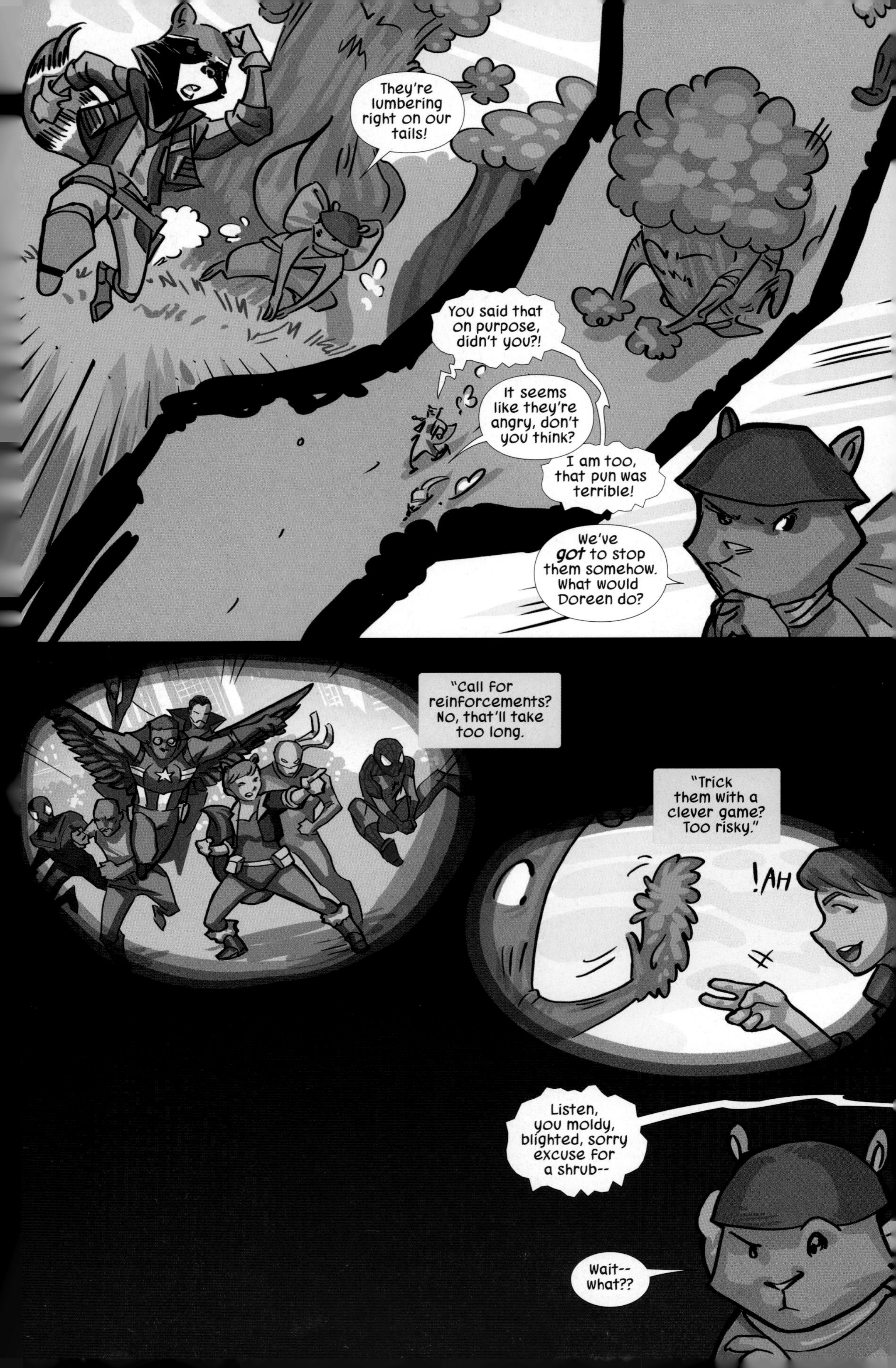

They're lumbering right on our tails!
You said that on purpose, didn't you?!
It seems like they're angry, don't you think?
I am too, that pun was terrible!
We've got to stop them somehow. What would Doreen do?
"Call for reinforcements? No, that'll take too long.
"Trick them with a clever game? Too risky."
!AH
Listen, you moldy, blighted, sorry excuse for a shrub--
Wait-- what??

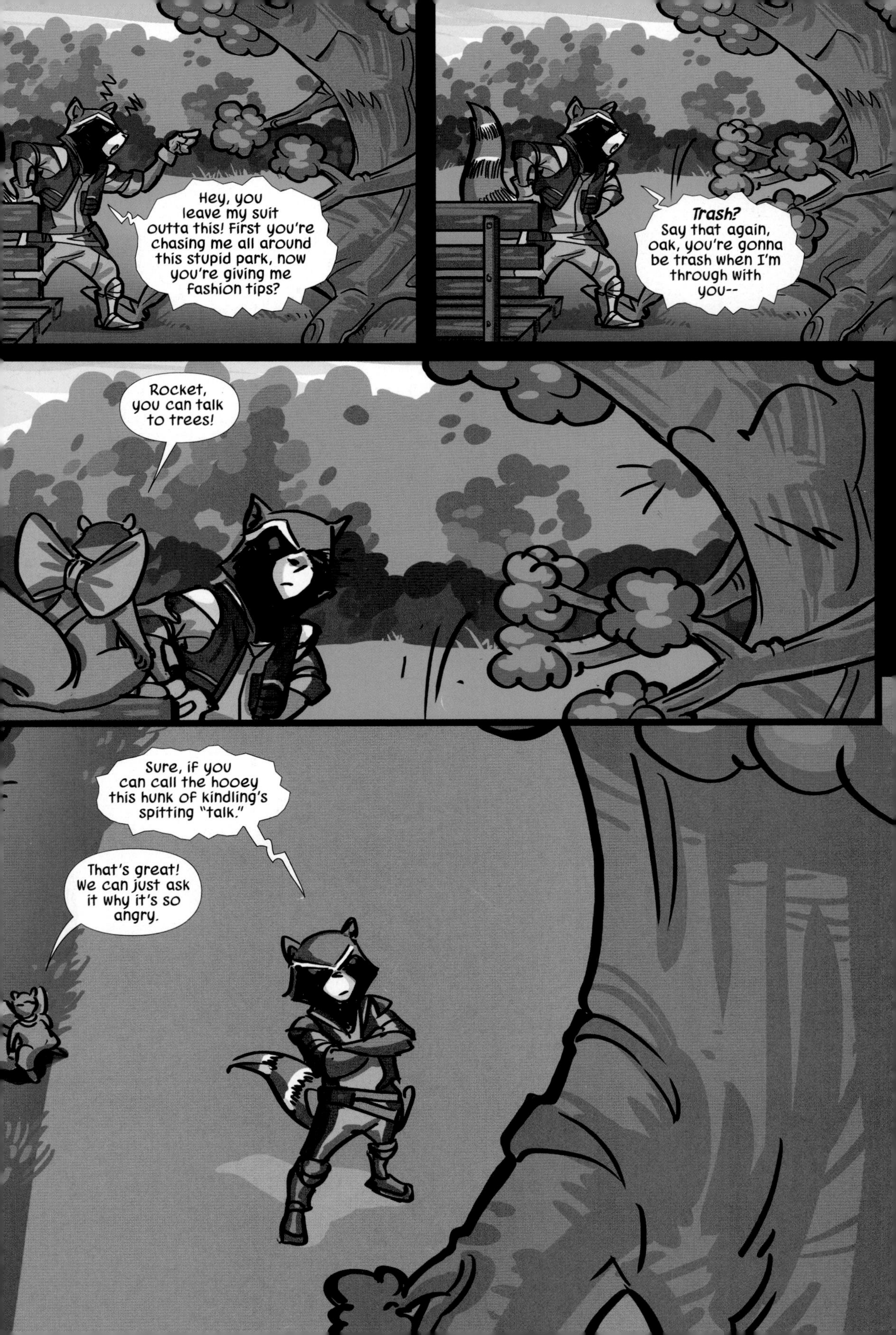

Hey, you leave my suit outta this! First you're chasing me all around this stupid park, now you're giving me fashion tips?
Trash? Say that again, oak, you're gonna be trash when I'm through with you--
Rocket, you can talk to trees!
Sure, if you can call the hooey this hunk of kindling's spitting "talk."
That's great! We can just ask it why it's so angry.

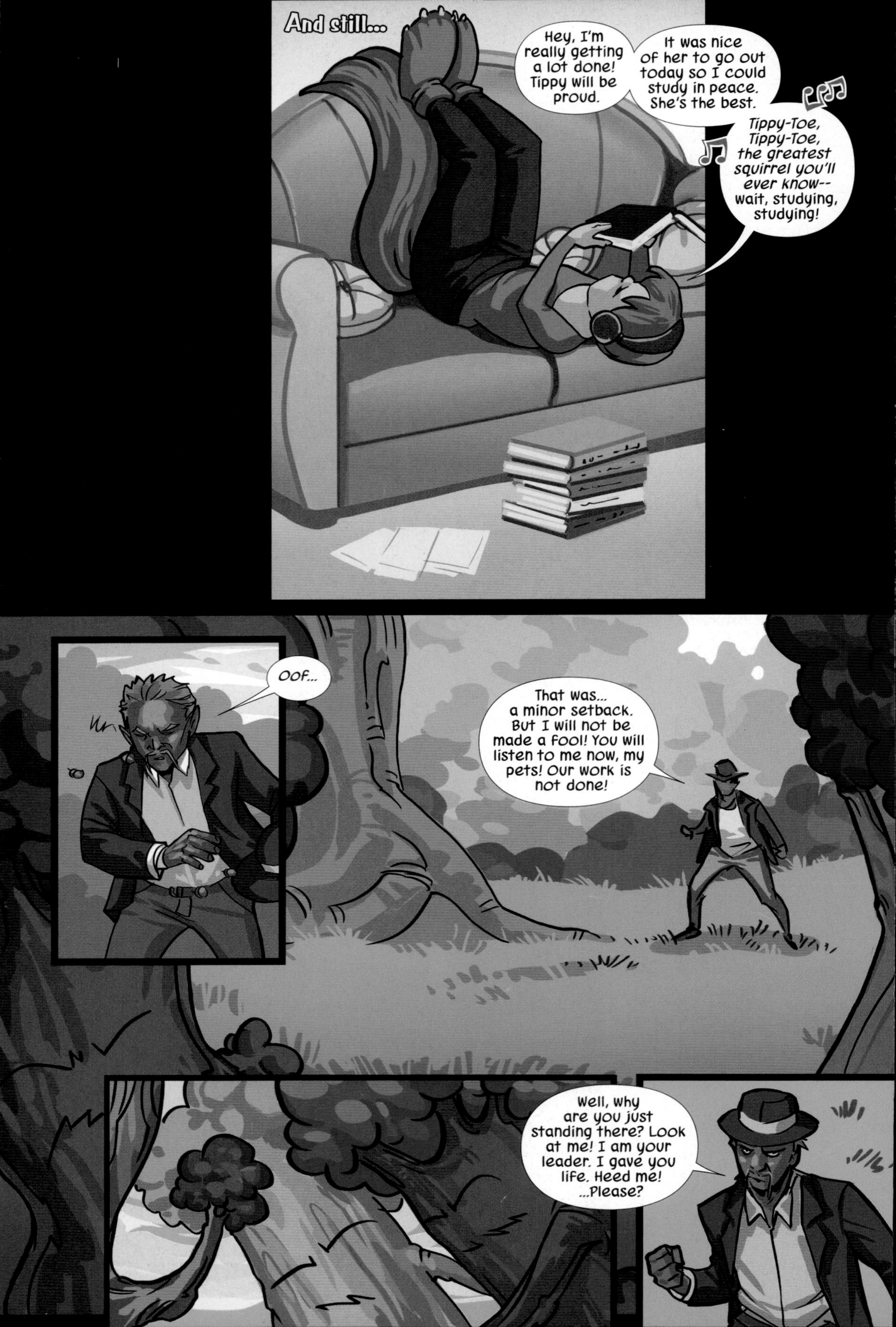

And still...
Hey, I'm really getting a lot done! Tippy will be proud.
It was nice of her to go out today so I could study in peace. She's the best.
Tippy-Toe, Tippy-Toe, the greatest squirrel you'll ever know-- wait, studying, studying!
Oof...
That was... a minor setback. But I will not be made a fool! You will listen to me now, my pets! Our work is not done!
Well, why are you just standing there? Look at me! I am your leader. I gave you life. Heed me! ...Please?

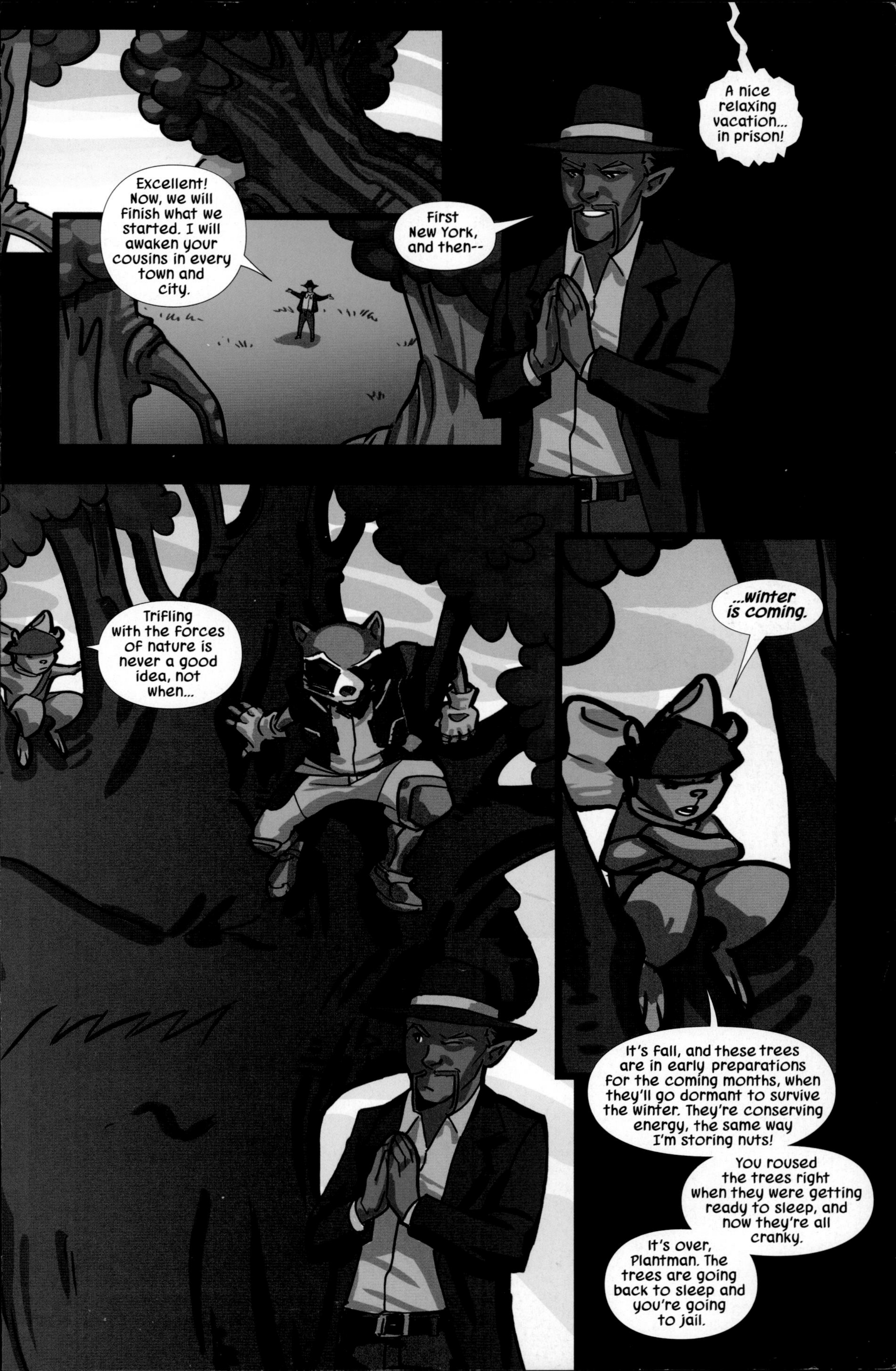

Excellent! Now, we will finish what we started. I will awaken your cousins in every town and city.
First New York, and then--
A nice relaxing vacation... in prison!
Trifling with the forces of nature is never a good idea, not when...
...winter is coming.
It's fall, and these trees are in early preparations for the coming months, when they'll go dormant to survive the winter. They're conserving energy, the same way I'm storing nuts!
You roused the trees right when they were getting ready to sleep, and now they're all cranky.
It's over, Plantman. The trees are going back to sleep and you're going to jail.

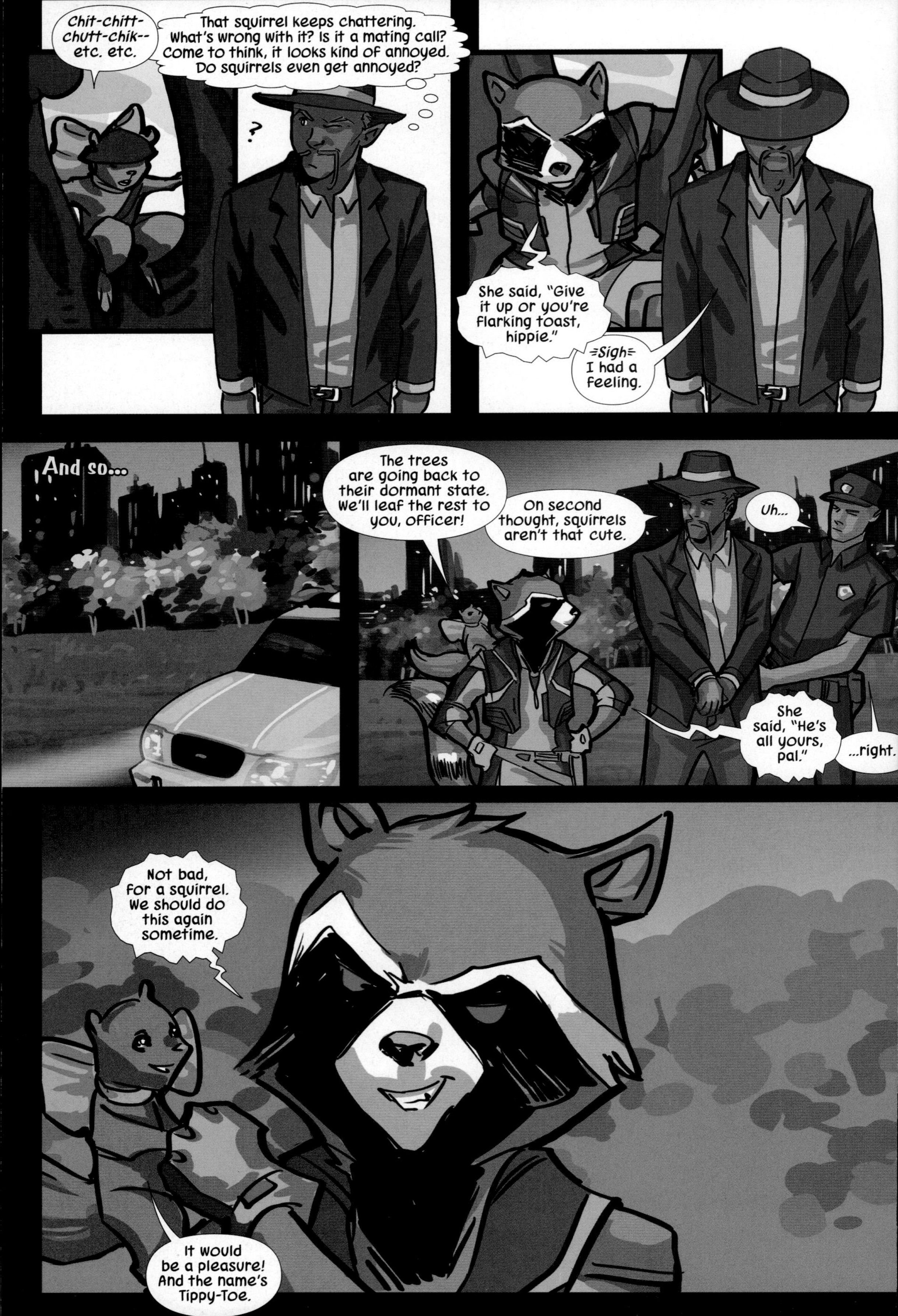
Chit-chitt-chutt-chik-- etc. etc.
That squirrel keeps chattering. What's wrong with it? Is it a mating call? Come to think, it looks kind of annoyed. Do squirrels even get annoyed?
?
She said, "Give it up or you're flarking toast, hippie."
=Sigh= I had a feeling.
And so...
The trees are going back to their dormant state. We'll leaf the rest to you, officer!
On second thought, squirrels aren't that cute.
Uh...
She said, "He's all yours, pal."
...right.
Not bad, for a squirrel. We should do this again sometime.
It would be a pleasure! And the name's Tippy-Toe.

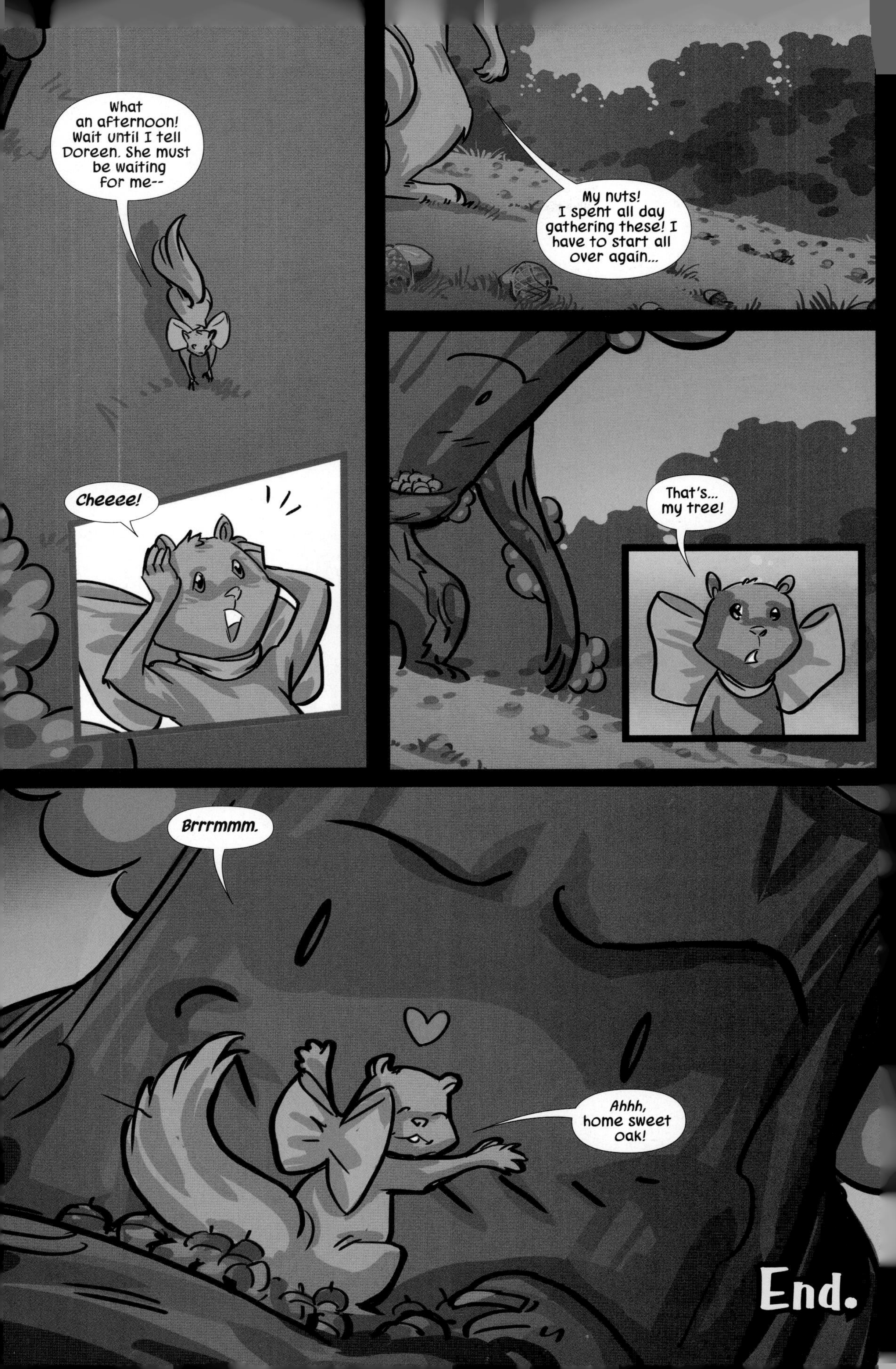
What an afternoon! Wait until I tell Doreen. She must be waiting for me--
My nuts! I spent all day gathering these! I have to start all over again...
Cheeee!
That's... my tree!
Brrrmmm.
Ahhh, home sweet oak!
End.

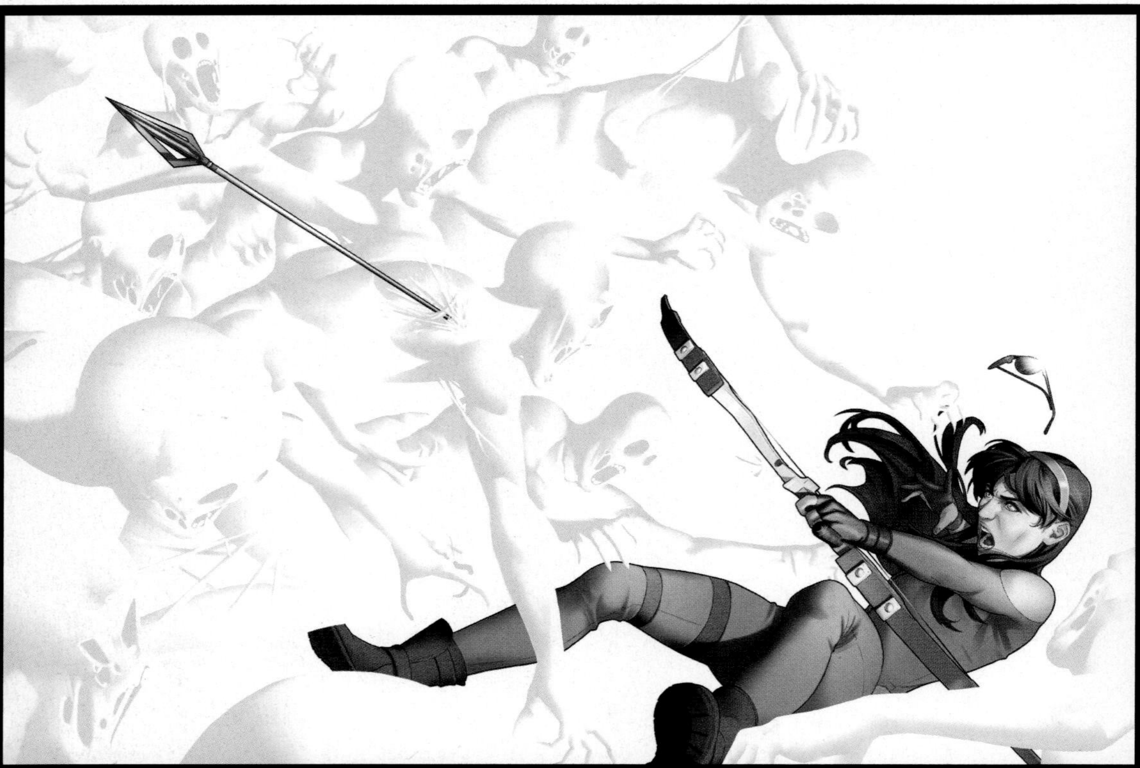

A YEAR OF MARVELS

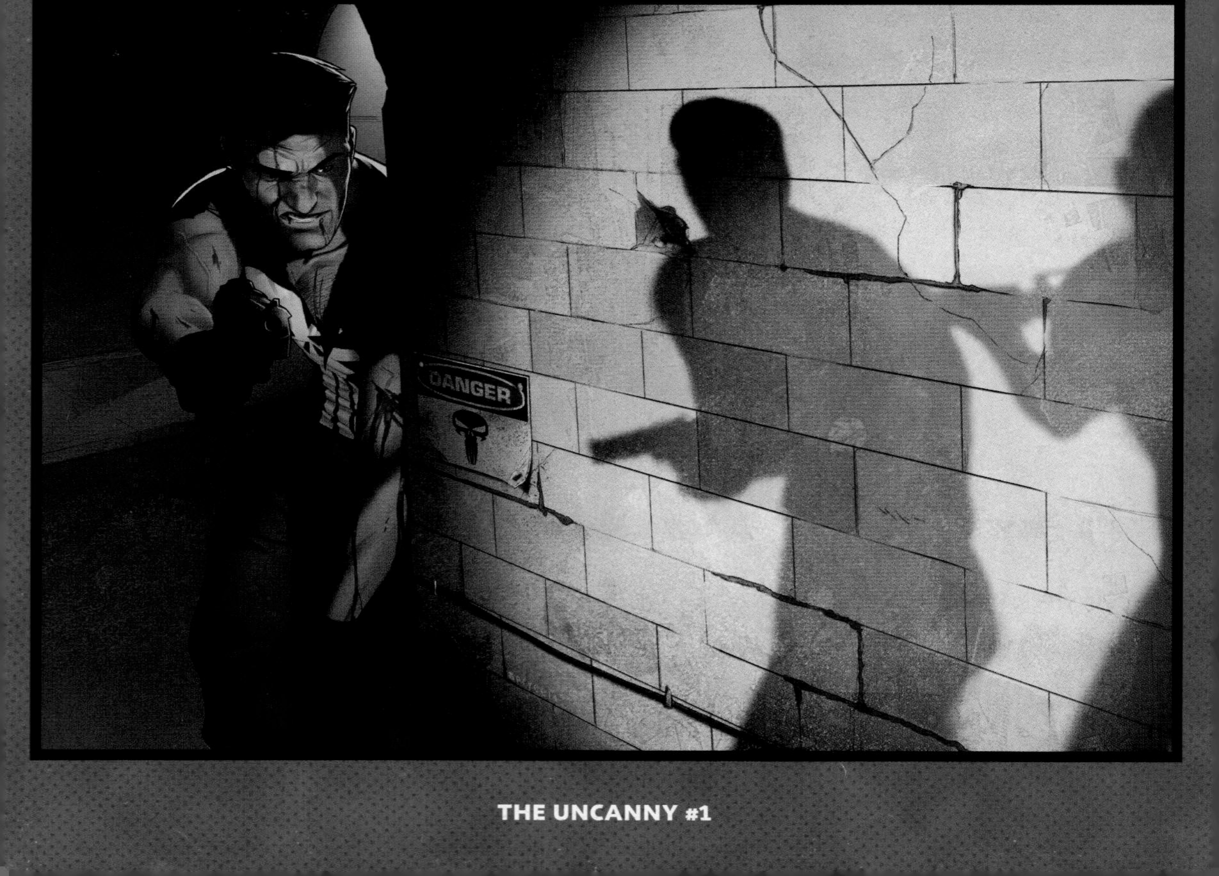
DANGER

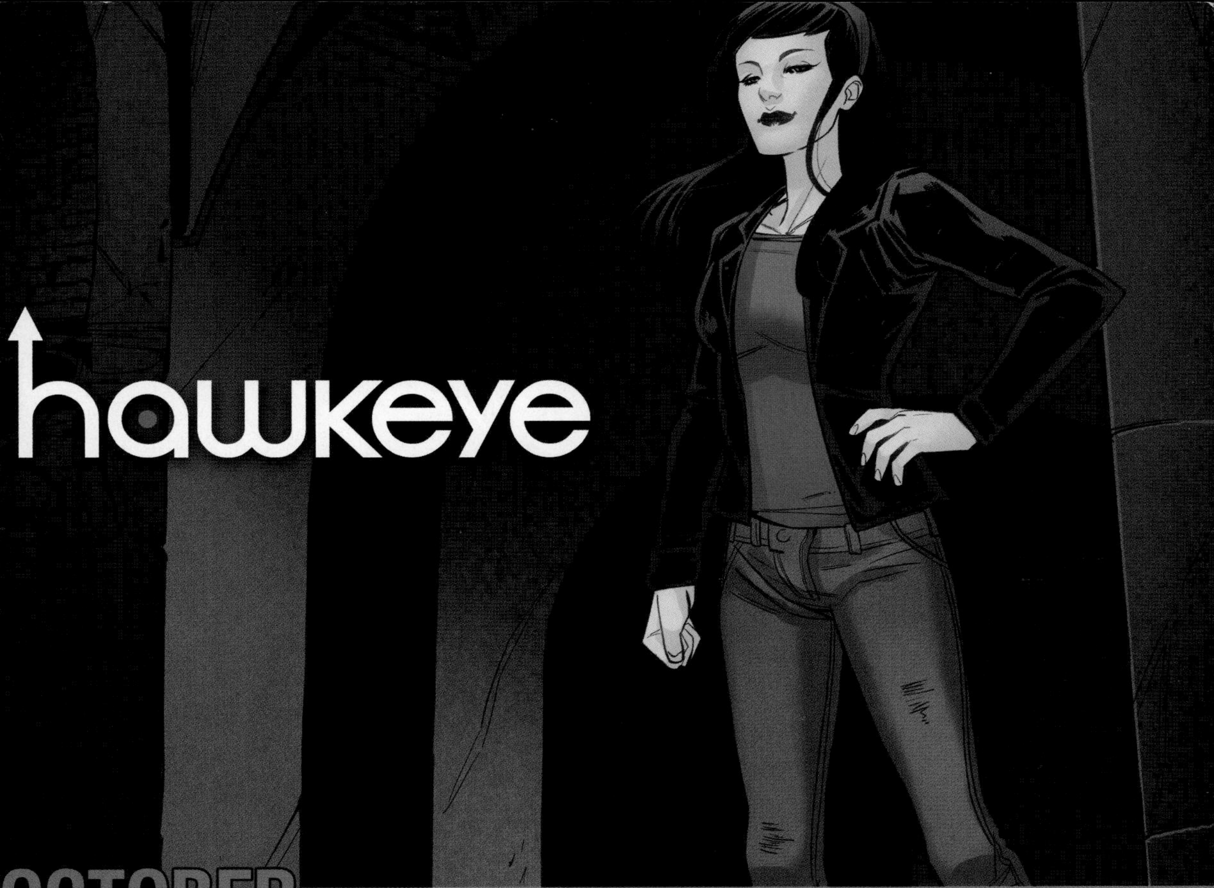
hawkeye

OCTOBER

SUNDAY	MONDAY	TUESDAY	WEDNESDAY	THURSDAY	FRIDAY	SATURDAY
1	2	3	4	5	6	7
8	9	10	11	12	13	14
15	16	17	18	19	20	21
22	23	24	25	26	27	28
29	30	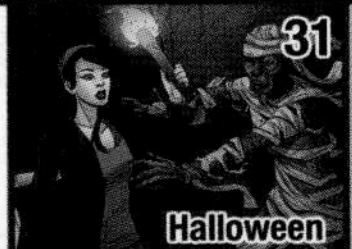 31 Halloween				

JEREMY WHITLEY WRITER
LAURA BRAGA ARTIST
GEOFFO LAYOUT ARTIST
RACHELLE ROSENBERG COLOR ARTIST
VC'S TRAVIS LANHAM LETTERING

JAMAL CAMPBELL COVER
ANNIE CHENG & TIM SMITH 3 PRODUCTION TEAM
CARLOS LAO PRODUCTION DESIGN
CHRISTINA HARRINGTON EDITOR
JORDAN D. WHITE & NICK LOWE SUPERVISING EDITORS

EDITOR IN CHIEF AXEL ALONSO CHIEF CREATIVE OFFICER JOE QUESADA PUBLISHER DAN BUCKLEY EXECUTIVE PRODUCER ALAN FINE

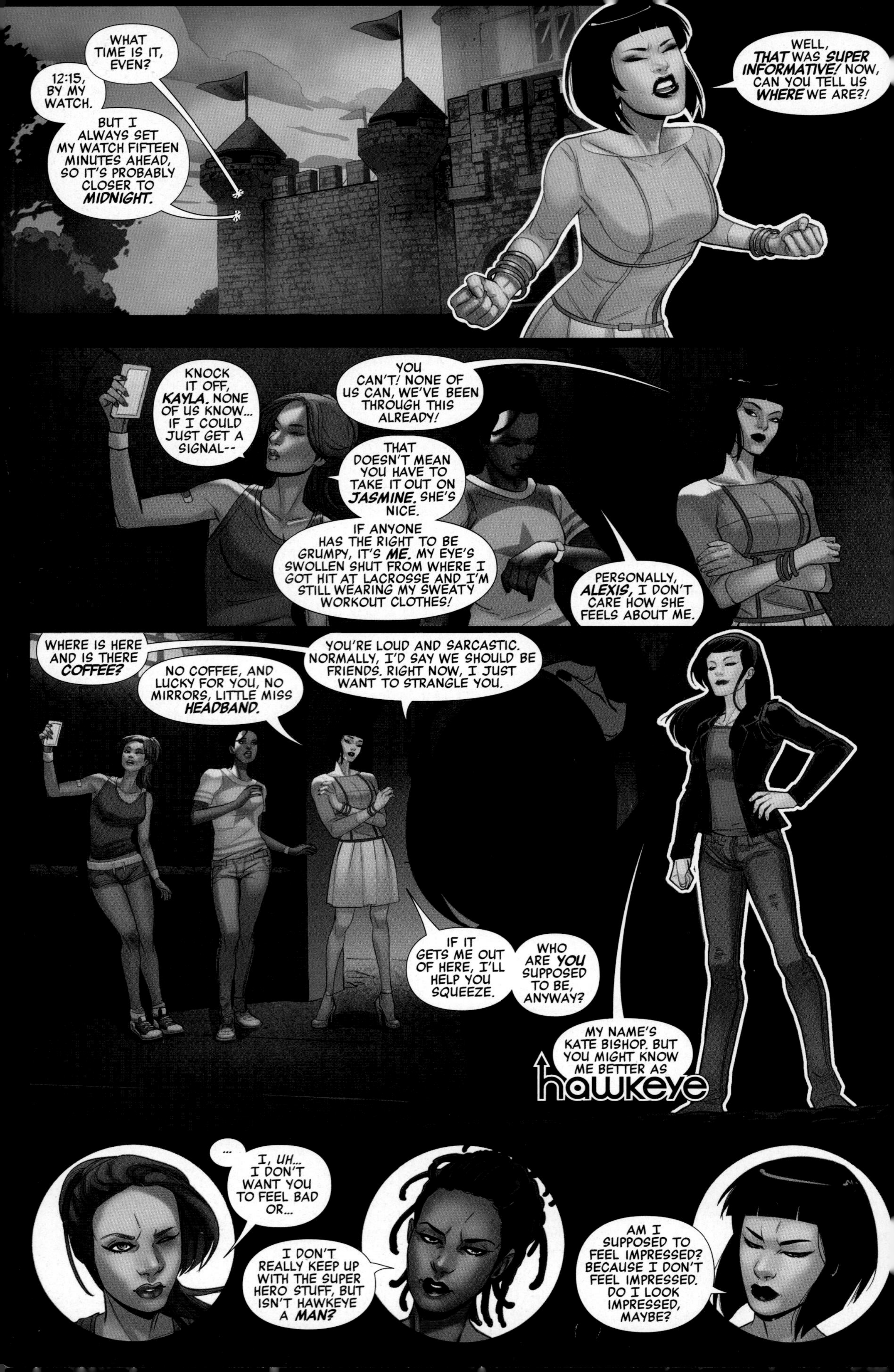
WHAT TIME IS IT, EVEN?
12:15, BY MY WATCH.
BUT I ALWAYS SET MY WATCH FIFTEEN MINUTES AHEAD, SO IT'S PROBABLY CLOSER TO MIDNIGHT.
WELL, THAT WAS SUPER INFORMATIVE! NOW, CAN YOU TELL US WHERE WE ARE?!
KNOCK IT OFF, KAYLA. NONE OF US KNOW... IF I COULD JUST GET A SIGNAL--
YOU CAN'T! NONE OF US CAN, WE'VE BEEN THROUGH THIS ALREADY!
THAT DOESN'T MEAN YOU HAVE TO TAKE IT OUT ON JASMINE. SHE'S NICE.
IF ANYONE HAS THE RIGHT TO BE GRUMPY, IT'S ME. MY EYE'S SWOLLEN SHUT FROM WHERE I GOT HIT AT LACROSSE AND I'M STILL WEARING MY SWEATY WORKOUT CLOTHES!
PERSONALLY, ALEXIS, I DON'T CARE HOW SHE FEELS ABOUT ME.
WHERE IS HERE AND IS THERE COFFEE?
NO COFFEE, AND LUCKY FOR YOU, NO MIRRORS, LITTLE MISS HEADBAND.
YOU'RE LOUD AND SARCASTIC. NORMALLY, I'D SAY WE SHOULD BE FRIENDS. RIGHT NOW, I JUST WANT TO STRANGLE YOU.
IF IT GETS ME OUT OF HERE, I'LL HELP YOU SQUEEZE.
WHO ARE YOU SUPPOSED TO BE, ANYWAY?
MY NAME'S KATE BISHOP. BUT YOU MIGHT KNOW ME BETTER AS
hawkeye
...
I, UH... I DON'T WANT YOU TO FEEL BAD OR...
I DON'T REALLY KEEP UP WITH THE SUPER HERO STUFF, BUT ISN'T HAWKEYE A MAN?
AM I SUPPOSED TO FEEL IMPRESSED? BECAUSE I DON'T FEEL IMPRESSED. DO I LOOK IMPRESSED, MAYBE?

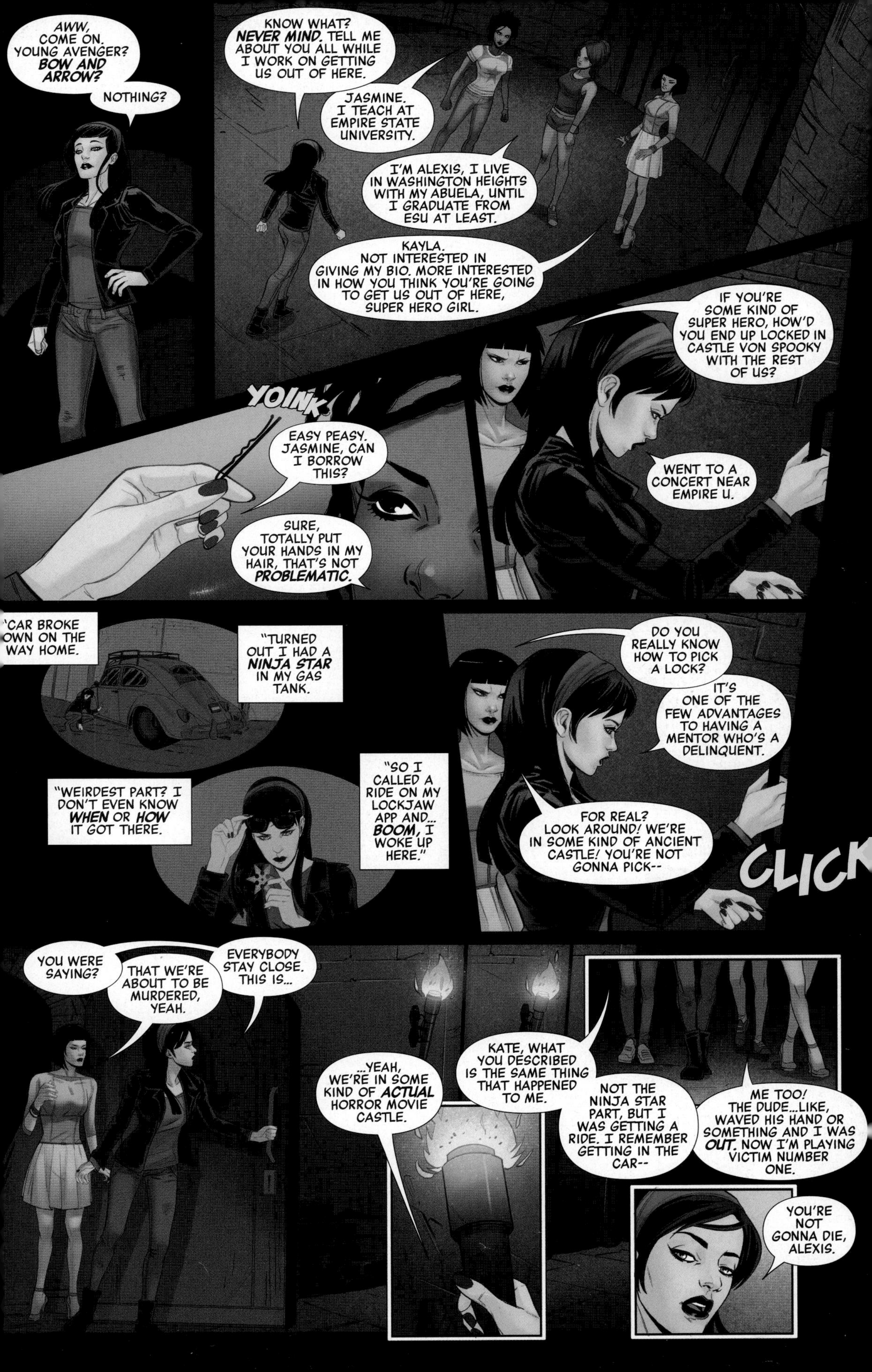
AWW, COME ON. YOUNG AVENGER? BOW AND ARROW?
NOTHING?
KNOW WHAT? NEVER MIND. TELL ME ABOUT YOU ALL WHILE I WORK ON GETTING US OUT OF HERE.
JASMINE. I TEACH AT EMPIRE STATE UNIVERSITY.
I'M ALEXIS, I LIVE IN WASHINGTON HEIGHTS WITH MY ABUELA, UNTIL I GRADUATE FROM ESU AT LEAST.
KAYLA. NOT INTERESTED IN GIVING MY BIO. MORE INTERESTED IN HOW YOU THINK YOU'RE GOING TO GET US OUT OF HERE, SUPER HERO GIRL.
YOINK
EASY PEASY. JASMINE, CAN I BORROW THIS?
SURE, TOTALLY PUT YOUR HANDS IN MY HAIR, THAT'S NOT PROBLEMATIC.
IF YOU'RE SOME KIND OF SUPER HERO, HOW'D YOU END UP LOCKED IN CASTLE VON SPOOKY WITH THE REST OF US?
WENT TO A CONCERT NEAR EMPIRE U.
"CAR BROKE DOWN ON THE WAY HOME.
"TURNED OUT I HAD A NINJA STAR IN MY GAS TANK.
"WEIRDEST PART? I DON'T EVEN KNOW WHEN OR HOW IT GOT THERE.
"SO I CALLED A RIDE ON MY LOCKJAW APP AND... BOOM, I WOKE UP HERE."
DO YOU REALLY KNOW HOW TO PICK A LOCK?
IT'S ONE OF THE FEW ADVANTAGES TO HAVING A MENTOR WHO'S A DELINQUENT.
FOR REAL? LOOK AROUND! WE'RE IN SOME KIND OF ANCIENT CASTLE! YOU'RE NOT GONNA PICK--
CLICK
YOU WERE SAYING?
THAT WE'RE ABOUT TO BE MURDERED, YEAH.
EVERYBODY STAY CLOSE. THIS IS...
...YEAH, WE'RE IN SOME KIND OF ACTUAL HORROR MOVIE CASTLE.
KATE, WHAT YOU DESCRIBED IS THE SAME THING THAT HAPPENED TO ME.
NOT THE NINJA STAR PART, BUT I WAS GETTING A RIDE. I REMEMBER GETTING IN THE CAR--
ME TOO! THE DUDE...LIKE, WAVED HIS HAND OR SOMETHING AND I WAS OUT. NOW I'M PLAYING VICTIM NUMBER ONE.
YOU'RE NOT GONNA DIE, ALEXIS.

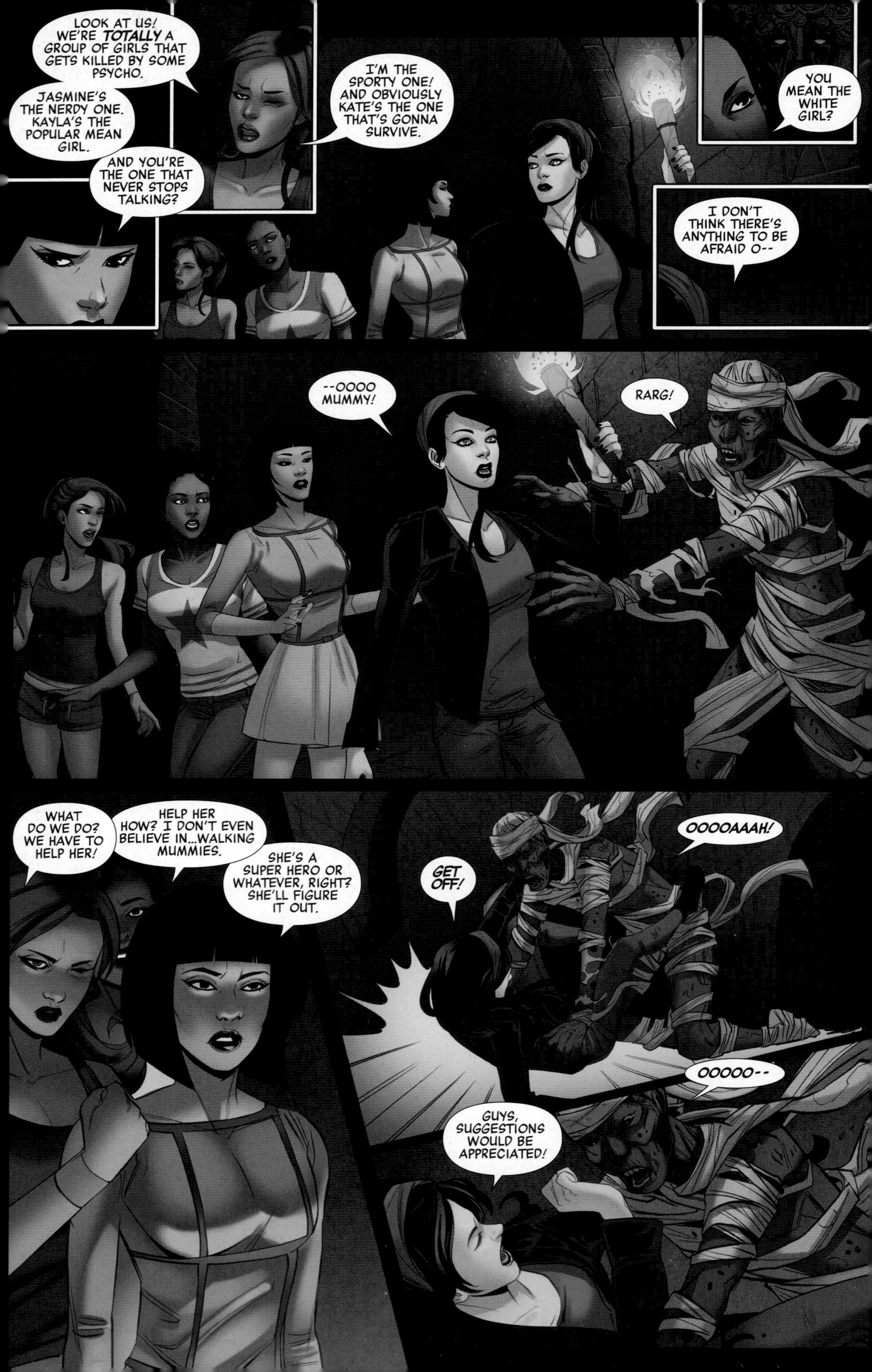
LOOK AT US! WE'RE TOTALLY A GROUP OF GIRLS THAT GETS KILLED BY SOME PSYCHO.
JASMINE'S THE NERDY ONE. KAYLA'S THE POPULAR MEAN GIRL.
I'M THE SPORTY ONE! AND OBVIOUSLY KATE'S THE ONE THAT'S GONNA SURVIVE.
AND YOU'RE THE ONE THAT NEVER STOPS TALKING?
YOU MEAN THE WHITE GIRL?
I DON'T THINK THERE'S ANYTHING TO BE AFRAID O--
--OOOO MUMMY!
RARG!
WHAT DO WE DO? WE HAVE TO HELP HER!
HELP HER HOW? I DON'T EVEN BELIEVE IN...WALKING MUMMIES.
SHE'S A SUPER HERO OR WHATEVER, RIGHT? SHE'LL FIGURE IT OUT.
GET OFF!
OOOOAAAH!
OOOOO--
GUYS, SUGGESTIONS WOULD BE APPRECIATED!

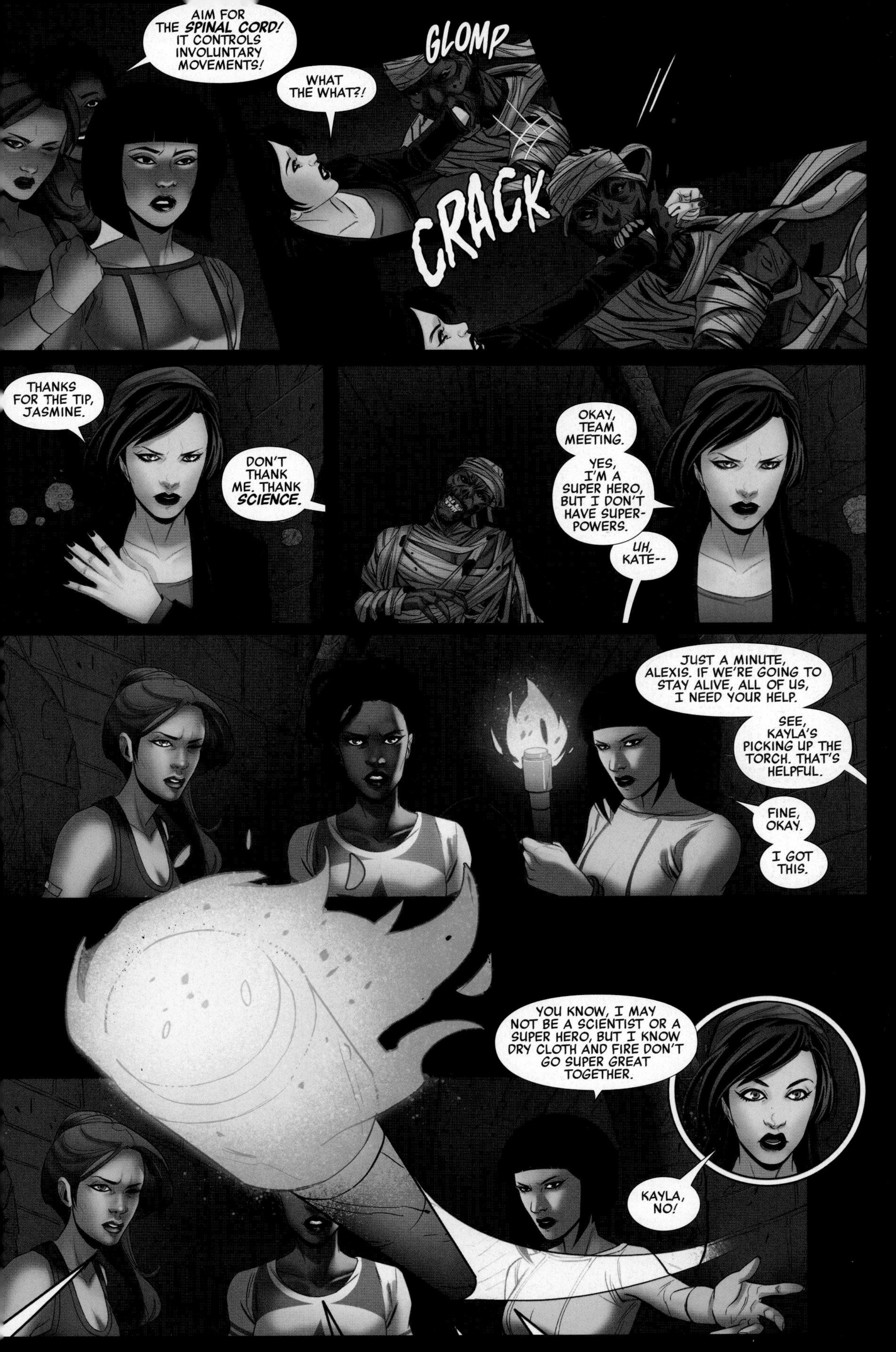
AIM FOR THE SPINAL CORD! IT CONTROLS INVOLUNTARY MOVEMENTS!
GLOMP
WHAT THE WHAT?!
CRACK
THANKS FOR THE TIP, JASMINE.
DON'T THANK ME. THANK SCIENCE.
OKAY, TEAM MEETING.
YES, I'M A SUPER HERO, BUT I DON'T HAVE SUPER-POWERS.
UH, KATE--
JUST A MINUTE, ALEXIS. IF WE'RE GOING TO STAY ALIVE, ALL OF US, I NEED YOUR HELP.
SEE, KAYLA'S PICKING UP THE TORCH. THAT'S HELPFUL.
FINE, OKAY.
I GOT THIS.
YOU KNOW, I MAY NOT BE A SCIENTIST OR A SUPER HERO, BUT I KNOW DRY CLOTH AND FIRE DON'T GO SUPER GREAT TOGETHER.
KAYLA, NO!

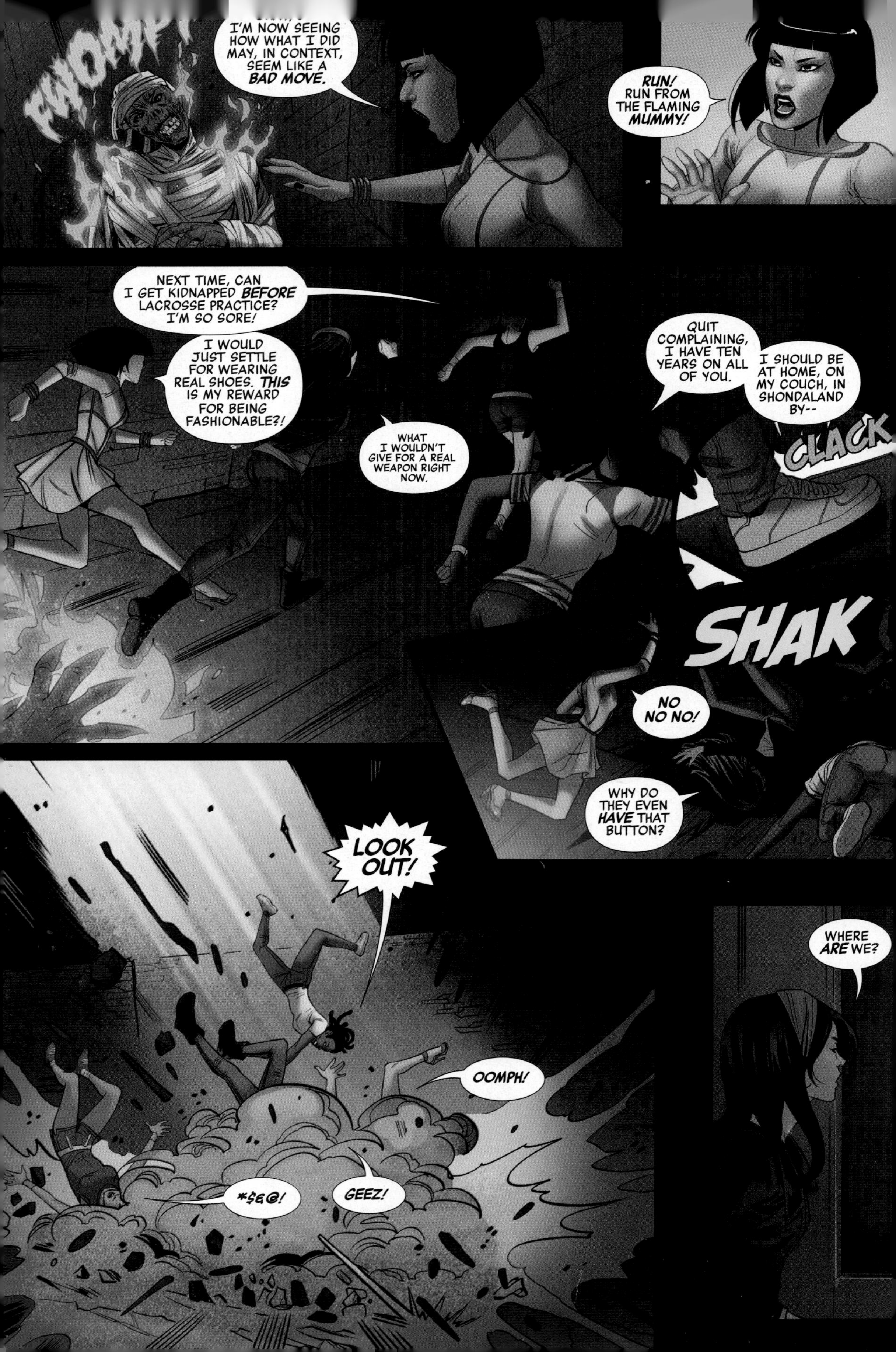

FWOMP
I'M NOW SEEING HOW WHAT I DID MAY, IN CONTEXT, SEEM LIKE A BAD MOVE.
RUN! RUN FROM THE FLAMING MUMMY!
NEXT TIME, CAN I GET KIDNAPPED BEFORE LACROSSE PRACTICE? I'M SO SORE!
I WOULD JUST SETTLE FOR WEARING REAL SHOES. THIS IS MY REWARD FOR BEING FASHIONABLE?!
WHAT I WOULDN'T GIVE FOR A REAL WEAPON RIGHT NOW.
QUIT COMPLAINING, I HAVE TEN YEARS ON ALL OF YOU.
I SHOULD BE AT HOME, ON MY COUCH, IN SHONDALAND BY--
CLACK
SHAK
NO NO NO!
WHY DO THEY EVEN HAVE THAT BUTTON?
LOOK OUT!
OOMPH!
*$&@!
GEEZ!
WHERE ARE WE?

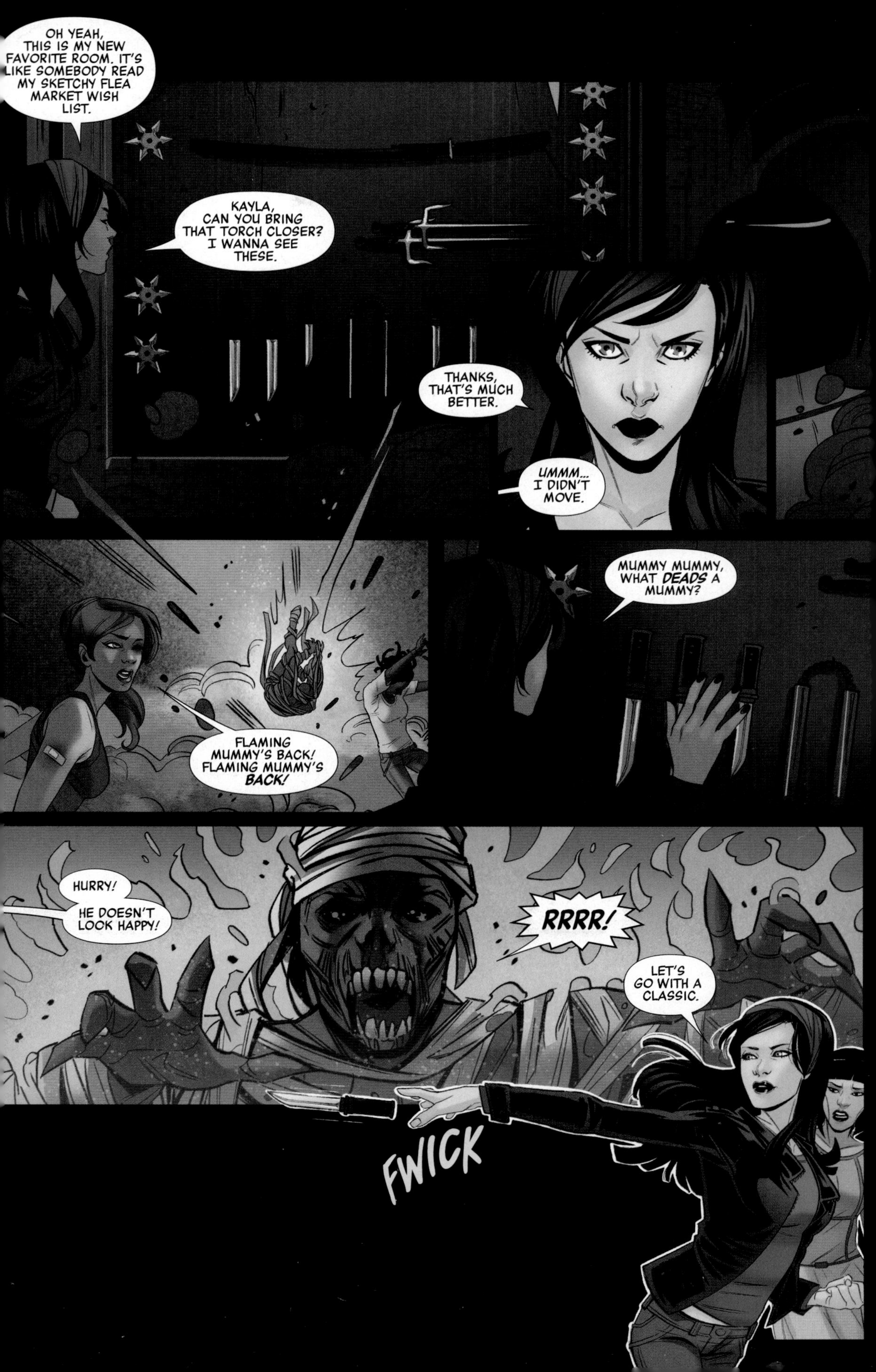
OH YEAH, THIS IS MY NEW FAVORITE ROOM. IT'S LIKE SOMEBODY READ MY SKETCHY FLEA MARKET WISH LIST.
KAYLA, CAN YOU BRING THAT TORCH CLOSER? I WANNA SEE THESE.
THANKS, THAT'S MUCH BETTER.
UMMM... I DIDN'T MOVE.
FLAMING MUMMY'S BACK! FLAMING MUMMY'S *BACK!*
MUMMY MUMMY, WHAT *DEADS* A MUMMY?
HURRY!
HE DOESN'T LOOK HAPPY!
RRRR!
LET'S GO WITH A CLASSIC.
FWICK

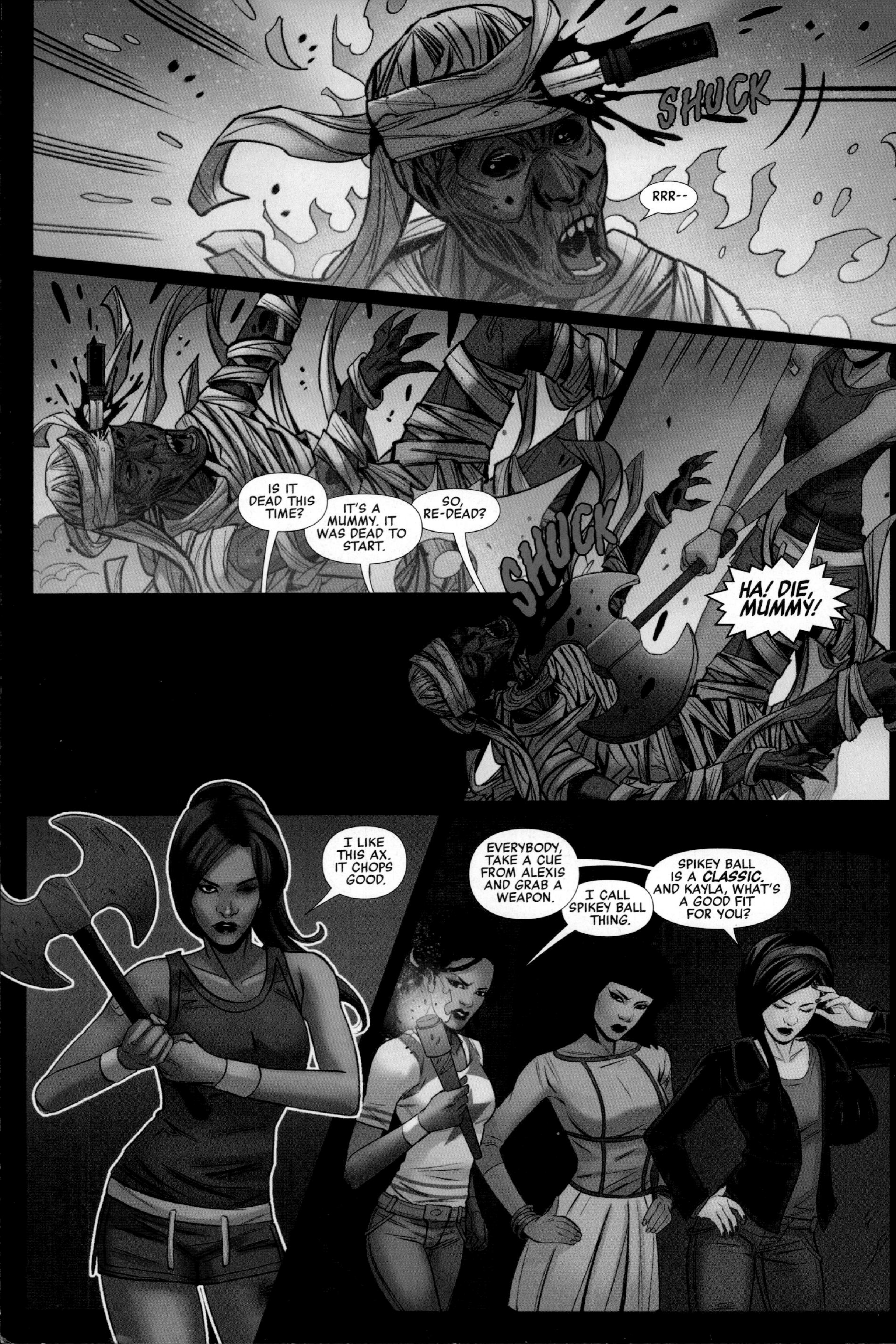
SHUCK
RRR--
IS IT DEAD THIS TIME?
IT'S A MUMMY. IT WAS DEAD TO START.
SO, RE-DEAD?
SHUCK
HA! DIE, MUMMY!
I LIKE THIS AX. IT CHOPS GOOD.
EVERYBODY, TAKE A CUE FROM ALEXIS AND GRAB A WEAPON.
I CALL SPIKEY BALL THING.
SPIKEY BALL IS A CLASSIC. AND KAYLA, WHAT'S A GOOD FIT FOR YOU?

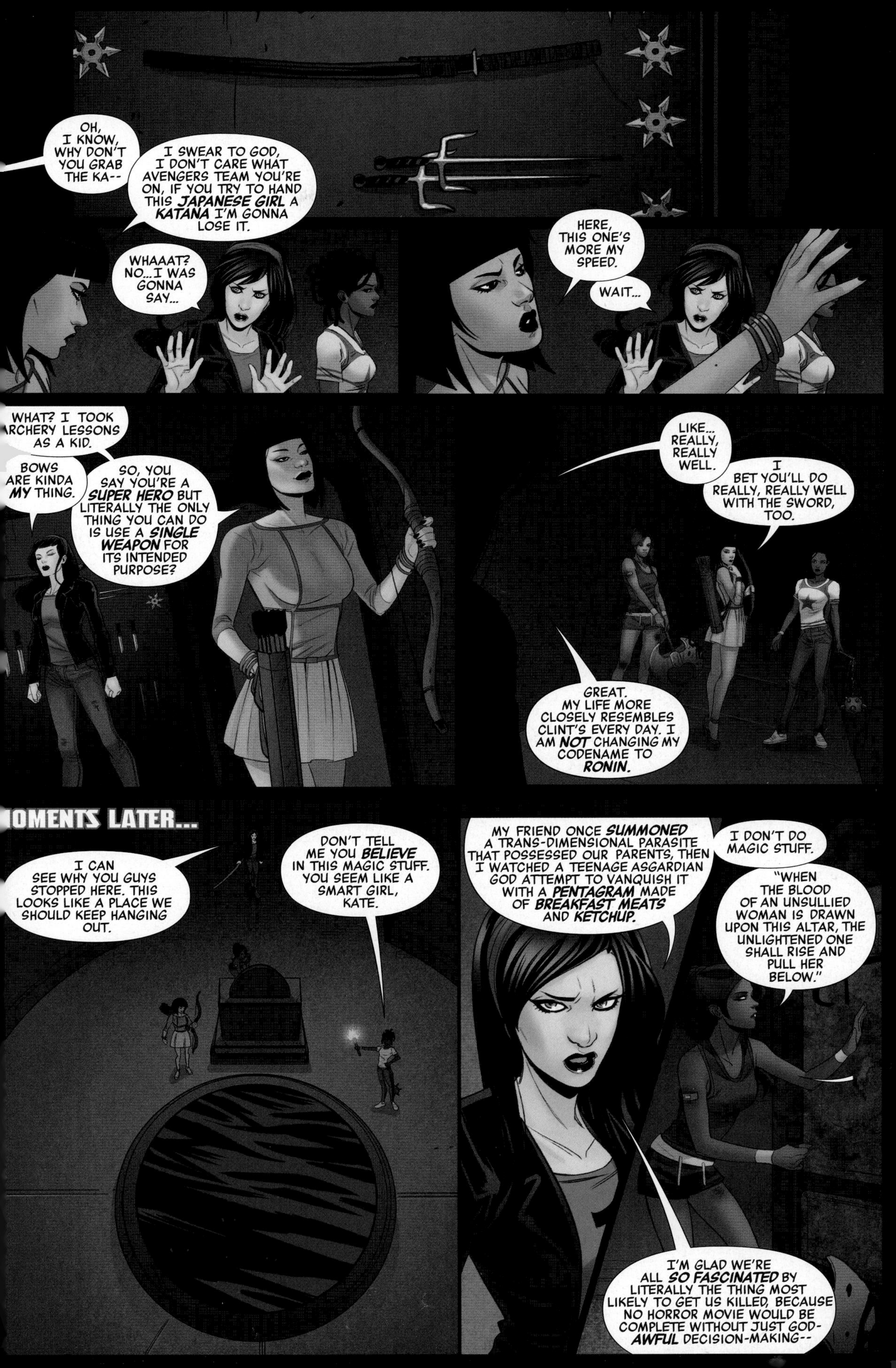

OH, I KNOW, WHY DON'T YOU GRAB THE KA--
I SWEAR TO GOD, I DON'T CARE WHAT AVENGERS TEAM YOU'RE ON, IF YOU TRY TO HAND THIS JAPANESE GIRL A KATANA I'M GONNA LOSE IT.
WHAAAT? NO...I WAS GONNA SAY...
HERE, THIS ONE'S MORE MY SPEED.
WAIT...
WHAT? I TOOK ARCHERY LESSONS AS A KID.
BOWS ARE KINDA MY THING.
SO, YOU SAY YOU'RE A SUPER HERO BUT LITERALLY THE ONLY THING YOU CAN DO IS USE A SINGLE WEAPON FOR ITS INTENDED PURPOSE?
LIKE... REALLY, REALLY WELL.
I BET YOU'LL DO REALLY, REALLY WELL WITH THE SWORD, TOO.
GREAT. MY LIFE MORE CLOSELY RESEMBLES CLINT'S EVERY DAY. I AM NOT CHANGING MY CODENAME TO RONIN.
MOMENTS LATER...
I CAN SEE WHY YOU GUYS STOPPED HERE. THIS LOOKS LIKE A PLACE WE SHOULD KEEP HANGING OUT.
DON'T TELL ME YOU BELIEVE IN THIS MAGIC STUFF. YOU SEEM LIKE A SMART GIRL, KATE.
MY FRIEND ONCE SUMMONED A TRANS-DIMENSIONAL PARASITE THAT POSSESSED OUR PARENTS, THEN I WATCHED A TEENAGE ASGARDIAN GOD ATTEMPT TO VANQUISH IT WITH A PENTAGRAM MADE OF BREAKFAST MEATS AND KETCHUP.
I DON'T DO MAGIC STUFF.
"WHEN THE BLOOD OF AN UNSULLIED WOMAN IS DRAWN UPON THIS ALTAR, THE UNLIGHTENED ONE SHALL RISE AND PULL HER BELOW."
I'M GLAD WE'RE ALL SO FASCINATED BY LITERALLY THE THING MOST LIKELY TO GET US KILLED, BECAUSE NO HORROR MOVIE WOULD BE COMPLETE WITHOUT JUST GOD-AWFUL DECISION-MAKING--

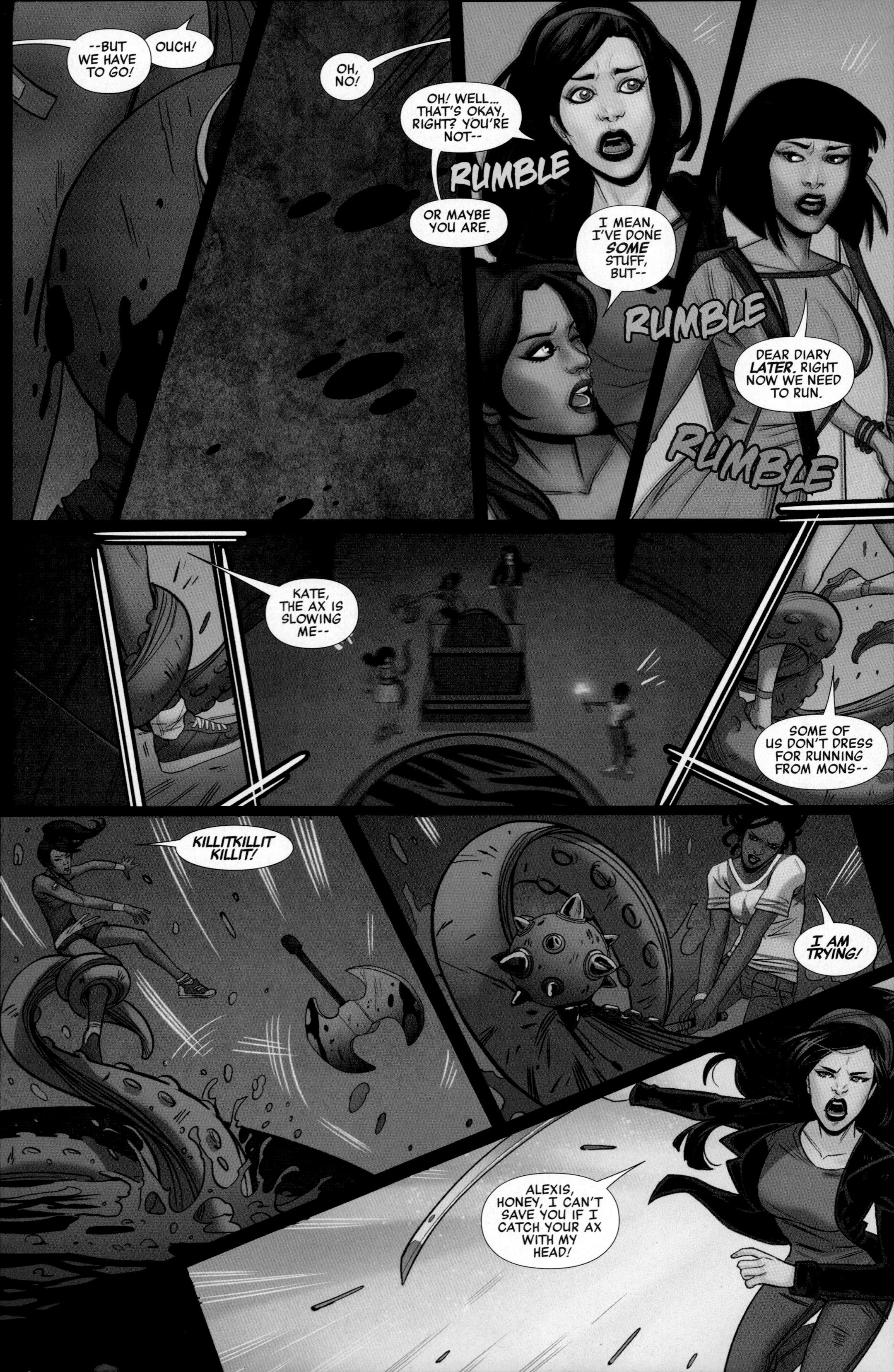
--BUT WE HAVE TO GO!
OUCH!
OH, NO!
OH! WELL... THAT'S OKAY, RIGHT? YOU'RE NOT--
RUMBLE
OR MAYBE YOU ARE.
I MEAN, I'VE DONE SOME STUFF, BUT--
RUMBLE
DEAR DIARY LATER. RIGHT NOW WE NEED TO RUN.
RUMBLE
KATE, THE AX IS SLOWING ME--
SOME OF US DON'T DRESS FOR RUNNING FROM MONS--
KILLITKILLIT KILLIT!
I AM TRYING!
ALEXIS, HONEY, I CAN'T SAVE YOU IF I CATCH YOUR AX WITH MY HEAD!

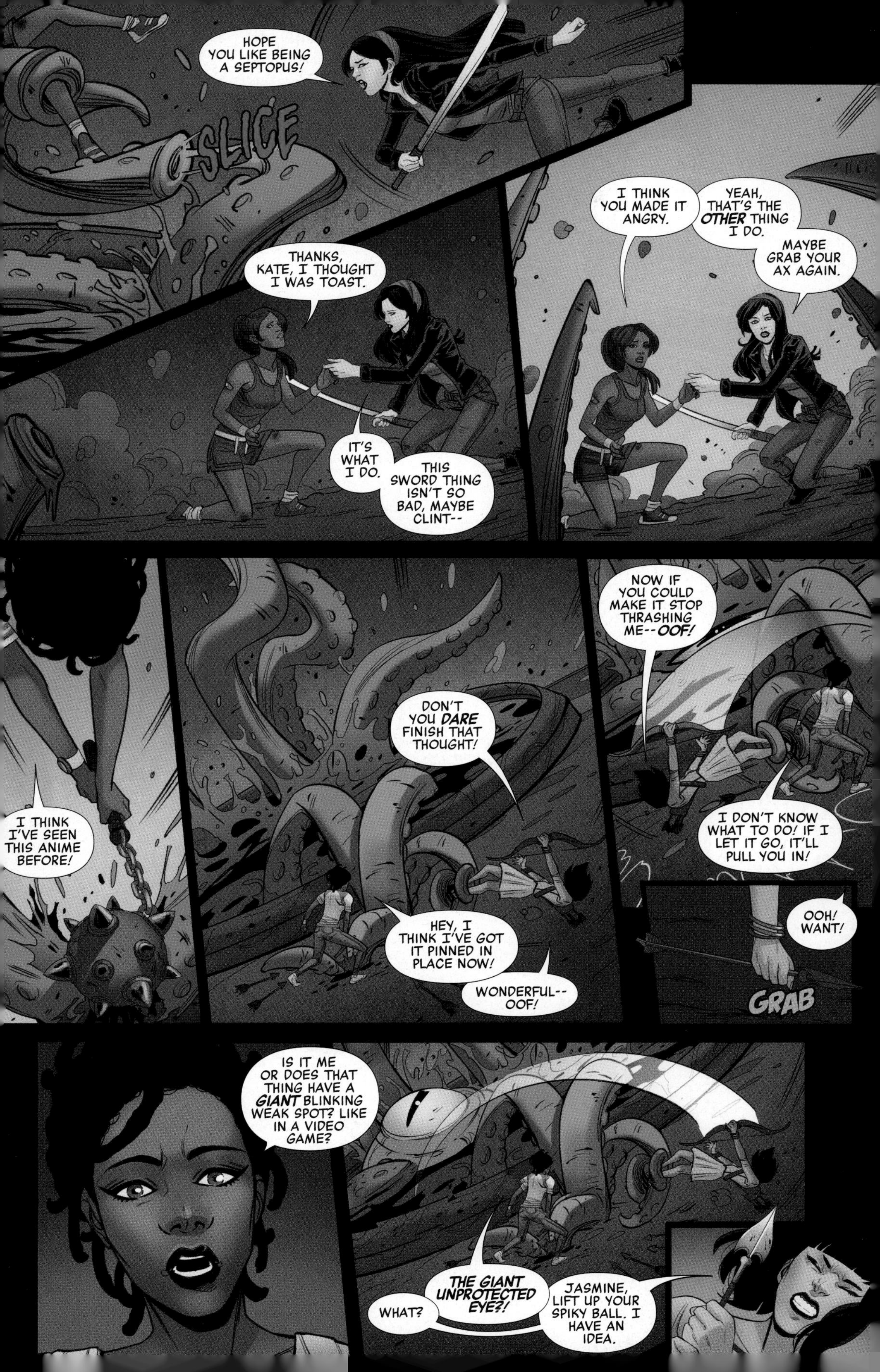
HOPE YOU LIKE BEING A SEPTOPUS!
SLICE
THANKS, KATE, I THOUGHT I WAS TOAST.
IT'S WHAT I DO.
THIS SWORD THING ISN'T SO BAD, MAYBE CLINT--
I THINK YOU MADE IT ANGRY.
YEAH, THAT'S THE OTHER THING I DO.
MAYBE GRAB YOUR AX AGAIN.
I THINK I'VE SEEN THIS ANIME BEFORE!
DON'T YOU DARE FINISH THAT THOUGHT!
HEY, I THINK I'VE GOT IT PINNED IN PLACE NOW!
WONDERFUL--OOF!
NOW IF YOU COULD MAKE IT STOP THRASHING ME--OOF!
I DON'T KNOW WHAT TO DO! IF I LET IT GO, IT'LL PULL YOU IN!
OOH! WANT!
GRAB
IS IT ME OR DOES THAT THING HAVE A GIANT BLINKING WEAK SPOT? LIKE IN A VIDEO GAME?
WHAT?
THE GIANT UNPROTECTED EYE?!
JASMINE, LIFT UP YOUR SPIKY BALL. I HAVE AN IDEA.

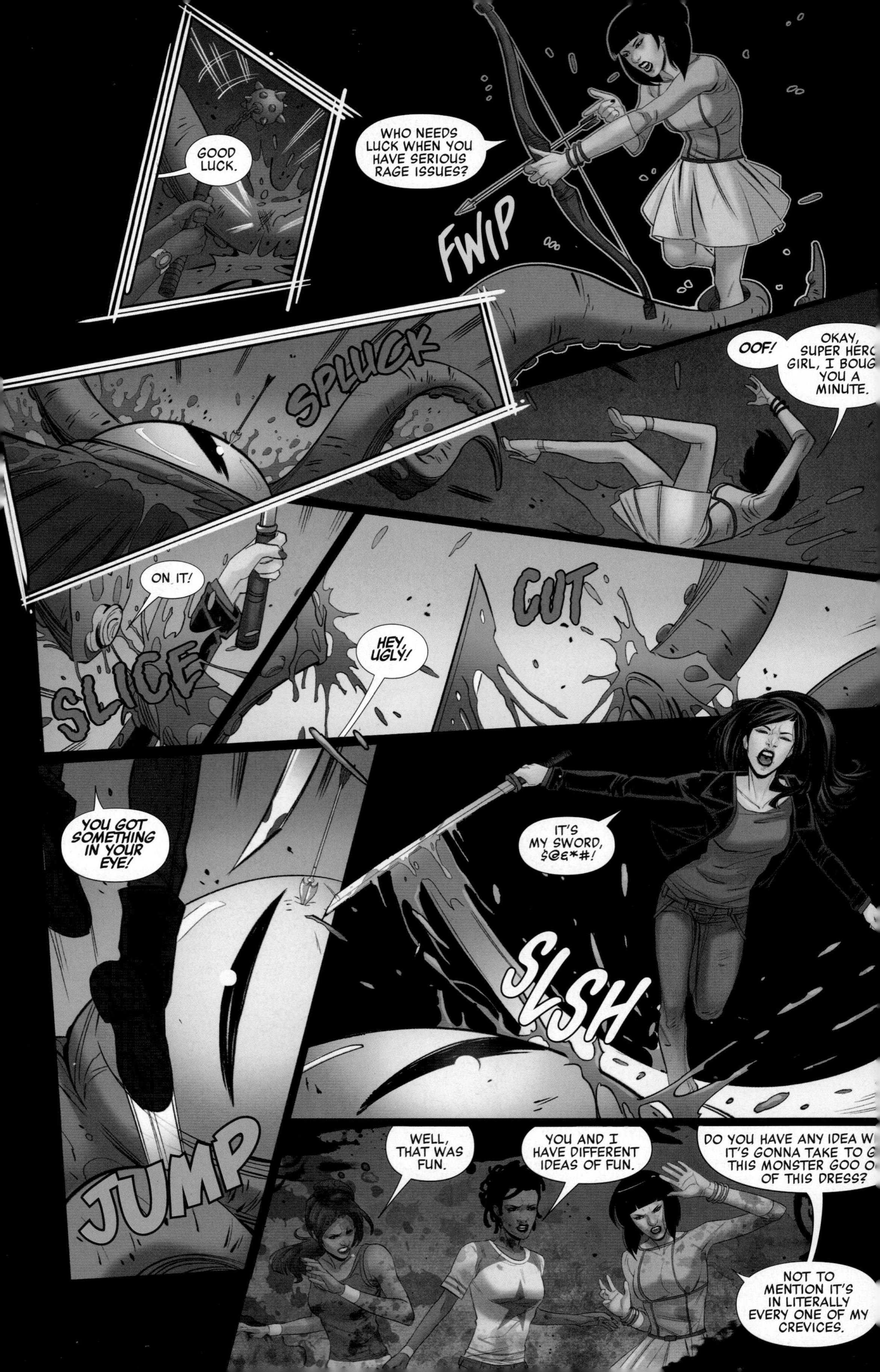

GOOD LUCK.
WHO NEEDS LUCK WHEN YOU HAVE SERIOUS RAGE ISSUES?
FWIP
SPLUCK
OOF!
OKAY, SUPER HERO GIRL, I BOUG YOU A MINUTE.
ON IT!
SLICE
CUT
HEY, UGLY!
YOU GOT SOMETHING IN YOUR EYE!
IT'S MY SWORD, $@€*#!
SLSH
JUMP
WELL, THAT WAS FUN.
YOU AND I HAVE DIFFERENT IDEAS OF FUN.
DO YOU HAVE ANY IDEA W IT'S GONNA TAKE TO G THIS MONSTER GOO O OF THIS DRESS?
NOT TO MENTION IT'S IN LITERALLY EVERY ONE OF MY CREVICES.

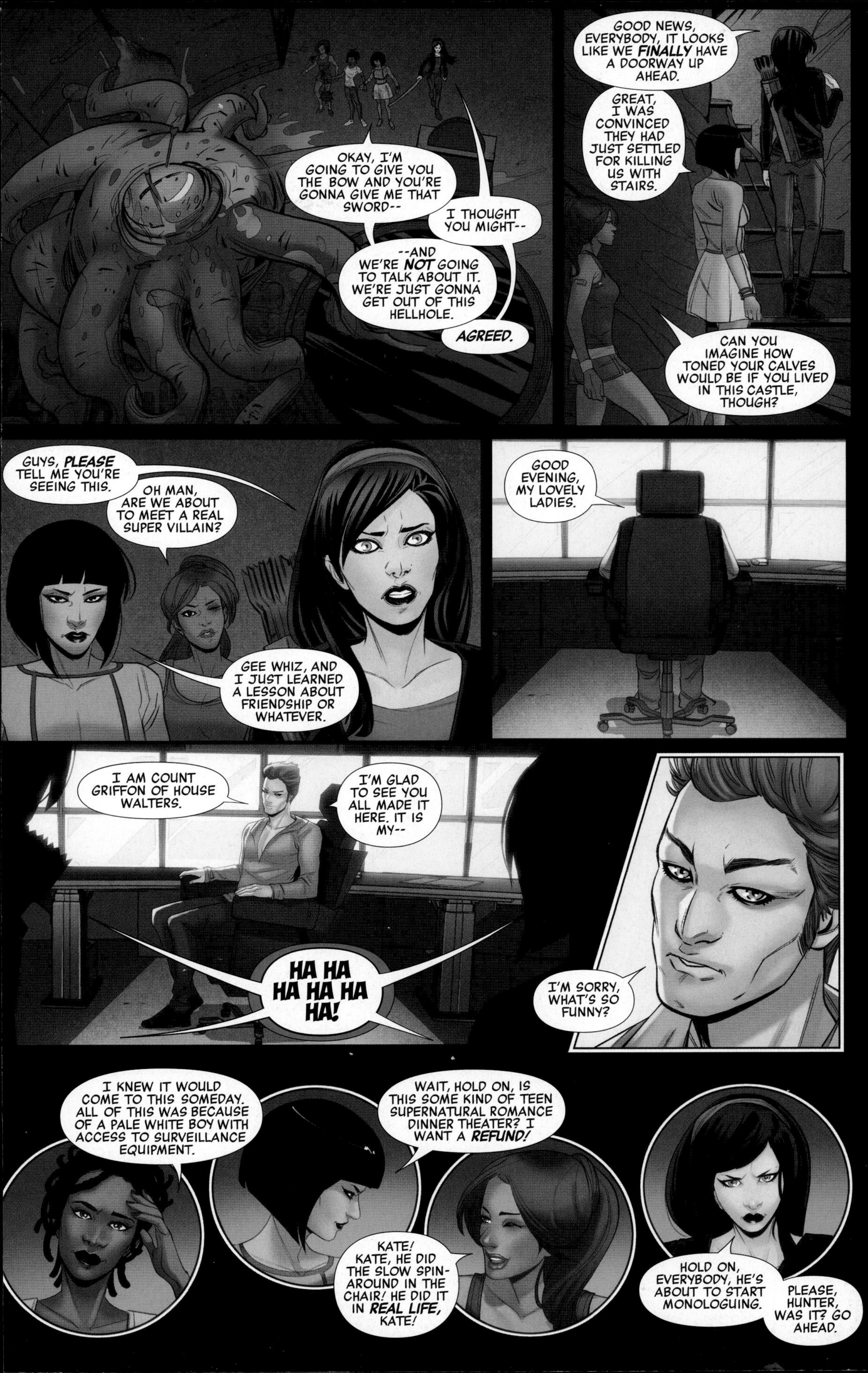
OKAY, I'M GOING TO GIVE YOU THE BOW AND YOU'RE GONNA GIVE ME THAT SWORD--
I THOUGHT YOU MIGHT--
--AND WE'RE NOT GOING TO TALK ABOUT IT. WE'RE JUST GONNA GET OUT OF THIS HELLHOLE.
AGREED.
GOOD NEWS, EVERYBODY, IT LOOKS LIKE WE FINALLY HAVE A DOORWAY UP AHEAD.
GREAT, I WAS CONVINCED THEY HAD JUST SETTLED FOR KILLING US WITH STAIRS.
CAN YOU IMAGINE HOW TONED YOUR CALVES WOULD BE IF YOU LIVED IN THIS CASTLE, THOUGH?
GUYS, PLEASE TELL ME YOU'RE SEEING THIS.
OH MAN, ARE WE ABOUT TO MEET A REAL SUPER VILLAIN?
GEE WHIZ, AND I JUST LEARNED A LESSON ABOUT FRIENDSHIP OR WHATEVER.
GOOD EVENING, MY LOVELY LADIES.
I AM COUNT GRIFFON OF HOUSE WALTERS.
I'M GLAD TO SEE YOU ALL MADE IT HERE. IT IS MY--
HA HA HA HA HA HA!
I'M SORRY, WHAT'S SO FUNNY?
I KNEW IT WOULD COME TO THIS SOMEDAY. ALL OF THIS WAS BECAUSE OF A PALE WHITE BOY WITH ACCESS TO SURVEILLANCE EQUIPMENT.
WAIT, HOLD ON, IS THIS SOME KIND OF TEEN SUPERNATURAL ROMANCE DINNER THEATER? I WANT A REFUND!
KATE! KATE, HE DID THE SLOW SPIN-AROUND IN THE CHAIR! HE DID IT IN REAL LIFE, KATE!
HOLD ON, EVERYBODY, HE'S ABOUT TO START MONOLOGUING.
PLEASE, HUNTER, WAS IT? GO AHEAD.

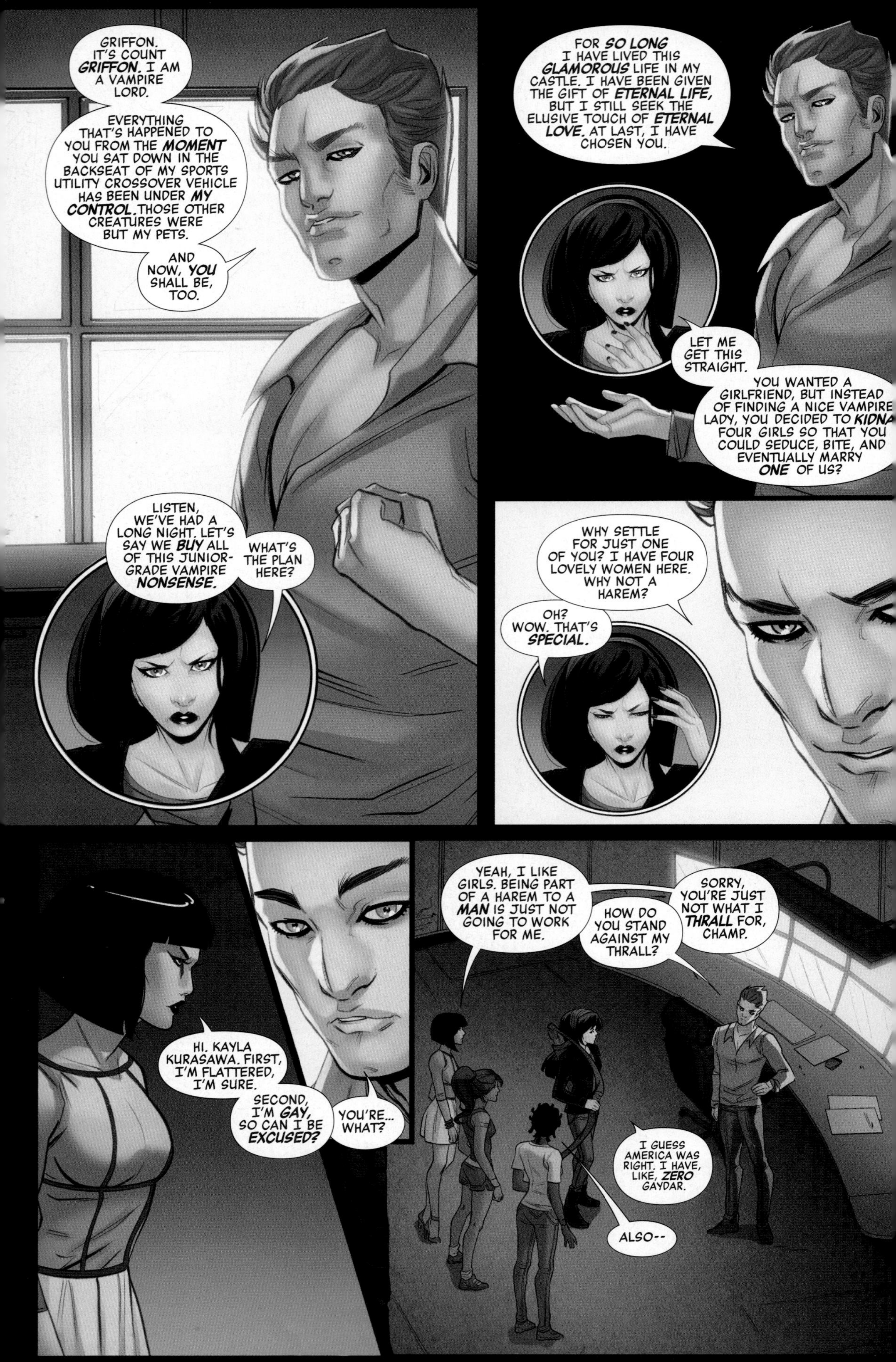
GRIFFON. IT'S COUNT GRIFFON. I AM A VAMPIRE LORD.
EVERYTHING THAT'S HAPPENED TO YOU FROM THE MOMENT YOU SAT DOWN IN THE BACKSEAT OF MY SPORTS UTILITY CROSSOVER VEHICLE HAS BEEN UNDER MY CONTROL. THOSE OTHER CREATURES WERE BUT MY PETS.
AND NOW, YOU SHALL BE, TOO.
LISTEN, WE'VE HAD A LONG NIGHT. LET'S SAY WE BUY ALL OF THIS JUNIOR-GRADE VAMPIRE NONSENSE.
WHAT'S THE PLAN HERE?
FOR SO LONG I HAVE LIVED THIS GLAMOROUS LIFE IN MY CASTLE. I HAVE BEEN GIVEN THE GIFT OF ETERNAL LIFE, BUT I STILL SEEK THE ELUSIVE TOUCH OF ETERNAL LOVE. AT LAST, I HAVE CHOSEN YOU.
LET ME GET THIS STRAIGHT.
YOU WANTED A GIRLFRIEND, BUT INSTEAD OF FINDING A NICE VAMPIRE LADY, YOU DECIDED TO KIDNA FOUR GIRLS SO THAT YOU COULD SEDUCE, BITE, AND EVENTUALLY MARRY ONE OF US?
WHY SETTLE FOR JUST ONE OF YOU? I HAVE FOUR LOVELY WOMEN HERE. WHY NOT A HAREM?
OH? WOW. THAT'S SPECIAL.
HI. KAYLA KURASAWA. FIRST, I'M FLATTERED, I'M SURE.
SECOND, I'M GAY, SO CAN I BE EXCUSED?
YOU'RE... WHAT?
YEAH, I LIKE GIRLS. BEING PART OF A HAREM TO A MAN IS JUST NOT GOING TO WORK FOR ME.
HOW DO YOU STAND AGAINST MY THRALL?
SORRY, YOU'RE JUST NOT WHAT I THRALL FOR, CHAMP.
I GUESS AMERICA WAS RIGHT. I HAVE, LIKE, ZERO GAYDAR.
ALSO--

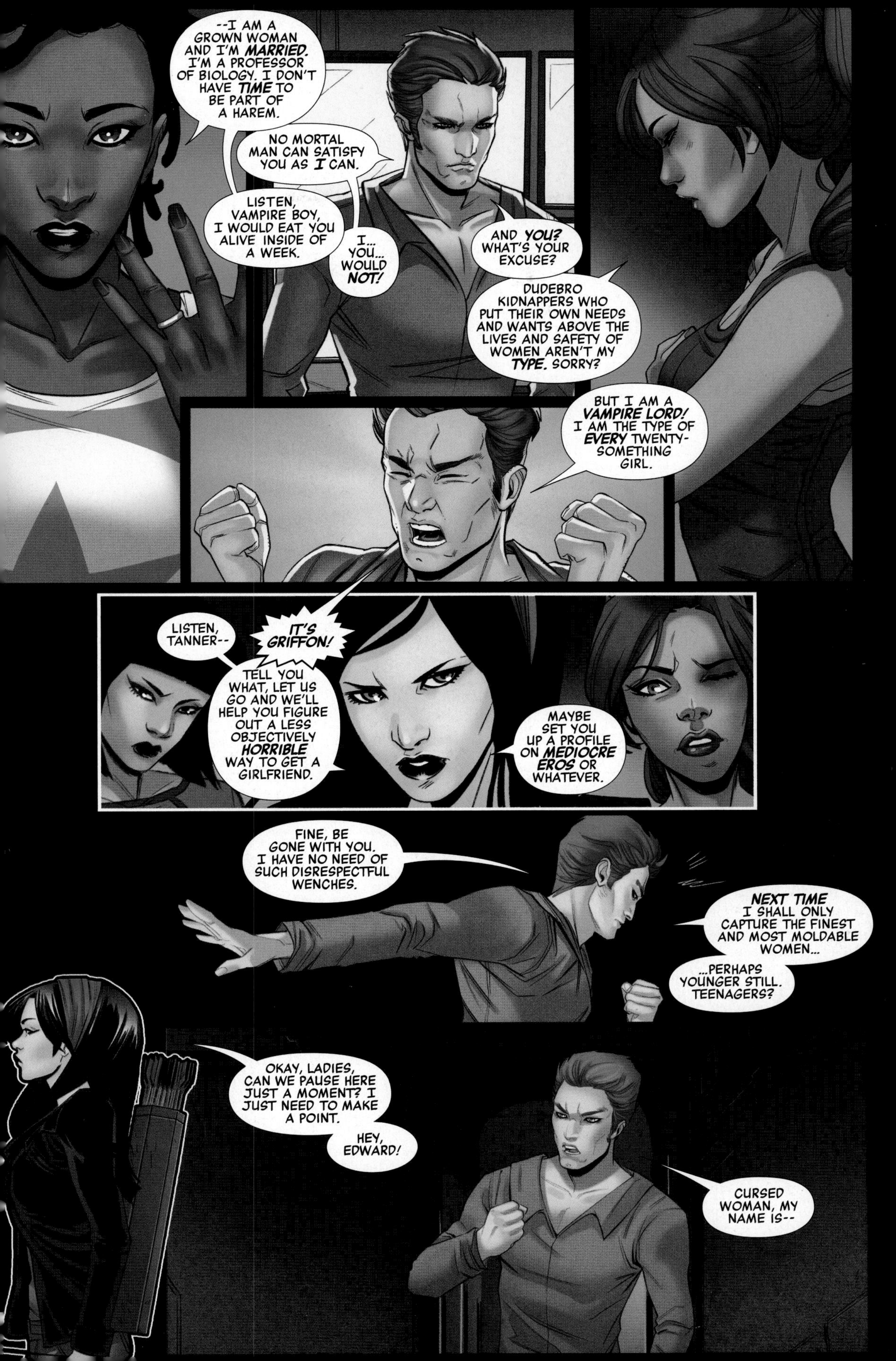
--I AM A GROWN WOMAN AND I'M MARRIED. I'M A PROFESSOR OF BIOLOGY. I DON'T HAVE TIME TO BE PART OF A HAREM.
NO MORTAL MAN CAN SATISFY YOU AS I CAN.
LISTEN, VAMPIRE BOY, I WOULD EAT YOU ALIVE INSIDE OF A WEEK.
I... YOU... WOULD NOT!
AND YOU? WHAT'S YOUR EXCUSE?
DUDEBRO KIDNAPPERS WHO PUT THEIR OWN NEEDS AND WANTS ABOVE THE LIVES AND SAFETY OF WOMEN AREN'T MY TYPE. SORRY?
BUT I AM A VAMPIRE LORD! I AM THE TYPE OF EVERY TWENTY-SOMETHING GIRL.
LISTEN, TANNER--
IT'S GRIFFON!
TELL YOU WHAT, LET US GO AND WE'LL HELP YOU FIGURE OUT A LESS OBJECTIVELY HORRIBLE WAY TO GET A GIRLFRIEND.
MAYBE SET YOU UP A PROFILE ON MEDIOCRE EROS OR WHATEVER.
FINE, BE GONE WITH YOU. I HAVE NO NEED OF SUCH DISRESPECTFUL WENCHES.
NEXT TIME I SHALL ONLY CAPTURE THE FINEST AND MOST MOLDABLE WOMEN...
...PERHAPS YOUNGER STILL. TEENAGERS?
OKAY, LADIES, CAN WE PAUSE HERE JUST A MOMENT? I JUST NEED TO MAKE A POINT.
HEY, EDWARD!
CURSED WOMAN, MY NAME IS--

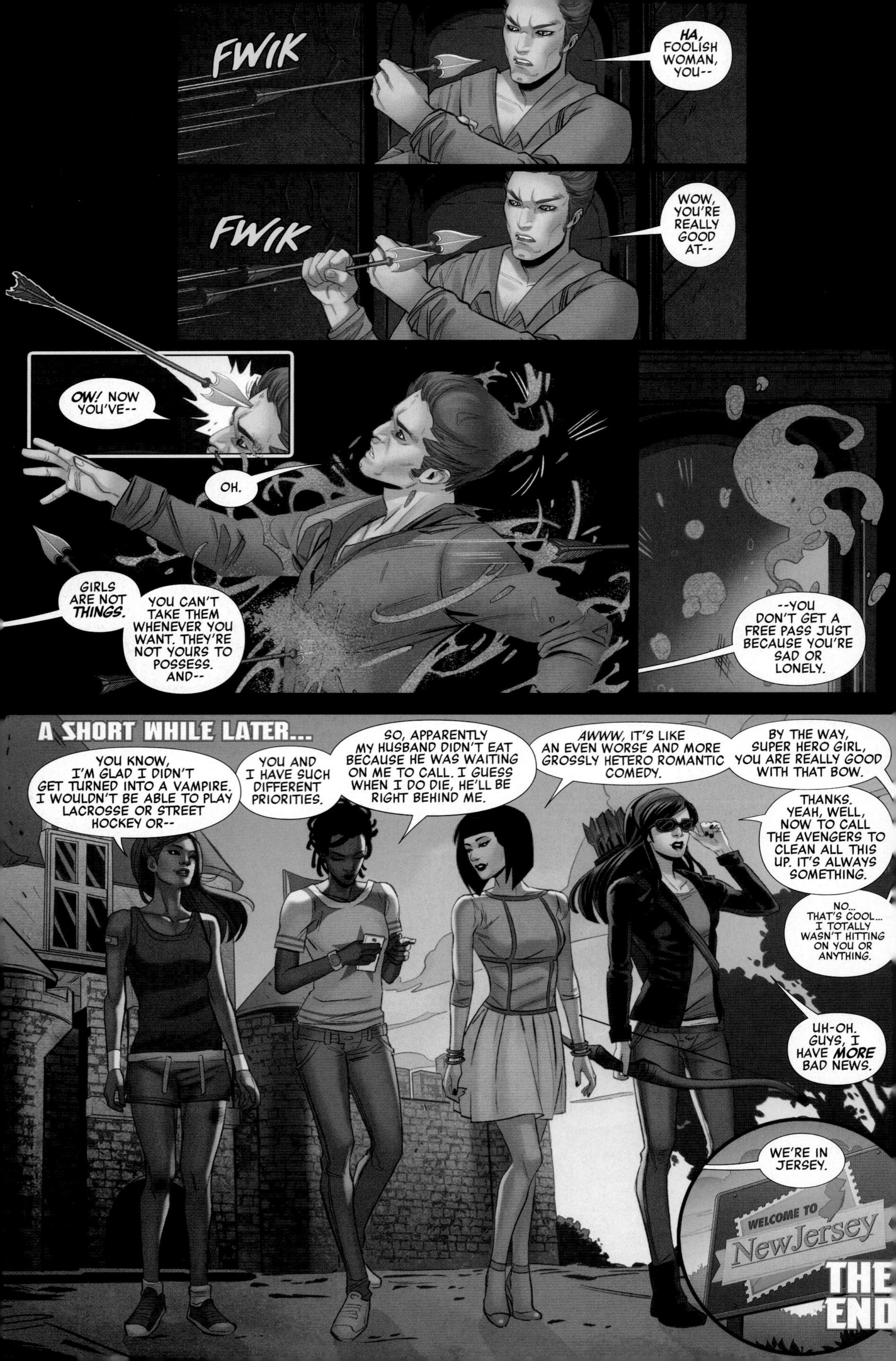
FWIK
HA, FOOLISH WOMAN, YOU--
FWIK
WOW, YOU'RE REALLY GOOD AT--
OW! NOW YOU'VE--
OH.
GIRLS ARE NOT THINGS.
YOU CAN'T TAKE THEM WHENEVER YOU WANT. THEY'RE NOT YOURS TO POSSESS. AND--
--YOU DON'T GET A FREE PASS JUST BECAUSE YOU'RE SAD OR LONELY.
A SHORT WHILE LATER...
YOU KNOW, I'M GLAD I DIDN'T GET TURNED INTO A VAMPIRE. I WOULDN'T BE ABLE TO PLAY LACROSSE OR STREET HOCKEY OR--
YOU AND I HAVE SUCH DIFFERENT PRIORITIES.
SO, APPARENTLY MY HUSBAND DIDN'T EAT BECAUSE HE WAS WAITING ON ME TO CALL. I GUESS WHEN I DO DIE, HE'LL BE RIGHT BEHIND ME.
AWWW, IT'S LIKE AN EVEN WORSE AND MORE GROSSLY HETERO ROMANTIC COMEDY.
BY THE WAY, SUPER HERO GIRL, YOU ARE REALLY GOOD WITH THAT BOW.
THANKS. YEAH, WELL, NOW TO CALL THE AVENGERS TO CLEAN ALL THIS UP. IT'S ALWAYS SOMETHING.
NO... THAT'S COOL... I TOTALLY WASN'T HITTING ON YOU OR ANYTHING.
UH-OH. GUYS, I HAVE MORE BAD NEWS.
WE'RE IN JERSEY.
WELCOME TO NewJersey
THE END

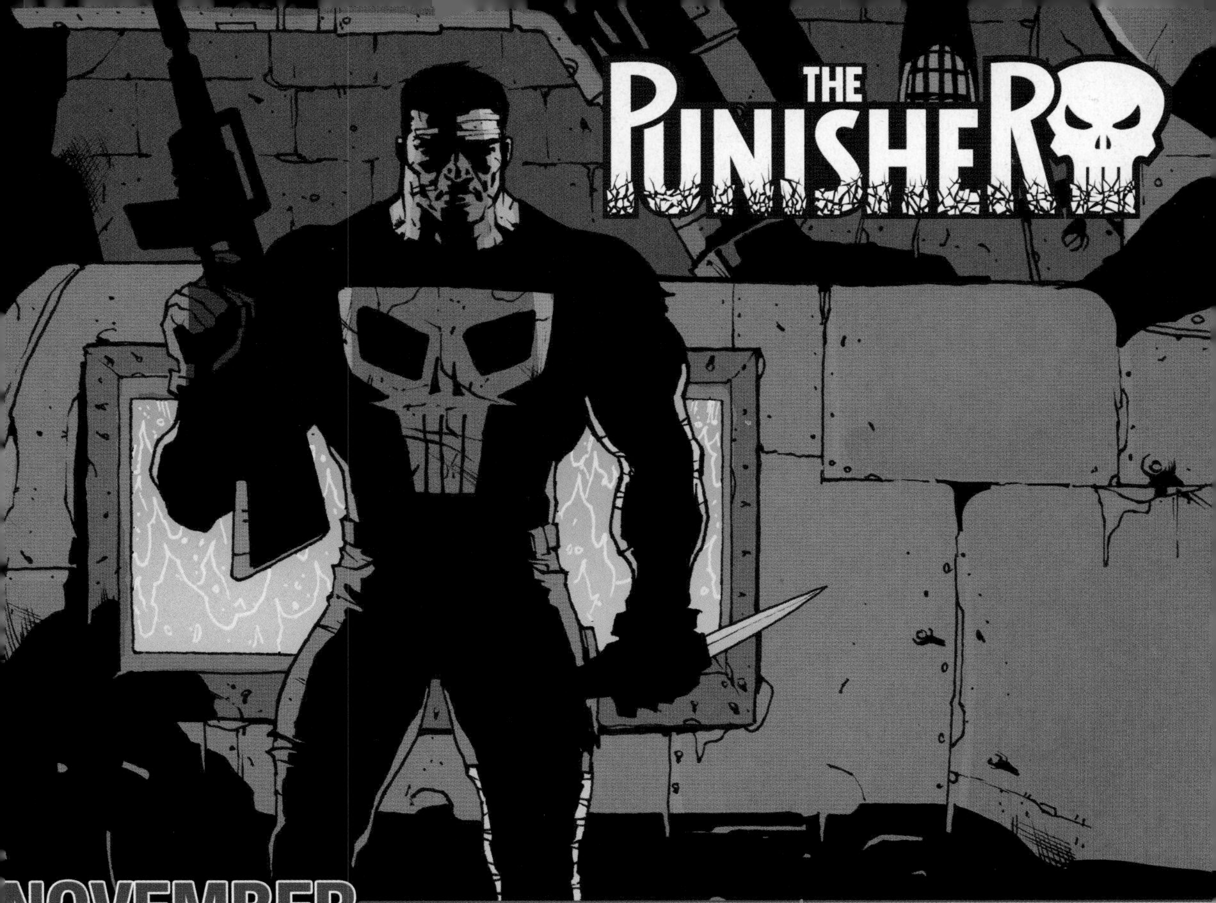
THE PUNISHER

NOVEMBER

SUNDAY	MONDAY	TUESDAY	WEDNESDAY	THURSDAY	FRIDAY	SATURDAY
			1	2	3	4
5	6	7	8	9	10	11 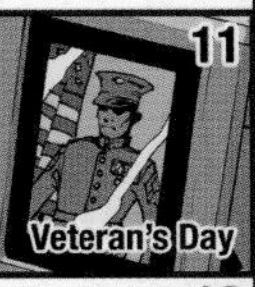 Veteran's Day
12	13	14	15	16	17	18
19	20	21	22	23 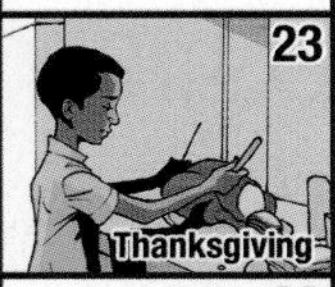 Thanksgiving	24	25
26	27	28	29	30		

ODD CASEY & ELLIOTT CASEY WRITERS
DANIEL GOVAR STORYBOARD ARTIST
PAUL DAVIDSON ARTIST
LEE LOUGHRIDGE COLORIST
VC'S TRAVIS LANHAM LETTERER

AMAL CAMPBELL COVER ART
ANNIE CHENG & TIM SMITH 3 PRODUCTION TEAM
CARLOS LAO DESIGN
JOEL WONG PRODUCTION
MARK BASSO EDITOR
JORDAN D. WHITE & NICK LOWE SUPERVISING EDITORS

EDITOR IN CHIEF **AXEL ALONSO** CHIEF CREATIVE OFFICER **JOE QUESADA** PUBLISHER **DAN BUCKLEY** EXECUTIVE PRODUCER **ALAN FINE**

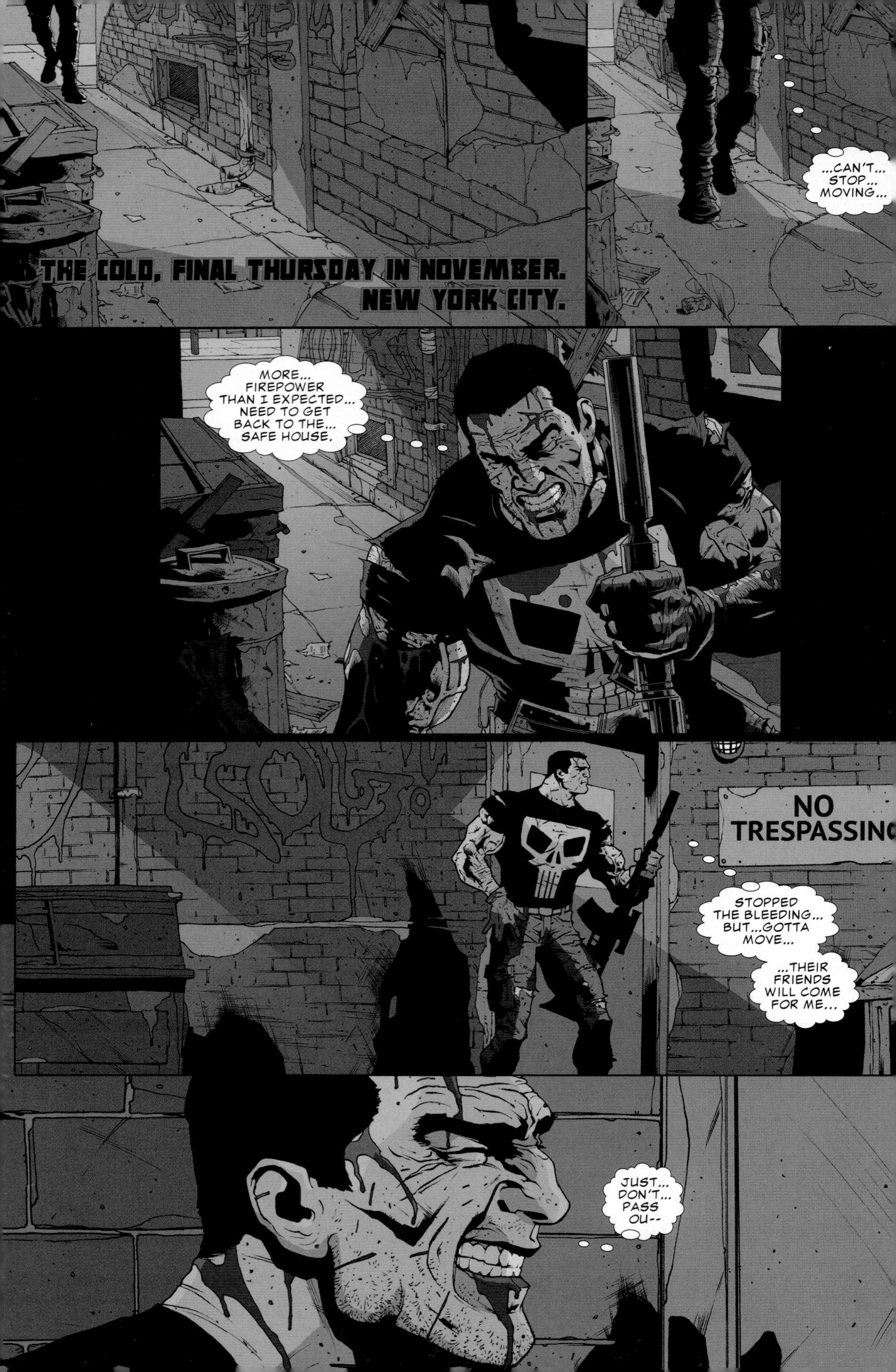
THE COLD, FINAL THURSDAY IN NOVEMBER.
NEW YORK CITY.
...CAN'T... STOP... MOVING...
MORE... FIREPOWER THAN I EXPECTED... NEED TO GET BACK TO THE... SAFE HOUSE.
NO TRESPASSING
STOPPED THE BLEEDING... BUT...GOTTA MOVE...
...THEIR FRIENDS WILL COME FOR ME...
JUST... DON'T... PASS OU--

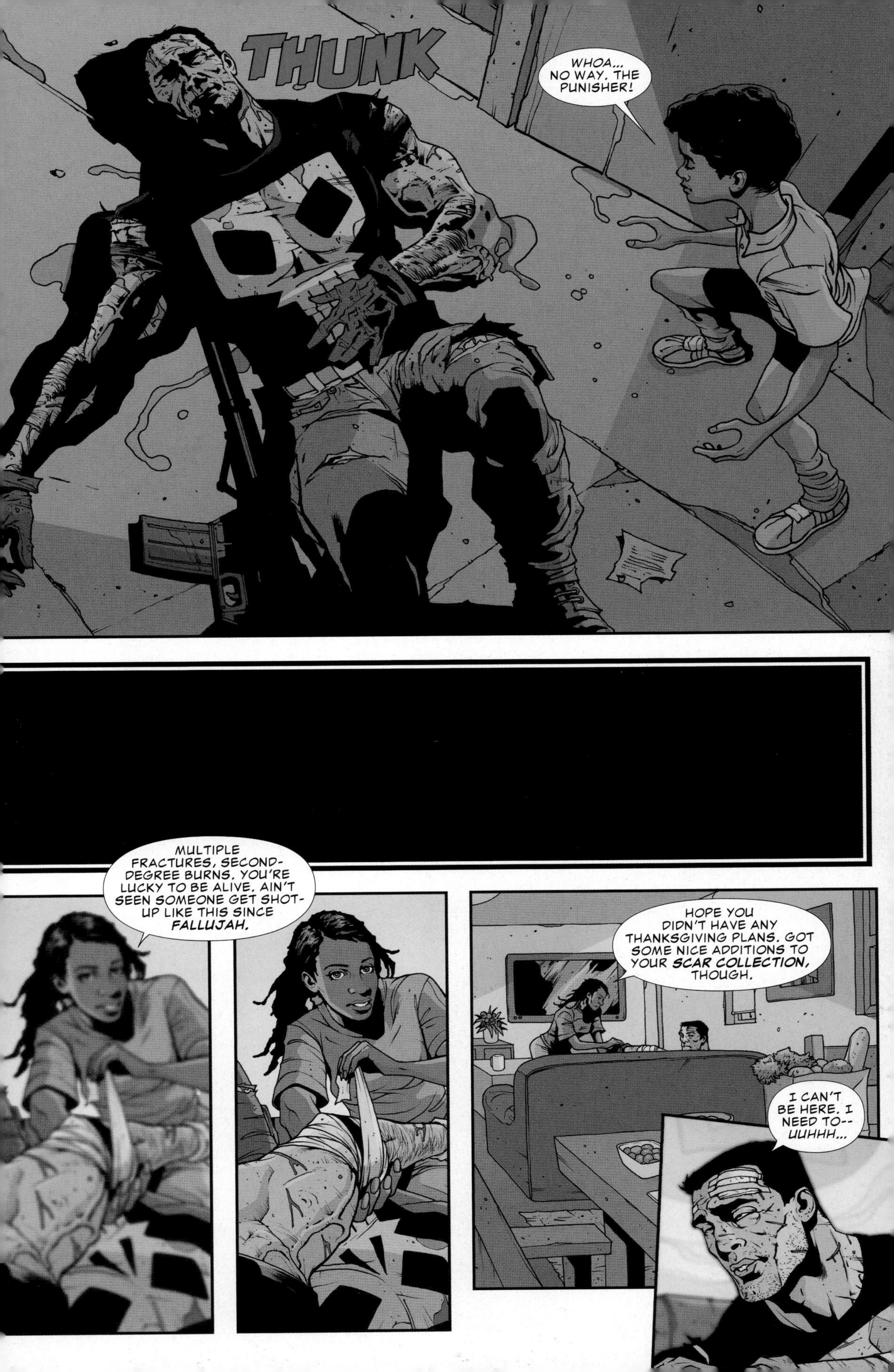
THUNK
WHOA... NO WAY. THE PUNISHER!
MULTIPLE FRACTURES, SECOND-DEGREE BURNS. YOU'RE LUCKY TO BE ALIVE. AIN'T SEEN SOMEONE GET SHOT-UP LIKE THIS SINCE *FALLUJAH.*
HOPE YOU DIDN'T HAVE ANY THANKSGIVING PLANS. GOT SOME NICE ADDITIONS TO YOUR *SCAR COLLECTION,* THOUGH.
I CAN'T BE HERE. I NEED TO-- UUHHH...

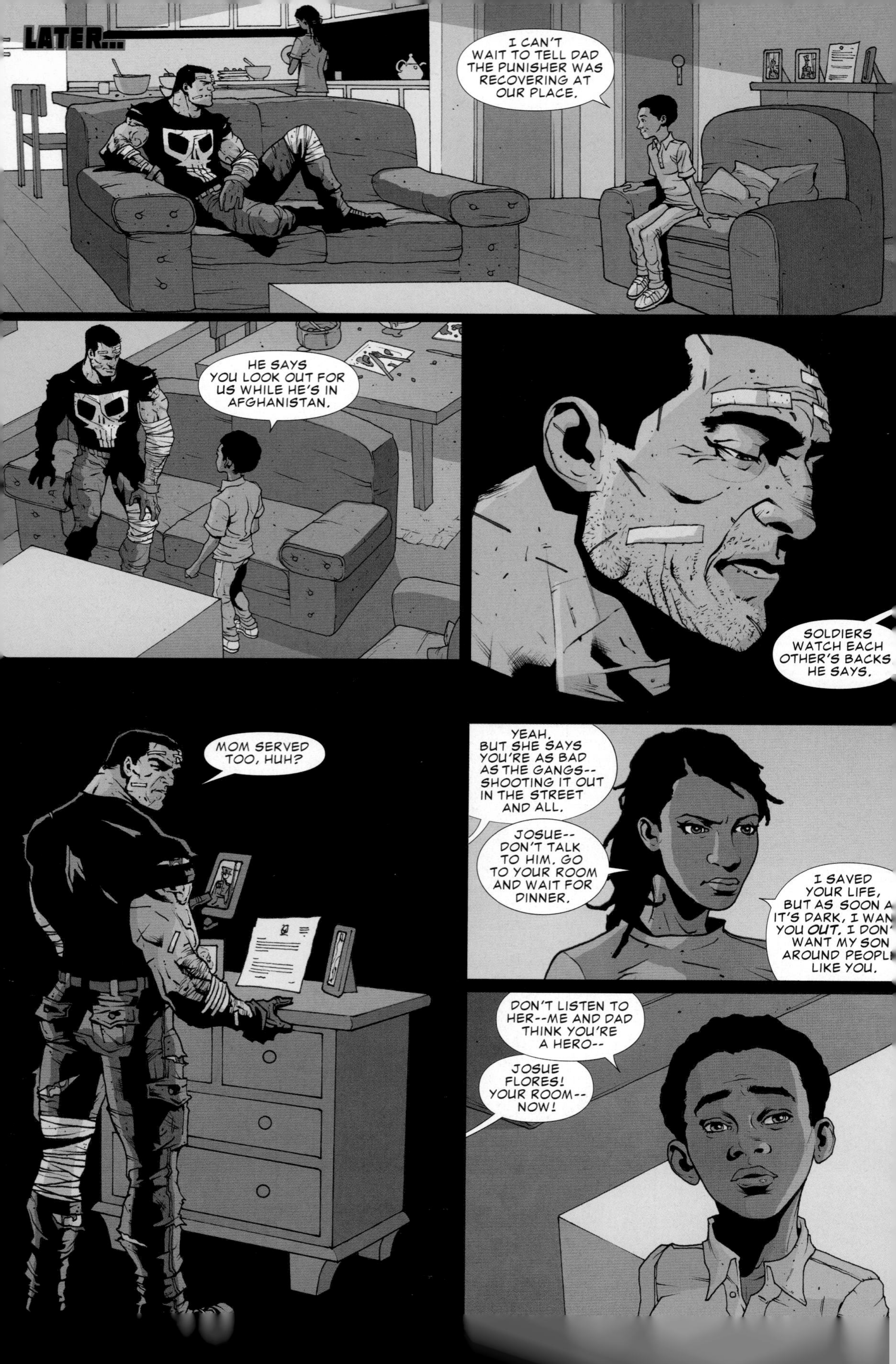
LATER...
I CAN'T WAIT TO TELL DAD THE PUNISHER WAS RECOVERING AT OUR PLACE.
HE SAYS YOU LOOK OUT FOR US WHILE HE'S IN AFGHANISTAN.
SOLDIERS WATCH EACH OTHER'S BACKS HE SAYS.
MOM SERVED TOO, HUH?
YEAH, BUT SHE SAYS YOU'RE AS BAD AS THE GANGS-- SHOOTING IT OUT IN THE STREET AND ALL.
JOSUE-- DON'T TALK TO HIM. GO TO YOUR ROOM AND WAIT FOR DINNER.
I SAVED YOUR LIFE, BUT AS SOON A IT'S DARK, I WAN YOU OUT. I DON' WANT MY SON AROUND PEOPL LIKE YOU.
DON'T LISTEN TO HER--ME AND DAD THINK YOU'RE A HERO--
JOSUE FLORES! YOUR ROOM-- NOW!

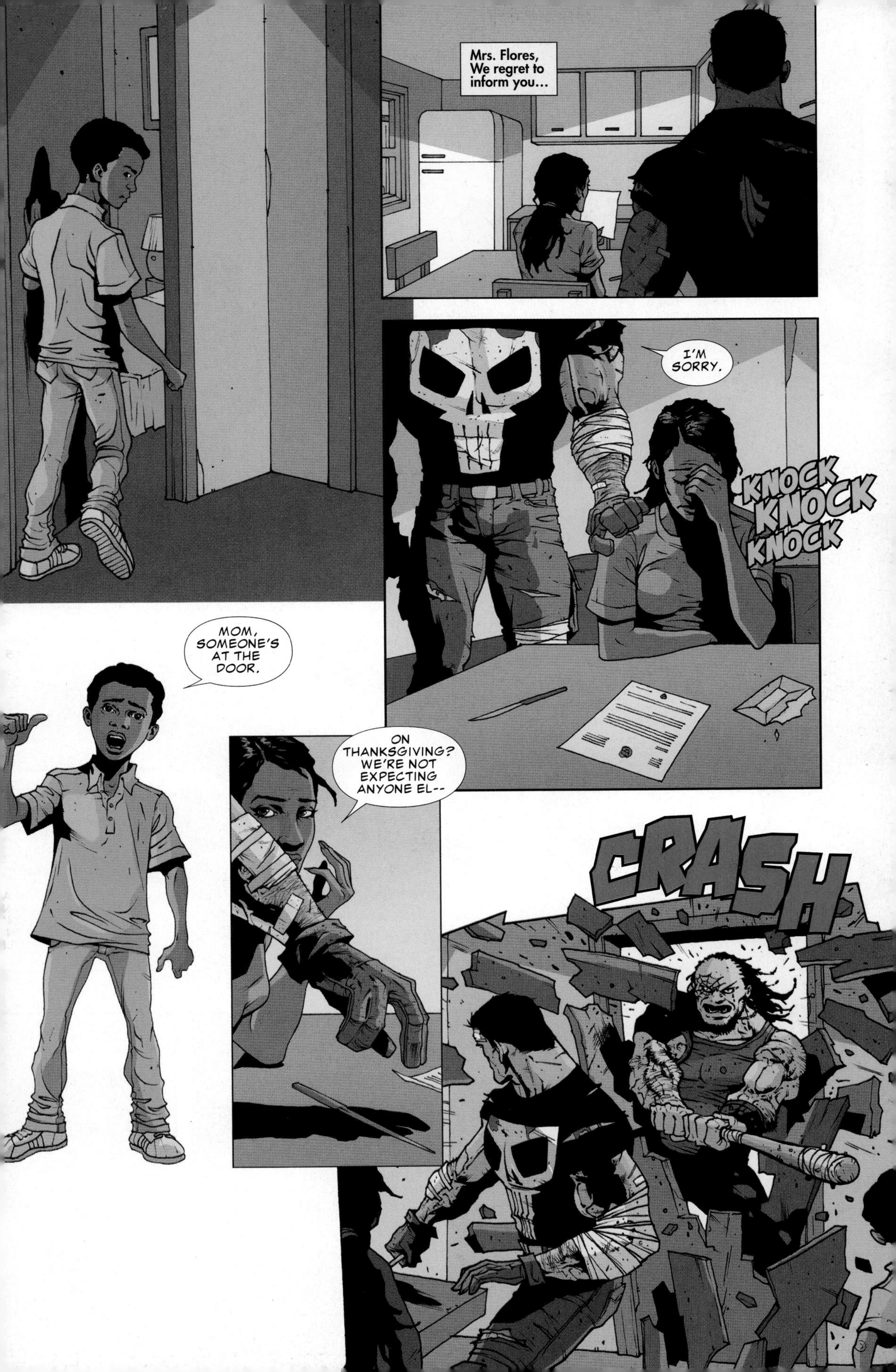

Mrs. Flores,
We regret to
inform you...
I'M SORRY.
KNOCK
KNOCK
KNOCK
MOM, SOMEONE'S AT THE DOOR.
ON THANKSGIVING? WE'RE NOT EXPECTING ANYONE EL--
CRASH

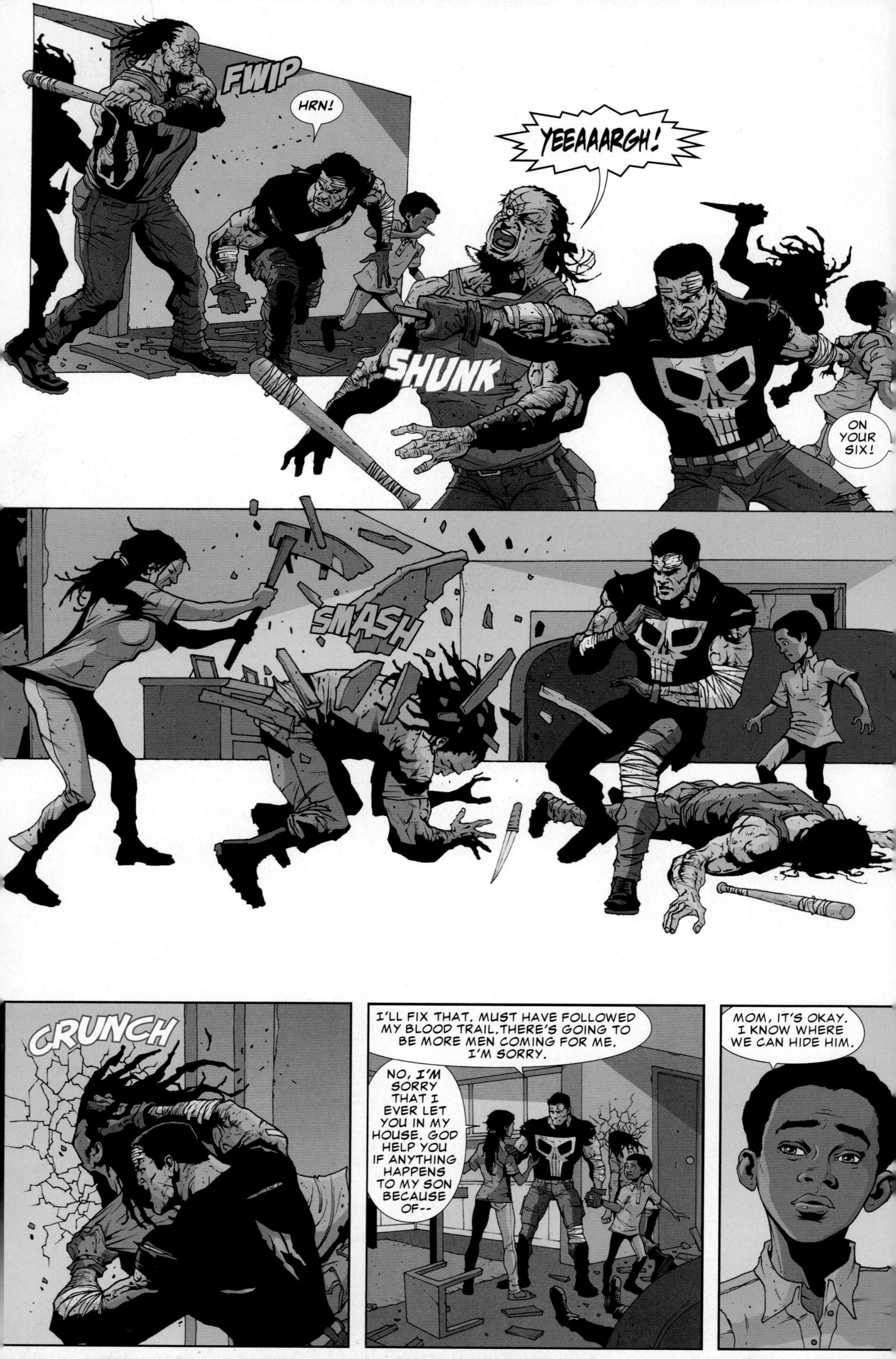
FWIP
HRN!
YEEAAARGH!
SHUNK
ON YOUR SIX!
SMASH
CRUNCH
I'LL FIX THAT. MUST HAVE FOLLOWED MY BLOOD TRAIL. THERE'S GOING TO BE MORE MEN COMING FOR ME. I'M SORRY.
NO, I'M SORRY THAT I EVER LET YOU IN MY HOUSE. GOD HELP YOU IF ANYTHING HAPPENS TO MY SON BECAUSE OF--
MOM, IT'S OKAY. I KNOW WHERE WE CAN HIDE HIM.

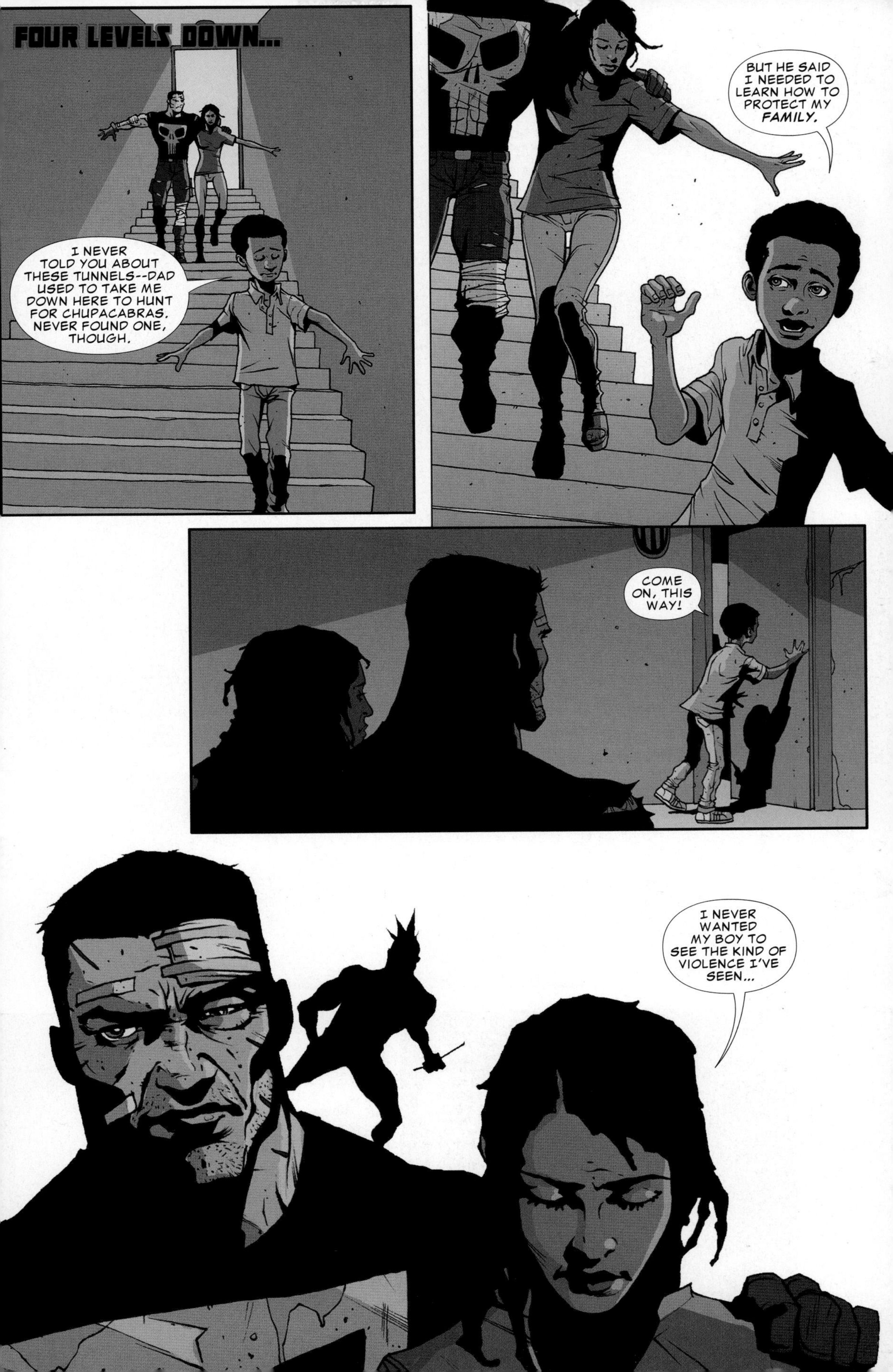
FOUR LEVELS DOWN...
I NEVER TOLD YOU ABOUT THESE TUNNELS--DAD USED TO TAKE ME DOWN HERE TO HUNT FOR CHUPACABRAS. NEVER FOUND ONE, THOUGH.
BUT HE SAID I NEEDED TO LEARN HOW TO PROTECT MY FAMILY.
COME ON, THIS WAY!
I NEVER WANTED MY BOY TO SEE THE KIND OF VIOLENCE I'VE SEEN...

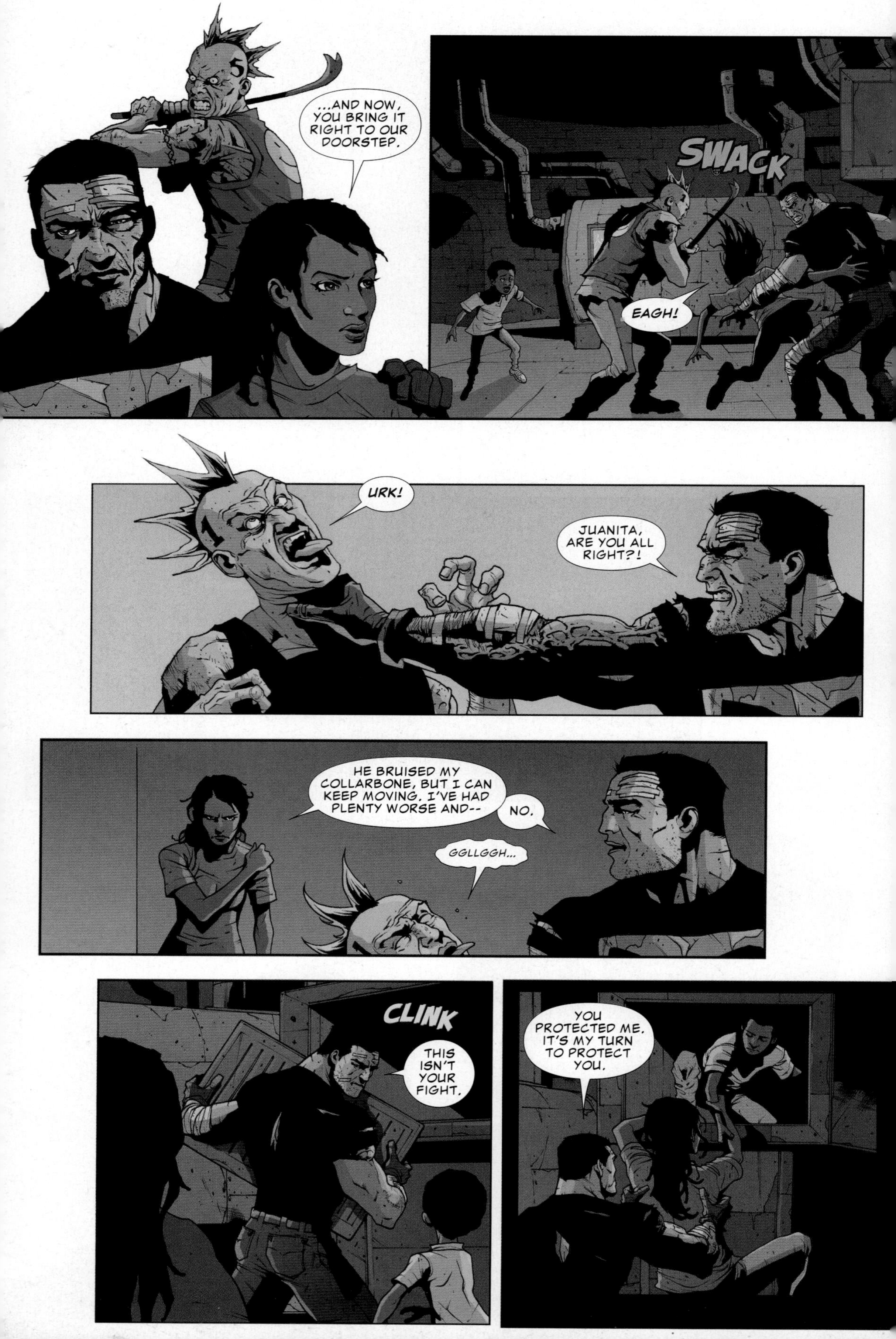
...AND NOW, YOU BRING IT RIGHT TO OUR DOORSTEP.
SWACK
EAGH!
URK!
JUANITA, ARE YOU ALL RIGHT?!
HE BRUISED MY COLLARBONE, BUT I CAN KEEP MOVING. I'VE HAD PLENTY WORSE AND--
NO.
GGLLGGH...
CLINK
THIS ISN'T YOUR FIGHT.
YOU PROTECTED ME. IT'S MY TURN TO PROTECT YOU.

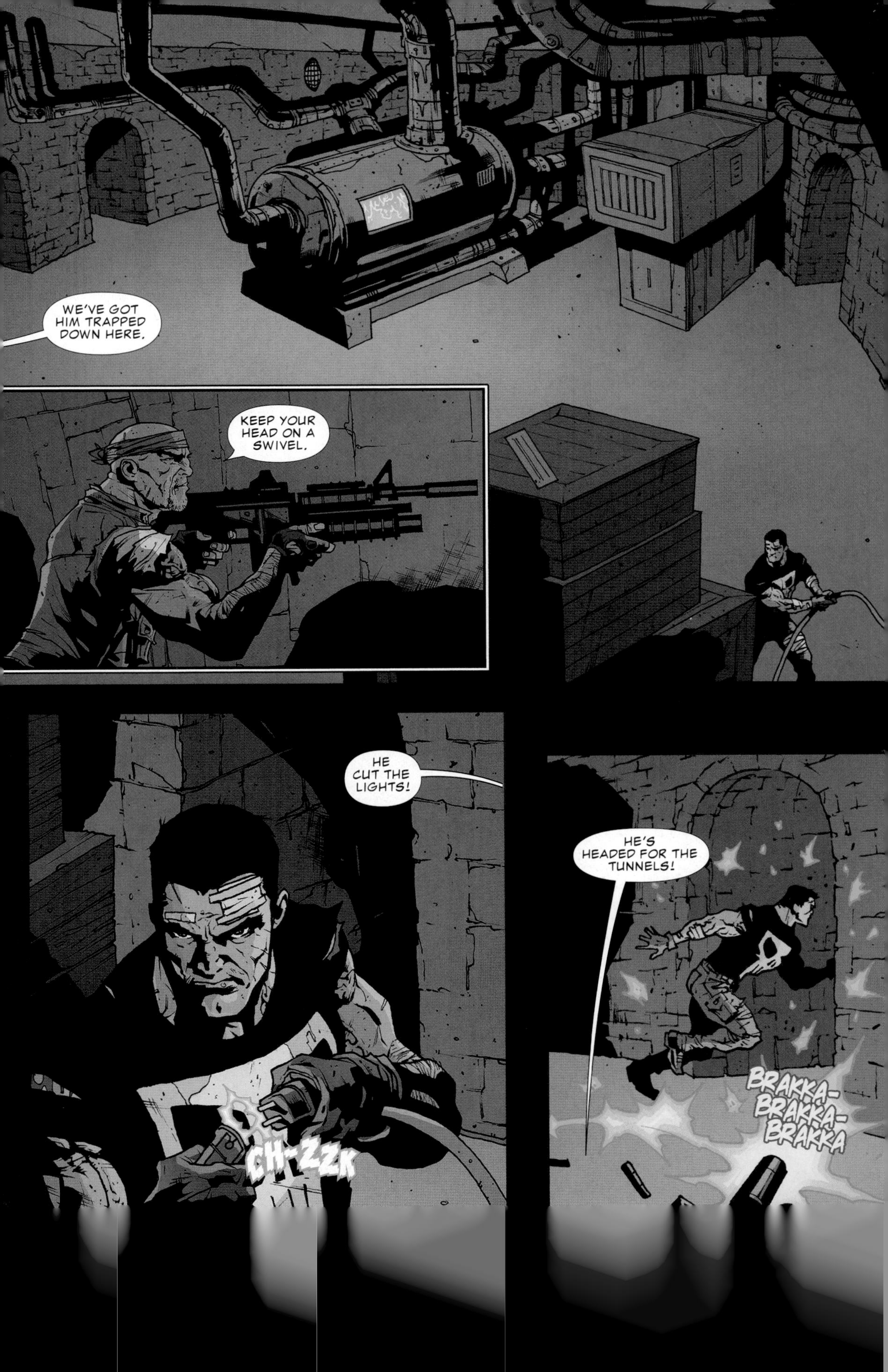
WE'VE GOT HIM TRAPPED DOWN HERE.
KEEP YOUR HEAD ON A SWIVEL.
HE CUT THE LIGHTS!
CH-ZZK
HE'S HEADED FOR THE TUNNELS!
BRAKKA-BRAKKA-BRAKKA

COME OUT AND FACE ME, PUNISHER.

COME OUT!!

BRAKKA-BRA BLAM CL

BRA CL

CLICK

YOU'RE EMPTY.

YEAH, WELL, KNIVES DON'T NEED NO--

MMFMFF--

CRACK

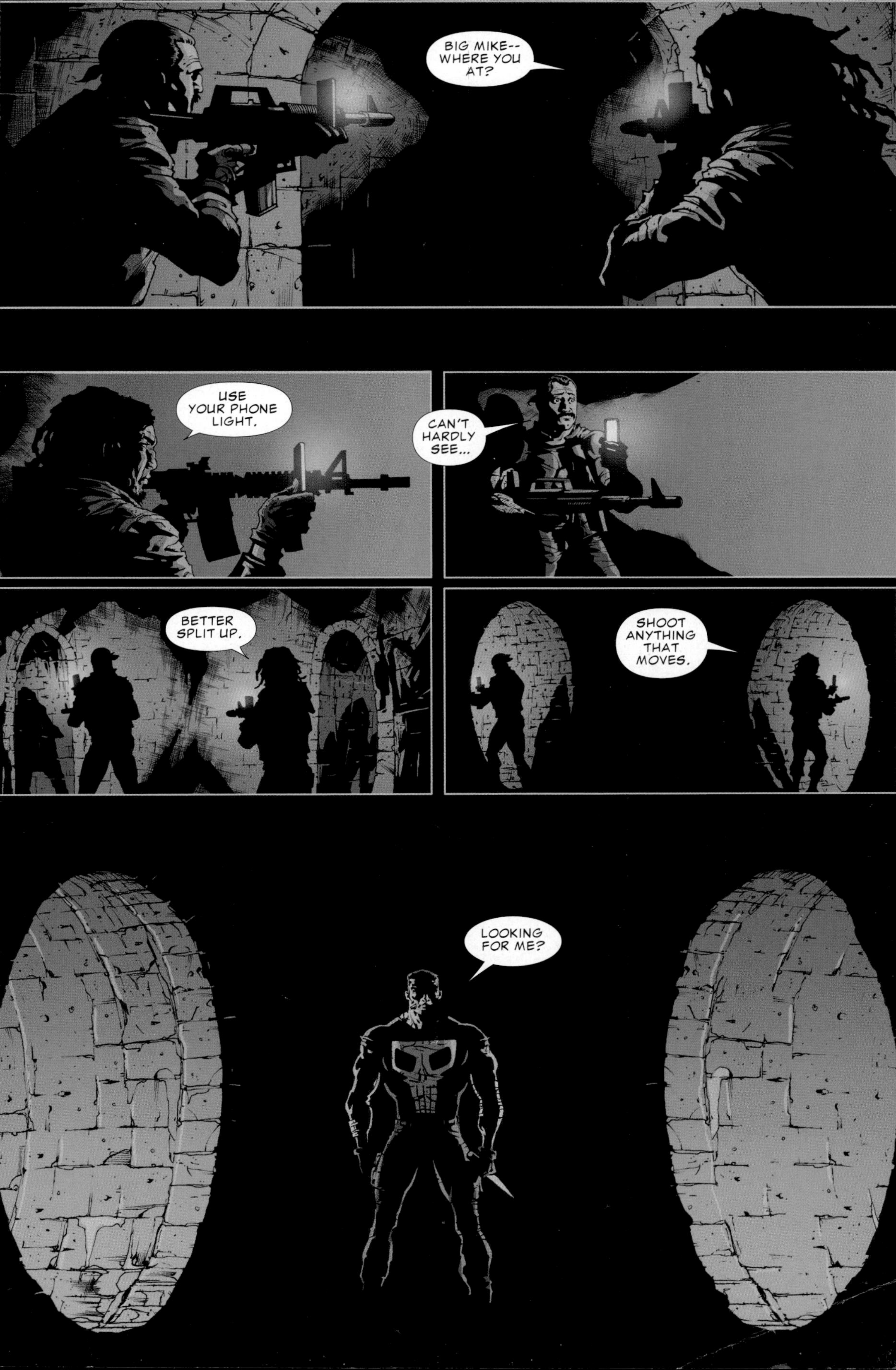
BIG MIKE-- WHERE YOU AT?
USE YOUR PHONE LIGHT.
CAN'T HARDLY SEE...
BETTER SPLIT UP.
SHOOT ANYTHING THAT MOVES.
LOOKING FOR ME?

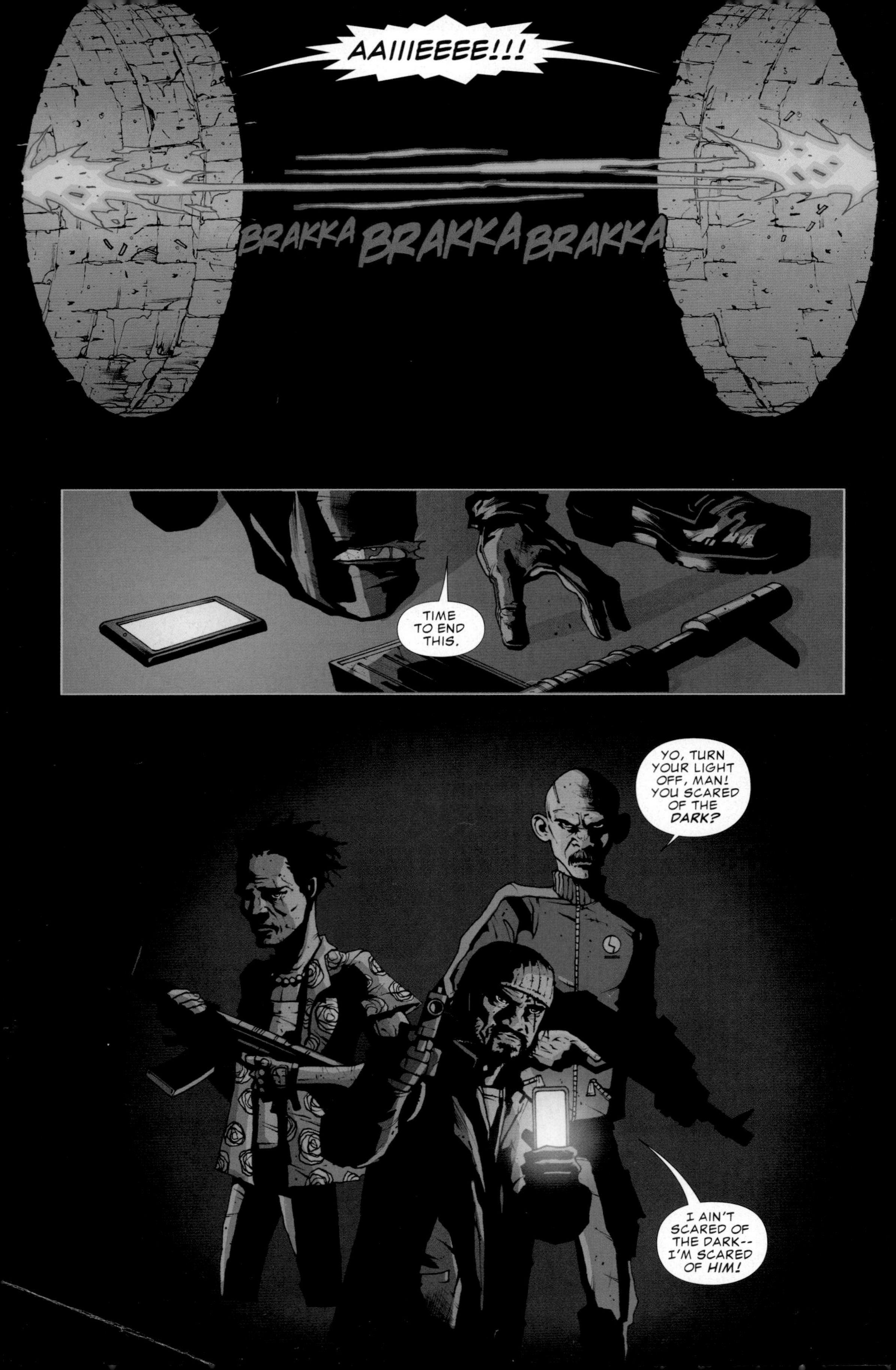
AAIIIEEEE!!!
BRAKKA BRAKKA BRAKKA
TIME TO END THIS.
YO, TURN YOUR LIGHT OFF, MAN! YOU SCARED OF THE DARK?
I AIN'T SCARED OF THE DARK-- I'M SCARED OF HIM!

A YEAR OF MARVELS

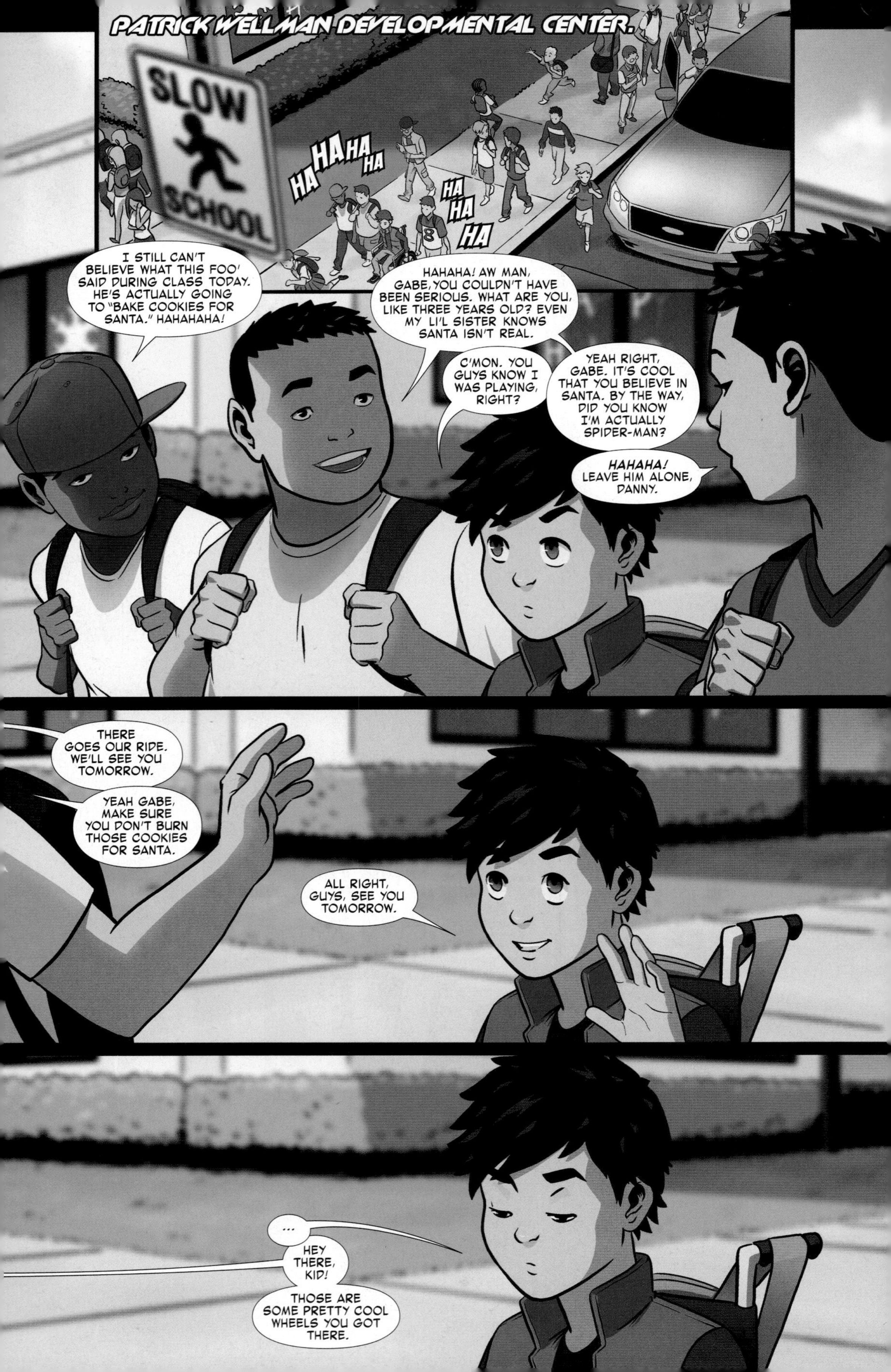
PATRICK WELLMAN DEVELOPMENTAL CENTER.
SLOW SCHOOL
HA HA HA HA
HA HA HA
I STILL CAN'T BELIEVE WHAT THIS FOO' SAID DURING CLASS TODAY. HE'S ACTUALLY GOING TO "BAKE COOKIES FOR SANTA." HAHAHAHA!
HAHAHA! AW MAN, GABE, YOU COULDN'T HAVE BEEN SERIOUS. WHAT ARE YOU, LIKE THREE YEARS OLD? EVEN MY LI'L SISTER KNOWS SANTA ISN'T REAL.
C'MON. YOU GUYS KNOW I WAS PLAYING, RIGHT?
YEAH RIGHT, GABE. IT'S COOL THAT YOU BELIEVE IN SANTA. BY THE WAY, DID YOU KNOW I'M ACTUALLY SPIDER-MAN?
HAHAHA! LEAVE HIM ALONE, DANNY.
THERE GOES OUR RIDE. WE'LL SEE YOU TOMORROW.
YEAH GABE, MAKE SURE YOU DON'T BURN THOSE COOKIES FOR SANTA.
ALL RIGHT, GUYS, SEE YOU TOMORROW.
...
HEY THERE, KID!
THOSE ARE SOME PRETTY COOL WHEELS YOU GOT THERE.

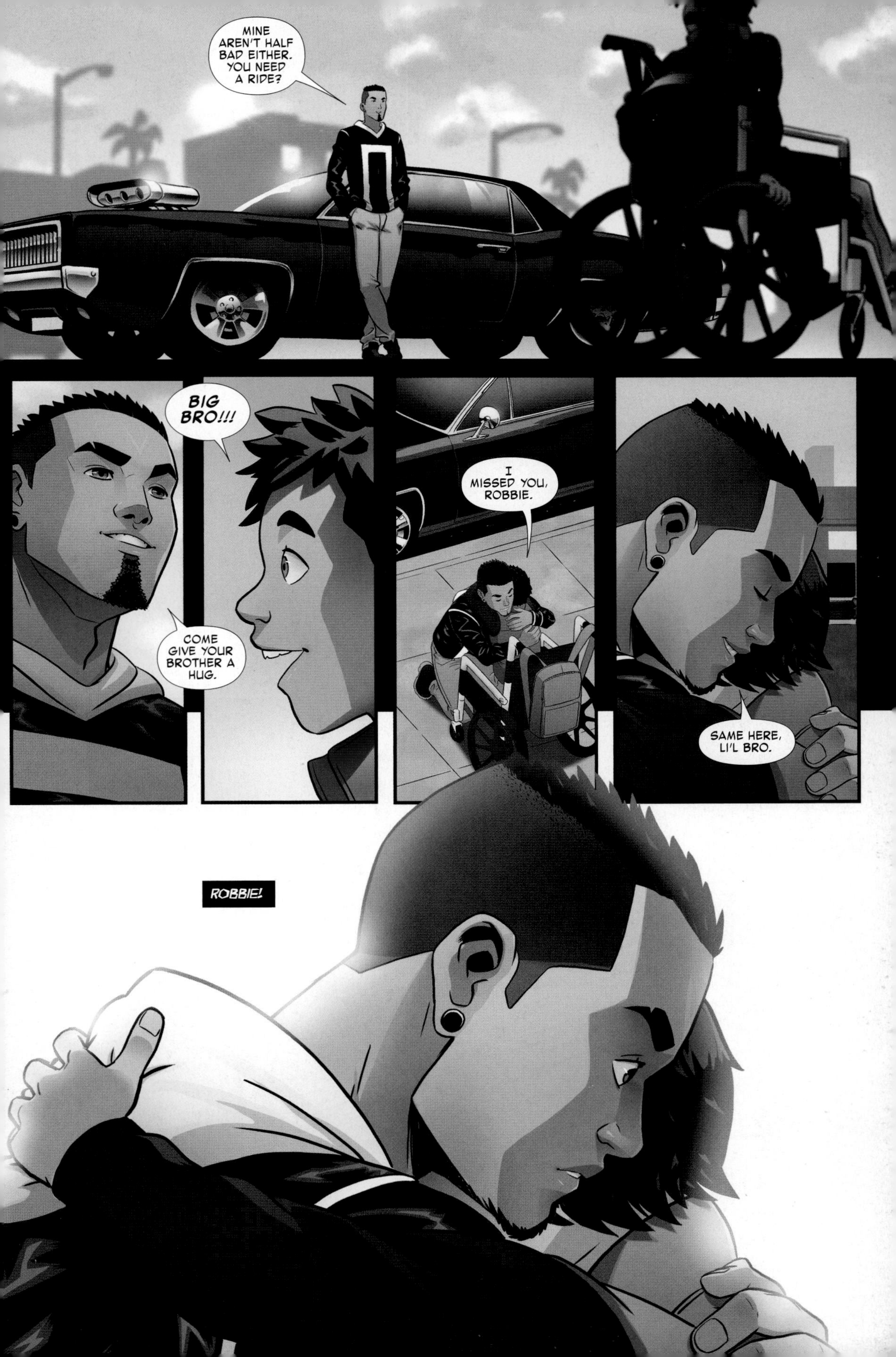
MINE AREN'T HALF BAD EITHER. YOU NEED A RIDE?
BIG BRO!!!
COME GIVE YOUR BROTHER A HUG.
I MISSED YOU, ROBBIE.
SAME HERE, LI'L BRO.
ROBBIE!

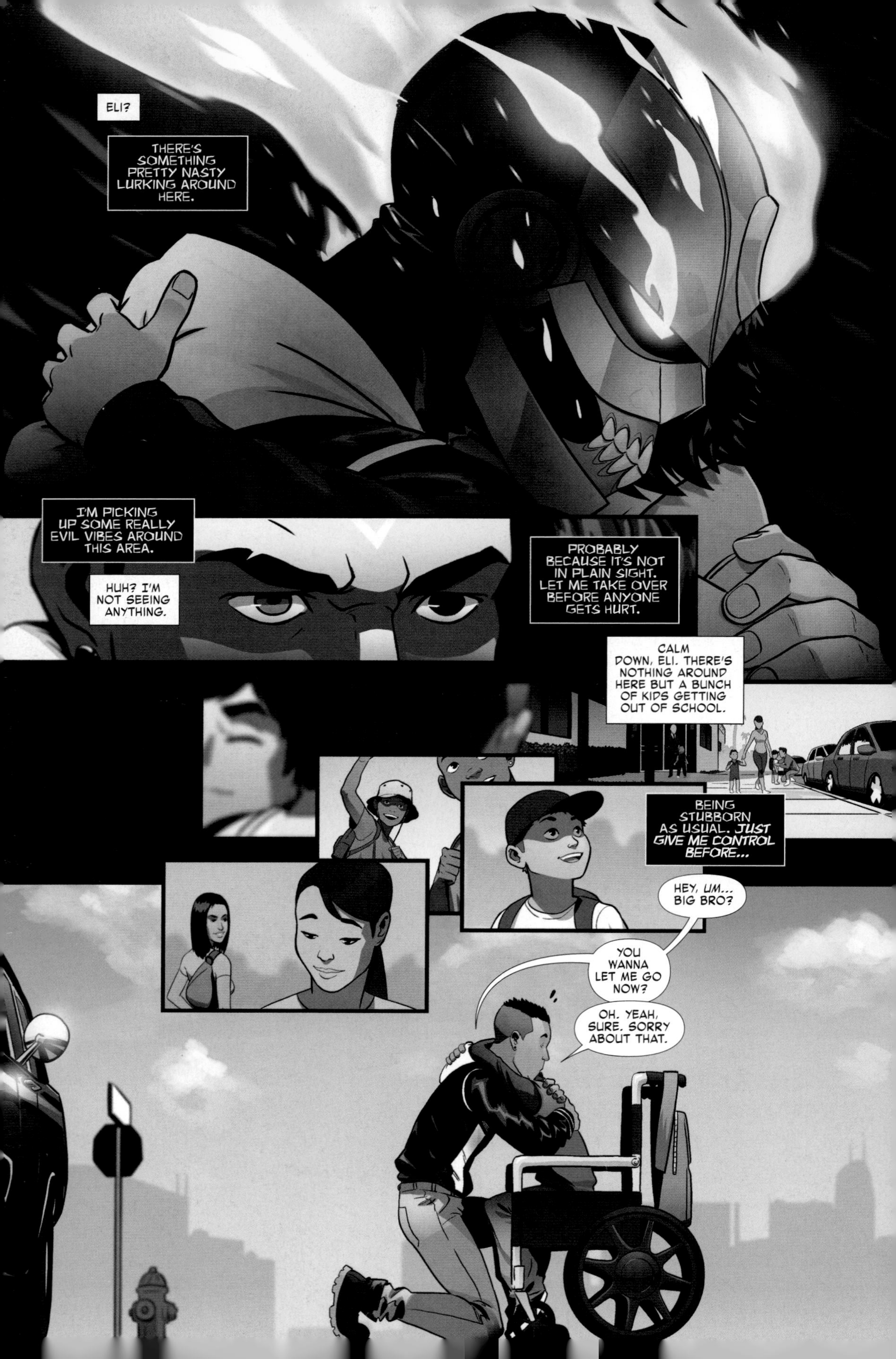
ELI?
THERE'S SOMETHING PRETTY NASTY LURKING AROUND HERE.
I'M PICKING UP SOME REALLY EVIL VIBES AROUND THIS AREA.
HUH? I'M NOT SEEING ANYTHING.
PROBABLY BECAUSE IT'S NOT IN PLAIN SIGHT. LET ME TAKE OVER BEFORE ANYONE GETS HURT.
CALM DOWN, ELI. THERE'S NOTHING AROUND HERE BUT A BUNCH OF KIDS GETTING OUT OF SCHOOL.
BEING STUBBORN AS USUAL. JUST GIVE ME CONTROL BEFORE...
HEY, UM... BIG BRO?
YOU WANNA LET ME GO NOW?
OH. YEAH, SURE. SORRY ABOUT THAT.

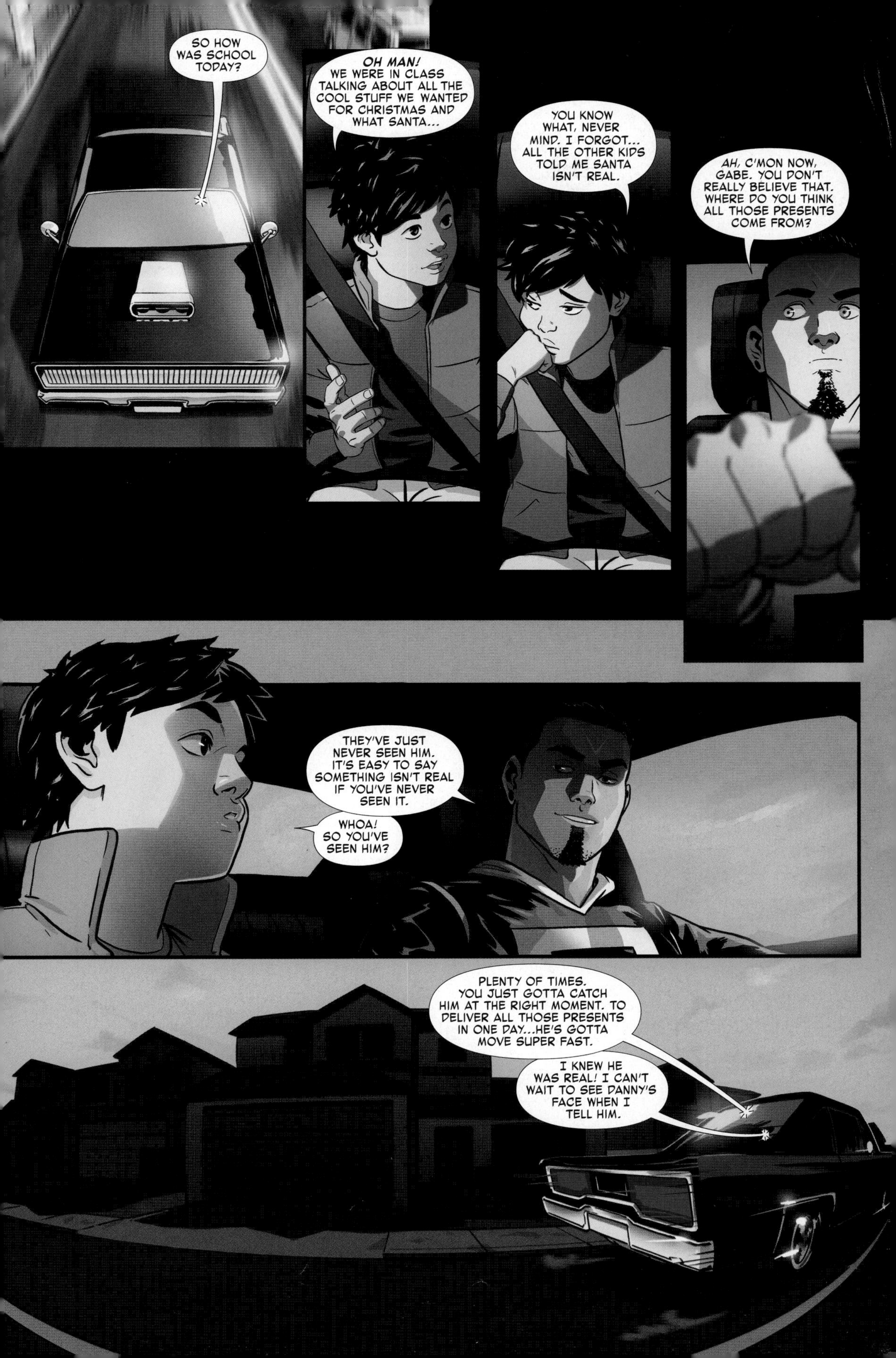
SO HOW WAS SCHOOL TODAY?
OH MAN! WE WERE IN CLASS TALKING ABOUT ALL THE COOL STUFF WE WANTED FOR CHRISTMAS AND WHAT SANTA...
YOU KNOW WHAT, NEVER MIND. I FORGOT... ALL THE OTHER KIDS TOLD ME SANTA ISN'T REAL.
AH, C'MON NOW, GABE. YOU DON'T REALLY BELIEVE THAT. WHERE DO YOU THINK ALL THOSE PRESENTS COME FROM?
THEY'VE JUST NEVER SEEN HIM. IT'S EASY TO SAY SOMETHING ISN'T REAL IF YOU'VE NEVER SEEN IT.
WHOA! SO YOU'VE SEEN HIM?
PLENTY OF TIMES. YOU JUST GOTTA CATCH HIM AT THE RIGHT MOMENT. TO DELIVER ALL THOSE PRESENTS IN ONE DAY...HE'S GOTTA MOVE SUPER FAST.
I KNEW HE WAS REAL! I CAN'T WAIT TO SEE DANNY'S FACE WHEN I TELL HIM.

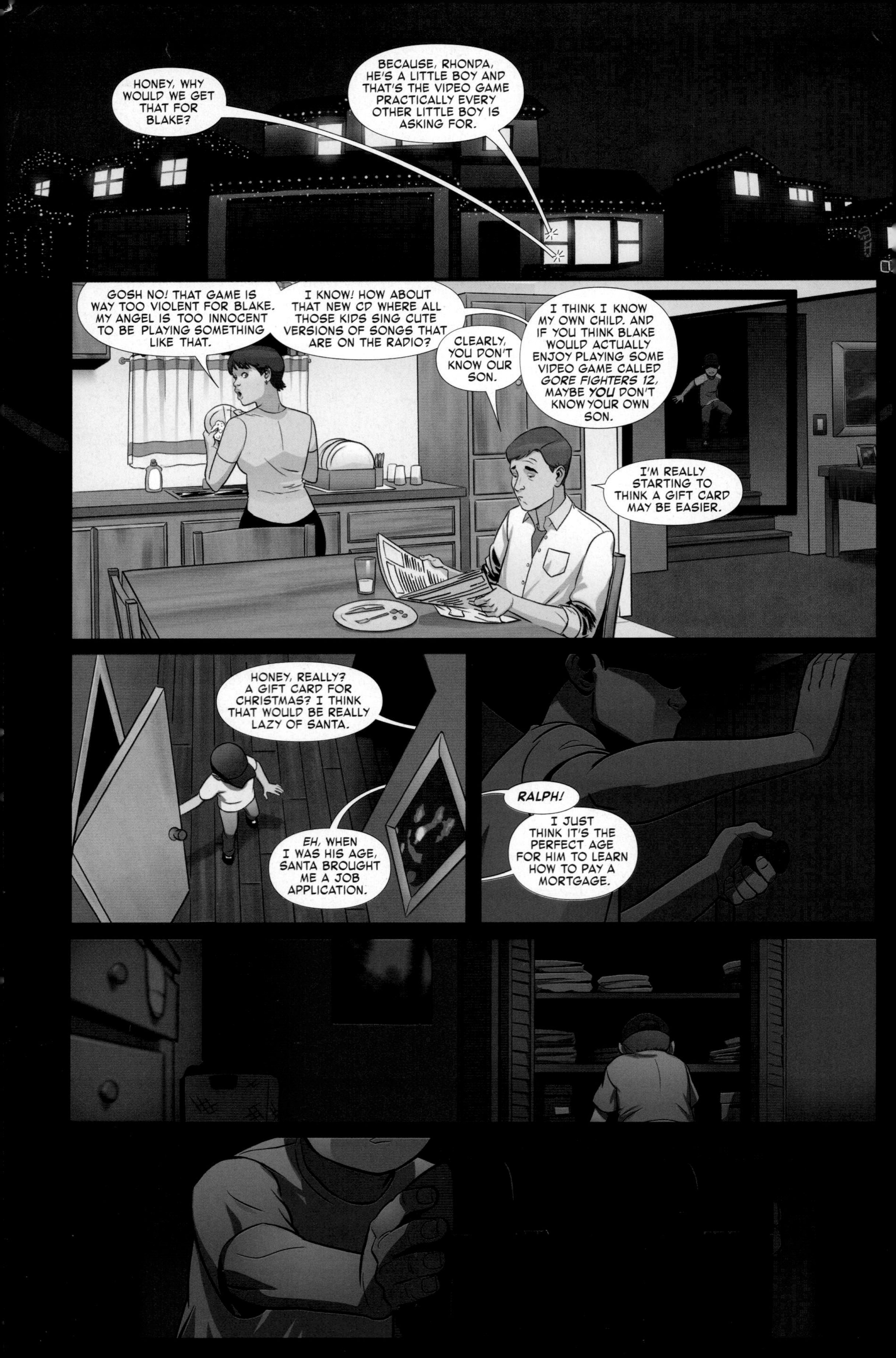
HONEY, WHY WOULD WE GET THAT FOR BLAKE?
BECAUSE, RHONDA, HE'S A LITTLE BOY AND THAT'S THE VIDEO GAME PRACTICALLY EVERY OTHER LITTLE BOY IS ASKING FOR.
GOSH NO! THAT GAME IS WAY TOO VIOLENT FOR BLAKE. MY ANGEL IS TOO INNOCENT TO BE PLAYING SOMETHING LIKE THAT.
I KNOW! HOW ABOUT THAT NEW CD WHERE ALL THOSE KIDS SING CUTE VERSIONS OF SONGS THAT ARE ON THE RADIO?
CLEARLY, YOU DON'T KNOW OUR SON.
I THINK I KNOW MY OWN CHILD. AND IF YOU THINK BLAKE WOULD ACTUALLY ENJOY PLAYING SOME VIDEO GAME CALLED GORE FIGHTERS 12, MAYBE YOU DON'T KNOW YOUR OWN SON.
I'M REALLY STARTING TO THINK A GIFT CARD MAY BE EASIER.
HONEY, REALLY? A GIFT CARD FOR CHRISTMAS? I THINK THAT WOULD BE REALLY LAZY OF SANTA.
EH, WHEN I WAS HIS AGE, SANTA BROUGHT ME A JOB APPLICATION.
RALPH!
I JUST THINK IT'S THE PERFECT AGE FOR HIM TO LEARN HOW TO PAY A MORTGAGE.

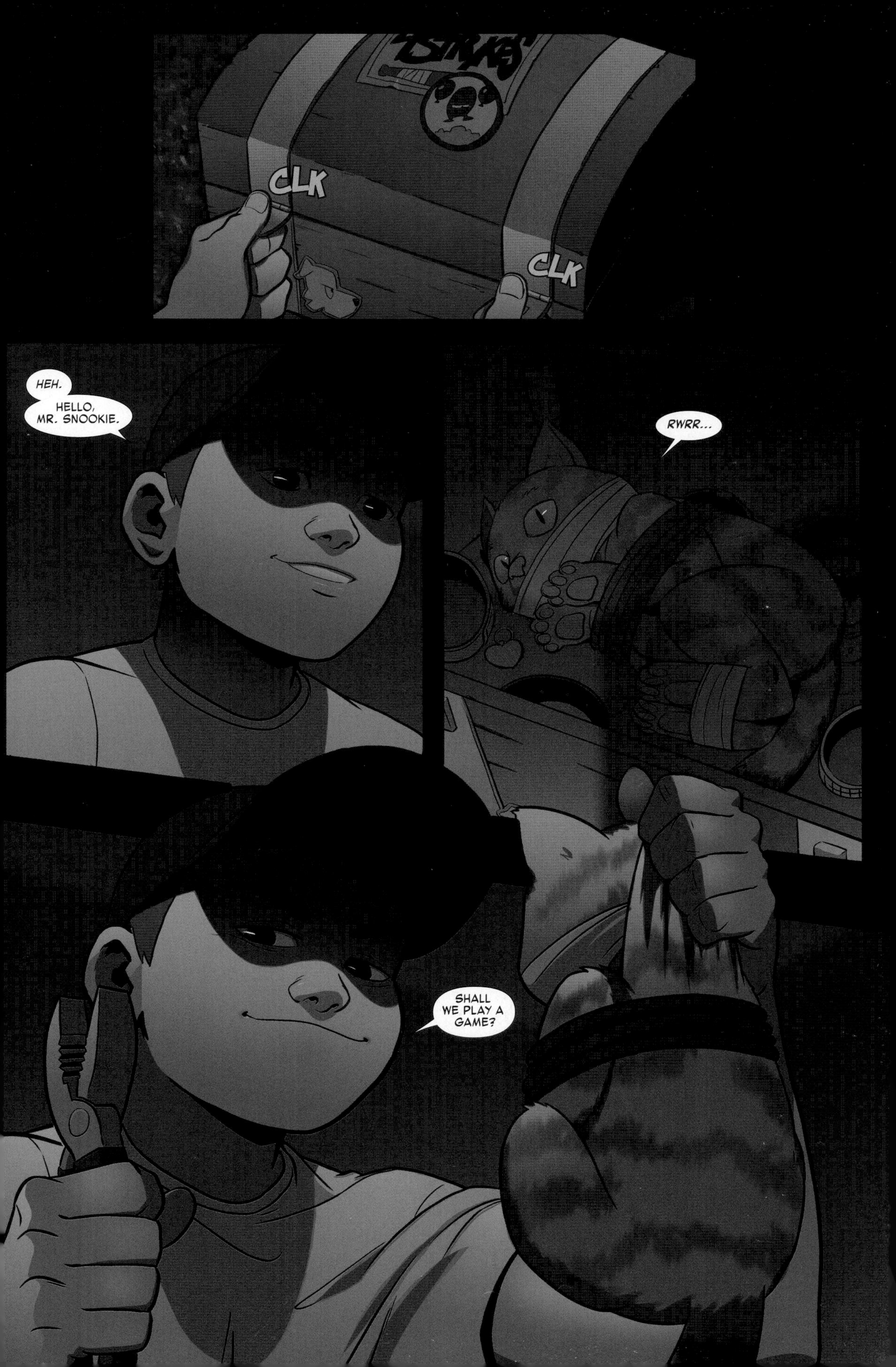
CLK
CLK
HEH.
HELLO, MR. SNOOKIE.
RWRR...
SHALL WE PLAY A GAME?

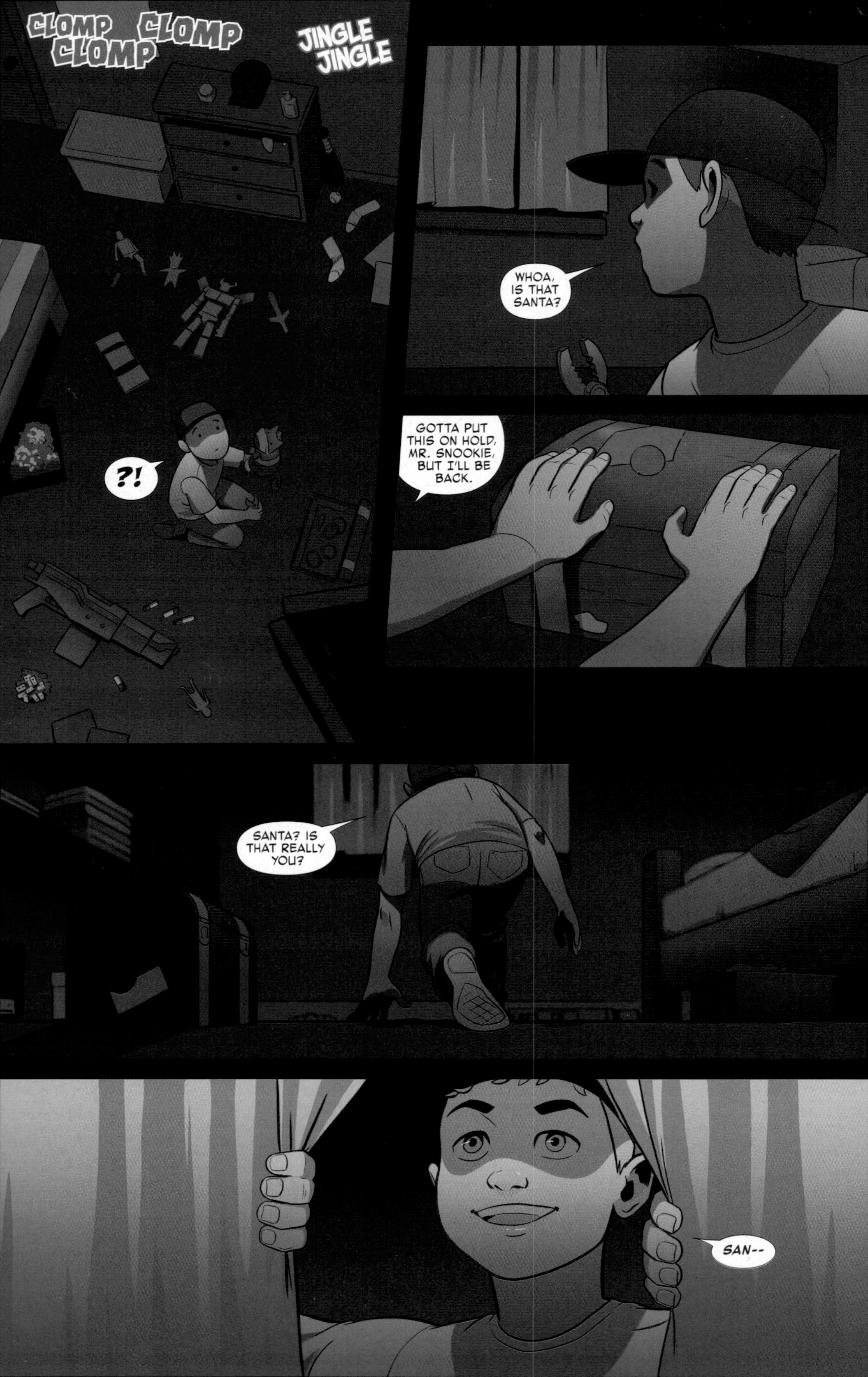
CLOMP CLOMP CLOMP
JINGLE JINGLE
?!
WHOA, IS THAT SANTA?
GOTTA PUT THIS ON HOLD, MR. SNOOKIE, BUT I'LL BE BACK.
SANTA? IS THAT REALLY YOU?
SAN--

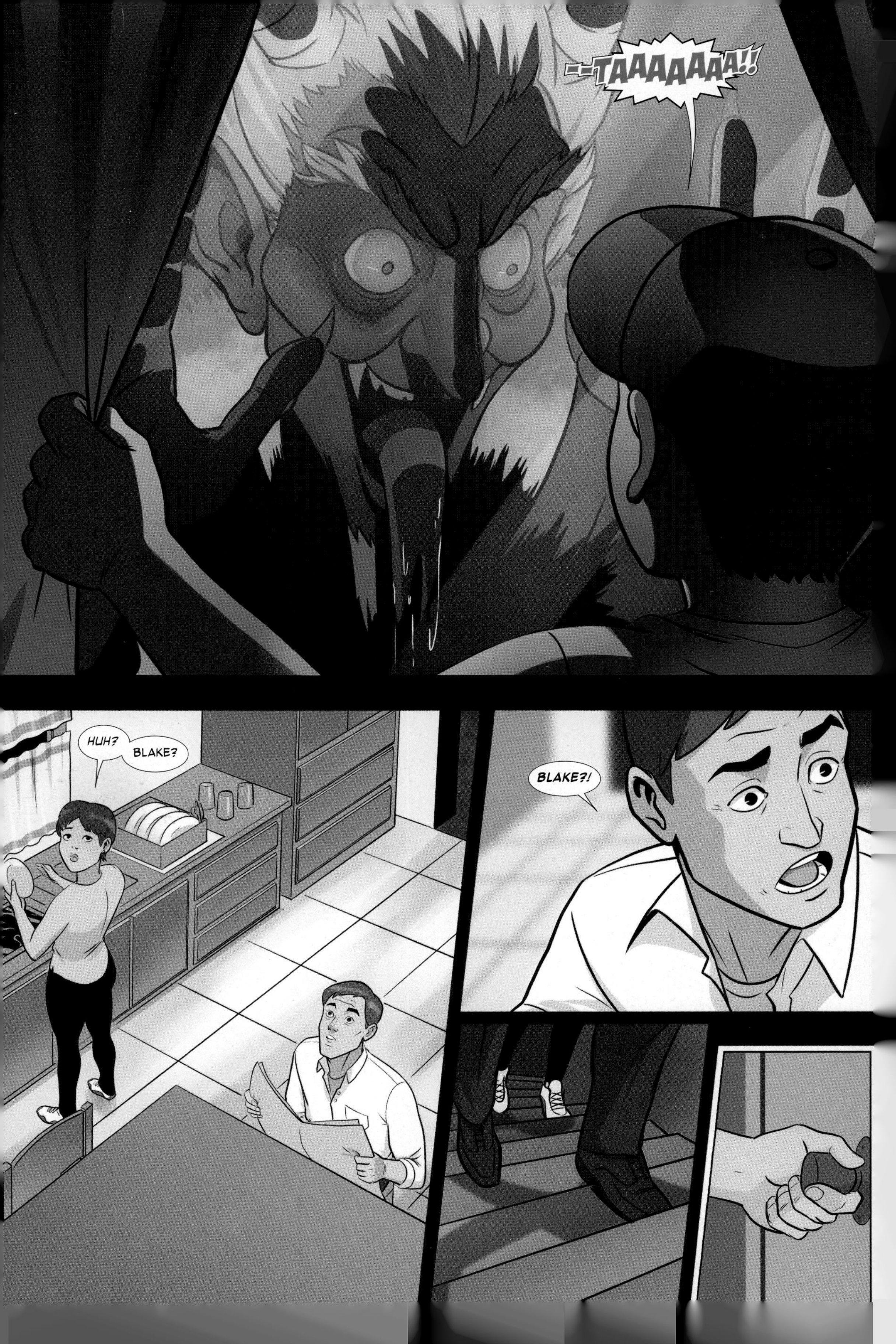
--TAAAAAAA!!
HUH?
BLAKE?
BLAKE?!

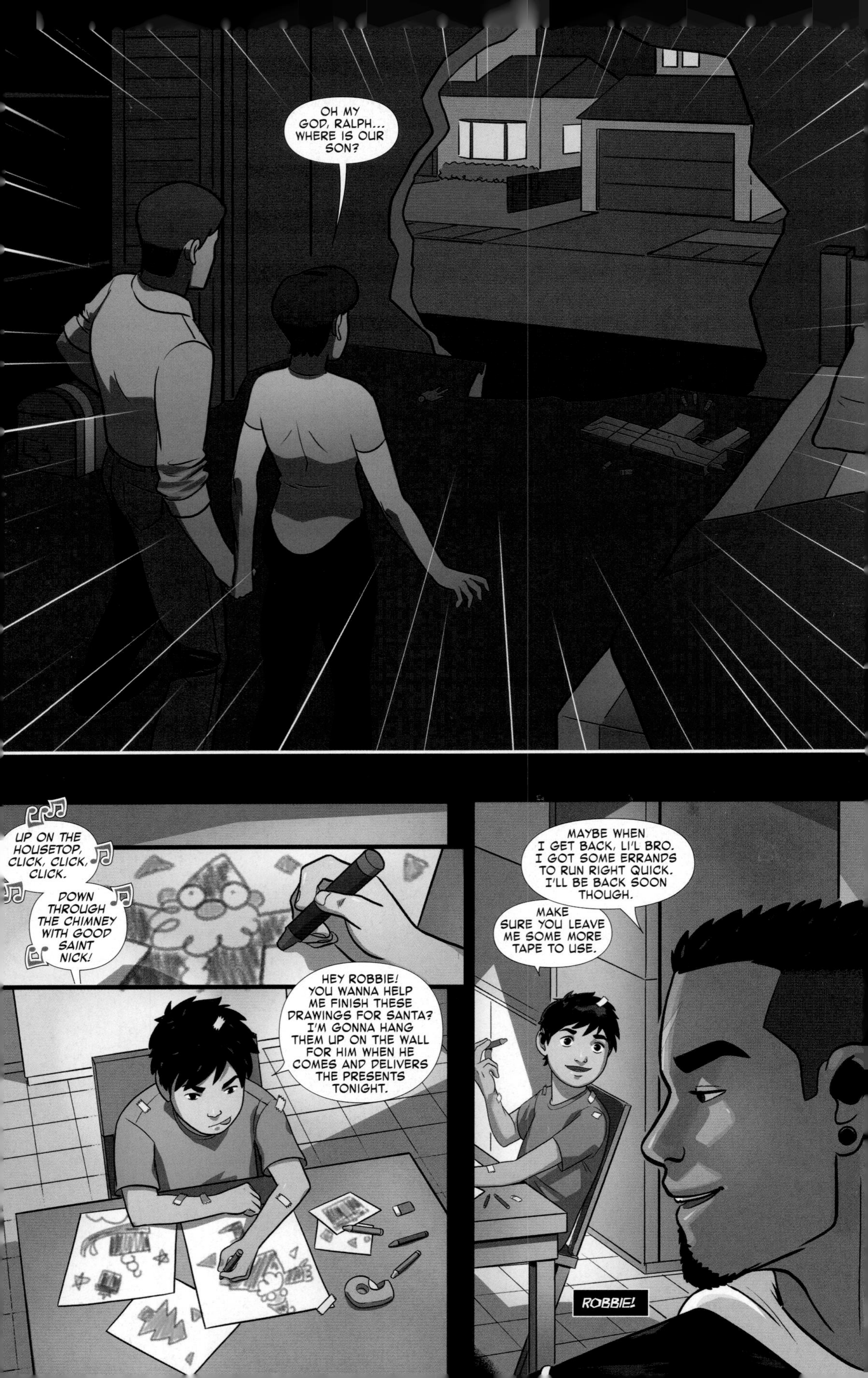
OH MY GOD, RALPH... WHERE IS OUR SON?
UP ON THE HOUSETOP, CLICK, CLICK, CLICK.
DOWN THROUGH THE CHIMNEY WITH GOOD SAINT NICK!
HEY ROBBIE! YOU WANNA HELP ME FINISH THESE DRAWINGS FOR SANTA? I'M GONNA HANG THEM UP ON THE WALL FOR HIM WHEN HE COMES AND DELIVERS THE PRESENTS TONIGHT.
MAYBE WHEN I GET BACK, LI'L BRO. I GOT SOME ERRANDS TO RUN RIGHT QUICK. I'LL BE BACK SOON THOUGH.
MAKE SURE YOU LEAVE ME SOME MORE TAPE TO USE.
ROBBIE!

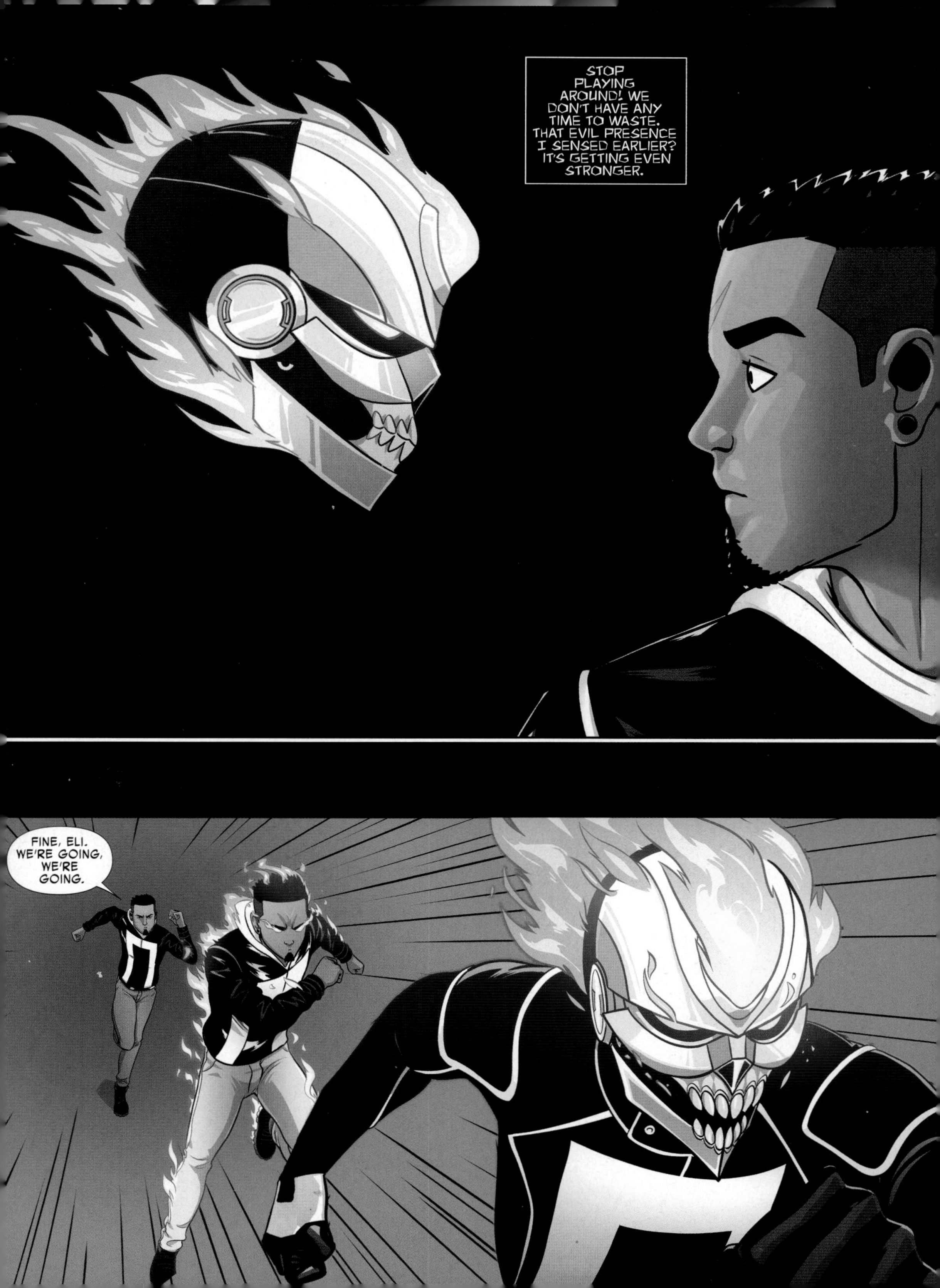
STOP PLAYING AROUND! WE DON'T HAVE ANY TIME TO WASTE. THAT EVIL PRESENCE I SENSED EARLIER? IT'S GETTING EVEN STRONGER.
FINE, ELI. WE'RE GOING, WE'RE GOING.

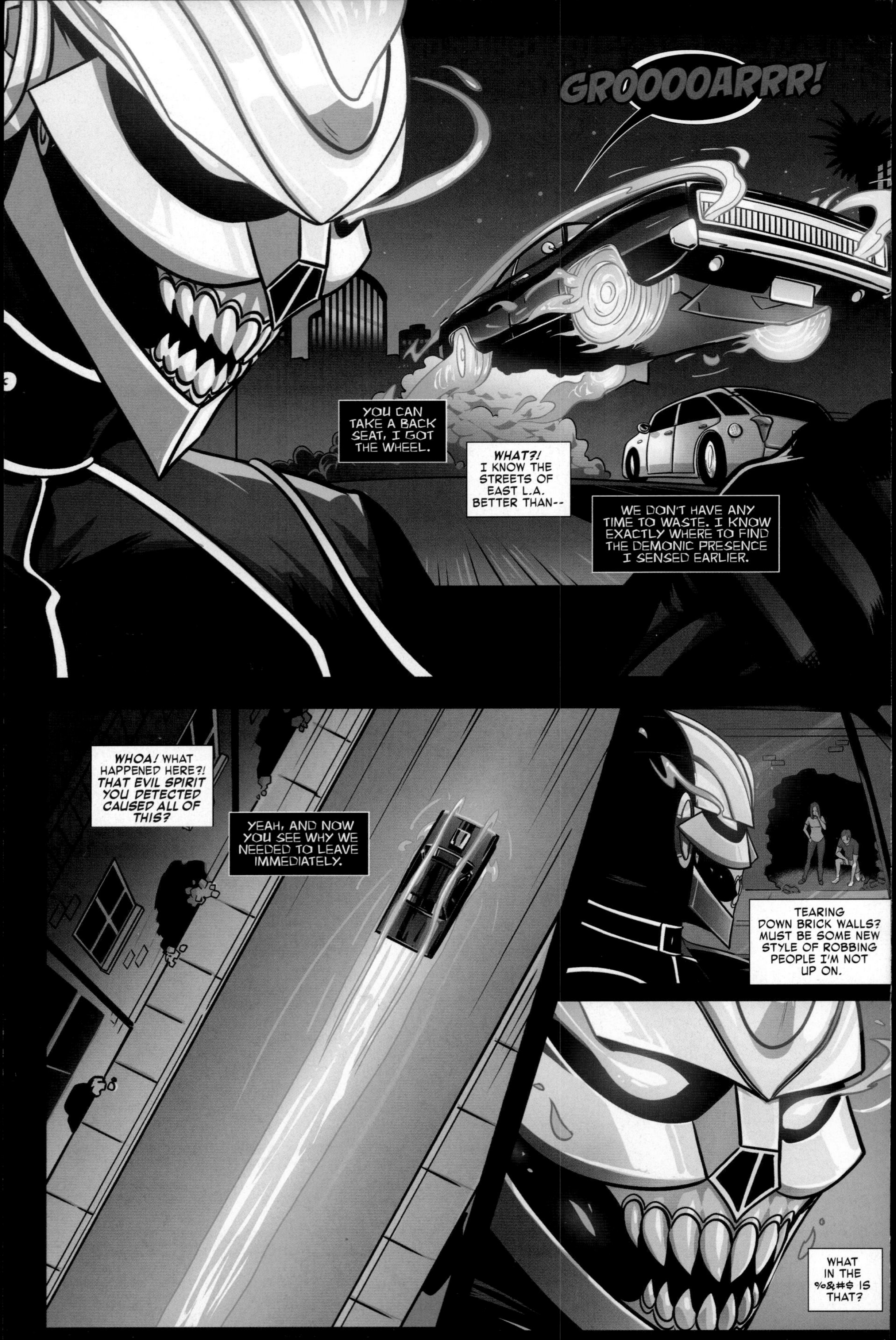
GROOOOARRR!
YOU CAN TAKE A BACK SEAT, I GOT THE WHEEL.
WHAT?! I KNOW THE STREETS OF EAST L.A. BETTER THAN--
WE DON'T HAVE ANY TIME TO WASTE. I KNOW EXACTLY WHERE TO FIND THE DEMONIC PRESENCE I SENSED EARLIER.
WHOA! WHAT HAPPENED HERE?! THAT EVIL SPIRIT YOU DETECTED CAUSED ALL OF THIS?
YEAH, AND NOW YOU SEE WHY WE NEEDED TO LEAVE IMMEDIATELY.
TEARING DOWN BRICK WALLS? MUST BE SOME NEW STYLE OF ROBBING PEOPLE I'M NOT UP ON.
WHAT IN THE %&#$ IS THAT?

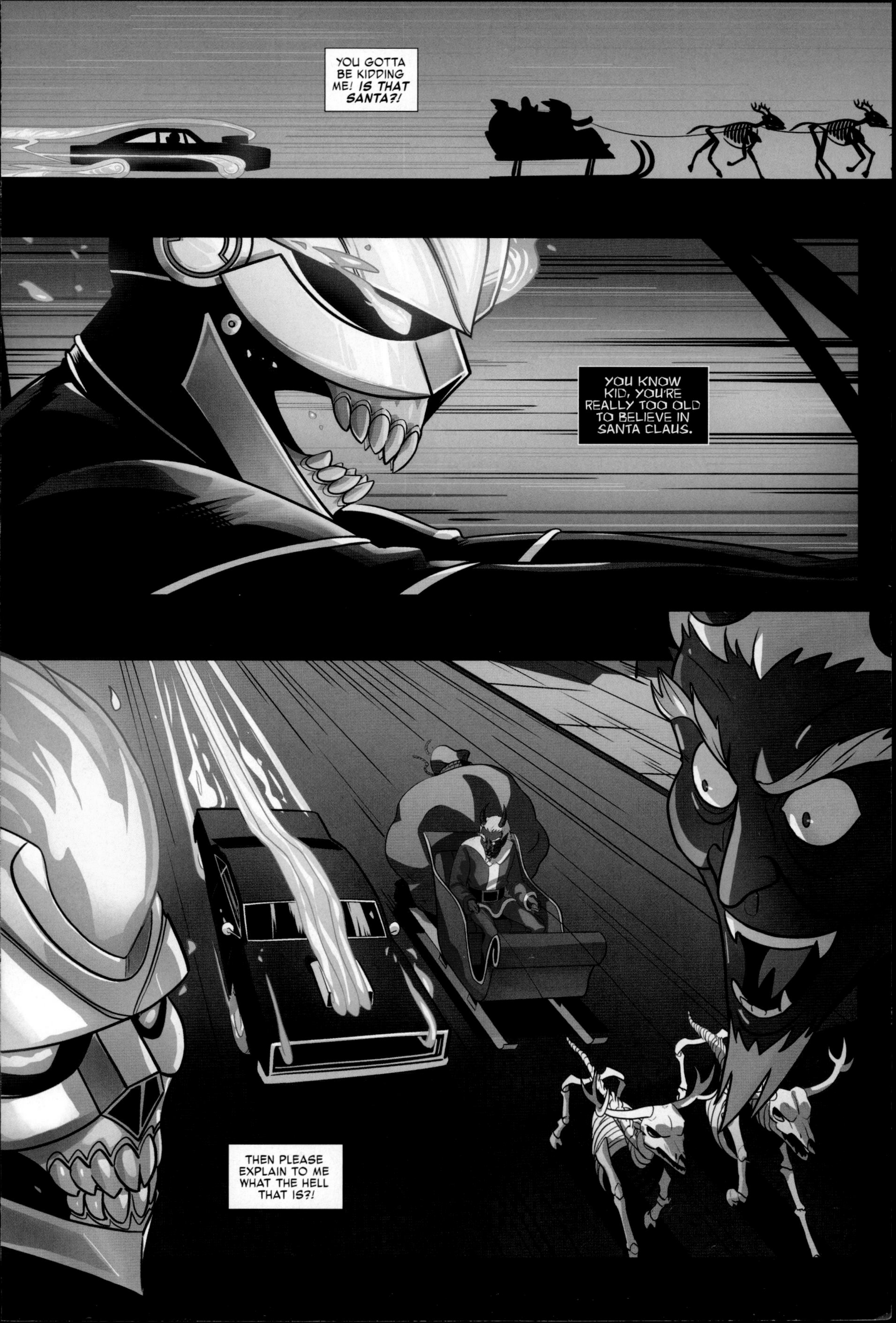
YOU GOTTA BE KIDDING ME! IS THAT SANTA?!
YOU KNOW KID, YOU'RE REALLY TOO OLD TO BELIEVE IN SANTA CLAUS.
THEN PLEASE EXPLAIN TO ME WHAT THE HELL THAT IS?!

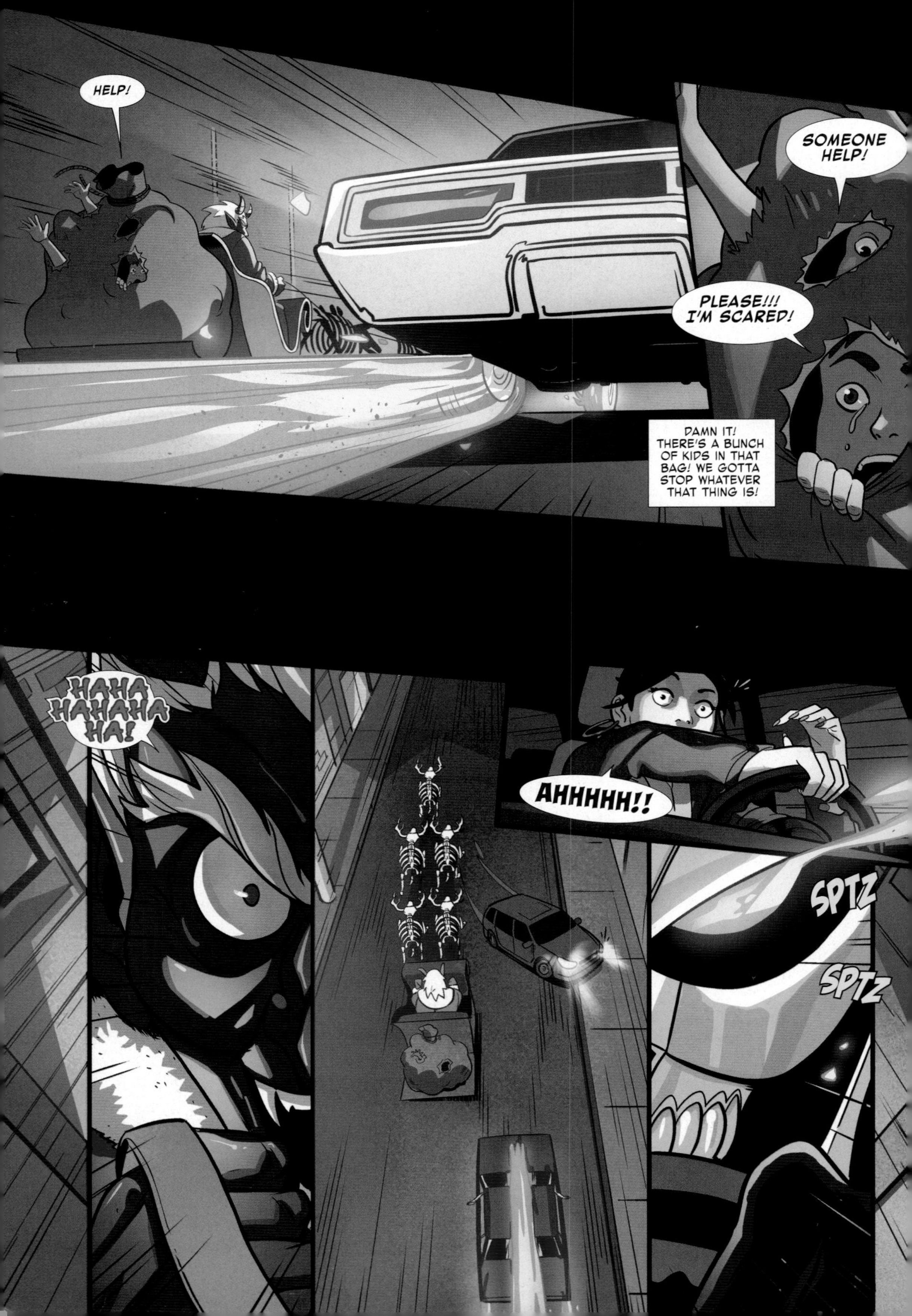
HELP!
SOMEONE HELP!
PLEASE!!! I'M SCARED!
DAMN IT! THERE'S A BUNCH OF KIDS IN THAT BAG! WE GOTTA STOP WHATEVER THAT THING IS!
HAHA HAHAHA HA!
AHHHHH!!
SPTZ
SPTZ

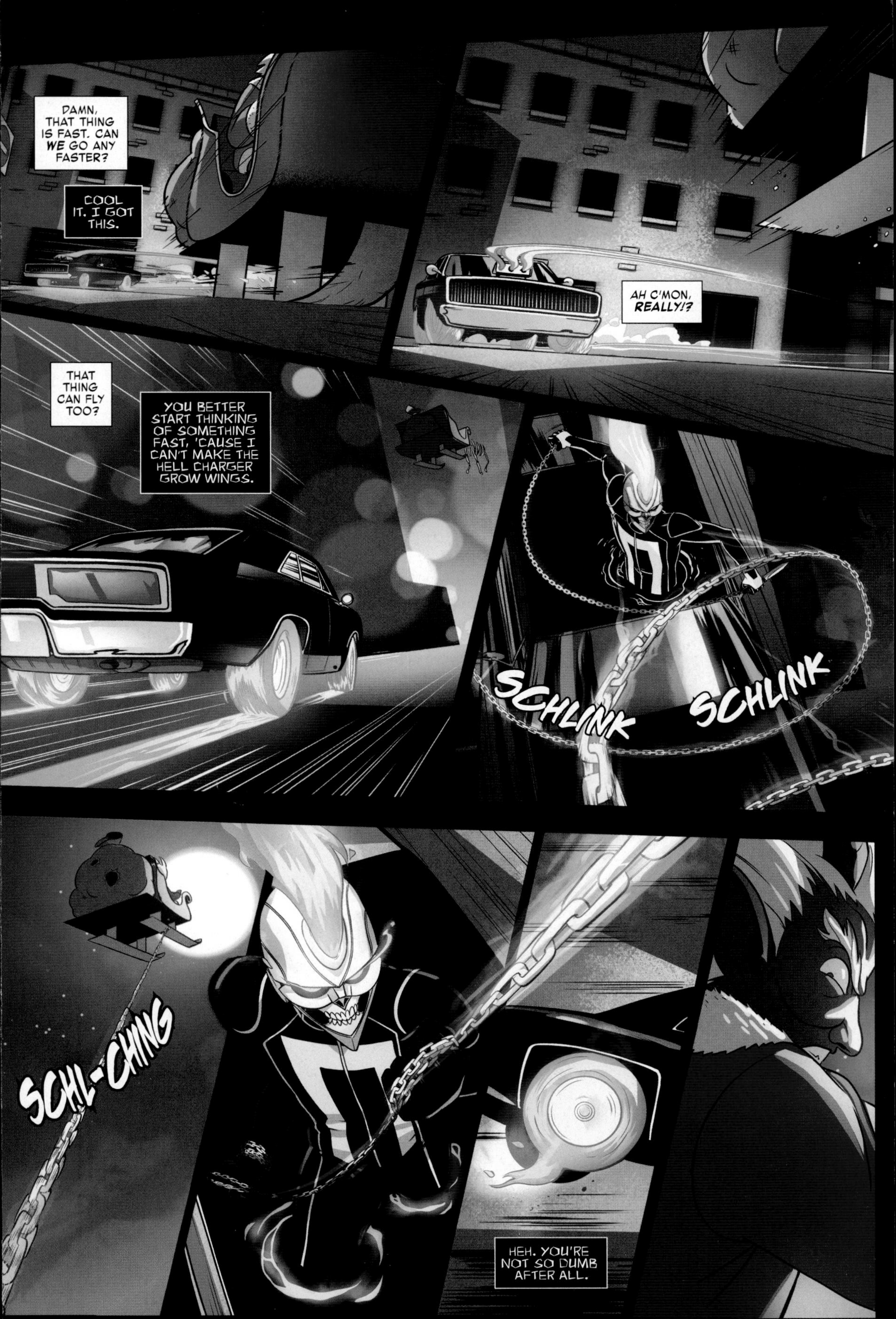
DAMN, THAT THING IS FAST. CAN WE GO ANY FASTER?
COOL IT. I GOT THIS.
AH C'MON, REALLY!?
THAT THING CAN FLY TOO?
YOU BETTER START THINKING OF SOMETHING FAST, 'CAUSE I CAN'T MAKE THE HELL CHARGER GROW WINGS.
SCHLINK
SCHLINK
SCHL-CHING
HEH. YOU'RE NOT SO DUMB AFTER ALL.

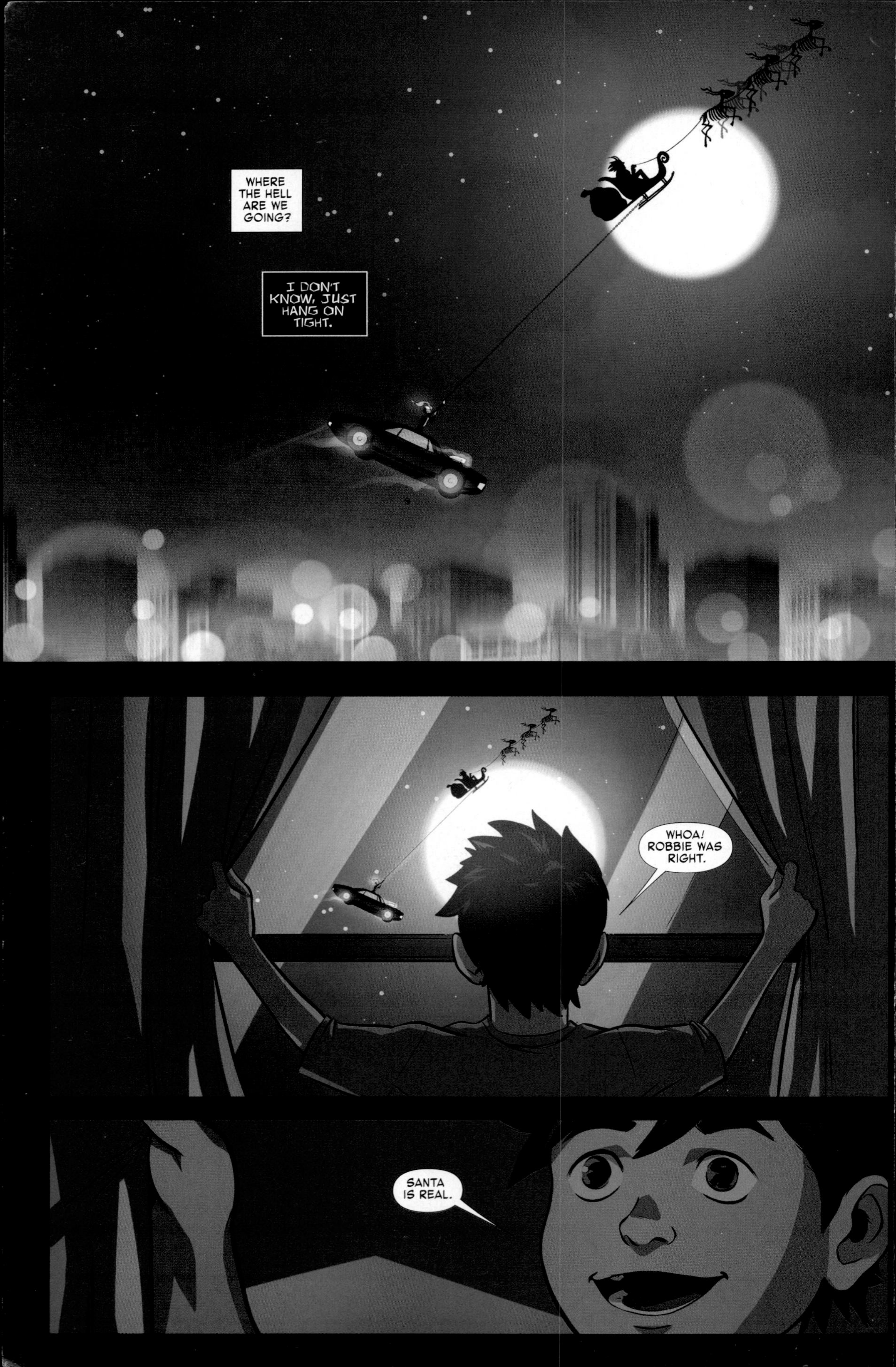
WHERE THE HELL ARE WE GOING?
I DON'T KNOW, JUST HANG ON TIGHT.
WHOA! ROBBIE WAS RIGHT.
SANTA IS REAL.

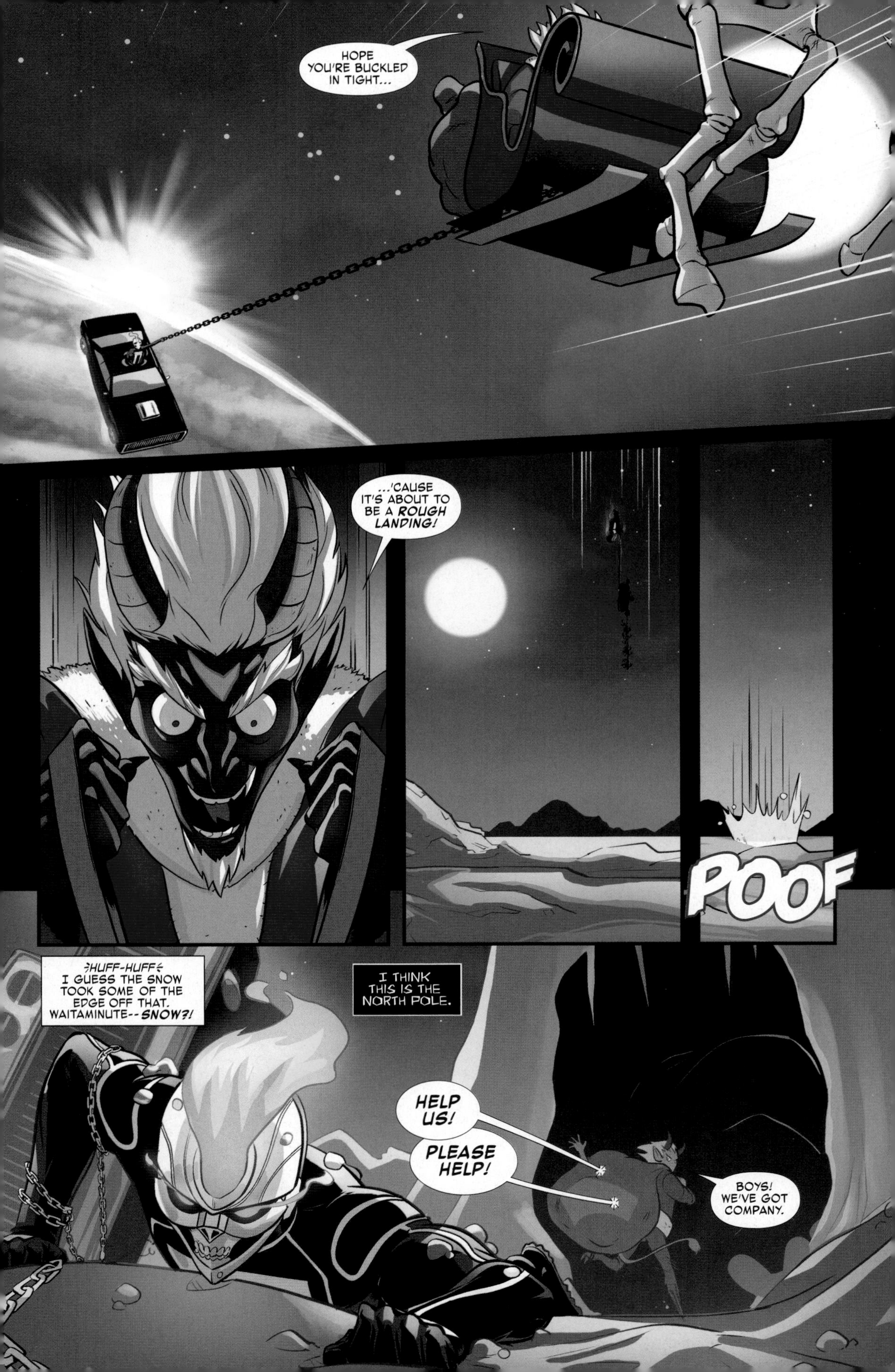
HOPE YOU'RE BUCKLED IN TIGHT...
...'CAUSE IT'S ABOUT TO BE A *ROUGH LANDING!*
POOF
HUFF-HUFF I GUESS THE SNOW TOOK SOME OF THE EDGE OFF THAT. WAITAMINUTE--*SNOW?!*
I THINK THIS IS THE NORTH POLE.
HELP US!
PLEASE HELP!
BOYS! WE'VE GOT COMPANY.

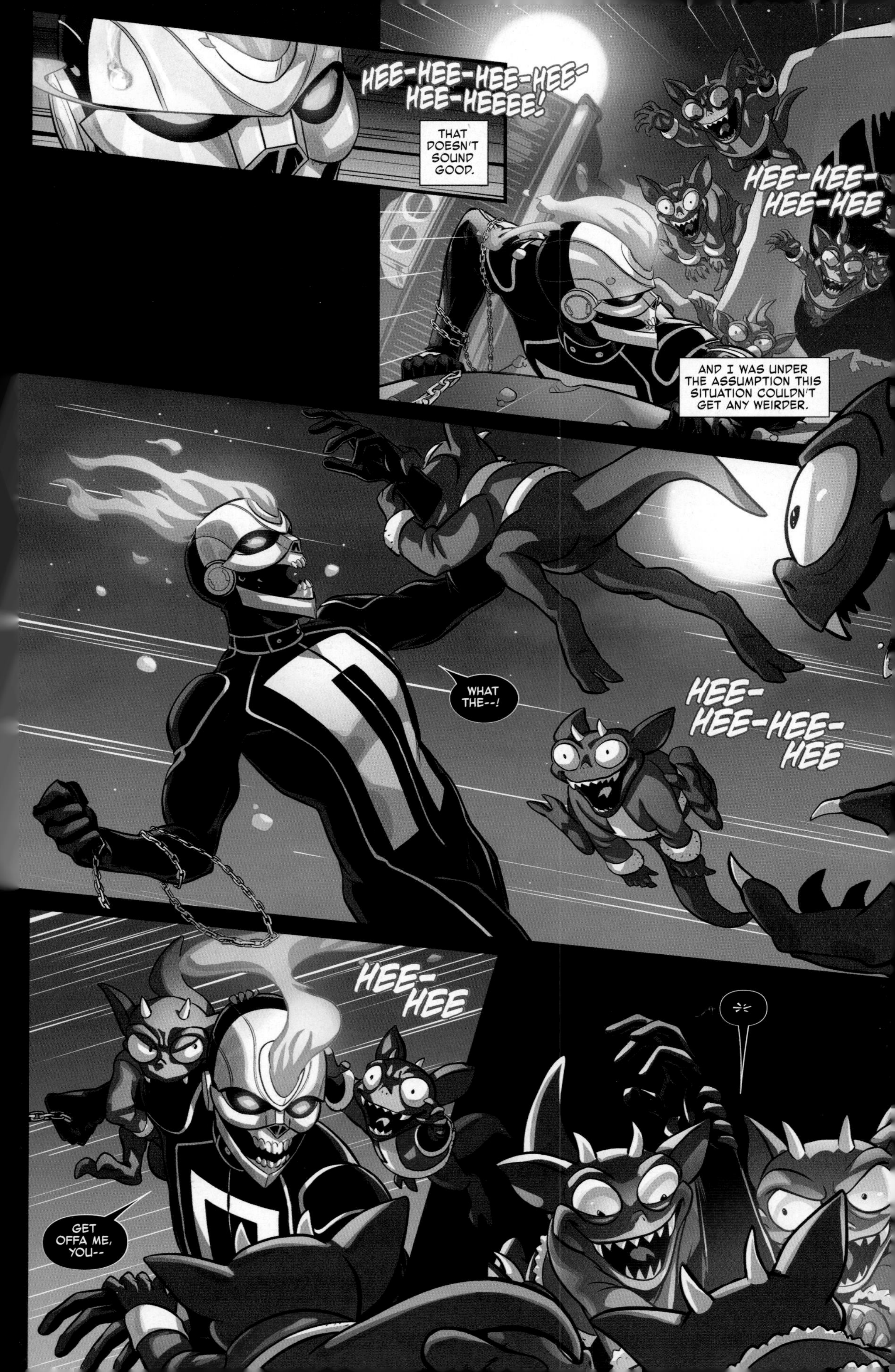
HEE-HEE-HEE-HEE-HEE-HEEEE!
THAT DOESN'T SOUND GOOD.
HEE-HEE-HEE-HEE
AND I WAS UNDER THE ASSUMPTION THIS SITUATION COULDN'T GET ANY WEIRDER.
WHAT THE--!
HEE-HEE-HEE-HEE
HEE-HEE
GET OFFA ME, YOU--

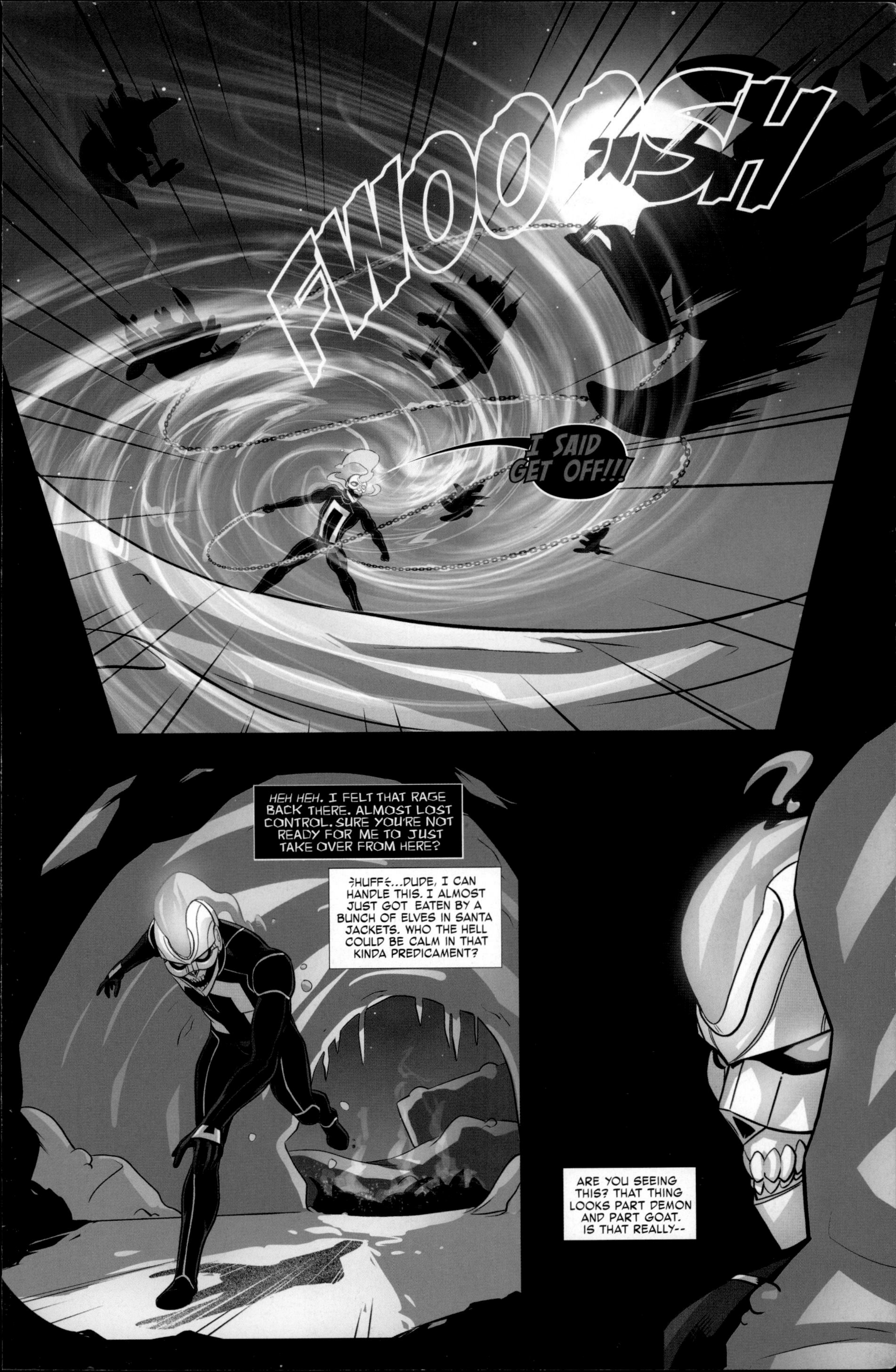
FWOOOSH
I SAID GET OFF!!!
HEH HEH. I FELT THAT RAGE BACK THERE. ALMOST LOST CONTROL. SURE YOU'RE NOT READY FOR ME TO JUST TAKE OVER FROM HERE?
HUFF...DUDE, I CAN HANDLE THIS. I ALMOST JUST GOT EATEN BY A BUNCH OF ELVES IN SANTA JACKETS. WHO THE HELL COULD BE CALM IN THAT KINDA PREDICAMENT?
ARE YOU SEEING THIS? THAT THING LOOKS PART DEMON AND PART GOAT. IS THAT REALLY--

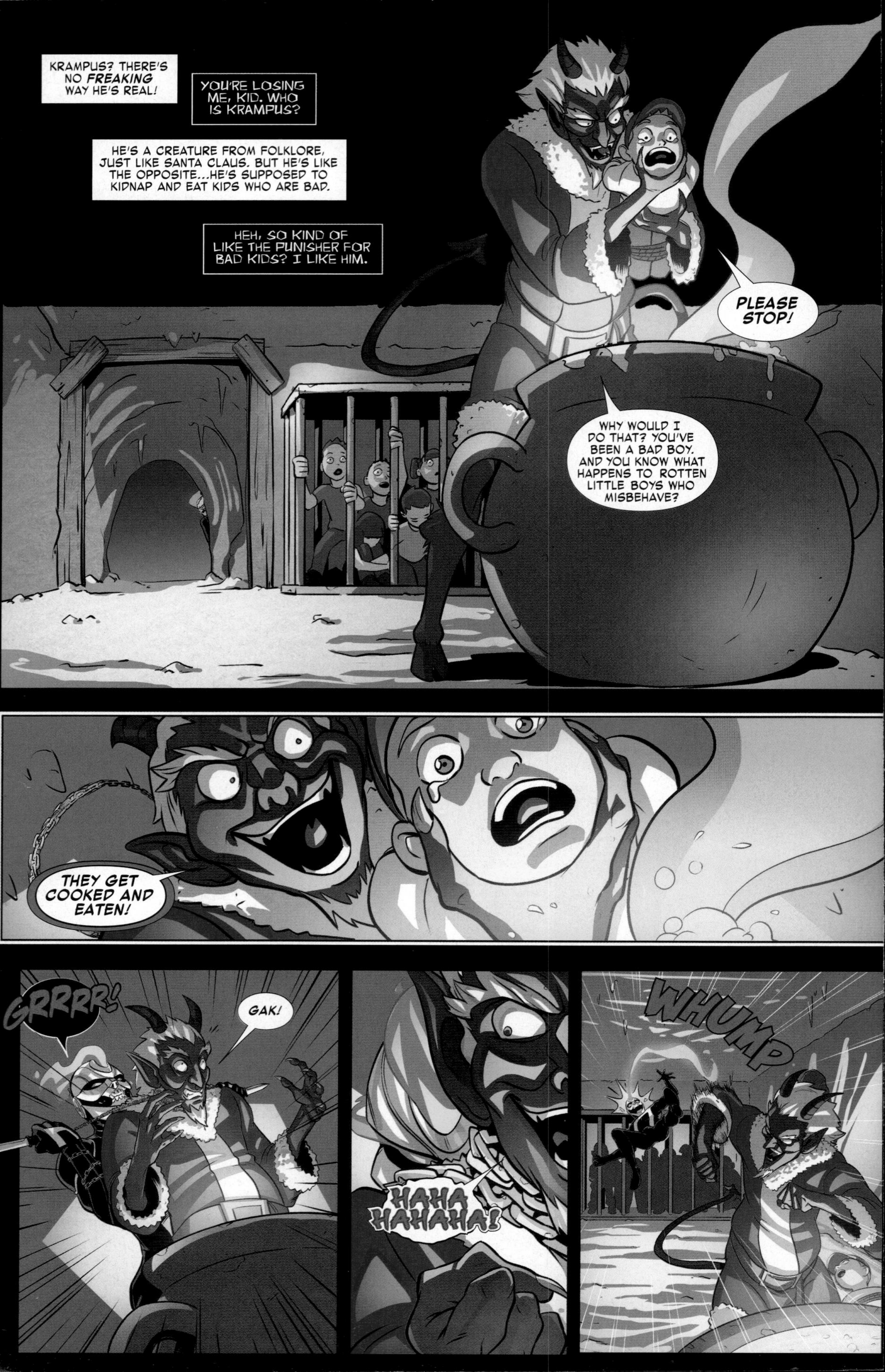
KRAMPUS? THERE'S NO FREAKING WAY HE'S REAL!
YOU'RE LOSING ME, KID. WHO IS KRAMPUS?
HE'S A CREATURE FROM FOLKLORE, JUST LIKE SANTA CLAUS. BUT HE'S LIKE THE OPPOSITE...HE'S SUPPOSED TO KIDNAP AND EAT KIDS WHO ARE BAD.
HEH, SO KIND OF LIKE THE PUNISHER FOR BAD KIDS? I LIKE HIM.
PLEASE STOP!
WHY WOULD I DO THAT? YOU'VE BEEN A BAD BOY. AND YOU KNOW WHAT HAPPENS TO ROTTEN LITTLE BOYS WHO MISBEHAVE?
THEY GET COOKED AND EATEN!
GRRRR!
GAK!
HAHA HAHAHA!
WHUMP

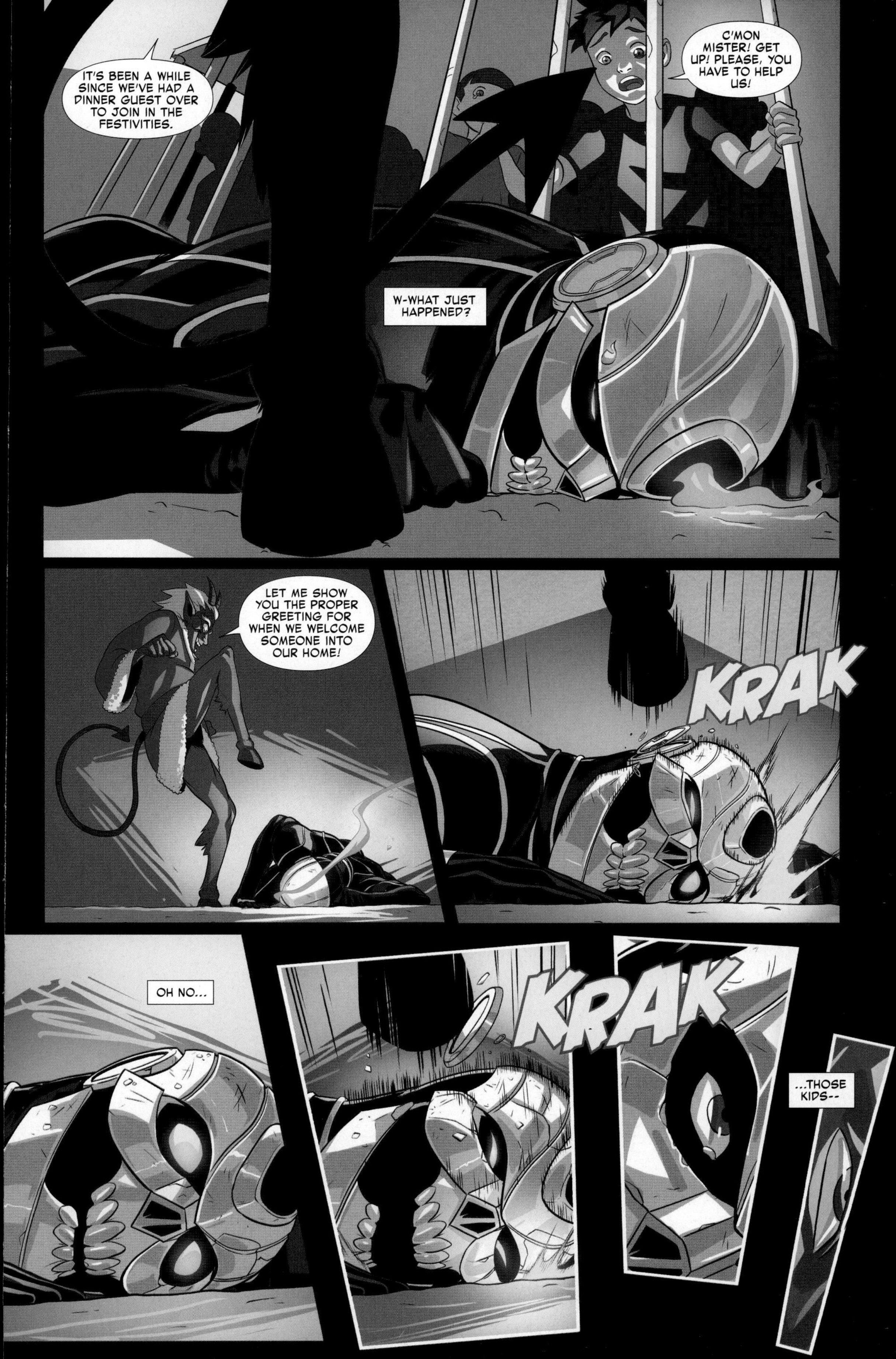
IT'S BEEN A WHILE SINCE WE'VE HAD A DINNER GUEST OVER TO JOIN IN THE FESTIVITIES.
C'MON MISTER! GET UP! PLEASE, YOU HAVE TO HELP US!
W-WHAT JUST HAPPENED?
LET ME SHOW YOU THE PROPER GREETING FOR WHEN WE WELCOME SOMEONE INTO OUR HOME!
KRAK
OH NO...
KRAK
...THOSE KIDS--

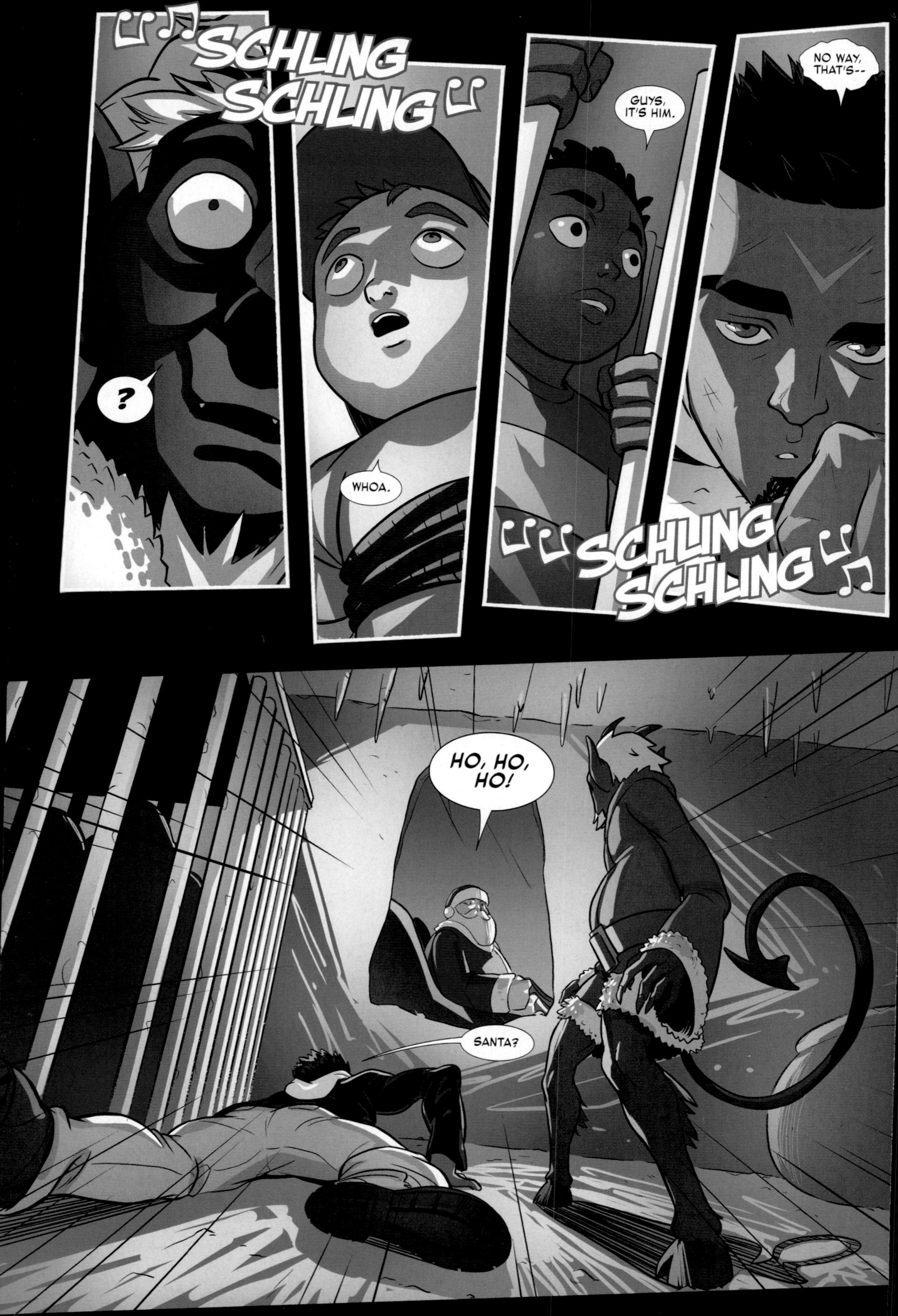
SCHLING SCHLING
?
WHOA.
GUYS, IT'S HIM.
NO WAY, THAT'S--
SCHLING SCHLING
HO, HO, HO!
SANTA?

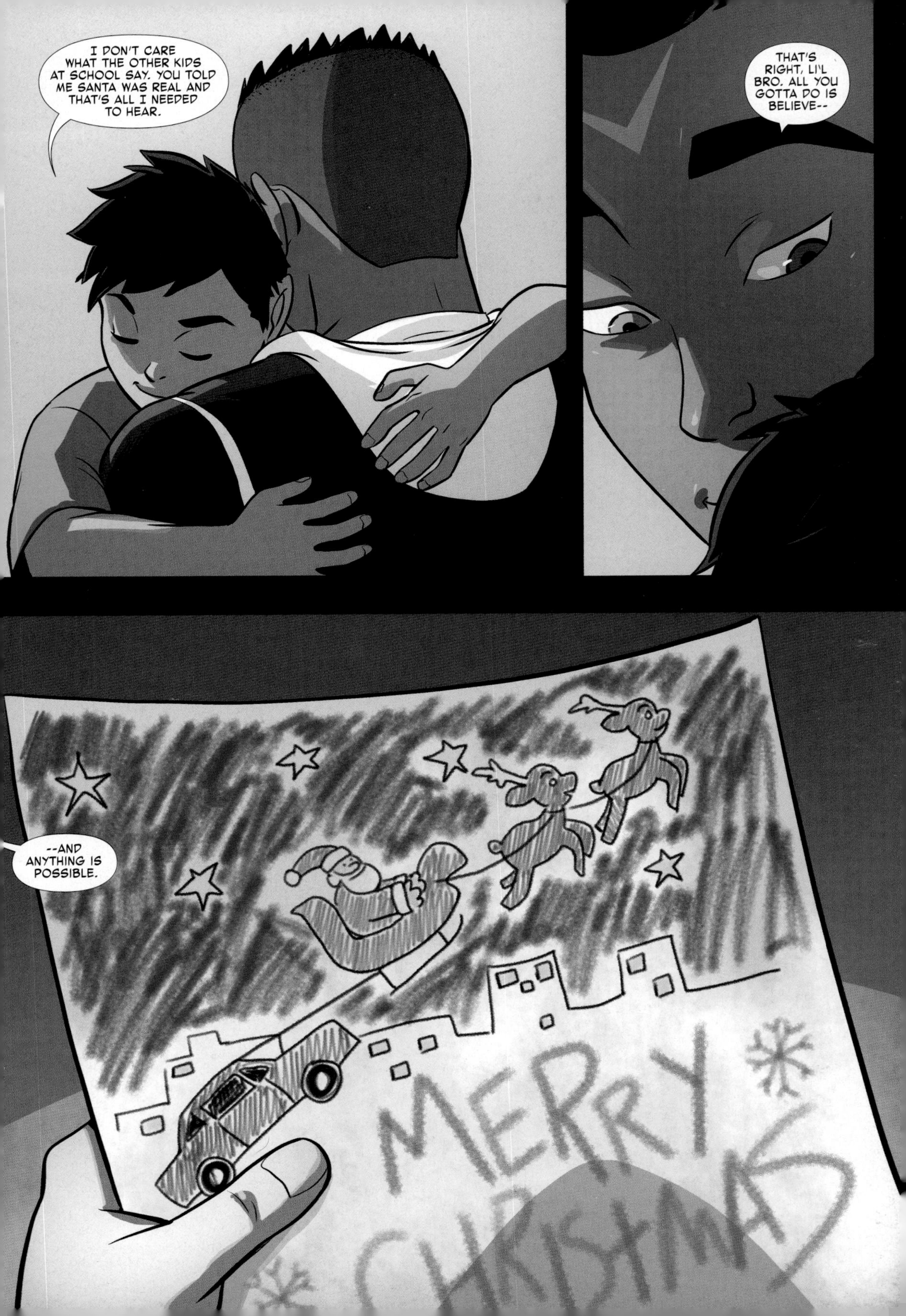
I DON'T CARE WHAT THE OTHER KIDS AT SCHOOL SAY. YOU TOLD ME SANTA WAS REAL AND THAT'S ALL I NEEDED TO HEAR.
THAT'S RIGHT, LI'L BRO. ALL YOU GOTTA DO IS BELIEVE--
--AND ANYTHING IS POSSIBLE.
MERRY CHRISTMAS

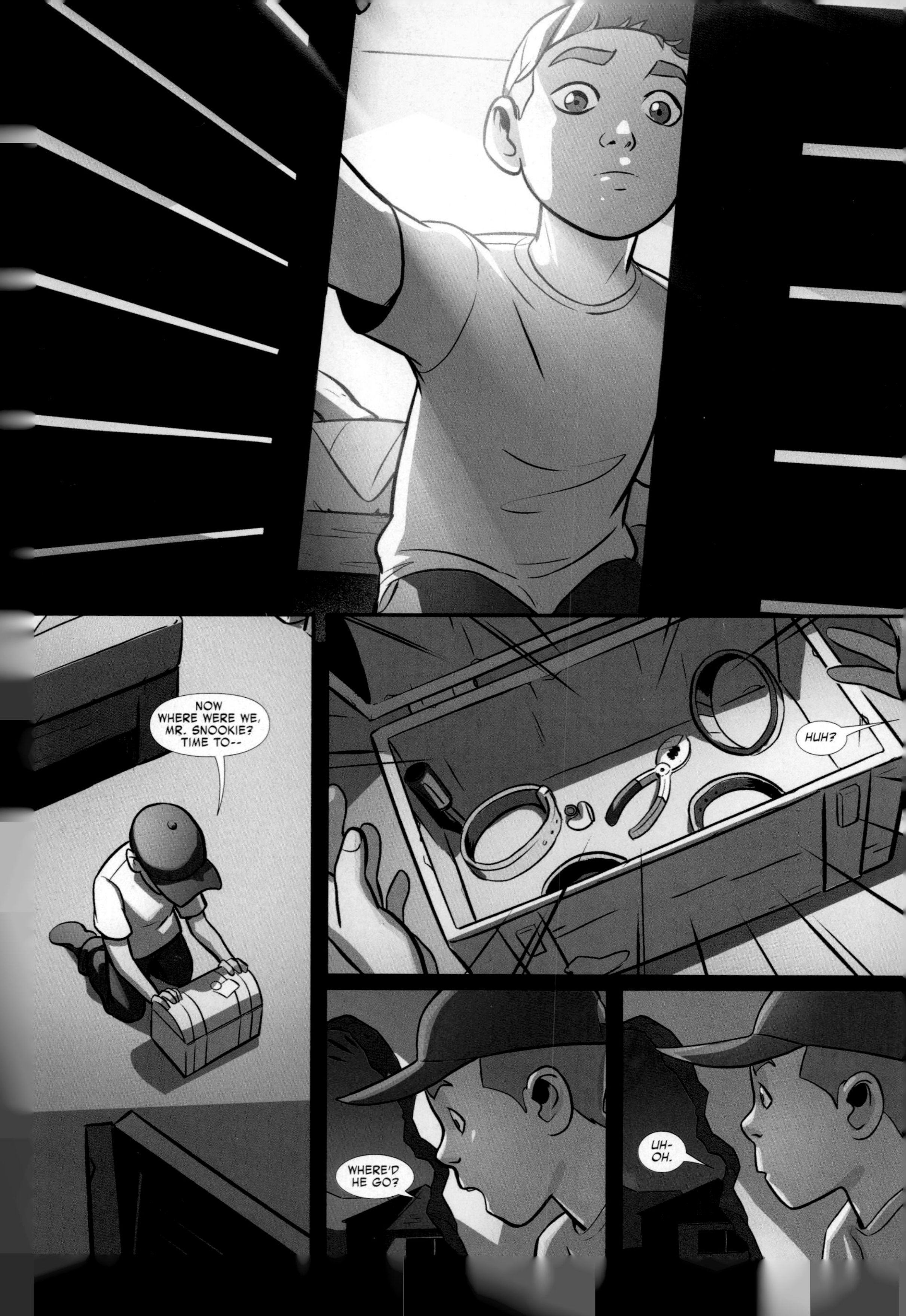
NOW WHERE WERE WE, MR. SNOOKIE? TIME TO--
HUH?
WHERE'D HE GO?
UH-OH.

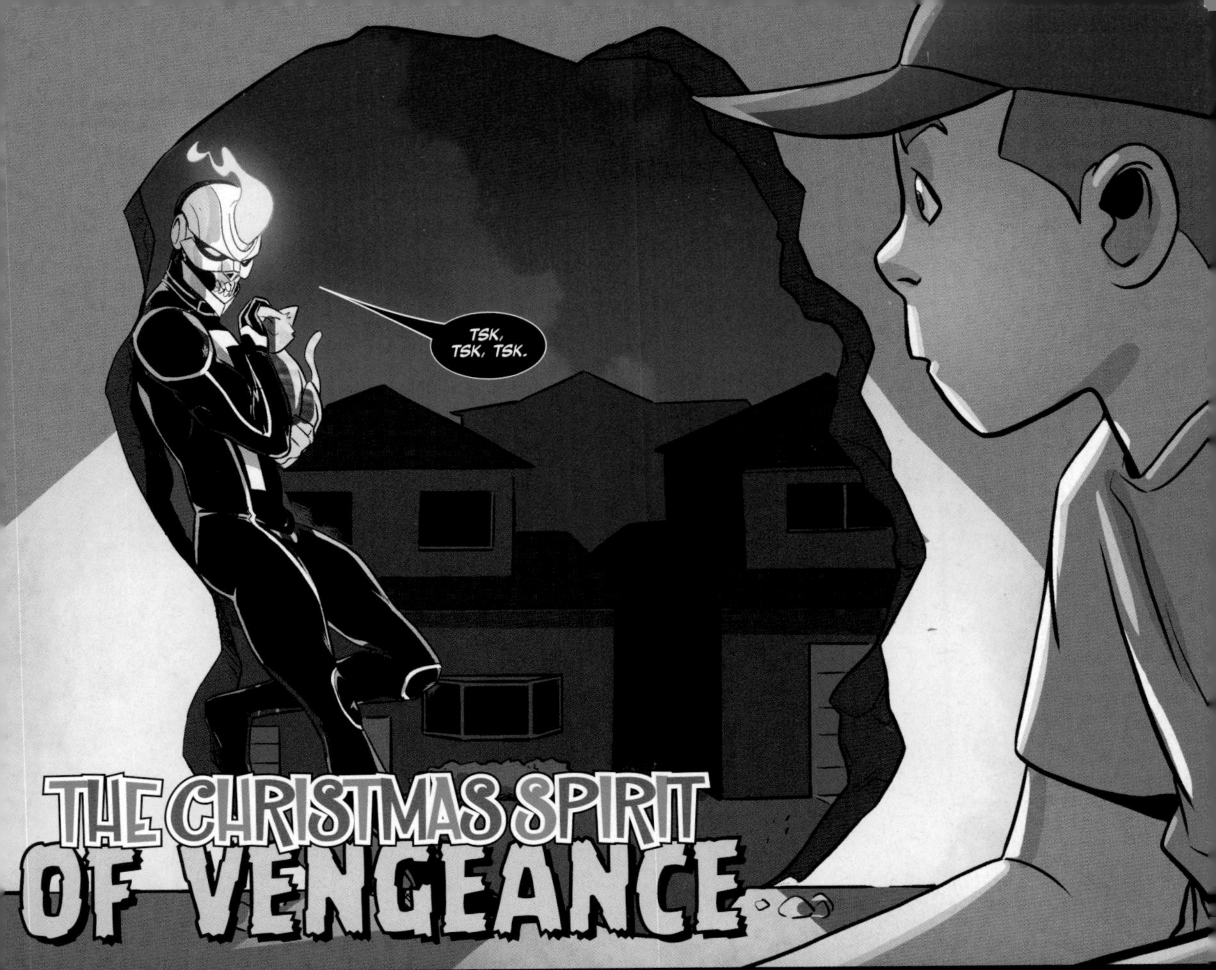
TSK, TSK, TSK.
THE CHRISTMAS SPIRIT OF VENGEANCE

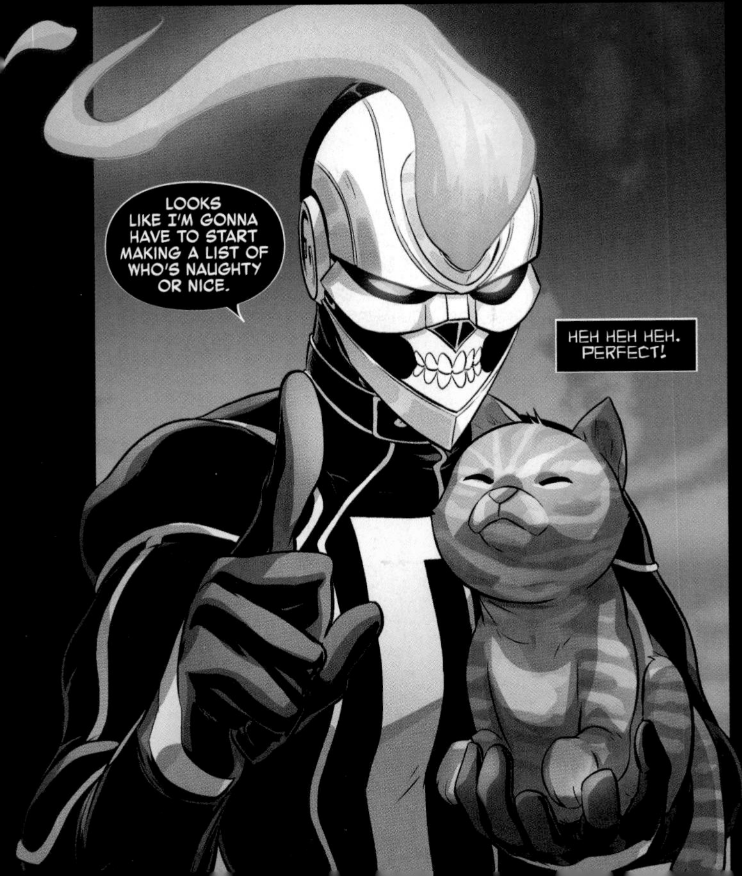
LOOKS LIKE I'M GONNA HAVE TO START MAKING A LIST OF WHO'S NAUGHTY OR NICE.
HEH HEH HEH. PERFECT!

METHOD MAN & ANTHONY PIPER & YVES BIGEREL
STORYTELLERS
ANTHONY PIPER & ANDRES MOSSA
COLOR ARTISTS
VC'S TRAVIS LANHAM
LETTERER
ANNIE CHENG
DIGITAL PRODUCTION AND LAYOUT
TIM SMITH 3
DIGITAL PRODUCTION MANAGER
CHRIS ROBINSON
EDITOR

Merry Christmas from Marvel Comics!

A YEAR OF MARVELS

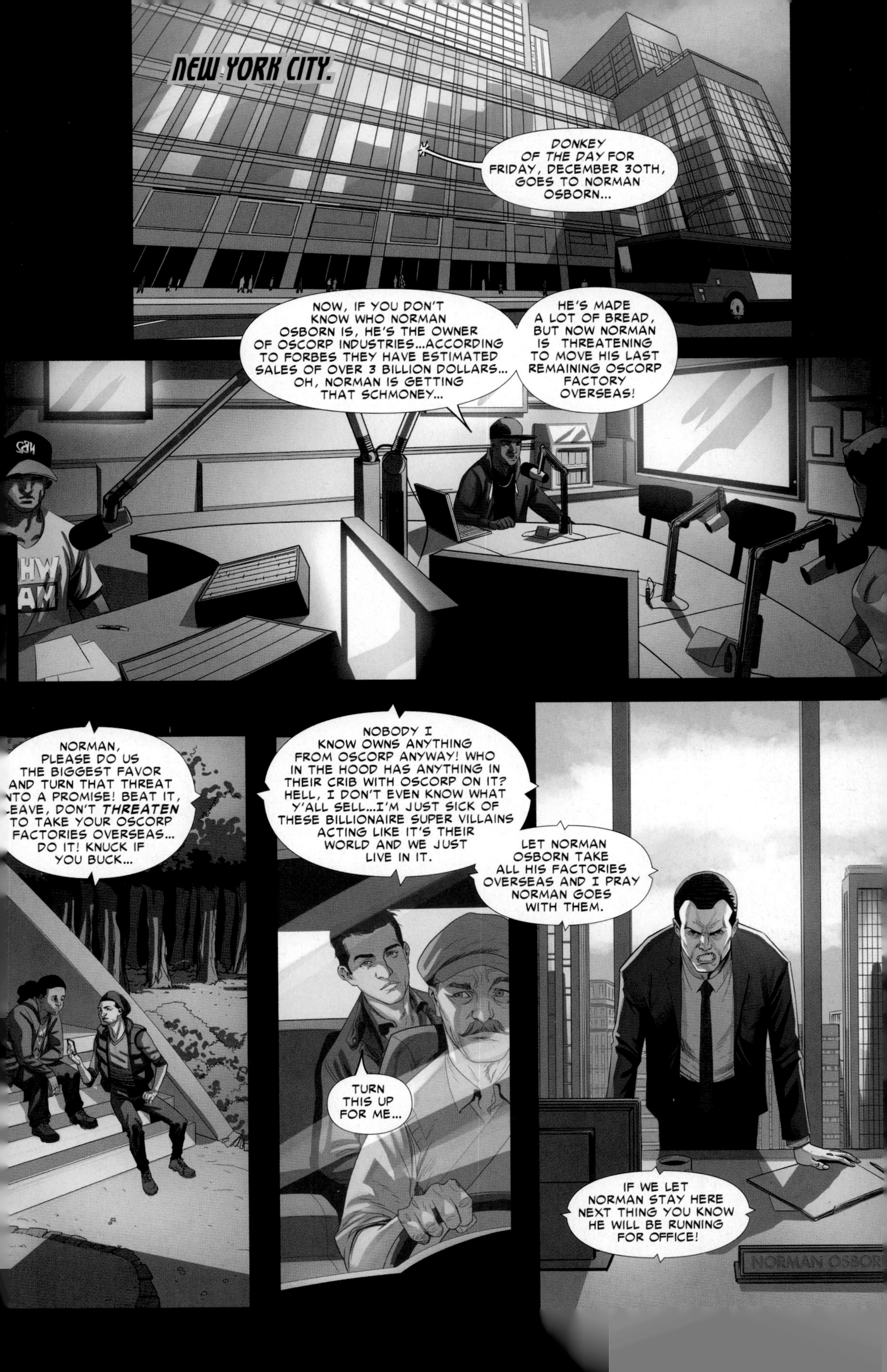
NEW YORK CITY.
DONKEY OF THE DAY FOR FRIDAY, DECEMBER 30TH, GOES TO NORMAN OSBORN...
NOW, IF YOU DON'T KNOW WHO NORMAN OSBORN IS, HE'S THE OWNER OF OSCORP INDUSTRIES...ACCORDING TO FORBES THEY HAVE ESTIMATED SALES OF OVER 3 BILLION DOLLARS... OH, NORMAN IS GETTING THAT SCHMONEY...
HE'S MADE A LOT OF BREAD, BUT NOW NORMAN IS THREATENING TO MOVE HIS LAST REMAINING OSCORP FACTORY OVERSEAS!
NORMAN, PLEASE DO US THE BIGGEST FAVOR AND TURN THAT THREAT INTO A PROMISE! BEAT IT, LEAVE, DON'T THREATEN TO TAKE YOUR OSCORP FACTORIES OVERSEAS... DO IT! KNUCK IF YOU BUCK...
NOBODY I KNOW OWNS ANYTHING FROM OSCORP ANYWAY! WHO IN THE HOOD HAS ANYTHING IN THEIR CRIB WITH OSCORP ON IT? HELL, I DON'T EVEN KNOW WHAT Y'ALL SELL...I'M JUST SICK OF THESE BILLIONAIRE SUPER VILLAINS ACTING LIKE IT'S THEIR WORLD AND WE JUST LIVE IN IT.
LET NORMAN OSBORN TAKE ALL HIS FACTORIES OVERSEAS AND I PRAY NORMAN GOES WITH THEM.
TURN THIS UP FOR ME...
IF WE LET NORMAN STAY HERE NEXT THING YOU KNOW HE WILL BE RUNNING FOR OFFICE!

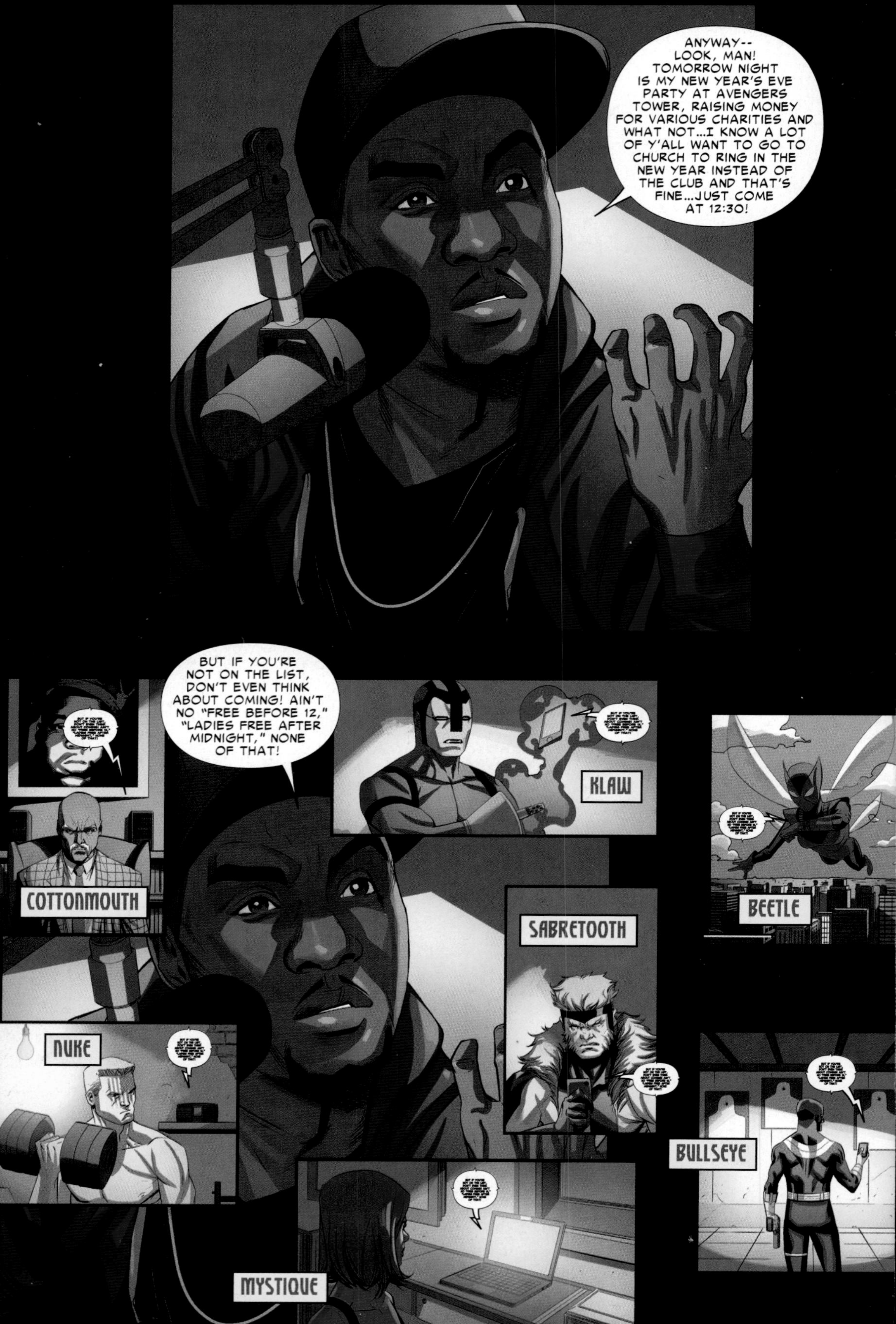

ANYWAY-- LOOK, MAN! TOMORROW NIGHT IS MY NEW YEAR'S EVE PARTY AT AVENGERS TOWER, RAISING MONEY FOR VARIOUS CHARITIES AND WHAT NOT...I KNOW A LOT OF Y'ALL WANT TO GO TO CHURCH TO RING IN THE NEW YEAR INSTEAD OF THE CLUB AND THAT'S FINE...JUST COME AT 12:30!
BUT IF YOU'RE NOT ON THE LIST, DON'T EVEN THINK ABOUT COMING! AIN'T NO "FREE BEFORE 12," "LADIES FREE AFTER MIDNIGHT," NONE OF THAT!
KLAW
COTTONMOUTH
BEETLE
SABRETOOTH
NUKE
BULLSEYE
MYSTIQUE

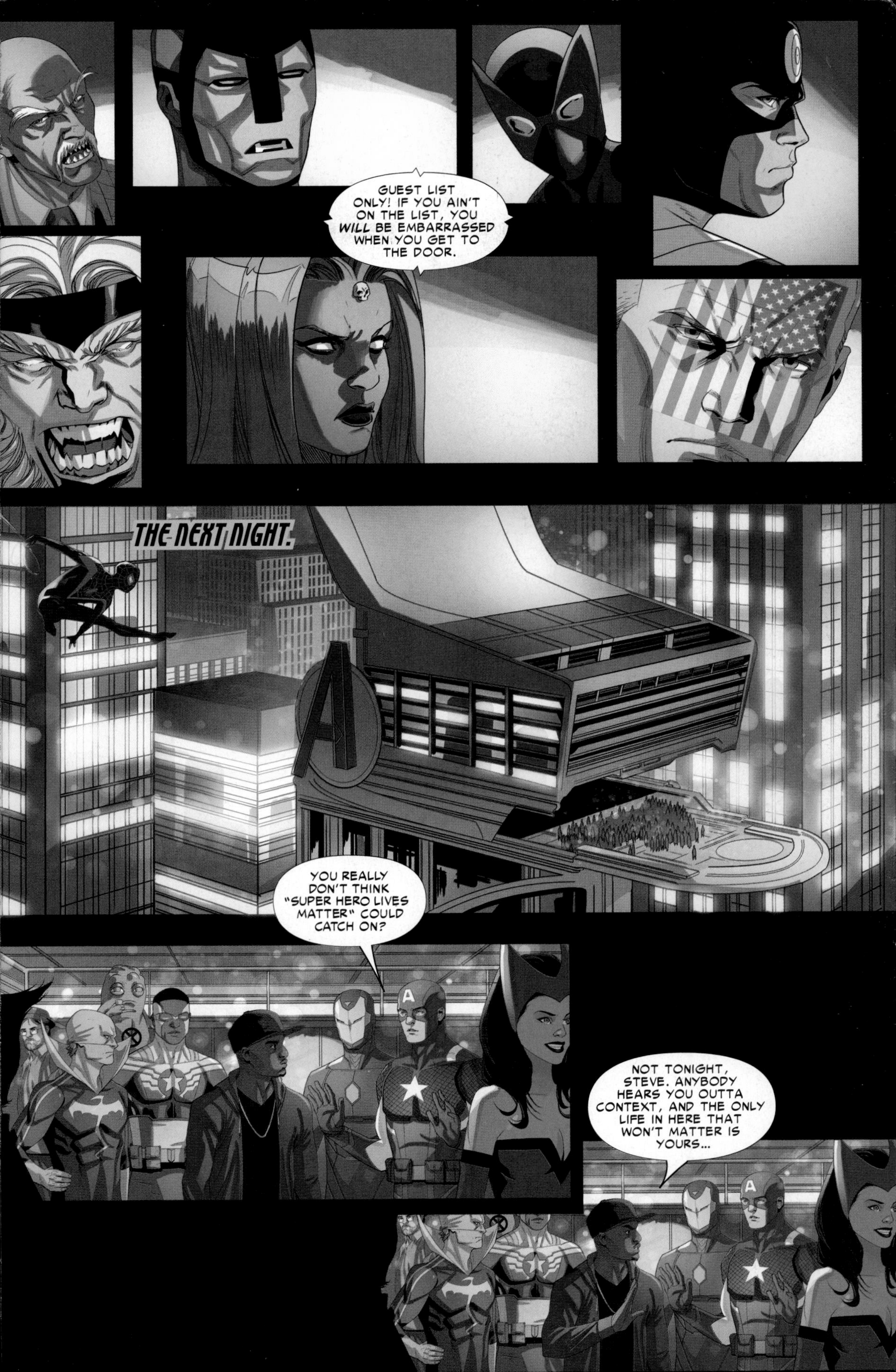
GUEST LIST ONLY! IF YOU AIN'T ON THE LIST, YOU WILL BE EMBARRASSED WHEN YOU GET TO THE DOOR.
THE NEXT NIGHT.
YOU REALLY DON'T THINK "SUPER HERO LIVES MATTER" COULD CATCH ON?
NOT TONIGHT, STEVE. ANYBODY HEARS YOU OUTTA CONTEXT, AND THE ONLY LIFE IN HERE THAT WON'T MATTER IS YOURS...

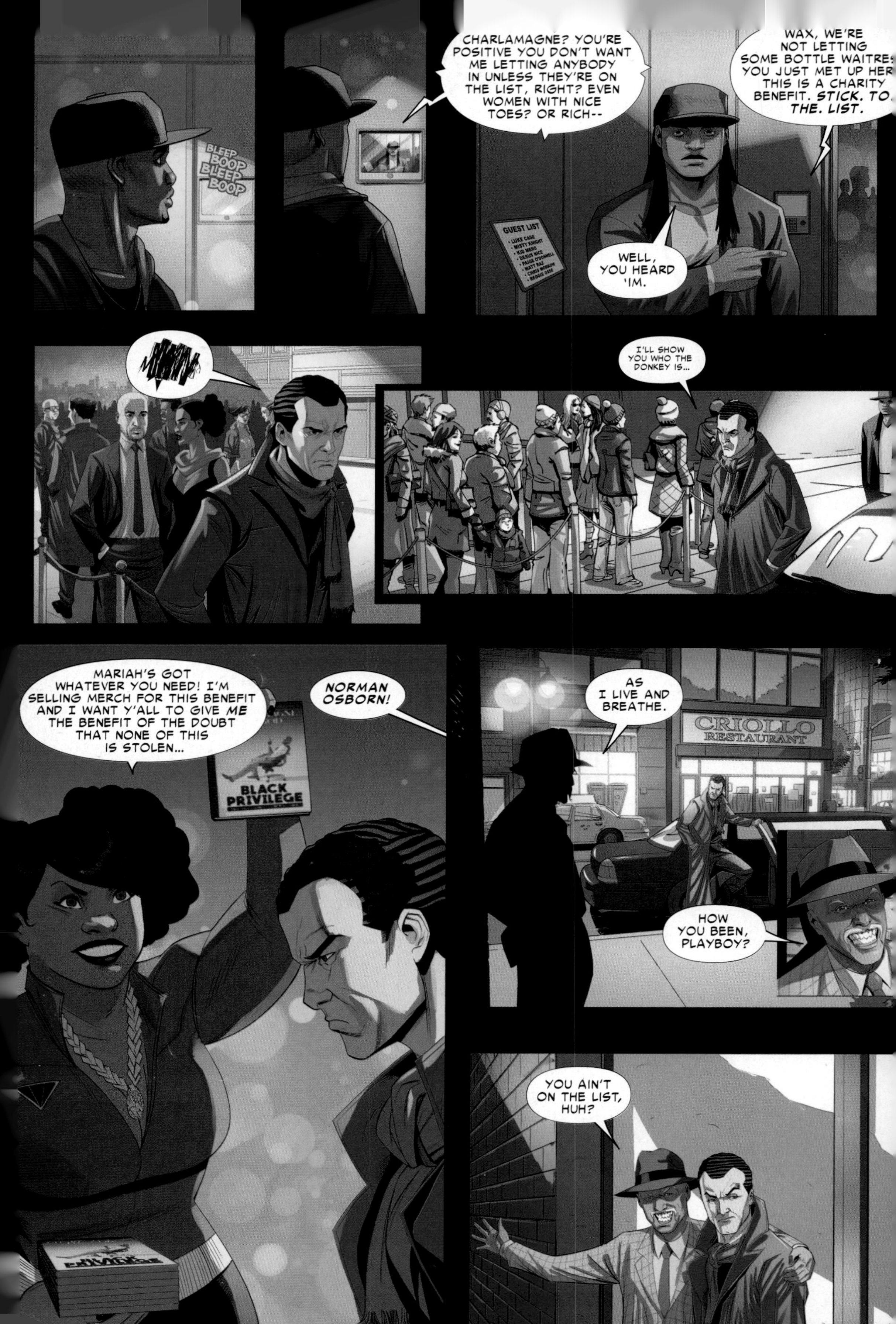
BLEEP BOOP BLEEP BOOP
CHARLAMAGNE? YOU'RE POSITIVE YOU DON'T WANT ME LETTING ANYBODY IN UNLESS THEY'RE ON THE LIST, RIGHT? EVEN WOMEN WITH NICE TOES? OR RICH--
WAX, WE'RE NOT LETTING SOME BOTTLE WAITRES YOU JUST MET UP HER THIS IS A CHARITY BENEFIT. STICK. TO. THE. LIST.
GUEST LIST
• LUKE CAGE
• MISTY KNIGHT
• KID MERO
• DESUS NICE
• PAIGE O'DONNELL
• MATT RAZ
• CHRIS MORROW
• REGGIE OSSE
WELL, YOU HEARD 'IM.
I'LL SHOW YOU WHO THE DONKEY IS...
MARIAH'S GOT WHATEVER YOU NEED! I'M SELLING MERCH FOR THIS BENEFIT AND I WANT Y'ALL TO GIVE ME THE BENEFIT OF THE DOUBT THAT NONE OF THIS IS STOLEN...
NORMAN OSBORN!
BLACK PRIVILEGE
AS I LIVE AND BREATHE.
CRIOLLO RESTAURANT
HOW YOU BEEN, PLAYBOY?
YOU AIN'T ON THE LIST, HUH?

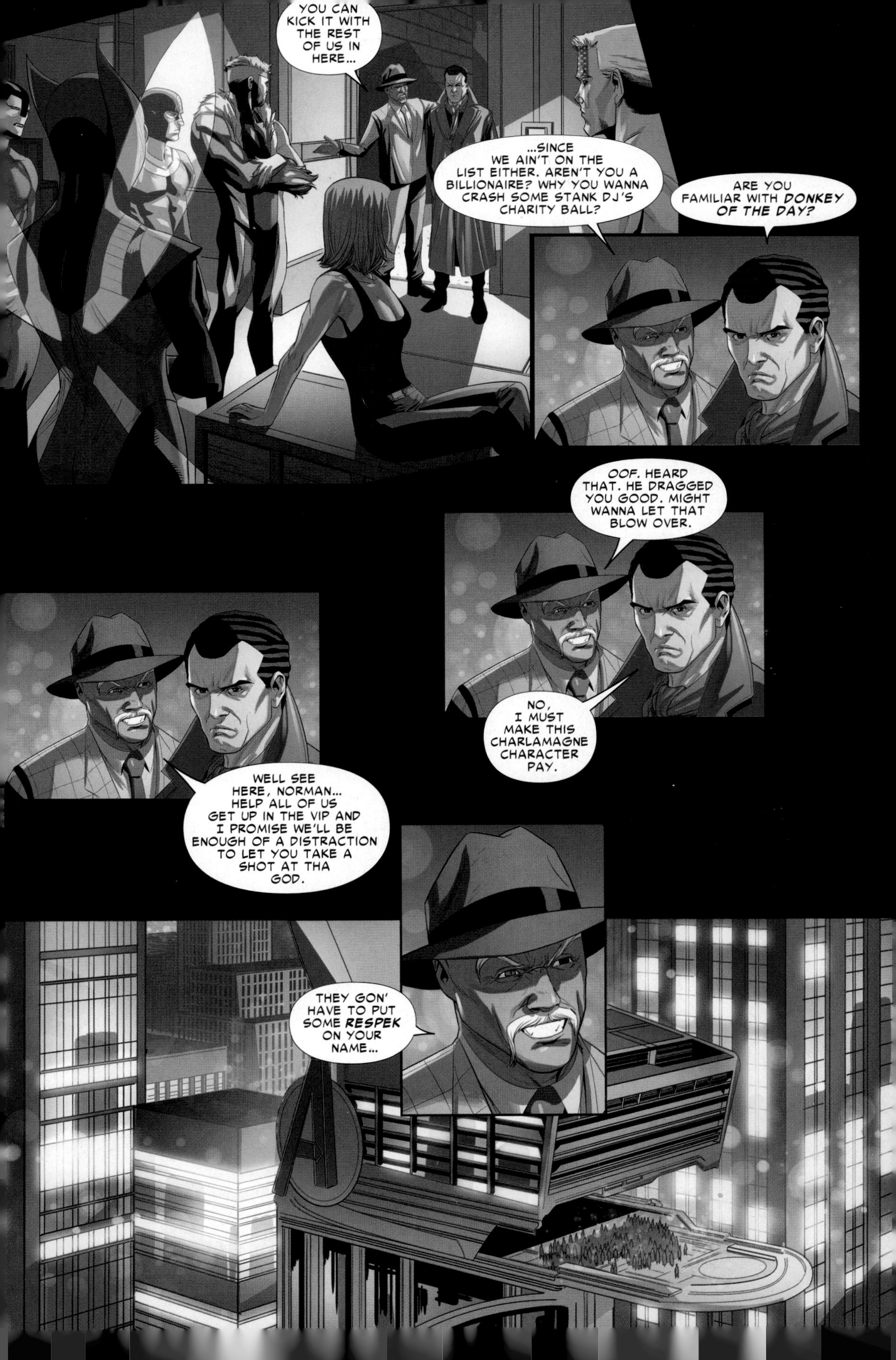
YOU CAN KICK IT WITH THE REST OF US IN HERE...
...SINCE WE AIN'T ON THE LIST EITHER. AREN'T YOU A BILLIONAIRE? WHY YOU WANNA CRASH SOME STANK DJ'S CHARITY BALL?
ARE YOU FAMILIAR WITH *DONKEY OF THE DAY?*
OOF. HEARD THAT. HE DRAGGED YOU GOOD. MIGHT WANNA LET THAT BLOW OVER.
NO, I MUST MAKE THIS CHARLAMAGNE CHARACTER PAY.
WELL SEE HERE, NORMAN... HELP ALL OF US GET UP IN THE VIP AND I PROMISE WE'LL BE ENOUGH OF A DISTRACTION TO LET YOU TAKE A SHOT AT THA GOD.
THEY GON' HAVE TO PUT SOME *RESPEK* ON YOUR NAME...

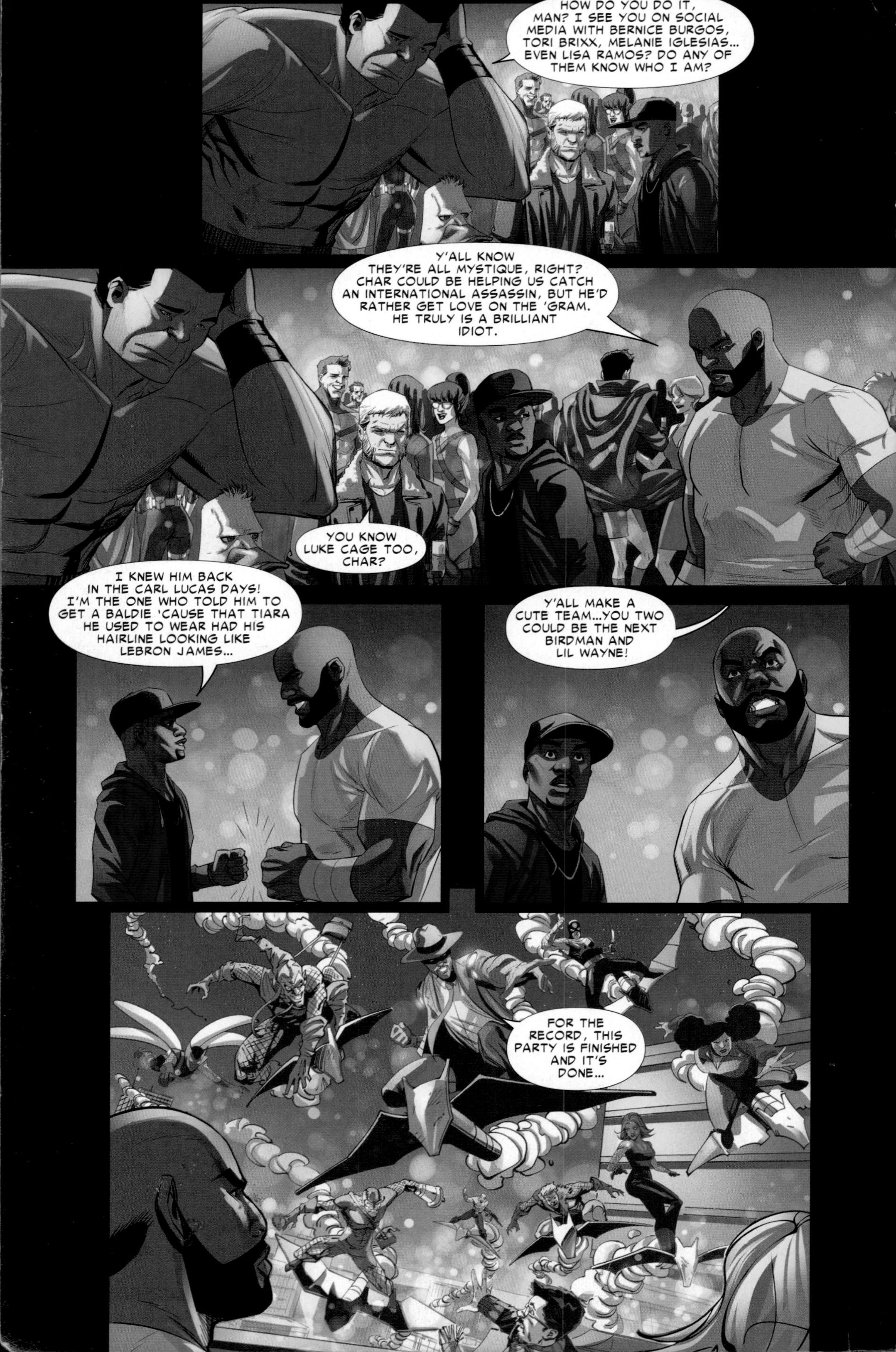
HOW DO YOU DO IT, MAN? I SEE YOU ON SOCIAL MEDIA WITH BERNICE BURGOS, TORI BRIXX, MELANIE IGLESIAS... EVEN LISA RAMOS? DO ANY OF THEM KNOW WHO I AM?
Y'ALL KNOW THEY'RE ALL MYSTIQUE, RIGHT? CHAR COULD BE HELPING US CATCH AN INTERNATIONAL ASSASSIN, BUT HE'D RATHER GET LOVE ON THE 'GRAM. HE TRULY IS A BRILLIANT IDIOT.
YOU KNOW LUKE CAGE TOO, CHAR?
I KNEW HIM BACK IN THE CARL LUCAS DAYS! I'M THE ONE WHO TOLD HIM TO GET A BALDIE 'CAUSE THAT TIARA HE USED TO WEAR HAD HIS HAIRLINE LOOKING LIKE LEBRON JAMES...
Y'ALL MAKE A CUTE TEAM...YOU TWO COULD BE THE NEXT BIRDMAN AND LIL WAYNE!
FOR THE RECORD, THIS PARTY IS FINISHED AND IT'S DONE...

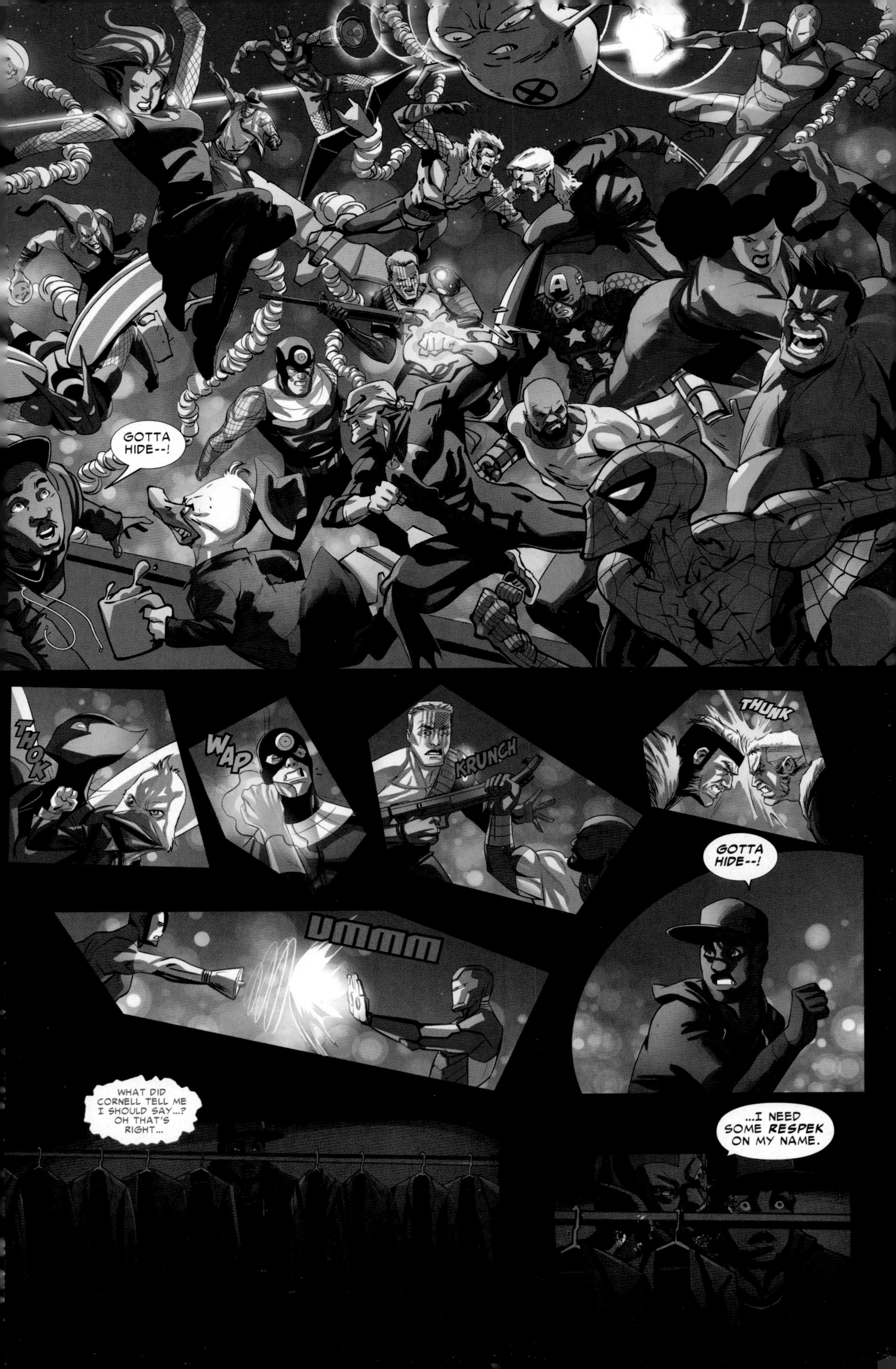
GOTTA HIDE--!
THOK
WAP
KRUNCH
THUNK
GOTTA HIDE--!
UMMMM
WHAT DID CORNELL TELL ME I SHOULD SAY...? OH THAT'S RIGHT...
...I NEED SOME RESPEK ON MY NAME.

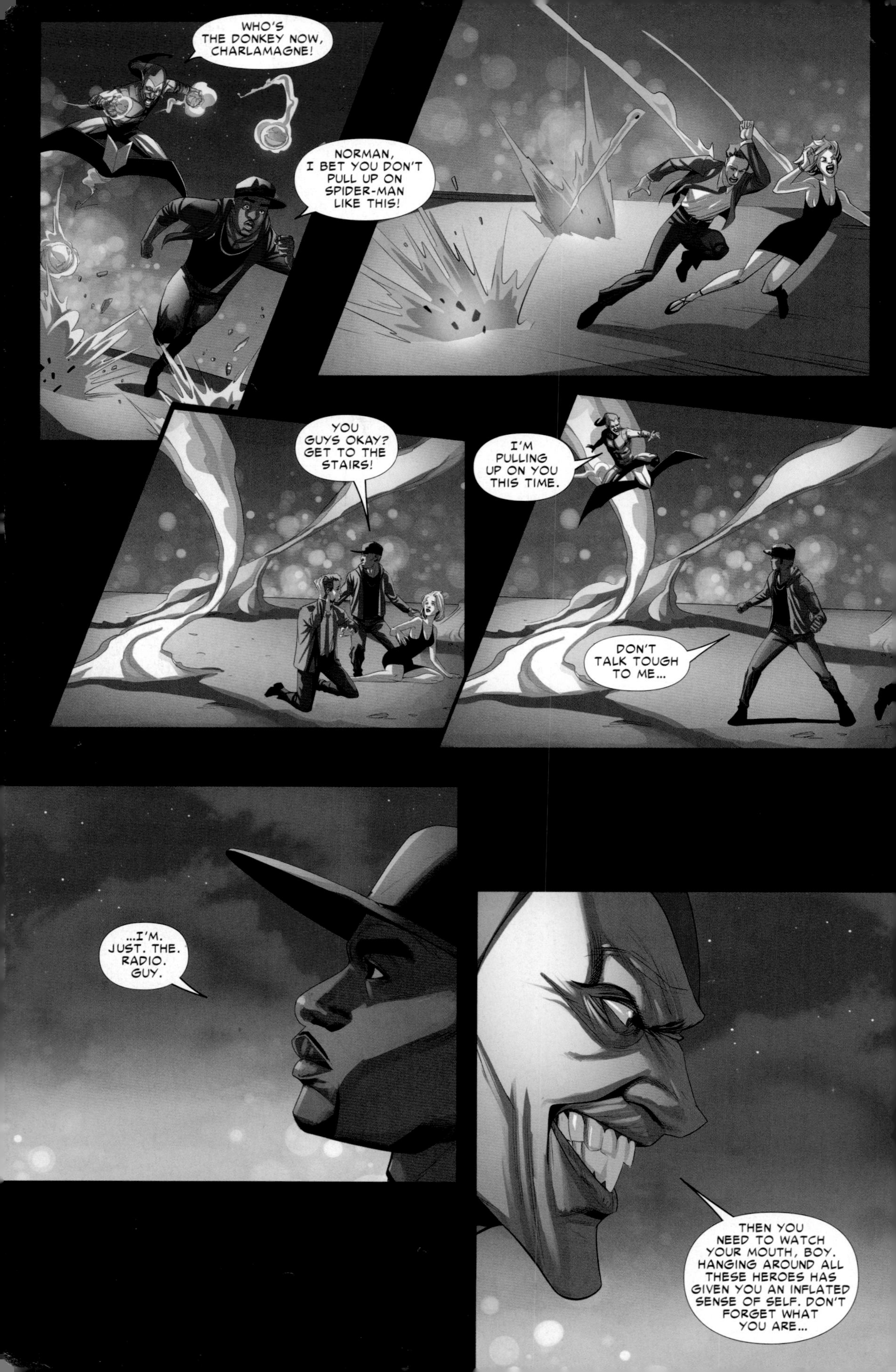
WHO'S THE DONKEY NOW, CHARLAMAGNE!
NORMAN, I BET YOU DON'T PULL UP ON SPIDER-MAN LIKE THIS!
YOU GUYS OKAY? GET TO THE STAIRS!
I'M PULLING UP ON YOU THIS TIME.
DON'T TALK TOUGH TO ME...
...I'M. JUST. THE. RADIO. GUY.
THEN YOU NEED TO WATCH YOUR MOUTH, BOY. HANGING AROUND ALL THESE HEROES HAS GIVEN YOU AN INFLATED SENSE OF SELF. DON'T FORGET WHAT YOU ARE...

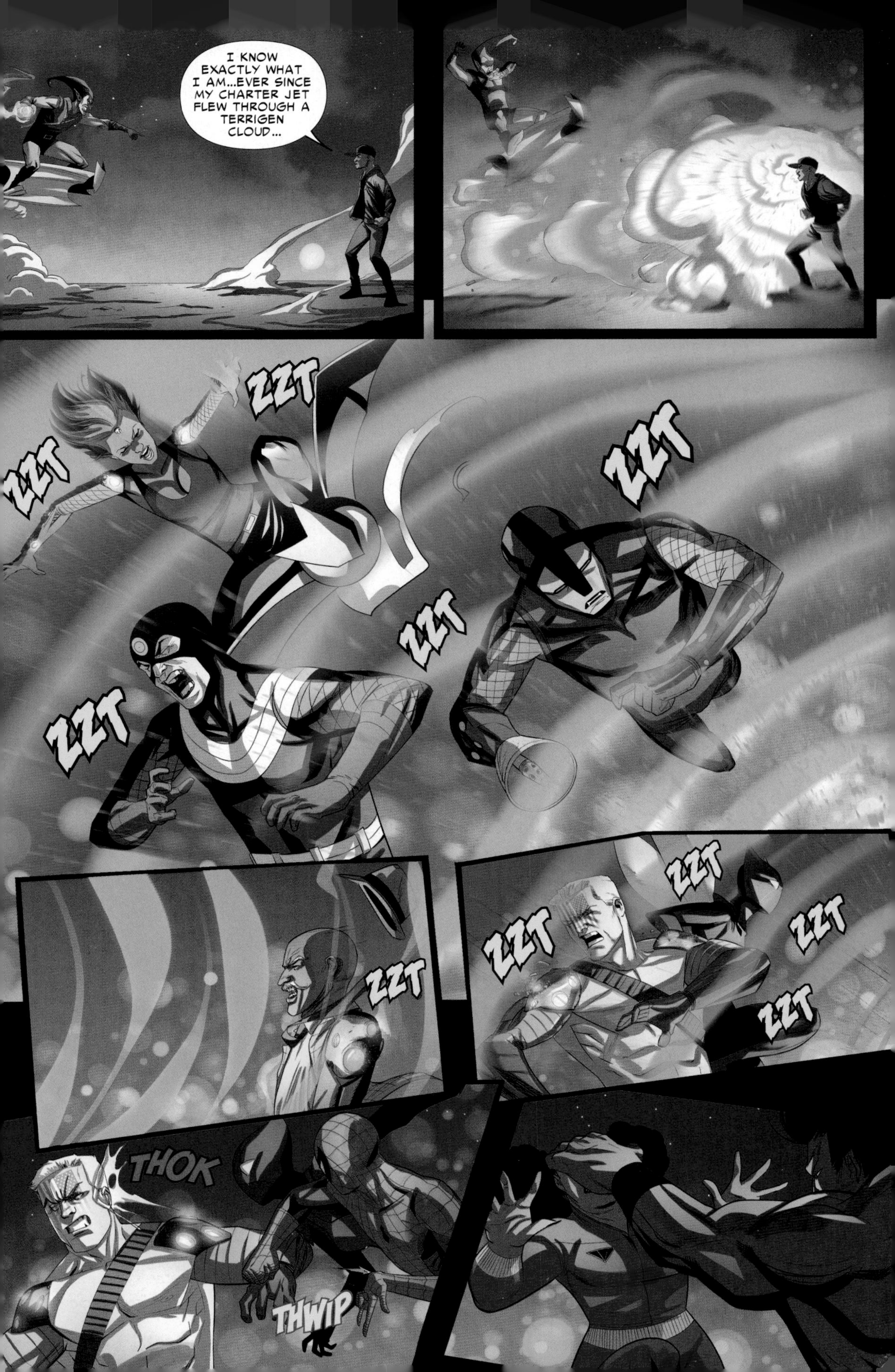

I KNOW EXACTLY WHAT I AM...EVER SINCE MY CHARTER JET FLEW THROUGH A TERRIGEN CLOUD...
ZZT
ZZT
ZZT
ZZT
ZZT
ZZT
ZZT
ZZT
ZZT
ZZT
THOK
THWIP

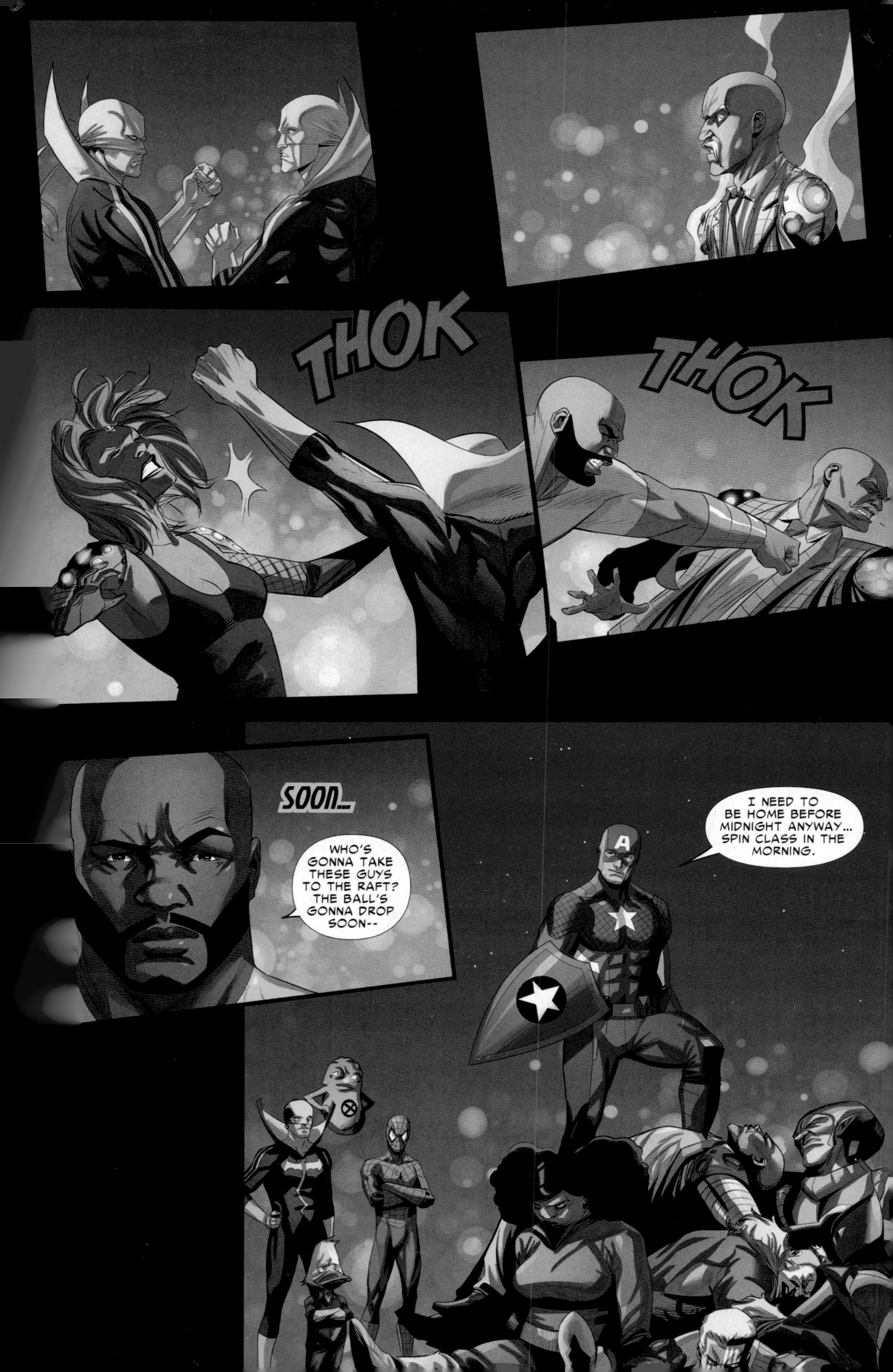
THOK
THOK
SOON...
WHO'S GONNA TAKE THESE GUYS TO THE RAFT? THE BALL'S GONNA DROP SOON--
I NEED TO BE HOME BEFORE MIDNIGHT ANYWAY... SPIN CLASS IN THE MORNING.

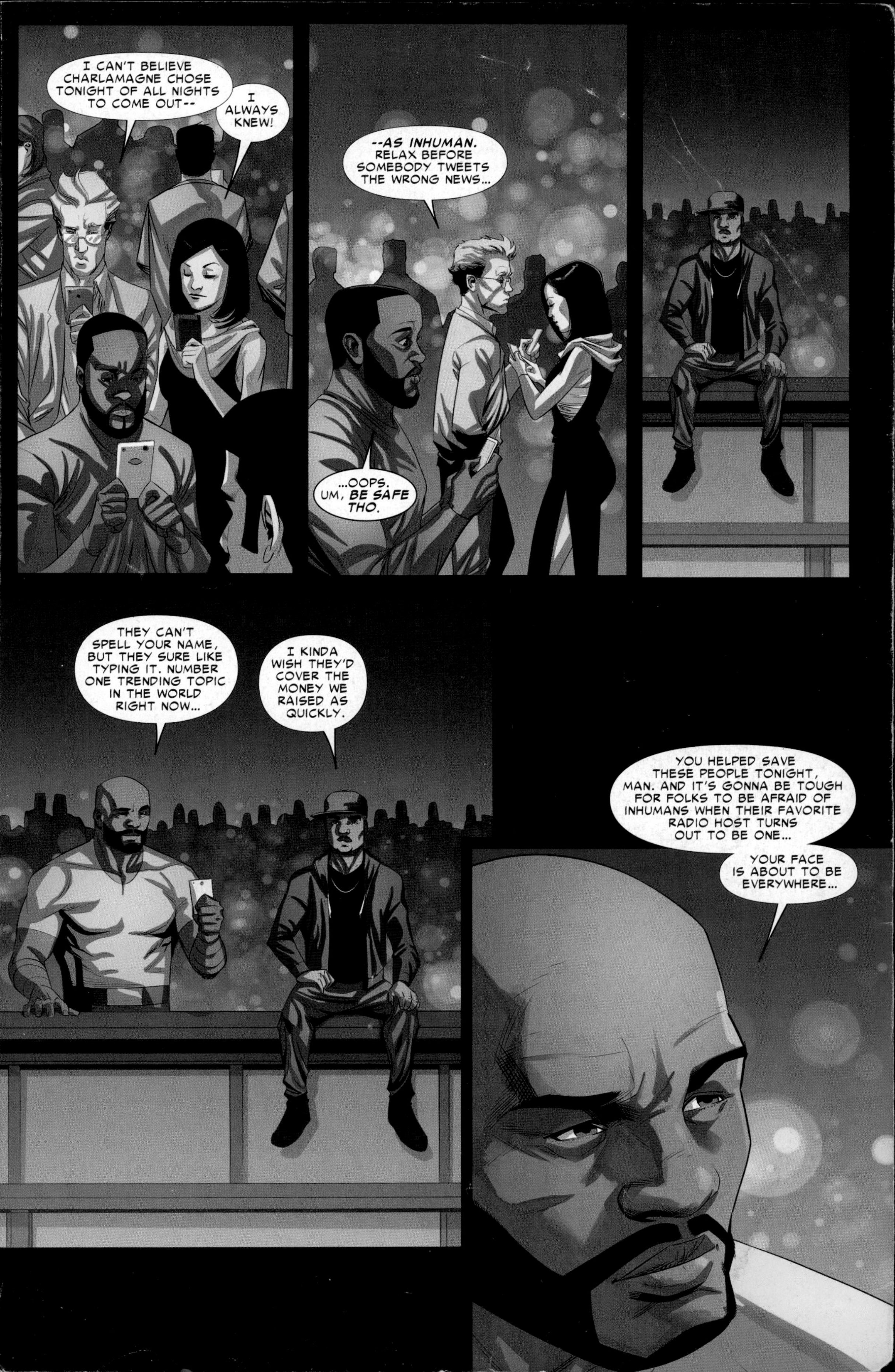
I CAN'T BELIEVE CHARLAMAGNE CHOSE TONIGHT OF ALL NIGHTS TO COME OUT--
I ALWAYS KNEW!
--AS INHUMAN. RELAX BEFORE SOMEBODY TWEETS THE WRONG NEWS...
...OOPS. UM, BE SAFE THO.
THEY CAN'T SPELL YOUR NAME, BUT THEY SURE LIKE TYPING IT. NUMBER ONE TRENDING TOPIC IN THE WORLD RIGHT NOW...
I KINDA WISH THEY'D COVER THE MONEY WE RAISED AS QUICKLY.
YOU HELPED SAVE THESE PEOPLE TONIGHT, MAN. AND IT'S GONNA BE TOUGH FOR FOLKS TO BE AFRAID OF INHUMANS WHEN THEIR FAVORITE RADIO HOST TURNS OUT TO BE ONE...
YOUR FACE IS ABOUT TO BE EVERYWHERE...

NEW YEAR'S RETRIBUTION

CHARLAMAGNE THA GOD WRITER
MAST LAYOUTS
NELSON BLAKE II with J.L. GILES ARTISTS
ANDRES MOSSA COLOR ARTIST
VC'S TRAVIS LANHAM LETTERER
ANNIE CHENG/TIM SMITH 3 DIGITAL PRODUCTION AND LAYOUT
TIM SMITH 3 DIGITAL PRODUCTION MANAGER
CHRIS ROBINSON EDITOR

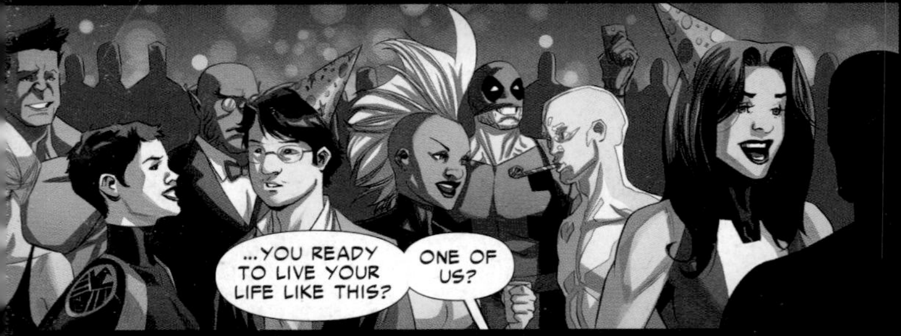
...YOU READY TO LIVE YOUR LIFE LIKE THIS?
ONE OF US?

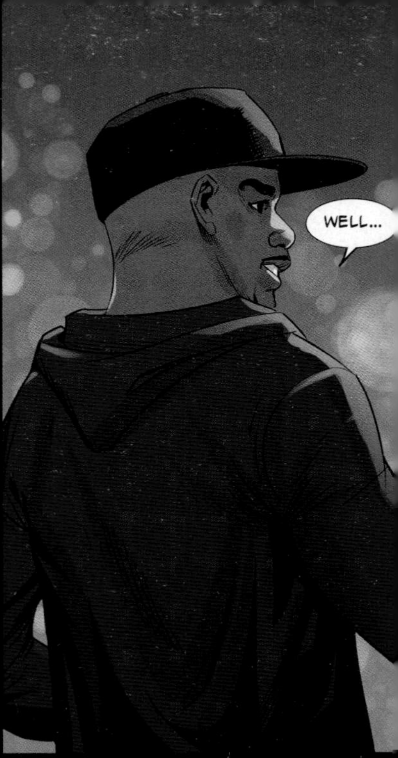
WELL...

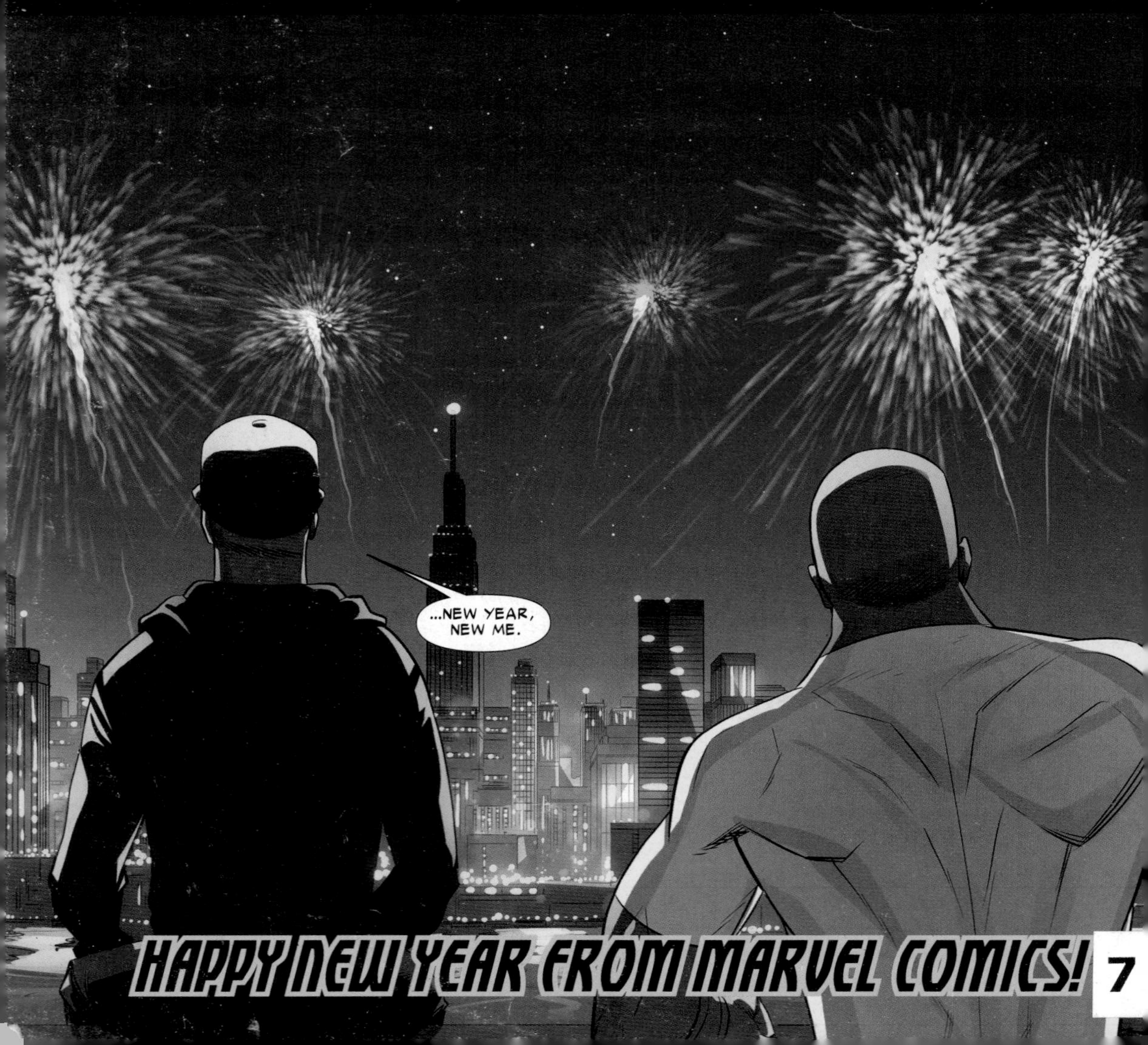
...NEW YEAR, NEW ME.
HAPPY NEW YEAR FROM MARVEL COMICS!